STRANGERS IN ZION

Strangers in Zion

Fundamentalists in the South,

1900–1950

William R. Glass

Mercer
University
Press
2001

ISBN 0-86554-756-4
MUP/H568

© 2001 Mercer University Press
6316 Peake Road
Macon, Georgia 31210-3960

First Edition.

∞The paper used in this publication meets the minimum
requirements of American National Standard for
Information Sciences—Permanence of Paper for Printed
Library Materials, ANSI Z39.48-1992.

Scripture quotations taken from the New American
Standard Bible®, Copyright© 1960, 1962, 1963, 1968,
1971, 1972, 1973, 1975, 1977, 1995 by the Lockman
Foundation Used by permission. (www.Lockman.org)

Library of Congress Cataloging-in-Publication Data

Glass, William R. (William Robert), 1952-
Strangers in Zion : fundamentalists in the South, 1900-1950 / by
William R. Glass.— 1st ed.
p. cm.
Includes bibliographical references and index.
ISBN 0-86554-756-4 (alk. paper)
1. Fundamentalism--Southern States—History—20th century.
2. Southern
States—Church history—19th century. I. Title.
BR535 .G57 2001
280'.4'097309041—dc21
2001004524

For

Lois P. Glass

1914–1988

"But a woman who fears the Lord, she shall be praised."

—Proverbs 31:30

TABLE OF CONTENTS

PREFACE   viii

ACKNOWLEDGMENTS   xxi

1: DEFINING FUNDAMENTALISM   1

2: ITINERANT FUNDAMENTALISTS   33

3: INTERDENOMINATIONAL FUNDAMENTALISTS   81

4: DENOMINATIONAL FUNDAMENTALISTS:

    THE PRESBYTERIANS   134

5: DENOMINATIONAL FUNDAMENTALISTS:

    THE BAPTISTS   185

6: SEPARATIST FUNDAMENTALISTS   226

7: CONCLUSION: SOUTHERN FUNDAMENTALISTS   275

SOURCES   283

INDEX   303

PREFACE

All scripture is inspired by God.
—2 Timothy 2:2

This book tells the story of the growth of Protestant fundamentalist theological traditions and institutions in the American South and the consequent emergence of patterns of fundamentalist conflict. Its central argument is that fundamentalists, whether they were Southern born and bred or were Northern transplants, were "strangers in Zion." In other words, despite the generally conservative character of Southern society and religion, fundamentalists during the first half of the twentieth century had difficulty making a home for themselves in the region. But they did gain a foothold that became the foundation for a more significant presence in the years after World War II. This study thus lays the groundwork for understanding the South's contribution to the growth of the religious right in the second half of the twentieth century.[1]

Moreover, this story has been virtually ignored by historians of fundamentalism and by historians of religion in the South. Scholars studying fundamentalism like George Marsden, Joel Carpenter, William Trollinger, and Margaret Bendroth rarely discuss Southern

---

[1]Among other works discussing the rise of the religious right but without much historical background are Michael D'Antonio, *Fall from Grace: The Failed Crusade of the Christian Right* (New Brunswick: Rutgers University Press, 1992); Michael Lienesch, *Redeeming America: Piety and Politics in the New Christian Right* (Chapel Hill: University of North Carolina Press, 1993); and Mark J. Rozell and Clyde Wilcox, *Second Coming: The New Christian Right in Virginia Politics* (Baltimore: Johns Hopkins University Press, 1996).

circumstances or at best incorporate them into a national pattern, obscuring specific regional developments.[2]

Despite the vibrant development of the field of Southern religion in the last several decades, its students generally minimize the fundamentalist presence on the Southern scene. They give considerable attention to the growth of Protestant evangelicalism in the antebellum period, to African American faith, and to the struggle for civil rights.[3] The best of denominational histories moves beyond simply chronicling the growth of a particular tradition to exploring the broader social and cultural context of that tradition.[4] In these studies fundamentalists are at best minor characters, if they appear at all. One significant exception is the cottage industry that analyzes the fundamentalist-moderate quarrel among Southern Baptists in the last two

[2]George Marsden, *Fundamentalism and American Culture: The Shaping of Twentieth-Century Evangelicalism, 1870–1925* (New York: Oxford University Press, 1980); Joel Carpenter, *Revive Us Again: The Reawakening of American Fundamentalism* (New York: Oxford University Press, 1997); William Vance Trollinger, Jr., *God's Empire: William Bell Riley and Midwestern Fundamentalism* (Madison: University of Wisconsin Press, 1990); and Margaret Lamberts Bendroth, *Fundamentalism and Gender, 1875 to the Present* (New Haven: Yale University Press, 1996).

[3]See for example, John B. Boles, *The Great Revival, 1787–1805: The Origins of the Southern Evangelical Mind* (Lexington: University Press of Kentucky, 1972) ; Jean Friedman, *The Enclosed Garden: Women and Community in Evangelical South,1830–1900* (Chapel Hill: University of North Carolina Press, 1990); Christine Leigh Heyrman, *Southern Cross: The Beginnings of the Bible Belt* (Chapel Hill: University of North Carolina Press, 1997); Randy J. Sparks, *On Jordan's Stormy Banks: Evangelicalism in Mississippi, 1773–1876* (Athens: University of Georgia Press, 1994); Paul Harvey, *Redeeming the South: Religious Cultures and Racial Identities among Southern Baptists, 1865–1925* (Chapel Hill: University of North Carolina Press, 1997); Mechal Sobel, *Trabelin' On: The Slave Journey to an Afro-Baptist Faith* (New York; Greenwood Press, 1979; reprint, Princeton: Princeton University Press, 1988). A comprehensive historiographical essay is John B. Boles, "The Discovery of Southern Religious History" in *Interpreting Southern History: Historiographical Essays in Honor of Sanford W. Higginbotham,* ed. John B. Boles and Evelyn Thomas Nolen (Baton Rouge: Louisiana State University Press, 1987) 510–48.

[4]Two recent studies about Southern Presbyterians illustrate this point: Rick L. Nutt, *Toward Peacemaking: Presbyterians in the South and National Security, 1945–1983* (Tuscaloosa: University of Alabama Press, 1994); and Joel L. Alvis, *Religion and Race: Southern Presbyterians, 1946 to 1983* (Tuscaloosa: University of Alabama Press, 1994).

decades. It has produced some fine works by Nancy Ammerman, Bill J. Leonard, Joe Barnhart, and David T. Morgan, but these authors do not push their discussion of the conflict's historical roots much earlier than World War II.[5] Two recent works suggest Southern fundamentalists are starting to receive their due. Mark Dalhouse's *An Island in a Lake of Fire* is a history of Bob Jones University, a major fundamentalist school, and Barry Hankins's *God's Rascal* is a biography of J. Frank Norris, the South's most notorious fundamentalist.[6] No book-length study exists to set the broader context for appreciating the contributions of these works. This book thus fills a significant gap in the historical literature on fundamentalism and on religion in the twentieth century South.

"Fundamentalist" and "fundamentalism" are fighting words, not only among those American Protestants who adopt these terms to describe themselves and their theology but also among historians who analyze this movement in American religious history. Over the last three decades, a scholarly consensus, based largely on the work of George Marsden, argues Protestant fundamentalism emerged around 1900 as a broad response to the modernization and secularization of American culture and specifically to the acceptance of liberal interpretations of traditional Protestant doctrines. A helpful distinction can be drawn between fundamentalism as a set of beliefs and as a movement with a specific agenda.[7] Fundamentalism's theological

---

[5]Nancy Ammerman, *Baptist Battles: Social Change and Religious Conflict in the Southern Baptist Convention* (New Brunswick: Rutgers University Press, 1990); Bill J. Leonard, *God's Last and Only Hope: The Fragmentation of the Southern Baptist Convention* (Grand Rapids: Eerdmans, 1990); Joe Edward Barnhart, *The Southern Baptist Holy War* (Austin: Texas Monthly Press, 1986); and David T. Morgan, *The New Crusades, the New Holy Land: Conflict in the Southern Baptist Convention, 1969–1991* (Tuscaloosa: University of Alabama Press, 1996).

[6]Mark Taylor Dalhouse, *An Island in the Lake of Fire: Bob Jones University, Fundamentalism, and the Separatist Movement* (Athens: University of Georgia Press, 1996); and Barry Hankins, *God's Rascal: J. Frank Norris and the Beginnings of Southern Fundamentalism* (Lexington: University Press of Kentucky, 1996).

[7]In *The Roots of Fundamentalism: British and American Millenarianism, 1800–1930* (Chicago: University of Chicago Press, 1970; reprint, Grand Rapids MI: Baker Book House, 1978) xvii, Ernest R. Sandeen distinguishes between the fundamentalist movement or its theological heritage, and the fundamentalist

roots grew in the soil of nineteenth-century evangelicalism, a broad
Protestant tradition that affirmed the Bible as the supreme authority
in all that it teaches and the necessity of a personal conversion experience for salvation.[8] Within these two main currents, four smaller
eddies were particularly important for the development of fundamentalism after the turn of the century.[9] First, a revivalistic heritage

---

controversy of the 1920s in which fundamentalists gave shape to their coalition
through efforts to address an agenda of concerns like liberal control of the
denominations and the teaching of evolution in public schools.

[8]See John D. Woodbridge, Mark A. Noll, and Nathan O. Hatch, *The Gospel in
America: Themes in the Story of America's Evangelicals* (Grand Rapids MI:
Zondervan Publishing House, 1979) 14; cf., Winthrop S. Hudson, *American
Protestantism* (Chicago: University of Chicago Press, 1961) 30. See also the essays in
David F. Wells and John D. Woodbridge, eds. *The Evangelicals: What They Believe,
Who They Are, Where They Are Changing*, rev. ed. (Grand Rapids MI: Baker Book
House, 1977); in particular, Kenneth S. Kantzer's essay, "Unity and Diversity in
Evangelical Faith" 58–87. More recently in *Evangelicalism: Comparative Studies of
Popular Protestantism in North America, the British Isles, and Beyond, 1700–1990*
(New York: Oxford University Press, 1994) 6, the editors, Mark A. Noll, David W.
Bebbington, and George A. Rawlyk, define evangelical as a movement within
Protestantism originating in the eighteenth century whose diverse adherents held four
core principles in common: the Bible as the main source of religious authority, the
necessity of a conversion experience, the importance of personal involvement in
missions and morality, and the centrality of the crucifixion to the Bible's message.

[9]The selection of these themes is based on their prominence in Marsden,
Fundamentalism, 32–39, 48–55, 72–80, 103–123. The key distinguishing feature of
fundamentalists for Marsden was their opposition to theological modernism and the
related cultural changes that supported this shift in theology, yet he recognized the
diversity of sources upon which fundamentalism drew. In "Fundamentalism as an
American Phenomenon: A Comparison with English Evangelicalism," *Church History*
46 (June 1977): 215, he maintained "'Fundamentalism' refers to a twentieth century
movement closely tied to the revivalist tradition of mainstream evangelical
Protestantism that militantly opposed modernist theology and the cultural change
associated with it. Fundamentalism shares traits with many other movements to
which it has been related (such as pietism, evangelicalism, revivalism, conservatism,
confessionalism, millenarianism, and the holiness and pentecostal movements), but it
has been distinguished most clearly from these by its militance in opposition to
modernism." In "The Fundamentalist Defense of the Faith," in *Change and
Continuity in Twentieth Century America: The 1920s*, ed. John Braeman, Robert H.
Bremner, and David Brody (Columbus: Ohio State University Press, 1968) 188, Paul
A. Carter was more blunt: "Without Modernism—and the anticlerical scientism
beyond it—there could have been no Fundamentalism."

included a concern for evangelizing the cities and expanding the work
of missionaries in foreign countries. Second, a new emphasis on personal holiness appeared, differing in expression from the perfectionist
traditions in Wesleyan circles, and imposed an individualistic moral
code on behavior. Third, an old understanding of the end times, premillennialism, won many new adherents through a modern
restatement of its pessimistic vision that civilization could be redeemed only by Christ's return to earth to rule for 1,000 years. Fourth,
liberal trends in theology provoked strong counter-affirmations of
certain doctrines like the authority and inspiration of the Bible and
the deity of Christ.[10]

The transformation of the adherents of these theological traditions
into an organized movement lay in the theological controversies
within the Northern denominations in the 1920s.[11] In 1920 Curtis Lee
Laws, editor of the Northern Baptist publication *Watchman-Exami-
ner*, coined the term "fundamentalist" to denote the party within the
Northern Baptist denomination that sought to reaffirm the core of
Christian orthodoxy while resisting control by theological liberals of
their Church.[12] The name quickly became the label applied to conservatives within Northern denominations who militantly opposed the
liberal interpretation of the Bible. While the specific fundamentals

---

[10]Other traditions participated in and supported these currents without becoming
fundamentalists. For example, even though these areas resemble the general shape of
Southern Protestantism, leaders of the main Southern denominations recognized and
criticized differences, most notably dispensational premillennialism, and resisted the
penetration of these traditions into their region. Moreover, fundamentalists
frequently wove these four areas into a tighter, more coherent system than the way in
which the individual elements were held and expressed among Southern Protestants.
Another example would be the Missouri Synod Lutherans. In *Fundamentalism and
the Missouri Synod: A Historical Study of Their Interaction and Mutual Influence*
(St. Louis MO: Concordia Publishing House, 1966), Milton L. Rudnick documented
the affinities these Lutherans had with fundamentalists but also their reluctance to
join in the movement.

[11]The earliest studies of fundamentalism focused on these developments and were
written by the liberal winners in the struggle. See for example, Stewart Cole, *The
History of Fundamentalism* (New York: Richard R. Smith, 1931).

[12]John W. Bradbury, "Curtis Lee Laws and the Fundamentalist Movement,"
Foundations 5 (January 1962): 55–56.

varied from list to list, fundamentalists agreed on the supernatural character of Christianity, the authority and inspiration of the Bible, and Jesus' substitutionary death on the cross as essential elements of Christianity.[13] Particularly among Northern Baptists and Presbyterians, the conflict was especially divisive as fundamentalists tried but failed in their efforts to impose doctrinal norms on their denominations and to drive out the liberals. While it may be anachronistic to speak of a fundamentalist movement before 1920, if used in a broader sense to include the theological streams that fed the twenties coalition, fundamentalism can be studied as an increasingly significant movement within American Protestantism.

A complementary effort to create a more generic definition of fundamentalism useful for making cross-cultural comparisons is the work spearheaded by Martin Marty and R. Scott Appleby on the Fundamentalism Project. Marty and Appleby suggest fundamentalism varies from culture to culture but has a "symbiotic relationship" with the secularism, relativism, and individualism of the modern world. Without the appearance of a modern, secular outlook in a society, no fundamentalism would appear, for fundamentalism defines itself in response to a society's particular experience with the social, intellectual, and economic changes associated with modernization. At the same time, fundamentalism provides for their followers a way of adjusting to modernization by providing a stable set of values and framework for interpreting the transformation, though usually one that is critical of change.[14]

This consensus undermines two popular assumptions about fundamentalism and the South. First, despite its past associations and its

---

[13]A comparison of the creed of the Niagara Bible Conference, reprinted in Sandeen, *Roots,* 273–77, with the five point declaration adopted by the General Assembly of Presbyterian Church in the U. S. A., Minutes of the General Assembly (1910) 272–73, and the Statement of Faith adopted by the World Conference on Christian Fundamentals, in World Conference on Christian Fundamentals, *God Hath Spoken* (Philadelphia: Bible Conference Committee, 1919) 11–12, reveals the diversity of the "fundamentals" defended by conservatives.

[14]Martin E. Marty and R. Scott Appleby, "Introduction: The Fundamentalism Project: A User's Guide," in *Fundamentalisms Observed,* ed. Martin E. Marty and R. Scott Appleby (Chicago: University of Chicago Press, 1991) vii–x.

present notoriety as the element of Southern religion that leads to the characterization of the region as the Bible belt, fundamentalism was not native to the South. It was primarily Northern and urban in origin and was a movement with a distinctive theology and marked by a militant opposition to liberal theology. This concern for doctrine led to particular patterns of denominational controversy in the North as fundamentalists tried to reverse the growing influence of liberals within their churches. The appearance of this system of beliefs in the South in the early twentieth century resulted from the enlistment of some Southern Protestants. This development led to disputes within Southern churches similar to those that arose in the North.

Moreover, fundamentalism was not synonymous with the anti-evolution campaigns of the twenties, an impression popularized by the press in the 1920s and subsequently confirmed by innumerable text-books.[15] To be sure, fundamentalists rallied to the battle to stop the teaching of evolution in the public schools, but Ferenc Szasz cogently argues two points: fundamentalists turned to antievolutionism while their campaign to oust liberals from the denominations was failing, and evolution came to symbolize for fundamentalists the cultural crisis that America faced in the 1920s. Also, he suggests funda-mentalists supported the antievolution campaign because William Jennings Bryan captured the fundamentalist movement to serve his

---

[15]In "Evolution, Fundamentalism, and the Historians: An Historiographical Review," *The Historian* 44 (November 1981): 16–23, William E. Ellis provides an excellent survey of the literature linking fundamentalism with antievolution campaigns. Two of the more influential works were Norman F. Furniss, *The Fundamentalist Controversy, 1918–1931* (New Haven CT: Yale University Press, 1954) and Ray Ginger, *Six Days or Forever? Tennessee v. John Thomas Scopes* (Boston: Beacon Press, 1958). In contrast, Edward J. Larson, in *Summer for the Gods: The Scopes Trial and America's Continuing Debate over Science and Religion* (Cambridge: Harvard University Press, 1997) 37, notes "Fundamentalism began as a response to theological developments within the Protestant church rather than to political or educational developments within American society." For older studies denying the centrality of antievolutionism to fundamentalism, see Nelson Hodges Hart, "The True and the False: The Worlds of an Emerging Evangelical Protestantism in America, 1890–1920" (Ph.D. diss., Michigan State University, 1976) viii–ix; and Donald George Tinder, "Fundamentalist Baptists in the Northern and Western States, 1920–1950" (Ph.D. diss., Yale University, 1969) 110–11.

crusade to reverse the disturbing cultural trends of the twenties.[16] Moreover, evolution gave fundamentalists an issue with broader and more direct popular appeal than trying to explain how theological liberalism threatened American civilization.[17] But while providing a platform to move their campaign out of the churches and into the streets, evolution proved to be their undoing when the coverage of the Scopes trial portrayed them as buffoons, bigots, and obscurantists.[18] Thus, while they are important elements, evolution and the Scopes trial are the wrong lenses through which to view the origins of fundamentalism in the South.

The argument is not that considering Southern developments will undermine or even significantly alter Marsden's interpretation. Quite the contrary, it is necessary for understanding what happened in the South. Nor will the Southern story challenge the Fundamentalism Project's suggestion that fundamentalism represents a reactive and adaptive response to modernization. Indeed, the South is a particularly good example of the relationship between modernization and fundamentalism. However, distinctive circumstances in the South affected the process. First, the social and cultural ferment that shaped fundamentalism had its impact in the South about a generation later. For example, regarding intellectual developments, Daniel Signal in *The War Within* argues Southern intellectual life moved from Victorian to modernist thought in the space of one generation, roughly from the end of World War I to the end of the

---

[16]Ferenc Morton Szasz, *The Divided Mind of Protestant America, 1880–1930* (University: University of Alabama Press, 1982) 107–135.

[17]Ellis, "Evolution," 16. Szasz makes this point in his dissertation, "Three Fundamentalist Leaders: The Roles of William Bell Riley, John Roach Straton, and William Jennings Bryan in the Fundamentalist-Modernist Controversy" (Ph.D. diss., University of Rochester, 1969) 163.

[18]In "When World Views Collide: Journalists and the Great Monkey Trial" (paper presented at the Annual Meeting of the Association for Education in Journalism and Mass Communication, Norman OK, 3–6 August 1986), Marvin N. Olansky shows how the journalists covering the trial filtered their reporting through their biases thus creating the stereotypes that endure to the present. For a similar evaluation of the impact of the Scopes Trial, see Robert E. Wenger, "Social Thought in American Fundamentalism, 1918–1933," (Ph.D. dissertation, University of Nebraska, 1973) 255–56.

World War II.[19] In terms of economic changes since Reconstruction, while some Southerners have tried to diversify the South's agricultural economy, significant changes came during and after World War II. In fact, this war marked a significant turning point in Southern history. The region was more diverse, more urban, and more industrial than before.[20] Second, Southern race relations also played a critical role in shaping Southern society. The necessity of maintaining Jim Crow gave a conservative cast to Southern culture, as almost any change, unless controlled and directed by the white elite, could be charged with threatening the Southern system of race relations and hence the basis of the Southern social order.[21] Here too World War II represented a significant turning point. The first challenges to Jim Crow began appearing during the war years, and a national consensus opposing segregation began building after the war. Third, the place of churches in Southern society was quite special as church leaders saw themselves as moral guardians of society and their institutions as central features of the region's culture. This connection grew, in part, from the clergy's role in defending slavery, rallying morale during the Civil War, and explaining defeat in the postbellum era.[22] But also evangelical Protestantism won the hearts of white Southerners, and its churches

---

[19]Daniel Joseph Signal, *The War Within: From Victorian to Modernist Thought in the South, 1919–1945* (Chapel Hill: University of North Carolina Press, 1985).

[20]Such is the suggestion of Morton Sosna in "More Important than the Civil War? The Impact of World War II on the South," in *Perspectives on the South: An Annual Review of Society, Politics, and Culture,* vol. 4, ed. James C. Cobb and Charles R. Wilson (University: University of Mississippi Press, 1987) 145–58.

[21]Though some of its conclusions and interpretations have been questioned, C. Vann Woodward's *The Strange Career of Jim Crow,* 3rd ed. (New York: Oxford University Press, 1974) has many valuable insights; cf., Howard N. Rabinowitz, "More than the Woodward Thesis: Assessing *The Strange Career of Jim Crow,*" *Journal of American History* 75 (December 1988): 842–56. For a perceptive historiographical essay, see Dan T. Carter, "From Segregation to Integration" in *Interpreting Southern History,* 408–433.

[22]Mitchell Snay, "American Thought and Southern Distinctiveness: The Southern Clergy and the Sanctification of Slavery," *Civil War History* 33 (December 1989): 311–28; Drew Gilpin Faust, "Christian Soldiers: The Meaning of Revivalism in the Confederate Army," *Journal of Southern History* 53 (February 1987): 63–90; and Charles Reagan Wilson, *Baptized in Blood: The Religion of the Lost Cause, 1865–1920* (Athens: University of Georgia Press, 1980).

functioned as an organizing institution for Southern communities.[23] These roles created intense loyalty among Southern Protestants to their denominations and in turn encouraged a popular perception of the South as Zion, a special land where Protestant values undergirded the social order.

While the South's cultural conservatism may appear to make the region a natural place for fundamentalism to flourish, other circumstances hindered its growth. Though fundamentalist doctrine resembled the main lines of conservative Southerner's theology, there were differences. Most Southern Protestants endorsed fundamentalist insistence on the supernatural character of Christianity and on the importance of evangelism, but premillennialism, particularly of the dispensational variety, was an important stumbling block to fundamentalist recruiting efforts among Southern Protestants. Additionally, as fundamentalists came to endorse separation not just from an immoral world but also from organizations that tolerated liberalism, Southern Protestants backed away from alliances with fundamentalists because of their allegiance to their own denominations and the perception that their denominations were orthodox. This fidelity also made fundamentalism suspect because of the movement's interdenominational cooperation. Many Southern Protestants felt ties to other organizations represented disloyalty to Southern denominations. These differences in theology and perspective form the main themes distinguishing conservative Southern Protestantism from fundamentalism. Thus fundamentalists became strangers in Zion.

Yet some Southerners joined the fundamentalist ranks. They initially learned fundamentalism in the same way as Northerners, from itinerant Bible teachers and in Bible conferences, and they generally gave these traveling preachers and their messages a warm reception. This significant Southern participation dating back to the beginning of the twentieth century helped to shape the institutional

---

[23]Donald G. Mathews, *Religion in the Old South* (Chicago: University of Chicago Press, 1977); Anne C. Loveland, *Southern Evangelicals and the Social Order, 1800–1860* (Baton Rouge: Louisiana State University Press, 1980); Ted Ownby, *Subduing Satan: Recreation and Manhood in the Rural South* (Chapel Hill: University of North Carolina Press, 1990); and Heyrman, *Southern Cross*.

development of the movement. Itinerant fundamentalist preachers regularly toured the South, introducing thousands of Southern laypeople and ministers to the doctrines and cultural concerns of fundamentalism. Fundamentalist institutions developed in the South in the 1920s and 1930s as they did in the North and were an important part of the emerging network of fundamentalist schools and organizations. Particularly important was the appearance of fundamentalist schools in the South because they expanded significantly the range of the broader fundamentalist movement's educational efforts by offering vocational training, graduate education, and graduate professional training for the pastorate. But even when some schools focused on the traditional fundamentalist concern for the training of laypeople, the Southern versions of Bible institutes and colleges should not be dismissed as mere imitations of Northern models but seen as an important step in building a Southern wing of the movement and broadening the movement's coalition. The appearance of these schools provoked the first sustained reaction in Southern denominations against fundamentalist presence in their region. During these same years, a theologically liberal faction of ministers, administrators, and seminary professors began taking a more prominent role in influencing policy and ascending to leadership positions within the bureaucracy and educational institutions in the largest Southern denominations. The result was the introduction of Northern patterns of fundamentalist controversy among Southern Protestants. These battles for the control of Southern denominations were fought with a fundamentalist passion and a fundamentalist perspective defining the terms of battle. These controversies over liberalism were of the type troubling Northern churches in the 1920s. These battles, particularly those among Southern Baptists and Southern Presbyterians, fostered the establishment of ongoing factions determined to resist and reverse the penetration of liberal theology in their churches. But a distinctive Southern accent sounded in these disputes. Among Southern Baptists, the characteristic fundamentalist militancy was most noted among Baptists concerned with the growing bureaucratization of their convention. Among Southern Methodists and Presbyterians, the issue over which the lines were drawn was reunion with Northern denominations. Southern conservatives objected on a variety of grounds but a central criticism was the fundamentalist complaint concerning the dominance of liberals in Northern organizations. For Methodists, the battle was barely a skirmish in the late 1930s resulting in reunion with the liberal Northern Methodists, but conservative Presbyterians stalled reunion until 1983. During these same years, disputes within the conservative factions over eschatology, in particular dispensationalism, and ecclesiological separation divided fundamentalists and prevented the development of a united Southern coalition.

In this story several important social and cultural factors had little influence in shaping the growth and development of fundamentalist traditions and conflict in the South. For example, African-Americans did not play much of a role. In this era of Jim Crow they were excluded from fundamentalist schools, relegated to balconies or special meetings if they wanted to hear fundamentalist itinerants, and segregated into separate synods, circuits, and denominations. The Great Depression did curtail the Southern trips of the touring preachers, but fundamentalist schools continued to grow though each faced financial crises that tested the faith of their founders and supporters. Veterans returning from World War II swelled enrollments as most fundamentalist schools qualified as institutions where GIs could use their benefits.

Finally, this story was one of conflict, hence Southern fundamentalists appear as an ornery, contentious lot, frequently exhibiting little in way of the Christian virtue of charity. Apart from the notorious exception of J. Frank Norris, most Southern fundamentalists did not look for fights for the sake of a fight, but neither did they did they run from confrontation nor seek grounds for accommodation with their foes. To do so, in their eyes, represented an unconscionable compromise in their stand for their beliefs. It cannot be stressed too strongly that their passion for battle was raised to such a fever pitch only because they deemed the stakes were so high. If they exaggerated the consequences of defeat by describing them in apocalyptic terms, they did so because they genuinely believed they were defending and trying to preserve that which gave meaning to their lives and provided a stable foundation for society.

ACKNOWLEDGMENTS

As tempting as it might be to claim the credit for whatever value this book might have and to lay the blame for its faults to those mentioned below, just the opposite is the case. While this book might not be the best evidence for it, I learned much about being an historian and doing historical research while in the classes of John Woodbridge at Trinity Evangelical Divinity School. Other apprentices should be so fortunate to have as skillful a master when learning the profession. While at Trinity, I met Joel Carpenter who suggested that studying fundamentalists in the South would make a good dissertation topic and gave me my first clue by directing me to the Bible conference at Atlanta's Tabernacle Baptist Church. That dissertation took shape under the direction of Dan T. Carter, Brooks Holifield, and Patrick Allit at Emory University, and again I was the beneficiary of their expertise in training novices as well as their knowledge of Southern history and American religion.

Everyone working in the field of Southern religion owes a debt to Samuel S. Hill for almost single handedly laying its foundation. At several points in the long process of research and writing, he provided encouraging words that this project was worth the effort. My thinking about religious history has been shaped by participation in two National Endowment for the Humanities seminars: one on religion in the South led by Charles Reagan Wilson and the other on American religious diversity led by Emma Lapsansky. I have had and continue to have many fruitful discussions about Southern religion with some of the participants, notably Charles Wilson, Samuel Shepherd, Paul Harvey, and Andrew Manis. Andy also played a crucial role in convincing the people at Mercer University Press that it should publish this book, a recommendation for which I am very grateful.

Very practical support (i.e., money) came from several sources, the most important being a dissertation research grant from Emory University, a grant from the Southern Baptist Historical Commission to use its extensive archives in Nashville, Tennessee, and two research grants from the Faculty Senate of Mississippi University for Women that enabled me to expand the analysis of Southern fundamentalists and the issue of reunion. My travels took me to a variety of institutions, and at each the librarians were quite helpful, patiently bringing out box after box of files and occasionally pointing me to sources I otherwise would have missed. Special Collections at the Woodruff Library of Emory University was where I started, but the Southern Baptist Historical Commission, the Presbyterian archives in Montreat, North Carolina, and those at Drew Theological Seminary provided access to invaluable official denominational records and manuscript collections. Without the cooperation of the librarians at fundamentalist schools, I could not have written this book. While they might not agree with my interpretation of their schools' places in the story of Southern fundamentalism, the staffs at Dallas Theological Seminary, Bob Jones University, Columbia Bible College, Southern Methodist College, and Bryan College were the most helpful. The University of North Carolina at Wilmington, Westminister College, Georgia College, and Mississippi University for Women provided funds for me to travel to conferences where I was able to try out my ideas and benefit from the insightful criticisms of Mark Noll, William Trollinger, and Mitchell Snay, among others. Three of these presentations have been published in slightly different forms, and I appreciate the criticisms of unnamed referees that helped me sharpen my arguments. I am grateful for permission from the editors of *American Baptist Quarterly* and the *Journal of the Social Sciences* to publish this material here.

Finally, while researching and writing can be solitary endeavors that isolate a person, friends in and out of the profession and my family reminded me of life outside the library. Suzanne White-Junod, Kathleen Berkeley, Barry Bergen, Rose Begemann, Lewis Gambill, and my colleagues in the Division of Humanities at Mississippi University for Women played a most valuable role in keeping me grounded in the real world, as did my brother and sister and their families. My greatest debt is owed to the one to whom this book is dedicated. It is an inadequate memorial to a person whose life exemplified the virtues of faith.

William R. Glass
—Szczytno, Poland

1

DEFINING FUNDAMENTALISM

Do not move the ancient boundary.
—Proverbs 23:10

In 1927 the editors of the *Christian Century* described the peace and harmony of the national conventions of several Northern denominations under the title "Fading Fundamentalism." Focused on the Baptists and Presbyterians, the editorial noted that the efforts "of well-organized super-conservatives, worked to a tense emotional state," had failed "to control denominational machinery and determine denominational standards." The calm of the 1926 conventions indicated "a distinct retrogression in the fundamentalist movement. And this year shows that what last year was a retreat has now become a rout."[1] While the editors were right in describing the fundamentalist withdrawal from the denominational battlefield, their tone, which suggested a belief that fundamentalism would disappear from American Protestantism, or remain only on its fringes, was mistaken for fundamentalists and their evangelical heirs remained and continue to be a vibrant, significant part of American religion.[2]

---

[1]"Fading Fundamentalism," *Christian Century* (16 June 1927): 742.

[2]In *American Evangelicalism: Conservative Religion and the Quandary of Modernity* (New Brunswick NJ: Rutgers University Press, 1983) 49, James David Hunter estimated that in 1980 22 percent of Americans were evangelical, 35 percent nonevangelical Protestants, 30 percent Catholic, 4 percent non-Christian, and 9 percent had no religious preference. On the continued presence and growth of

Christian Century published the obituary while the patient was still alive.

Whether adopted as a badge of honor or leveled as a charge of opprobrium, the term fundamentalist requires careful definition. Over the last three decades, a scholarly consensus has built that Protestant fundamentalism emerged in the late nineteenth and early twentieth centuries as a response most broadly to the secularization of American culture and specifically to the acceptance of liberal interpretations of traditional Protestant doctrines.[3] Nurtured in a cycle of Bible conferences, fundamentalism sought to reaffirm the supernatural character of Christianity, to defend the authority and inerrancy of the Bible, to promote holy living by imposing an individualistic code of ethics, and to encourage evangelism in America and overseas as a solution to vexing social issues. Because it seemed to explain both obscure prophetic passages in the Bible and current world events, dispensational premillennialism attracted many fundamentalists to its interpretation of the end times.[4] After World

---

evangelicalism, see the essays in *Evangelicalism and Modern America,* ed. George Marsden (Grand Rapids MI: Eerdmans, 1984).

[3]George M. Marsden's *Fundamentalism and American Culture: The Shaping of Twentieth Century American Evangelicalism,* 1875–1925 (New York: Oxford University Press, 1981) provides the most forceful statement of this interpretation while Ferenc Morton Szasz's *The Divided Mind of Protestant America, 1880–1930* (University: University of Alabama Press, 1982) gives a good general narrative of these events.

[4] Premillennialism is a prophetic scheme that describes deteriorating world conditions redeemed by Christ's return to establish an earthly kingdom. The dispensational version divides world history into seven periods (or dispensations) in which God sets certain standards for humanity to win God's favor but in each age people fail and suffer God's judgement. The current age (the sixth) will end with Christ's return to rule a millennial kingdom. In *The Roots of Fundamentalism: British and American Millenarianism, 1800–1930* (Chicago: University of Chicago Press, 1970; reprint, Grand Rapids MI: Baker Book House, 1978), Ernest Sandeen describes in detail the development of this prophetic scheme but overestimates its contribution to the origins of fundamentalism. See George M. Marsden, "Defining Fundamentalism," *Christian Scholar's Review* 1 (1971): 141–51. Marsden expanded and refined his critique in *Fundamentalism and American Culture.* A good general discussion of premillennialism is Timothy Weber, *Living in the Shadow of the Second*

War I, fundamentalists fought two battles, one to reverse the troubling trends they perceived in American society, developments symbolized by the teaching of evolution, and the other to wrest control of denominations from theological liberals. Defeated on both fronts, fundamentalists retreated and built a decentralized array of Bible colleges, mission organizations, publications, and radio programs.[5]

A closer examination of these Northern developments is needed to tell the story necessary for understanding the growth of fundamentalist traditions and institutions in the South. Moreover, it is important to remember that to limit fundamentalism to a particular set of doctrinal points, fundamentalists to conservative denominational politicians, and the movement's cultural concerns to a crusade against evolution is to slight the rich heritage of nineteenth century evangelicalism from which the movement grew. In the last thirty years historians exploring fundamentalism have considerably revised earlier treatments and portrayed fundamentalism as an authentic conservative tradition in the history of American Protestantism. In 1968 Paul Carter suggested the direction for subsequent studies by insisting historians take seriously fundamentalists' claims that they were "defending what the Fundamentalists honestly believed was all that gave meaning to human life, 'the faith once delivered to the saints.'"[6] In short, to appreciate the nature and character of fundamentalism, the faith it defended must be understood.[7]

Coming: *American Premillennialism, 1875–1982*, rev. ed. (Grand Rapids MI: Zondervan, 1983).

[5]For a good discussion of these events, see Joel A. Carpenter, *Revive Us Again: The Reawakening of American Fundamentalism* (New York: Oxford University Press, 1997) 13–32.

[6]Paul A. Carter, "The Fundamentalist Defense of the Faith," in *Change and Continuity in Twentieth Century America: The 1920s*, ed. John Braeman, Robert H. Bremner, and David Brody, 179–213 (Columbus: Ohio State University Press, 1968) 212. Carter specifically rejected as inadequate interpretations those that tied fundamentalists of the twenties to the political right, that described fundamentalism as a rural revolt against urban values, that it was an anti-intellectual movement, and that it railed against the findings of science with the dogma of religion.

[7]In ibid., 188, note 21, Carter suggested that "a study between Fundamentalism per se and apocalyptic millennialism would add much to our understanding of religion and society in America." Ernest Sandeen's *The Roots of Fundamentalism*

The theological dimensions of fundamentalism developed in the intellectual and social ferment of the late nineteenth century. Arthur Schlesinger, Sr., called the last quarter of the nineteenth century "a critical period in American religion" in part because new intellectual currents challenged the ascendant position of evangelical theology through an attack on its foundation—the authority of the Bible. The conclusions of higher criticism, the implications—both scientific and social—of Darwin's evolutionary theory, and comparative study of other religions called into question the historical accuracy of biblical narratives, the uniqueness of man's place in the cosmos, and the validity of Christianity's claim to being the only authentic way to God.[8] Ferenc Szasz extended the period through the first third of the

---

supplied that analysis and was the first monograph to explore fundamentalism's theological heritage. The heart of his thesis was that fundamentalism represented an alliance between advocates of a new interpretation of biblical prophecy called dispensationalism and conservative scholars at Princeton Seminary who developed a new statement of the doctrine of inspiration that included the inerrancy of the Bible. Subsequent studies have charged Sandeen with too narrowly defining the "roots" but all have emphasized the importance of theology to understanding the dynamics of the movement. Many of these efforts have been dissertations. Some of the more insightful include: Robert E. Wenger, "Social Thought in American Fundamentalism, 1918–33," (Ph.D. diss., University of Nebraska, 1973); Walter Edmund Ellis, "Social and Religious Factors in the Fundamentalist-Modernist Schisms among Baptists in North America, 1895–34" (Ph.D. diss., University of Pittsburgh, 1974); Nelson Hodges Hart, "The True and the False: The Worlds of an Emerging Evangelical Protestantism in America, 1890–1920" (Ph.D. diss., Michigan State University, 1976); and Joel A. Carpenter, "The Renewal of American Fundamentalism, 1930–1945" (Ph.D. diss., Johns Hopkins University, 1984). In *Voices of Fundamentalism: Seven Biographical Studies* (Philadelphia: Westminster Press, 1976), C. Allyn Russell explored the diversity among fundamentalists through biographical sketches of their leaders. The most important and most comprehensive of these works is George Marsden's *Fundamentalism and American Culture*. In it, Marsden broadens considerably the nineteenth theological stream that fed fundamentalism and expands the context by discussing the social, intellectual, and cultural factors that shaped its development. Szasz's *Divided Mind* covers much the same ground as Marsden but does so with a more straightforward narrative and more attention to controversy over evolution.

[8]Arthur M. Schlesinger, Sr., "A Critical Period in American Religion, 1875–1900," *Massachusetts Historical Society Proceedings* 64 (October 1930–June 1932): 524–27. Schlesinger also noted challenges to religion's social program that came from the era's industrialization, urbanization, and immigration. Two studies, originating as dissertations under Schlesinger's guidance, expanded Schlesinger's

twentieth century by suggesting that the challenges Schlesinger described created conflict in American Protestantism that were resolved by the fundamentalist-modernist controversies of the 1920s. These battles permanently divided American Protestantism into two distinct theological camps largely without respect to denominational lines.[9]

Most troubling, and directly related to the development of fundamentalism, was the question of religious authority, particularly whether and in what way the Bible remained the normative rule of Protestant faith and practice.[10] In the late nineteenth century the hegemony of evangelicals over Protestant understanding of the Bible began breaking down. After studying under European scholars using higher critical methods to analyze the Bible,[11] American seminary professors introduced to ministerial students the fruits of their education. The professors applied the tools of historical analysis to the Bible and offered some disturbing theories. For example, they suggested that Moses did not write the first five books of the Old Testament but that the Pentateuch was the product of several authors edited by a redactor many years after the events. The implications were that the Bible was in error in attributing authorship to Moses and that Jesus was mistaken in affirming this tradition. Moreover, by comparing the practices and doctrines of Old Testament Jews with those of their neighbors, these scholars found striking similarities and concluded that the Jews' faith was influenced by, if not to some degree

---

observations about this latter point. See Aaron Abell, *The Urban Impact on American Protestantism, 1865–1900* (Cambridge MA: Harvard University Press, 1943; reprint, Hamden CT: Archon Books, 1962) and Henry F. May, *Protestant Churches and Industrial America* (New York: Harper and Brothers, 1949).

[9]Szasz, *Divided Mind*; note particularly the conclusion, 136–38.

[10]Such is the argument of ibid., 1–8.

[11]Biblical scholars distinguish between higher and lower criticism in that lower involves a close analysis and comparison of the extant copies of the original manuscripts of the books of the Bible in order to arrive at the most accurate text. Higher criticism focuses on issues of authorship, genuineness, authenticity, and literary form. It employs a rigorous historical analysis of the text, the same that would be given to any ancient document. See F. F. Bruce, *The New Testament Documents: Are They Reliable?* (Grand Rapids MI: Eerdmans, 1959) for a discussion of the distinction between the two.

derived from, other religions. Thus the Bible became simply a record, occasionally a faulty one too, of the development of the religious faith of the Jews culminating in stories about one remarkable Jew by the name of Jesus of Nazareth.

For many Protestants, the results of this kind of investigation called into question the authority and inspiration of the Bible and required a reassessment of these doctrines. Protestants had three broad choices.[12] Two of these choices proceeded from the assumption that the old doctrines were either irrelevant or needed to be reformulated to make them fit the changing social and intellectual environment.[13] The more radical choice was to adjust the doctrines to the findings of science and the biblical critics. Seminary professors, particularly those at the Divinity School of the University of Chicago, blazed this trail of complete accommodation. If particular doctrines, like the divinity of Jesus, or events, like miracles or the resurrection, could not be verified by science or historical inquiry, then they must be discarded as relics from an unenlightened, superstitious era. At best, Christianity became a noble code of ethics, indeed perhaps the best, but one whose authority was grounded in the scientific method.[14]

The other liberal option placed the basis for authority for religious belief and practices in experience. According to Winthrop Hudson, the result was that "the believer was no longer under compulsion to find his security in biblical proof texts. He could accept the conclusions of the biblical scholars with relative equanimity and appropriate the results of other scientific disciplines without great

---

[12]In *The Lively Experiment: The Shaping of Christianity in America* (New York: Harper and Row, 1963) 168–75, Sidney E. Mead outlined these three choices.

[13]Two fine studies of the development of liberalism are Kenneth Cauthen, *The Impact of American Religious Liberalism* (New York: Harper and Row, 1962) and William R. Hutchison, *The Modernist Impulse in American Protestantism* (Cambridge MA: Harvard University Press, 1976). An insightful analysis of liberalism's development during World War II and after is Mark Hulsether's *Building a Protestant Left: Christianity and Crisis Magazine, 1941–1993* (Knoxville: University of Tennessee Press, 1999).

[14]Mead, *Lively Experiment*, 173–74; Winthrop S. Hudson, *Religion in America: An Historical Account of the Development of American Religious Life*, 2nd ed., (New York: Charles Scribner's Sons, 1973) 274–77.

difficulty because his faith was validated by the inward testimony of the heart."[15] Championed by pastors, this new definition of the place of religious authority had an apologetic purpose and conservative intent. Faced with findings of science and higher criticism, these pastor-theologians tried to maintain the most important tenets of Protestantism. For them, the Bible and its stories were still important but valuable as a "record not of dogma but of experience."[16]

The third avenue was to affirm and restate evangelical orthodoxy and to try to refute the findings of these scholars. This alternative was the path followed by the fundamentalists' forebears and was best exemplified in a series of twelve pamphlets called *The Fundamentals*, published in 1910-1915.[17] Financed by oil millionaires from California and distributed to a variety of Christian workers, including every pastor, these booklets focused on defending traditional statements of biblical doctrines with articles written by a cross-section of evangelical pastors, scholars, missionaries, and itinerant Bible teachers. Avoiding divisive issues like church polity, baptism, and eschatology, the authors explained doctrines like the deity of Christ, sin, salvation, and the Trinity, affirmed the reality of miracles and the supernatural, and discussed evangelism and world missions. The largest group of essays on one topic, accounting for one-third of the total, responded to the critics with a defense of the authority, authenticity, and inspiration of the Bible.[18] These essays represented a moderate response to the liberals and a popular presentation of the fundamentalist position on the Bible.[19]

---

[15]Hudson, *Religion*, 272.

[16]Ibid., 273.

[17]*The Fundamentals*, 12 vols. (Chicago: Testimony Publishing Co., 1910–1915). Both Sandeen, *Roots*, 188–207, and Marsden, *Fundamentalism*, 118–23, have good overviews of the origins and contents of these pamphlets.

[18]Sandeen, *Roots*, 203–204, divided the articles as follows: out of ninety total, twenty-nine concerned the Bible, thirty-one defended doctrines, and thirty discussed a variety of other topics, like evangelism, missions, and cults.

[19]The classic scholarly response was A. A. Hodge and B. B. Warfield's essay, "Inspiration," *Princeton Review* 2 (April 1881): 225–60; reprinted in *The Princeton Defense of Plenary Verbal Inspiration* ed. Mark A. Noll (New York: Garland Publishing, 1988), 40–75. Noll's introductory essay provides a useful overview of how

The essayists in *The Fundamentals* defended the verbal, plenary inspiration of the Bible, meaning that inspiration extended to each word of each book in the Scriptures.[20] The Bible was not simply the record of the religious experience of the Jews nor did it merely contain the Word of God but it was the very word of God.[21] For fundamentalists, inspiration referred to the product, the books of the Bible, and not to the individual authors.[22] But they vigorously denied that the authors were mere scribes taking dictation from God and accounted for variation in style by suggesting that God prepared and then used their differences to communicate his ideas.[23] Moreover, neither their limitations nor those of language prevented God from delivering his message of salvation to lost humanity. The result was an infallible guide to faith and practice, without error even in areas

---

conservative professors at Princeton Theological Seminary defended the inspiration of the Bible against liberal criticism. Indeed, the nine essays in this volume represent an excellent sample of conservative scholarship. In *Roots*, 103–131, Sandeen has an extended analysis of the development of Princeton position on inspiration; cf., Marsden, *Fundamentalism*, 109–118.

[20]The task of defining and proving inspiration fell to James M. Gray, of Moody Bible Institute, in "The Inspiration of the Bible—Definition, Extent and Proof," *The Fundamentals*, 3:7–41. The evangelist L. W. Munhall contributed a rather superficial essay in "Inspiration," *The Fundamentals*, 7:21–37. Other articles "proved" or defended the Bible's inspiration in the manner indicated by their titles: William G. Moorehead, "The Moral Glory of Jesus Christ a Proof of Inspiration," *The Fundamentals*, 3:42–60; George S. Bishop, "The Testimony of the Scriptures to Themselves," *The Fundamentals*, 7:38–54; Arthur T. Pierson, "The Testimony of the Organic Unity of the Bible to Its Inspiration," *The Fundamentals*, 8:55–71; and A. C. Gaebelein, "Fulfilled Prophecy as Proof of the Bible's Inspiration," *The Fundamentals*, 9:55–86.

[21]Gray, "The Inspiration of the Bible," 10; Munhall, "Inspiration," 28; Hodge and Warfield, "Inspiration," 52.

[22]Gray, "The Inspiration of the Bible," 9–10.

[23]Hodge and Warfield's metaphor is particularly striking: "God predetermined all the matter and form of the several books largely by the formation and training of the several authors, as an organist determines the character of his music as much when he builds his organ and when he tunes his pipes, as when he plays his keys." "Inspiration," 45. See also, Munhall, "Inspiration," 33–34; and Gray, "The Inspiration of the Bible," 14.

where it commented on history and science.[24] The Bible's inerrancy, though, extended only to the original documents as they came from the pen of Moses, David, Luke, or Paul.[25] This position helped fundamentalists account for contradictions in Scripture by attributing errors to the copyists or faulty translation. They did not retreat to this thesis for every difficulty the critics raised because they believed that the careful study of the various copies of the New Testament had restored "in 999 cases out of every thousand the very word of the original text."[26] The remaining problems and the alleged conflicts with science and other historical sources resulted from "erroneous interpretations of the Bible and immature conclusions of science."[27]

---

[24]Hodge and Warfield acknowledged that the Bible was not intended to teach science or history but they insisted that "all the affirmations of Scripture of all kinds, whether of spiritual doctrine or duty, or of physical or historical fact, or of psychological or philosophical principle, are without error, when the *ipsissima verba* of the original autographs are ascertained and interpreted in their natural and intended sense." "Inspiration," 52–53.

[25]Scholars are debating the extent to which inerrancy in the original autographs represented an innovation by fundamentalists for apologetic purposes. Sandeen, *Roots*, 127–30, argues that A. A. Hodge and B. B. Warfield formulated and defended this thesis to make the inerrancy of the Bible incontestable. Without the original documents, no critic could prove that God inspired an error. Hodge and Warfield, though, clearly believed that they were restating the historic position of the church on inspiration (see "Inspiration," 55) as did the essayists in *The Fundamentals* (see Munhall, "Inspiration," 23–28). For two opposing views in the current debate, see Jack Rogers and Donald K. McKim, *The Authority and Interpretation of the Bible: An Historical Approach* (San Francisco: Harper and Row, 1979), who suggest that the doctrine of inerrancy was the intellectual product of seventeenth century scholasticism, and John D. Woodbridge, *Biblical Authority: A Critique of the Rogers/McKim Proposal* (Grand Rapids MI: Zondervan, 1982). For analysis, see George M. Marsden, *Reforming Fundamentalism: Fuller Seminary and the New Evangelicalism* (Grand Rapids MI: Eerdmans, 1987) 277–90.

[26]Gray, "The Inspiration of the Bible," 12. Gray exaggerated, but not by much. According to Bruce, *New Testament Documents*, 19–20 disputed passages of the New Testament account for only five percent of the entire New Testament and affect no doctrine that is not clearly stated in another undisputed passage.

[27]Gray, "Inspiration," 32. Fundamentalists insisted that this inerrant text be interpreted literally, and for Hodge and Warfield, "Inspiration," 53, literal meant understanding the text in its "natural and intended sense." Moreover, fundamentalist methods of exegesis recognized the presence in the Bible of literary devices like allegory, hyperbole, and metaphor. They differed with liberals on where such forms were

Inerrancy was crucial to the fundamentalist defense of the Bible because it sustained the authority and the truthfulness of the Bible's
message. Admitting the presence of a minor factual error might cast
doubt on the Bible's veracity on major issues like the efficacy of
Christ's death on the cross.[28]

Historians have labeled the two liberal parties as scientific
modernists and evangelical liberals,[29] but most fundamentalists did
not distinguish between the two, using the terms liberal or modernist
almost interchangeably. In any case, the rise of theological liberalism
was the most important development for sparking the emergence of
fundamentalism. The liberals' redefinitions of Protestant orthodoxy
were precisely the points of the fundamentalist response. As liberals
questioned the historical accuracy and scientific reliability of the
Bible, fundamentalists asserted its inerrancy. When liberals
emphasized the ethical teachings of Jesus and his life as an example for
humanity to follow, fundamentalists told of his virgin birth, his
ability to work miracles, his death on the cross for the world's sins,
and his resurrection. As liberals gave the ethical teachings of the Bible

---

employed. For example, the story of the Garden of Eden and the Fall were historical
events for fundamentalists not an allegory of the awakening of a moral conscience in
humanity. Even among themselves, no consensus developed as to where the line should
be drawn. For example, Gray believed that prophecies concerning Christ's return to
earth to rule would be fulfilled in a literal millennial kingdom while Hodge and
Warfield argued that they were being fulfilled in the Church's activities in the world.

[28]Hodge and Warfield, "Inspiration," 41–42, appear to deny this connection
arguing that the Bible's inspiration "is not . . . a principle fundamental to the truth of
the Christian religion. . . . Nor should we ever allow it to be believed that the truth of
Christianity depends entirely upon the any doctrine of Inspiration whatever." Yet
later in the essay, they said that the views of the Bible that admit the possibility of
error in the text "threaten not only to shake the confidence of men in the Scriptures,
but the very Scriptures themselves as an objective ground of faith." Ibid., 56.
Moreover, their assertion that the burden of proof lies with those who claim errors
exist (56–57) as well as their efforts to answer the critics (57–74) suggests that
inerrancy was more important to their defense of the truthfulness of Christianity
than the earlier comment implied.

[29]Hudson, Religion, 269–77. In A Religious History of the American People, 2 vols.
(New Haven: Yale University Press, 1975; Image Books edition, Garden City NJ:
Doubleday and Co., 1975) 2: 238–47, Sydney E. Ahlstrom noted that within these two
broad types of liberalism were several other subgroups.

a social application in the Social Gospel, fundamentalists preached with greater fervor the simple gospel of faith in Christ for the forgiveness of sins. In short, fundamentalists fought to maintain the supernatural in their interpretation of historic Christian doctrines.

Defending the authority of the Bible and affirming its doctrines and the supernatural character of Christianity were not the only theological dimensions to fundamentalism. Fundamentalists were also heirs to the fervent zeal of the nineteenth century's evangelicals for evangelism and world missions. In fact, on a practical level, preaching the gospel message of salvation at times seemed to exceed the concern for biblical authority. Of course the two were intimately tied together. The Bible told the story of salvation; thus the liberals' attack on its genuineness and authenticity discredited the message that people needed to hear to save their souls from eternal punishment. On the other hand, believing the message and being "born again" erased the doubts raised by the critics' assault on the Bible. In other words, conversion confirmed the supernatural character of the Scriptures and the truthfulness of its doctrines.[30] To be sure, the reasoning was circular, but it was a circle not easily broken and an apologetic tool that untrained laypeople could employ without having to answer the critics on the same scholarly level. Even preachers did not resist the temptation to employ this tactic. Speaking on "Experience—the Only Competent Critic," Leonard Broughton, an Atlanta pastor, accused the critics of unbelief. If they were truly converted individuals, they would know the truthfulness of the Bible because they would have experienced God's answers to prayers, his provision of strength in times of temptation, and his comfort in mourning.[31]

The last quarter of the nineteenth century saw a tremendous expenditure of energy to evangelize the cities. Motivated by a concern that at times became a fear of the changes resulting from the era's urbanization   and   industrialization,   the   forerunners   of

---

[30]While superficially similar to the evangelical liberals in this regard, fundamentalists asserted that experience had to be based on truth. From the fundamentalist perspective, liberals divorced the two.

[31]Leonard G. Broughton, "Experience—the Only Competent Critic," *Golden Age*, 9 March 1911, 4, 14–16.

fundamentalism renewed their efforts to convert the urban masses.[32] This concentration on evangelism reflected a common evangelical notion that the most effective means of dealing with social problems was through converting individuals. Such a belief, though, did not short circuit, at least not yet, the development of a variety of programs of social relief. Some evangelical churches sponsored employment bureaus to help the unemployed find jobs, rescue missions for alcoholics, evening vocational classes that taught white-collar skills, dispensaries providing free health care for the poor, gymnasiums, and kindergartens for children with working parents.[33] Fundamentalists gave these activities an evangelistic twist. Designed not only to meet

---

[32]Although he moved away from conservative theological positions, Josiah Strong alerted evangelicals and other Protestants to the dangers of the era's social changes in his shrill *Our Country: Its Possible Future and Its Present Crisis* (New York: Baker and Taylor, 1885).

[33]In the 1890s, churches that implemented these kinds of programs were called "institutional churches." Such a congregation expanded its ministry beyond the traditional worship services to include provisions of relief from the problems of the changing urban environment. Scholars have generally seen their activities as the practical application of the liberal's Social Gospel. See Charles Howard Hopkins, *The Rise of the Social Gospel in American Protestantism* (New Haven: Yale University Press, 1940) 319; and Abell, *Urban Impact,* 164–93. More recent investigations reveal that evangelicals developed similar programs in their churches. For example, in *Salvation in the Slums: Evangelical Social Work, 1865–1920* (Metuchen NJ: The Scarecrow Press, 1977), Norris Magnuson argues that the motivation for the men and women in groups like the Salvation Army and rescue missions grew out of a commitment to evangelism and personal holiness. In "The Cross and the Social Order: Calvinist Strategies for Social Improvement, 1870–1920," *Fides et Historia* 17 (Fall–Winter 1984): 39–55, Gary Scott Smith suggests that even the most theologically conservative of Reformed Protestants developed programs to aid the poor, the immigrants, child workers, and inmates in prisons. A Southern expression of this trend was the work of Leonard Broughton who began a dispensary in his church that later became the Georgia Baptist Hospital. William R. Glass, "The Ministry of Leonard G. Broughton at Tabernacle Baptist Church, 1898–1912: A Source of Southern Fundamentalism," *American Baptist Quarterly* 4 (March 1985): 42–43. In "Social Thought," 230–32, Wenger described how Mark A. Matthews, fundamentalist pastor of First Presbyterian Church of Seattle, organized kindergartens, day nurseries, and a branch of the Red Cross in his congregation. For an analysis of institutional programs in an evangelical church, see William R. Glass, "Liberal Means to Conservative Ends: Bethany Presbyterian Church and the Institutional Church Movement," *American Presbyterians* 68 (Fall 1990): 181–92.

the needs of the urban poor, they were used to attract people, who otherwise might not attend where they heard gospel preaching, to evangelical churches.[34] The returns were meager, but more promising with more obvious results was the work of itinerant evangelists.

Spearheading these campaigns was Dwight L. Moody, and the shape of the fundamentalist movement owes much to the energy and activities of this man.[35] Born and raised in rural Massachusetts, Moody found that his efforts to carve out a career in the shoe business of 1850s Chicago robbed him of time he wished to devote to religious activities. After a long inner struggle, he resigned from the shoe company and devoted all his time to fulfilling his obligations as a member of the Plymouth Congregational Church, teaching Sunday school to immigrant children, and working for the Chicago Young Men's Christian Association.[36] His work with the latter two movements took Moody to England on two occasions. During his

---

[34]In *Fundamentalism*, 80–85, Marsden links the creation of these programs to a renewed interest in holiness teachings that stressed the empowerment of the Holy Spirit for service in the church. He correctly notes that the application of holiness teachings to service "meant first of all verbal evangelism; yet in the 1890s it often meant social work among the poor as well" (80). He fails, though, to acknowledge adequately the evangelistic purpose given to this social work. This interpretation suggests a rather cynical evaluation of evangelicals' motives, that these programs were the bait hiding the hook of conversion. But if these activities are evaluated within the evangelical hierarchy of values, which put conversion as the most significant experience of a person's life, then the use of social work could be seen as a legitimate means to win an audience for the message evangelicals believed crucial for everyone to hear. Furthermore, the fact that no evidence remains that the offer of help was predicated on the recipient's response to the gospel suggests that the programs were a genuine effort to meet the needs of the poor in the cities. See the references cited in the previous note, particularly Magnuson, Smith, Glass, and Wenger.

[35]See Marsden, *Fundamentalism*, 32–39, for an analysis of Moody's contribution to fundamentalism.

[36]Moody's life had been the subject of many biographies. Most are hagiographic in character but the best of these is by his son: William R. Moody, *D. L. Moody* (New York: Macmillan, 1930). The best researched work on Moody is James Findlay, *Dwight L. Moody: American Evangelist, 1837–1899* (Chicago: University of Chicago Press, 1969). Moody's theology has been summarized and analyzed in Stanley N. Gundry's excellent work, *Love Them In: The Proclamation Theology of D. L. Moody* (Chicago: Moody Press, 1976). For details on Moody's early life, see Moody, *D. L. Moody*, 24–68 and Findlay, *Dwight L. Moody*, 44–91.

second tour in the early 1870s, he evoked such a remarkable outpouring of religious sentiment and gained such acclaim that when he returned to America in 1875 he was besieged with requests from pastors and laymen to conduct evangelistic campaigns in their cities.[37] Until his death in 1899, Moody was the dean of American evangelists and inspired many imitators.[38]

The excitement aroused by the activity of professional evangelists did not exhaust the fervor of Gilded Age Protestants. At the congregational level, some ministers turned their pulpits into platforms for revivals and the aisles in their churches into sawdust trails under the influence of evangelists. Biographers of prominent late nineteenth-century evangelicals recorded how these men changed their ministries after seeing an evangelist at work in their cities. Generally these men were moderately successful pastors of orthodox but complacent churches, preachers of some ability but lacking a consistent, evangelistic thrust in their sermons and a warm, vital piety in their lives. While an evangelist preached in their towns, these pastors came to a new understanding of their roles as church leaders, giving greater emphasis to evangelistic messages in their preaching and

---

[37]Findlay, *Dwight L. Moody*, 124, 127–28.

[38]A detailed account and analysis of these men is Richard James Anderson's "The Urban Revivalists, 1880–1910" (Ph.D. diss., University of Chicago, 1974). For example, Samuel Porter Jones plied the gospel message so effectively in the old Confederate states that he became known as the "Moody of the South." Raymond Charles Rensi, "Sam Jones: Southern Evangelist" (Ph.D. diss., University of Georgia, 1972) 56; see 14–17 for a discussion of Jones's indebtedness to Moody for revival techniques. For an assessment of Jones's career, see Kathleen Minnix, *Laughter in the Amen Corner: The Life of Evangelist Sam Jones* (Athens: University of Georgia Press, 1993) 236–44. Moody's mantle fell on R. A. Torrey, the man who left his position at Moody Bible Institute to continue the services when Moody suffered his fatal heart attack in 1899. Though respected, especially for an evangelistic tour that took him around the world from 1901 to 1905, Torrey never had the same success and acclaim as Moody and in 1911 left the revival circuit to become dean of the Los Angeles Bible Institute. William G. McLoughlin, *Modern Revivalism: Charles Grandison Finney to Billy Graham* (New York: Ronald Press Co., 1959) 282–329, 366–69.

leading their congregations in developing programs to meet the needs of the poor in their cities.[39]

This evangelistic heritage as shaped by the circumstances of the Gilded Age bequeathed to fundamentalism an emphasis on preaching the gospel and converting individuals as the central task of their churches. Though examples of broader social concern were available, after 1900 many evangelicals dropped most of these activities from their ministries for a variety of reasons. In part, the evangelistic results of these endeavors were so slim that they did not justify the programs' continuation; in any case, the traditional methods of evangelism reaped a larger harvest. More determinative, though, was that after 1900 these kinds of activities became identified with the liberals' Social Gospel; thus evangelical support of social work called into question the sponsor's orthodoxy, particularly during the controversies of the 1920s.[40] Moreover, evangelistic endeavors affirmed in practice and in some ways were more basic to the fundamentalist defense of the Bible than scholarly rebuttals and pastoral polemics against the modernists. Through the means of personal witnessing, pulpit evangelism, support of itinerant preachers, or mission work overseas, fundamentalists discharged these duties. The importance of these efforts to the fundamentalist battle with the modernists was they validated in a person's experience the fundamentalist understanding of the Bible. As Donald Tinder observed about Baptist fundamentalists in the North, they believed

---

[39]See these biographies: C. P. Headley, *George F. Pentecost: Life, Labors, and Bible Studies* (Boston: James H. Earle, 1880) 120–21, 131; Ernest B. Gordon, *Adoniram Judson Gordon: A Biography, with Letters and Illustrative Extracts Drawn from Unpublished or Uncollected Sermons and Addresses* (New York: Fleming H. Revell, 1896) 95, 100–108; Delavan Leonard Pierson, *Arthur T. Pierson: A Spiritual Warrior, Mighty in Scripture, a Leader in the Modern Missionary Crusade* (New York: Fleming H. Revell, 1920) 127–33; A. E. Thompson, *The Life of A. B. Simpson* (New York: The Christian Alliance Publishing Co., 1920) 53–60, 63–66; and Ford C. Ottman, *J. Wilbur Chapman: A Biography* (Garden City NJ: Doubleday, Page, and Co., 1920) 30, 53–56.

[40]See Donald Dayton, *Discovering an Evangelical Heritage* (New York: Harper and Row, 1976) and David Moberg, *The Great Reversal: Evangelism versus Social Concern* (Philadelphia: Lippincott, 1972). Marsden has detailed and insightful analysis of the loss of social concern among evangelical Protestants in *Fundamentalism*, 85–93.

"that unless a person were converted to a vital relationship with God, there was little value in and less likelihood of convincing him of the Fundamentalist view of Scripture. So the Fundamentalist's primary efforts were directed to the preaching at home and abroad of the message that had awakened and sustained his own religious interests."[41]

Another theological element crucial for defining fundamentalism was an emphasis on holiness. The late nineteenth century saw a revival of interest among American evangelicals in the person and work of the Holy Spirit in the life of the believer.[42] It differed from the older perfectionist theology in Wesleyan circles in denying that sin could be eradicated from the Christian's life yet was indebted to that tradition for the notion that the Holy Spirit empowered the Christian to resist sin. It also differed from the Pentecostal doctrines developed at the turn of the century in denying that speaking in tongues was evidence of being filled and controlled by the Holy Spirit.[43] It described the Christian life as a battle with the sinful tendencies of the old nature. The key to the conquest of sin and thus to a life of personal holiness was a "complete surrender" of one's life to God and an appropriation of the power of the Holy Spirit by an act of faith. The Christian took this step subsequent to regeneration and had to renew

---

[41]Donald George Tinder, "Fundamentalist Baptists in the Northern and Western States, 1920–1950" (Ph.D. diss., Yale University, 1969) 109.

[42]In *Fundamentalism*, 72–80, Marsden has a perceptive analysis of the development of this teaching, its relation to other similar traditions, its introduction to American Protestants, and its importance to fundamentalism. See also, Bruce Shelly, "Sources of Pietistic Fundamentalism," *Fides et Historia* 5 (Fall 1972–Spring 1973): 68–78.

[43]For a brief discussion of the rise of Pentecostalism, see Vinson Synan, "Theological Boundaries: the Arminian Tradition," in *The Evangelicals: What They Believe, Who They Are, Where They Are Changing*, rev. ed., ed. David F. Wells and John Woodbridge (Grand Rapids MI: Baker Book House, 1977) 42–49. A more detailed treatment is Synan's *The Holiness Pentecostal Movement in the United States* (Grand Rapids, MI: Eerdmans, 1971). For pentecostalism's theological debt to these new teachings, see William W. Menzies, " The Non-Wesleyan Origins of the Pentecostal Movement," in *Aspects of Pentecostal-Charismatic Origins*, ed. by Vinson Synan (Plainfield NJ: Logos International, 1975) 83–98.

this commitment daily. The result was that the Christian had power for service and power to overcome the temptations of the world.[44]

Holiness reinforced the fundamentalist insistence on the supernatural character of Christianity. After all, these teachings emphasized the active presence of the Holy Spirit in believers' lives to help them overcome temptation to sin, to guide them in making decisions, and to direct them in understanding the Bible. Moreover, the Holy Spirit provided power for the Church to pursue its main task of evangelizing the world. In the analysis of fundamentalists the Church lacked power because it tolerated sin in its members, and spiritual power to energize home and world missions could not be channeled through unclean vessels. Therefore, in terms of behavior, these teachings became the foundation for fundamentalist attacks on a variety of petty vices like drinking, card-playing, dancing, and lewd language. Fundamentalist condemnation of recreational activities like attending plays, and later movies, and reading popular fiction were found in the context of discussions of how the Holy Spirit enabled Christians to resist temptation.[45] In this, fundamentalists emphasized "separation from the world." In other words, Christians were to present to the world a way of life that marked them as different. Rarely did twentieth-century fundamentalists give these teachings much of a social application;[46] increasingly during the 1920s

---

[44]The classic statement of this teaching, and one which is still in print, is Hannah Whitall Smith's *The Christian's Secret to a Happy Life* (Westwood NJ: Revell, 1952). Other typical expositions include F. B. Meyer, *Steps into the Blessed Life* (Philadelphia: Henry T. Altemus, 1896) 7–22, 105–118; R. A. Torrey, *The Person and Work of the Holy Spirit as Revealed in Scripture and in Personal Experience* (Chicago: Fleming H. Revell, 1910; reprint, Grand Rapids MI: Zondervan, 1968) 116–18, 174–83, 190–95, 221–24; and S. D. Gordon, "The Power of the Holy Spirit," *Record of Christian Work*, May 1905, 295–99.

[45]See for example, these editorial comments: "Movies and Morals," *Moody Bible Institute Monthly*, June 1924, 496; "As to Hair-bobbing," *Moody Bible Institute Monthly*, October 1924, 54; "Christian College Theatricals," *Sunday School Times*, 3 December 1921, 690. For other examples see the discussion in chapter 2 of the presentation of this theme at the Atlanta Bible Conference.

[46]Marsden, in *Fundamentalism*, 80–85, suggests that these teachings stimulated concern for and work to aid the poor in the cities among late nineteenth century

and 1930s they used these holiness teachings to define how the believer functioned in a society in which cultural values no longer supported an evangelical definition of morality. Donald Tinder's comments about fundamentalist Northern Baptists could be applied to those in other traditions: "Acceptance of these prohibitions, when coupled with doctrinal orthodoxy, signified one's identity with the fundamentalist community. No fundamentalist ever said that these constituted the sum of Christian ethics, or even its most important aspects. They did serve to set Fundamentalists off as having a different style of life from many of those around them."[47]

A final important dimension in the theological boundaries of fundamentalism requires discussion: the growing acceptance of premillennialism as an interpretation of the prophetic passages in the Bible. Including premillennialism here is somewhat misleading because not all fundamentalists were premillennialists. In *The Roots of Fundamentalism* Ernest Sandeen documented the importance of premillennialism to fundamentalism, but other studies have shown that his thesis does not adequately acknowledge the nineteenth-century evangelical tradition that nurtured fundamentalism and failed to explain the nature of the coalition of conservatives that formed in the controversies of the 1920s.[48] For example, premillennialism held little attraction for conservatives in the Reformed tradition yet among Northern Presbyterians they rallied to the fundamentalist banner in the battle against modernist control of their denomination in the 1920s and 1930s.[49] Nevertheless,

---

evangelicals, but note the comments above about the evangelistic twist given to this work.

[47]Tinder, "Fundamentalist Baptists," 192. On 193–95, Tinder discusses the activities prohibited by the fundamentalist moral code.

[48]The former criticism was the main point Marsden in "Defining Fundamentalism;" and the latter was that of LeRoy Moore in "Another Look at Fundamentalism: A Response to Ernest R. Sandeen," *Church History* 37 (June 1968): 195–202. Moore was responding to Sandeen's article "Toward a Historical Interpretation of the Origins of Fundamentalism," *Church History* 36 (March 1967): 66–83. Marsden amplified and sustained his critique in *Fundamentalism*.

[49]J. Gresham Machen is the most notable example of this point. Machen was an amillennialist, believing that the Bible did not teach the establishment of a millennial

premillennialist presence in the fundamentalist movement played a critical role in shaping the coalition and determining its fate.

Premillennialists believe that Christ will return to earth to establish a kingdom of perfect peace and righteousness that will last for 1,000 years.[50] Prior to the millennium, the world will experience God's wrath on its sinfulness in an unprecedented scale in a seven year period called the tribulation. Premillennialism was not a new eschatology; until the eighteenth century it was prominent in Protestant theology. Then postmillennialism supplanted it with an interpretation that suggested the Church was responsible for establishing the millennium as a way preparing the world for Christ's return.[51] The triumph of postmillennialism in the nineteenth century among American Protestants was aided by the excesses of William Miller's futile attempts in the early 1840s to predict the precise date of Christ's return. Moreover, postmillennialism was an eschatology in step with the optimism of the Jacksonian era. Combined with the revivalist's emphasis on man's ability, it energized and sustained a variety of reform causes particularly in the Northern states.[52]

Premillennialism, though discredited by the Millerites, did not disappear. In fact, in the years after the Civil War, a new version of

---

kingdom and that the prophecies concerning it were fulfilled in some measure in the Christian Church. See C. Allyn Russell, "J. Gresham Machen—Scholarly Fundamentalist," in *Voices*, 142–43. Along this same line, the famous five points which the General Assembly of the Northern Presbyterian Church declared in 1910 to be essential doctrines did not include a statement on Christ's return. See Presbyterian Church in the USA, *Minutes of the General Assembly*, 1910, 272–73.

[50]In *Living*, 9–12, Weber gives a succinct overview of the varieties of Christian millennialism. Though focused on one issue, the discussion in *The Meaning of the Millennium: Four Views*, ed. Robert G. Clouse (Downers Grove IL: Inter-Varsity Press, 1977), is also quite useful. For a modern statement of classic premillennial doctrine, see George E. Ladd, *The Blessed Hope* (Grand Rapids MI: Eerdman's, 1956).

[51]In "Jonathan Edwards: A New Departure in Eschatology," *Church History* 27 (March 1959): 25–40, C. C. Goen traces this shift to the millennial speculations of Jonathan Edwards.

[52]See Timothy L. Smith, *Revivalism and Social Reform: American Protestantism on the Eve of the Civil War* (New York: Abingdon Press, 1957; reprint, Gloucester MA: Peter Smith, 1976) for a discussion of the relationship between religion and reform in antebellum America.

premillennialism began winning adherents, but there was a difference. This version came to be called dispensationalism.[53] Providing a comprehensive framework for understanding biblical history, its advocates the division of human history into a series of "dispensations," or ages, usually seven, in which God sets the conditions for humanity to gain his favor and blessing. In each age mankind failed to meet God's standards and incurred God's judgment. The present age, the sixth, is the era of the church or the age of grace. Like the others, this era will end in failure, with God's judgment expressed in the tribulation. Immediately prior to these years, the Church, that is all true believers in Christ for their salvation, will be "raptured," or miraculously swept up into God's presence before the tribulation begins. Christ will return to rule with the saints during the millennium (the seventh age), after which Satan is finally and completely vanquished, and a new heaven and earth established.

Introduced in the 1860s and 1870s to Americans by John Nelson Darby, a British clergyman, and by the Plymouth Brethren movement, dispensationalism remained on the fringes of American Protestantism until it became the subject of several prophetic conferences and standard fare on summer Bible conferences held at popular resorts during the late nineteenth and early twentieth centuries.[54] Itinerant Bible teachers took dispensationalism to those unable to attend the conferences while the publication of the Scofield Reference Bible in 1909 by Oxford University Press made a popular version of

---

[53]Sandeen, *Roots*, 3–102, provides the best account of the development of dispensationalism and its introduction to American Protestants. Two modern scholarly statements of this scheme are Charles C. Ryrie, *Dispensationalism Today* (Chicago: Moody Press, 1965) and John F. Walvoord, *The Blessed Hope and the Tribulation* (Grand Rapids MI: Zondervan, 1976). An extraordinarily popular presentation is Hal Lindsey's *The Late Great Planet Earth* (Grand Rapids MI: Zondervan, 1970).

[54]Sandeen, *Roots*, 132–61, discusses the importance of these conferences to the dissemination of dispensational teaching. The Niagara Bible Conference, the "mother of them all—the Monte Cassino and the Port Royale of the movement" (according to ibid., 132), has been given extended and careful treatment by Walter Unger in "'Earnestly Contending for the Faith:' The Role of the Niagara Bible Conference in the Emergence of American Fundamentalism" (Ph.D. diss., Simon Fraser University, 1982).

dispensationalism widely available. Its pessimistic vision of civilization's future seemed to be confirmed in the social conflict of closing decades of the nineteenth century and in World War I. Moreover, by insisting that biblical prophecy provided a map of future events and that the prophecies would be fulfilled literally, dispensationalists looked to current events to as a way of marking the progress of God's plans to bring this age to an end. Thus part of dispensationalism's appeal lay in its advocates' ability to point to current events in confirmation of their interpretations, even if occasionally they seemed to shape their interpretation to fit the event.[55]

Historic premillennialism benefited from dispensationalism's rise and experienced renewed interest, but it was difficult to distinguish its growth among American Protestants from the newer interpretation. Both described the events of the end times in approximately the same chronology; both insisted on a literal fulfillment of prophecy; and both maintained a pessimistic assessment of the course of human history. Historic premillennialists, though, were troubled by dispensationalism's rigid division of biblical history, which in some variations implied that God had different methods of salvation in each dispensation.[56] Indeed, some dispensationalists seemed to suggest that in certain eras God saved people on the basis of their deeds, not their faith. Historic premillennialists were more flexible about the timing of the rapture, accepting interpretations that placed the removal of the Church before, during, or after the tribulation. For dispensationalists the rapture could occur only before the tribulation.

While quibbling over such interpretations may seem like an exercise in the esoterica of medieval theology, an important issue was at stake that had implications for the broader fundamentalist cause. Multiple, conflicting interpretations raised the question of which was the right one and ultimately undermined fundamentalist claims of an authoritative understanding of the Bible's message and the unity of

---

[55]See Weber, *Living in the Shadow*, 231–32, for further discussion of this point.

[56]See chapter 4 for a discussion of how historic premillennialists in the Southern Presbyterian Church fought in the 1940s to distinguish themselves from dispensationalists their denomination was in the process of condemning.

the movement. While the issue of determining the timing of the rapture by itself did not cause the movement to split, the question of eschatology became more important to identifying an ally in the fight against liberalism during and after the denominational battles of the twenties. Because they insisted on a literal reading of prophetic passages in Scripture, premillennialists evinced a fundamentalist perspective on the Bible and its teachings. Moreover, premillennialism emphasized the supernatural by positing divine intervention as the solution to deteriorating world conditions. Premillennialism also encouraged holy living. At its crudest, believing in the imminent return of Christ restrained immoral behavior by posing the question, "Would you really want to be doing *that* when Jesus comes?"[57] Additionally, premillennialism explained the increasing defection of Christians from orthodoxy by describing this apostasy as a sign of the end of the age. Finally premillennialism stimulated evangelism in that discharging the duty to preach the gospel to all nations hastened the day of Christ's return. By the early 1940s, premillennialists, particularly the dispensational variety, dominated fundamentalism to the extent that Lewis Chafer, in a speech to the convention of the World Christian Fundamentals Association, answered yes to the question "Is Premillennialism Fundamental?"[58] Such a reply reflected the narrowing of the fundamentalist coalition to those holding a certain

---

[57]Weber, *Living in the Shadow*, 234.

[58]Chafer acknowledged that premillennialism was not "fundamental" to some things like a person's salvation, but he asserted that "premillennialism is foundational to the right interpretation of Scripture and right interpretation is foundational to all that concerns the Church of God." Lewis Sperry Chafer, "Is Premillennialism Fundamental?" (typescript manuscript in Lewis Sperry Chafer Papers, Mosher Library, Dallas Theological Seminary, Dallas TX) (hereinafter cited as LSC Papers). On his appearance at the convention, see Paul W. Rood to LSC, 15 March 1943, and LSC to Paul W. Rood, 23 March 1943, in LSC Papers. It is important to note that while Chafer used the term "premillennialism" he meant dispensationalism. Chafer employed the broader term to gloss over the differences in interpretations and to try to win some legitimacy and acceptance for the more controversial eschatological scheme. Significantly, Chafer wrote this speech when Southern Presbyterians were in the process of condemning dispensationalism as inconsistent with church doctrine. Thus the speech may be regarded as Chafer's efforts to reply to criticisms circulating in the Southern denomination. See chapter 4.

interpretation of biblical prophecy. The effect was to help weaken and divide the movement by alienating theological conservatives who held other views on prophecy.

What transformed the twentieth-century heirs of these theological streams into fundamentalists in the 1920s was the growing influence liberals exercised in the denominations, especially among the Baptists and Presbyterians in the North.[59] A variety of issues split conservatives from liberals, but the most divisive was the presence of liberal missionaries on foreign fields and liberal professors in the seminaries. In both denominations fundamentalists attempted to force the denominational conventions to adopt an explicit statement of doctrinal standards to which all ministers, professors, missionaries, and administrators would have to subscribe. Such action would then allow fundamentalists to initiate proceedings to remove those who deviated from the creeds. By the mid-twenties, though, fundamentalists were in retreat in both denominations, riven by factions within the conservative ranks and outmaneuvered in denominational politics by the liberals. In both denominations the balance of power lay with a large group of theologically conservative pastors and laymen. They agreed with fundamentalists that liberalism strayed too far from historic Protestant doctrines, but they abandoned the fundamentalist cause when it appeared on the verge of dividing their churches.

Fundamentalism was not simply a set of interpretations of Protestant doctrines nor was it only a coalition of conservative denominational politicians trying to resist liberal domination of their churches. Fundamentalists also built a network of churches, schools, conferences, mission societies, and publications to sustain their movement and to give it an institutional structure.[60] This network was a

---

[59]Marsden, *Fundamentalism*, 178–80, Sandeen, *Roots*, 264–65, and Szasz, *Divided Mind*, 101–104, discussed briefly the controversies in other denominations but much of their discussion of the denominational controversies of the 1920s focused on events among Northern Baptists and Presbyterians.

[60]In "Fundamentalist Institutions and the Rise of Evangelical Protestantism, 1929–1942," *Church History* 49 (March 1980): 62–75, Joel A. Carpenter describes and analyzes these developments.

loose affiliation without formal structural ties between the various parts, and its foundations were laid in the Gilded Age. The defeats in denominational politics in the twenties stimulated its further development. The Bible conferences played critical roles in spreading the holiness teachings and new interpretations of prophecy while the schools institutionalized and expanded the work of the conferences. Initially intended to train lay workers for the churches, as their curricula expanded the schools began sending their graduates into the churches as pastors and on to the mission field under the sponsorship of independent, interdenominational agencies.

In addition to their educational work many of these schools published magazines. While containing news of the schools' progress for alumni and supporters, these magazines also carried a variety of inspirational material, Bible study aids, reports on missionary activity, and developments in the broader fundamentalist movement. *Serving and Waiting* of the Philadelphia School of the Bible and *King's Business* of the Bible Institute of Los Angeles were two of the more noted,[61] but setting the pace in the 1920s was the *Moody Bible Institute Monthly* (formerly the *Institute Tie* and to become later simply *Moody Monthly*). Under the editorship of James Gray, the magazine moved from being only an informational newsletter to an elaborate publication featuring the material mentioned above plus editorial comments on current affairs.[62] Though not associated with a school but equally important to the movement was the *Sunday School Times*, a weekly publication giving evangelical commentary on and study aids for the International Sunday School Lesson Plans. Designed primarily to assist Sunday school teachers, the *Times* also carried articles on holiness, prophecy, current events, archeology, apologetics, missions, critiques of liberal theology, and news of fundamentalist leaders.[63] Essentially, these magazines became substitutes for

---

[61]Ibid., 66–67.

[62]Gene A. Getz, *MBI: The Story of the Moody Bible Institute* (Chicago: Moody Press, 1969) 254–64.

[63]*Sunday School Times* became a major evangelical publication under Henry Clay Trumball in the 1870s and 1880s. For a description of his accomplishments and editorial policies, see Philip E. Howard, *The Life Story of Henry Clay Trumball:*

denominational publications for laypeople and important for nurturing the fundamentalist vision of Christianity and of church affairs.

The schools took the fundamentalist message to the broader public in another way. Within two years of the first commercial radio broadcast in 1920, the Bible Institute of Los Angeles established its own radio station.[64] In 1926 Moody Bible Institute followed suit, creating WMBI, and its programming became the model for other fundamentalist stations. With a mix of Bible studies, evangelistic messages, religious music, news of the Institute and its alumni, extension classes, and fundamentalist commentary on current affairs, WMBI not only kept supporters informed of the needs and activities of the school but also served Midwestern fundamentalists as a point of identification with the broader movement.[65]

In a similar way, a host of evangelists and Bible teachers used the airwaves to convert the lost and instruct the faithful, but their programs also served as links in the emerging network of institutions that battled to preserve the fundamentalist version of Christianity.[66] The religious programming that appeared on the major networks was relegated to Sunday morning and dominated by liberals by the 1930s. Frustrated by the networks' decisions, fundamentalists found individual stations more open to including their broadcasts and built a patchwork network for their programs. Some were pastors like Donald Gray Barnhouse of Philadelphia's Tenth Presbyterian Church whose "Bible Study Hour" emphasized exposition of biblical texts. On the other hand, Charles Fuller's "Old Fashioned Revival Hour" featured revival hymns and evangelistic sermons and grew out of the broadcasts of his Southern California church's worship services. Fuller's popularity became such that he resigned in 1933 from the

---

Missionary, Army Chaplain, Editor, and Author (Philadelphia: Sunday School Times Co., 1905) 300–309. Under his son, Charles Trumball, the *Times* moved into the fundamentalist camp.

[64]Carpenter, "Fundamentalist Institutions," 67.

[65]Getz, *MBI*, 277–313; note the schedule on 282 detailing the programs for a week in 1927 and 304–313 for the diversity of programs broadcast over WMBI.

[66]Carpenter, "Fundamentalist Institutions," 70–72.

ministry for full-time work as a radio evangelist. By 1940, his program was heard from coast to coast over the Mutual Broadcasting Network by an estimated 15 to 20 million listeners.[67]

Fundamentalist efforts to create an inclusive, interdenominational organization that could present a united front of conservative Protestantism to the liberals and the world consistently foundered on doctrinal differences, personalities, and the issue of separation. The most notable effort in the 1920s along this line was the World Christian Fundamentals Association (WCFA). Organized in 1919 and a product of the premillennialist wing of fundamentalism, it was an effort to create an interdenominational fellowship of conservative churchmen for the purposes of defending the conservative interpretation of the Bible as well as coordinating their battle against liberalism in their denominations.[68] Over 6,000 delegates attended the first conference held in Philadelphia with William Bell Riley presiding. Pastor of First Baptist Church of Minneapolis, Riley was the driving force behind the WCFA in its early years. Following the initial convention, Riley plunged into nationwide effort to enlist recruits by conducting conferences across the country with the purpose of creating local and state chapters. Membership was open to individuals or organizations that signed the WCFA's nine-point doctrinal statement and paid a nominal fee.[69] By 1924, Riley's magazine reported that over 250 follow-up conferences had been held in thirty-two states and several Canadian provinces. Hampered by including premillennialism in it doctrinal statement, divided by conflicts among its leaders, and alienated from potential allies because of its confrontational tactics, the WCFA never reached its goal of

---

[67]See Daniel P. Fuller, *Give the Winds a Mighty Voice: The Story of Charles E. Fuller* (Waco TX: Word Books, 1972) 103–136, for the origins of Fuller's radio ministry; cf., Marsden, *Reforming Fundamentalism*, 14–16.

[68]Marsden, *Fundamentalism*, 158; Sandeen, in *Roots*, 243–47, suggests that the WCFA was virtually a fundamentalist denomination because the WCFA committees on Bible conferences, religious publications, Christian schools, and missionary work had similar functions to parallel agencies in the denominations.

[69]Russell, "William Bell Riley: Organizational Fundamentalist," in *Voices*, 97–99. See also, Szasz, *Divided Mind*, 89–92.

uniting Protestant conservatives under its fundamentalist banner.[70] After Riley left the leadership, the WCFA declined but maintained a precarious existence through the 1930s until it was eclipsed in the 1940s by two new organizations: the American Council of Christian Churches, representing the more militant, separatist descendants of the twenties fundamentalists, and the National Association of Evangelicals, providing a forum for cooperation for moderate fundamentalists.[71]

While a united fundamentalist front to attack liberalism proved to be illusory, fundamentalists were able to cooperate in sustaining organizations within certain doctrinal traditions and for a more focused purpose. Among the former, the most notable were the various associations, fellowships, and denominations created to unite independent congregations or churches that withdrew from liberal-dominated denominations. The General Association of Regular Baptists, Conservative Baptist Association, Independent Fundamental Churches of America, Orthodox Presbyterian Church, and Bible Presbyterian Church grew out of congregations and ministers leaving established denominations and were part of the fastest growing segment in American Protestantism in an era of religious decline.[72]

---

[70]In "William Bell Riley," 100–101, Russell notes that Riley's use of the WCFA to spearhead his fight against evolution also weakened its effectiveness.

[71]See Carpenter, *Revive*, 141–60, for a discussion and analysis of the origins of these two organizations; cf., Louis Gasper, *The Fundamentalist Movement, 1930–1956* (The Hague: Mouton and Company, 1963; reprint, Grand Rapids MI: Baker Book House, 1981) 23–37. For an internal perspective of these organizations, see Carl McIntire, *Twentieth Century Reformation* (Collinswood NJ: Christian Beacon Press, 1946) 180–92; and James DeForest Murch, *Cooperation Without Compromise: A History of the National Association of Evangelicals* (Grand Rapids MI: Eerdmans, 1956).

[72]Brief sketches of these organizations, and others, can be found in George W. Dollar, *A History of Fundamentalism in America*, 2nd ed. (Orlando FL: Daniels Publishing Co., 1983) 214–23, 237–40. On religious decline, see Robert T. Handy, "The American Religious Depression, 1926–1935," *Church History* 29 (March 1960): 3–16. While not discussing these groups, Joel Carpenter suggests that the growth of fundamentalist institutions in the thirties undermines Handy's thesis. See "Fundamentalist Institutions," 73–74.

The growth of missionary agencies and the creation of youth organizations demonstrates fundamentalists' ability to support institutions for specific purposes.[73] Some independent mission boards like the China Inland Mission or the Sudan Interior Mission worked in certain areas of the world, while others like the Independent Board for Presbyterian Foreign Missions established churches within a particular denominational tradition. Still others specialized their activities to accomplish a specific task. The goal of Wycliffe Bible Translators was to provide a written version of the Bible in every language group in the world.[74] The rise of fundamentalist youth groups in the 1940s directed this missionary activity to evangelizing American high school and college students. Youth for Christ and Young Life for teenagers and Inter-Varsity Christian Fellowship for those in college set the example that a variety of other organizations followed in the 1950s and 1960s.[75]

The relevance of looking at the creation of this institutional network for understanding fundamentalism is suggested in an observation of Lewis Sperry Chafer, founder of Dallas Theological Seminary. With the establishment of his school, he noted that a prospective fundamentalist minister could go from high school through seminary in fundamentalist institutions by attending prep school at Stony Brook in New York, college at Wheaton in Illinois, and seminary in Dallas. Such a pedigree would assure conservative churches that the candidate for pastor had been nurtured in the womb of the fundamentalist movement.[76] But the creation of this network of institutions implies a broader application of Chafer's remark. By World War II, fundamentalists had created "a shelter in a time of storm" that preserved and perpetuated not only their interpretations of Christian

---

[73]For an overview, see Carpenter, *Revive*, 161–86.

[74]James Hefley and Marti Hefley, *Uncle Cam: The Story of William Cameron Townsend, Founder of Wycliffe Bible Translators and the Summer Institute of Linguistics* (Waco, TX: Word Books, 1974).

[75]For brief overview and analysis, see Bruce Shelley, "The Rise of Evangelical Youth Movements," *Fides et Historia* 18 (January 1986): 47–63.

[76]Lewis Sperry Chafer to Paul Gaebelein, 20 December 1930, in LSC Papers.

doctrine but also a particular version of Christian living.[77] Fundamentalist laypeople attended churches where they heard sermons on fundamentalist living, spent their spare time participating in a variety of evangelistic projects, supported financially fundamentalist missionaries, and encouraged their children to attend Bible colleges and institutes. In their homes they listened to fundamentalist preachers on their radios, read fundamentalist magazines, and sent their children to fundamentalist youth groups.[78] Their understanding of biblical authority gave them a sense of stability and continuity in an era of shifting moral and religious values. For more ardent students of prophecy, premillennialism provided a comprehensive framework for understanding history and interpreting current events, while fundamentalist holiness prescribed a piety centered on Bible study, prayer, evangelism, and moral living. In short, fundamentalism by 1940 had strong similarities to an ethnic subculture with institutions designed to guard its traditions and pass them on to future generations.[79]

---

[77]The phrase comes from the Ira Sankey hymn, "A Shelter in the Time of Storm." Ira Sankey, James McGranahan, George T. Stebbins, and Philip P. Bliss, *Gospel Hymns, Nos. 1 to 6, Complete* (New York: Da Capo Press, 1972) 234.

[78]The degree and the extent to which any individual, family, or church actually pursued these activities is not the point of these comments but rather to emphasize the comprehensive character of the emerging fundamentalist subculture. Though Hunter does not distinguish between evangelical and fundamentalist, he does offer some quantitative measure of religious practices among conservative Protestants in *American Evangelicalism,* 65–68.

[79]George Marsden makes this provocative suggestion in "From Fundamentalism to Evangelicalism: A Historical Analysis," in Wells and Woodbridge, *The Evangelicals,* 149–53, and reaffirmed it in *Fundamentalism,* 204–205. In the latter, Marsden notes certain inadequacies of this analogy. First, fundamentalists did not voluntarily experience the shift "from the old world of the nineteenth century to the new world of the twentieth century," thus their feelings of alienation led them "to a militant defense of the old order." Second, unlike most immigrants, fundamentalists were not "trying to adjust to a new culture or break into the centers of influence in the culture" but believed that they were being pushed out of their dominant position. Cf., the similar comments of Carpenter in "Renewal," 37–38, where he suggests that the holiness behavioral restrictions along with the creation of independent, fundamentalist-controlled institutions gave the fundamentalist movement "many of the features of an ethnic subculture, since it offered a comfortable envelopment of mediating institutions to people who did not feel at home in Modern America."

In a development largely overlooked by most historians of fundamentalism meaningful Southern participation dating to the beginning of the twentieth century helped to shape the institutional development of the movement. Itinerant fundamentalist preachers regularly toured the South, introducing thousands of Southern laypeople and ministers to the doctrines and concerns of fundamentalism. Particularly important was the appearance of fundamentalist schools in the South because they expanded significantly the range of the broader fundamentalist movement's educational efforts by offering vocational training, graduate education, and graduate professional training for the pastorate. But even when some schools focused on the traditional fundamentalist concern for the training of laymen, the Southern versions of Bible institutes and colleges should not be dismissed as mere imitations of Northern models but seen as an important step in building a Southern wing of the movement and broadening the movement's coalition. Moreover, beginning in the 1930s and with increasing intensity in the 1940s, Southern denominations experienced controversies over liberalism of the type that troubled Northern churches in the 1920s. These battles, particularly those among Southern Baptists and Southern Presbyterians, fostered the establishment of ongoing factions determined to resist and reverse the penetration of liberal theology in their churches. During these same years, disputes within the conservative factions over eschatology, in particular dispensationalism, and ecclesiological separation divided fundamentalists and pre-vented the development united coalition.

Largely missing from this analysis is a careful evaluation of developments among Southern Protestants. The picture that emerges is that fundamentalism was Northern and urban in origin but that portrait neglects several significant factors. Though they built their careers in the North and Midwest, fundamentalist leaders like William Bell Riley, J. Gresham Machen, and A. C. Dixon, had significant ties to the South either by family or education.[80] Some

---

[80]Five of the seven fundamentalist leaders profiled by Russell in *Voices* fit this description. Of the five, only J. Frank Norris built his career in the South.

Southern Protestants supported Bible conferences similar to those in the North and gave a warm reception to itinerant fundamentalist Bible teachers. Southerners supported the crusade against Darwin's theories by enacting laws proscribing their teaching and prosecuting violators. The South became home to schools that expanded the scope of fundamentalist educational efforts. And Southern denominations in the 1930s and 1940s experienced battles for their control that represented the expansion of controversies that plagued Northern churches in the 1920s. For example, the creation of fundamentalist factions in Southern denominations in the 1930s and 1940s is one of the more obvious ways that the history of fundamentalism in the South has been neglected. Apart from George Marsden's cryptic remark that during the 1930s and 1940s "the center of gravity of fundamentalism distinctly shifted from the North to the South,"[81] historians of fundamentalism have ignored Southern developments, or at best, incorporated them into a national pattern. These factions sparked controversies among southerners that represented the first serious and prolonged disputes among southerners similar to those among Northern denominations in the 1920s. In fact, they represent the movement of 1920s battles into Southern denominations. As in the North, Baptists and Presbyterians were the most troubled while Methodist fundamentalists quickly left their denomination to form their own organization.[82] Moreover, historians of Southern denominations also have paid scant attention to these developments. Ernest Trice Thompson devoted only a few pages to denominational fundamentalists among Southern Presbyterians with his discussion of their activities providing a minor counterpoint to his main theme of

---

[81]Marsden, "From Fundamentalism to Evangelicalism," 147.

[82]For this reason, greater attention will be paid to events in the Southern Presbyterian church and the Southern Baptist Convention as case studies of the development of fundamentalist style controversies in Southern denominations. The story of Methodist fundamentalism will be analyzed to illustrate the development of independent fundamentalist organizations in the South in chapter 6.

the denomination's liberalization.[83] But they were far more successful in stalling the liberal agenda than Thompson was willing to admit. Southern Baptist historians preferred to ignore dissent and concentrate on their denomination's growth into a national church, the success of the Cooperative Program, and its world-wide missionary activities.[84] However, events of the 1940s deserve closer inspection because they were the preliminary skirmishes that developed into the "Southern Baptist holy war" of the 1980s.[85] The result of slighting Southern developments has been a failure to evaluate adequately what Southern activities meant for the broader fundamentalist movement and their impact on Southern denominations. The rest of this book tells that story.

---

[83] Earnest Trice Thompson, *Presbyterians in the South*, 3 vols. (Richmond VA: John Knox Press, 1973) 3:486–90. See chapter 4 for further development of this argument.

[84] See for example, Robert A. Baker, *The Southern Baptist Convention and Its People, 1607–1972* (Nashville: Broadman Press, 1974) 342–51.

[85] See chapter 5. This description comes from the title of Joe Edward Barnhart's *The Southern Baptist Holy War* (Austin: Texas Monthly Press, 1986). Barnhart did not trace the historical roots this controversy.

2

ITINERANT FUNDAMENTALISTS

Blessed are the feet of those that bring news of good tidings.
—*Romans 10:13*

In 1903, Leonard G. Broughton, pastor of Atlanta's Tabernacle Baptist Church and the director of the Tabernacle Bible Conference, reminded the conferees of the doctrinal themes of his conference, and in so doing placed the conference in fundamentalist theological traditions emerging in the North. He told his audience that "this conference stands for all old fashioned religion." These words meant that the speakers emphasized evangelism: they taught "that the worst of men can be saved and saved instantly." Moreover, the conferees learned how to live a "Spirit-filled life," one "sanctified" and pleasing to God. Broughton believed "that every Christian may enjoy the power of Pentecost insofar as God may order his life." Finally, the conference stood "for the premillennial coming of Christ. We hold that the world will never be saved until Jesus comes to reign among men, hence we are praying, 'Even so, come Lord Jesus.'"[1]

---

[1]N.a., "Many Attend First Session," *Atlanta* (GA) *Constitution*, 28 February 1903, 2 (hereinafter cited as *AC*). Similar expressions of the themes could be found in the early years of the conference. See n.a., "Bible Conference to Begin Tonight," *AC*, 6 March 1899, 4; n.a., "Conference on at Tabernacle," *AC*, 1 March 1902, 5; n.a., "Bible Conference Opened Last Night," *Atlanta* (GA) *Journal*, 1 March 1902, 2 (hereinafter cited as *AJ*); and n.a., "Great Audience Hears Dr. Morgan," *AC*, 24 February 1904, 3.

These statements not only describe the doctrinal emphases of the conference but also represent the central tenets of Broughton's theology.[2] The only element missing is a defense of the inspiration and authority of the Bible. Moreover, Broughton's words align him and his conference with the several movements in American Protestantism that merged in the 1920s to form the fundamentalist coalition. This conference was one of the earliest ways by which Southern Protestants learned the interests and doctrines of Northern fundamentalism before 1920. During the years 1900 to 1930 Northern fundamentalist preachers toured the South speaking in conferences like the one in Atlanta, conducting city-wide evangelistic services, or preaching for a week or more in a local church. From these traveling fundamentalists southerners heard of the growing threat of theological liberalism, of the premillennial second coming of Christ, of the power of the Holy Spirit enabling individuals to live a pure life, and of the importance of defending the inspiration of the Bible. Southerners responded enthusiastically to what they heard. Large crowds attended the conferences and revival meetings while some churches regularly hosted fundamentalist preachers. But southerners did not go to the barricades with their Northern brethren in the denominational controversies of 1920s despite the efforts of northerners to create a Southern wing of their movement. Southern Protestants did not see their denominations succumbing to theological liberalism; for the most part, their denominations still affirmed and defended orthodoxy. For another, the three main Protestant denominational families—Baptist, Methodist, and Presbyterian—remained divided into sectional churches. The disease was in the Northern denominations, and the absence of institutional ties insulated and protected Southern churches. Nevertheless, these conferences, revivals, and traveling preachers sowed the first seeds of fundamentalism in the South.

---

[2]For a more detailed discussion of Broughton's beliefs, see William R. Glass, "The Ministry of Leonard G. Broughton at Tabernacle Baptist Church, 1898–1912: A Source of Southern Fundamentalism," *American Baptist Quarterly* 4 (March 1985): 35–60. Material from this article is reprinted with the permission of American Baptist Historical Society, Valley Forge, PA 19482.

In the late nineteenth and early twentieth centuries, Bible conferences played a central role in the diffusion of fundamentalist ideas. The work of Dwight Moody left its imprint on this aspect of fundamentalism by popularizing a pattern for conferences when he developed the General Conference for Christian Workers in the 1880s. Drawing on the examples of conferences begun in the 1870s concerning prophecy held in Northern summer resorts and those concerning holiness held in Keswick, England,[3] Moody, in 1880, invited all Christians "who are hungering for intimate fellowship with God and for power to do His work" to gather in Northfield, Massachusetts, for a "convocation for prayer."[4] With 300 in attendance, the meetings were led by H. B. Hartzler and Moody and in the following year by Andrew Bonar, a Scottish clergyman. No conferences were held from 1882–1884 while Moody toured the British Isles, but upon his return in 1885 they began again and were held annually.[5] The main focus of these early conferences was devotional, the intention being to deepen the piety of the participants with the hope of bringing revival to the church. During the 1890s, the scope of the conferences expanded. Doctrinal concerns like the authority and inspiration of the Bible, the second coming of Christ, and the person and work of the Holy Spirit found a place on conference programs along with discussions of foreign missions, rescue work in the slums, and practical training in Sunday school work and evangelism. The

---

[3]For discussions of these conferences, see Ernest R. Sandeen, *The Roots of Fundamentalism: British and American Millenarianism, 1800–1930* (Chicago: University of Chicago Press, 1970; reprint, Grand Rapids MI: Baker Book House, 1978) 132–61; and George Marsden, *Fundamentalism and American Culture: The Shaping of Twentieth Century Evangelicalism* (New York: Oxford University Press, 1980) 75–79.

[4]Quoted in William R. Moody, *The Life of Dwight L. Moody* (New York: Fleming H. Revell, 1900) 362. The General Conference for Christian Workers was one of several conferences held at Northfield during the summer months. Conferences for young women and college students were annual events from the late 1880s. See Teunis S. Hamlin, "The Evolution of Northfield," *Northfield Echoes* 3 (Fall 1896): 21–22. For the various conferences conducted at Northfield, see ibid., 1 (Winter 1894): 66–67; 2 (Winter 1895): 73–75; 3 (Winter 1896): 77–80; 4 (Winter 1897): 93–95; and 5 (Winter 1898): 96.

[5]Moody, *Life*, 362–63.

call for the seventeenth conference in 1899 reflected the broadening of conference topics. Moody invited "all of God's people who are interested in the study of His word, in a revival of the spiritual life of the Church, and in the evangelization of the World" to attend.[6] The conservative theological positions presented at the conferences attracted thousands of laypeople and ministers from the major Protestant denominations,[7] and this evangelical ecumenicity fostered a widespread dissemination of the theology peculiar to these conferences and encouraged clerical alliances across denominational lines. Both of these results had important consequences for the growth of the fundamentalist coalition after 1910. Not only did these kinds of conferences produce theologically informed laymen, albeit within a narrow perspective, but they also served as forums in which fundamentalist leaders met to discuss the progress of their movement. In some ways, they functioned as a denominational convention of the fundamentalist coalition.[8]

---

[6]Quoted in ibid., 373; cf., A. T. Pierson, "The Story of the Northfield Conferences," *Northfield Echoes* 1 (Summer 1894): 1–13 and James Findlay, *Dwight L. Moody: American Evangelist, 1837–1899* (Chicago: University of Chicago Press, 1969) 340–42. Moody also encouraged the efforts of Solomon Dickey to begin a Bible conference at Winona Lake, Indiana, by appointing one of his associate evangelists, J. Wilbur Chapman, to assist Dickey. Starting in 1895, this conference grew under Chapman's leadership to where it almost rivaled Northfield in popularity. Ibid., see also Ford C. Ottman, *J. Wilbur Chapman: A Biography* (Garden City NJ: Doubleday, Page, and Co., 1920) 97–98.

[7]The presence of Social Gospeler Josiah Strong, evolutionary theologian Henry Drummond, and liberal New Testament scholar William Rainey Harper should not obscure the strong conservative flavor of the meetings. According to Findlay, *Dwight L. Moody*, 411, Moody "frequently" invited such men, but an analysis of the conference programs shows that traditional concerns and conservative speakers dominated the meetings. See *Northfield Echoes* 1 (Fall 1894): 581–83; 2 (Fall 1895): 619–21; 3 (Fall 1896): 527–30; 5 (Fall 1898): 511–12; 6 (Fall 1899): 510–12. In *Roots*, 174–76 Sandeen documents the presence of millenarians at the conferences while the prominence of holiness teachers in the programs provoked such criticism that William Moody sought to refute the charge that Northfield was an American Keswick. See William Moody, Editorial comment, *Record of Christian Work*, November 1899, 593–94.

[8]Sandeen, *Roots*, 132–45. Other scholars have acknowledged the importance of Bible conferences in popularization of fundamentalist ideas. For Stewart Cole, *The History of Fundamentalism* (New York: Richard R. Smith, 1931) 31–35, these

Southern conferences of the same type were an important link in the early fundamentalist network. One of the earliest and largest was the Tabernacle Bible Conference in Atlanta, and its schedule, format, and topics were typical of other fundamentalist meetings in the South. Its prominence and success owed much to the energy and vision of its founder, Leonard G. Broughton. Born in 1865 and raised in the rural poverty of central North Carolina, Broughton, with the financial assistance of an uncle, attended Wake Forest College and earned an MD from the Kentucky School of Medicine in Louisville. Returning to practice medicine in Wilson County and then in Reidsville, Broughton built a fairly successful practice and acquired a reputation within the North Carolina medical profession through the publication of several articles and the election to offices in the state medical society.[9] But Broughton was living in a time of spiritual turmoil. He was converted and baptized at age fourteen and soon afterward felt called by God to preach. He stifled these impressions through the years of his education and medical work, but during a bout with typhoid fever that left him bedridden for six months, he resolved to give up medicine and enter the ministry.[10] In 1891 he became the pastor of a struggling mission church in Winston, North Carolina, and succeeded in establishing it with a strong membership. He was ordained in 1893 before moving on to the pulpit of Calvary Baptist Church in Roanoke, Virginia.[11]

---

conferences represented the efforts of conservatives to preserve and reinforce a traditional statement of Christian doctrine, an effort that continued with the fundamentalists. Similarly, Norman F. Furniss, *The Fundamentalist Controversy, 1918–1931* (New Haven CT: Yale University Press, 1954) 11, saw the movement strengthening the religious conservatism of the people with its "polemic and organizational activity preparing the way directly for the fundamentalist movement." Worthy of note is that current fundamentalists acknowledge these conferences to be a part of their heritage. See George W. Dollar, *A History of Fundamentalism in America*, 2nd ed. (Orlando FL: Daniels Publishing Co., 1983) 27–28, 76, 261.

[9]N.a., "Leonard Gaston Broughton," *Baptist Biography*, ed. by B. J. W. Graham (Atlanta: Index Publishing Co., 1917) 46.

[10]Leonard G. Broughton, "Divine Reciprocity in Matters of Benevolence," *Golden Age*, 16 March 1911, 15.

[11]N.a., "Broughton," *Baptist Biography*, 47-48.

While at Calvary, Broughton conducted evangelistic services at different churches around the South, and one campaign took him to Second Baptist Church in Atlanta. He immediately recognized that his desire to expand the work of the church beyond the traditional worship services could be realized in a large city. He decided that should he be offered the pastorate of a church in Atlanta, he would accept it provided the membership agreed to implement his program.[12] In 1897, Third Baptist Church called Broughton to its pulpit, and the membership agreed to Broughton's condition that the church relocate from West Atlanta to a central location downtown. A group of members objected, so Broughton and about 200 people left Third Baptist in 1898 to establish Tabernacle Baptist.[13] By 1902, the church had built an auditorium seating 3,000, seen its membership grow to over 1,300, sponsored an annual Bible conference, begun an infirmary to care for the poor, and opened a home for single working women.[14] Within ten years, the Tabernacle received over 3,000 members and had over 1,500 enrolled in Sunday School.[15]

How and when Broughton came to accept and teach fundamentalist doctrine is unclear, but he probably learned his fundamentalism through trips to Moody's General Conference for Christian Workers in the 1890s. In 1901, he confessed that "no greater influence ever operated on my life" than the sermons he heard at the conferences.[16] He was disturbed, though, because the expense and time of traveling to Northfield prohibited most southerners from hearing the teaching that he believed had been so beneficial in his Christian life.[17] Broughton determined to reproduce the Northfield conference in the South. His move to Atlanta was one step in fulfilling that dream

---

[12]Leonard G. Broughton, "Tabernacle Tenth Anniversary," *Golden Age*, 11 March 1909, 1.

[13]Vivian Perkins and William F. Doverspike, "The Baptist Tabernacle," *History of Atlanta Baptist Churches*, James L. Baggott, ed. (Atlanta: privately published, no date) 5.

[14]N.a., "The Baptist Tabernacle," *AC*, 12 October 1902, E-8.

[15]Broughton, "Tabernacle Tenth Anniversary," 2.

[16]N.a., "Big Conference Is on at Tabernacle," *AC*, 16 March 1901, 7.

[17]Leonard G. Broughton, "The Faith Invisible," *Golden Age*, 13 March 1909, 2.

because the city was well connected by rail to all parts of the South, and the establishment of the Tabernacle was another that provided the conference with a suitable auditorium and a supportive constituency. This aspect of Broughton's work is important for understanding his significance as a source of Southern fundamentalism. Had Broughton remained a solitary figure preaching fundamentalist doctrine in Atlanta, he might be an interesting anomaly, but because he consciously sought to give his Bible conference a fundamentalist flavor, Broughton was one of the earliest individuals to bring northerners into the South to introduce Southern laymen and pastors to the theological currents shaping fundamentalism in the North.

In 1898, with Moody's encouragement, Broughton began making plans to hold a spring conference at the Tabernacle. Moody's death the following year did not slow the progress of the Tabernacle conference. Indeed ties with Northern traditions became stronger as speakers from Northfield and Moody's Bible Institute in Chicago regularly made the trek South for the Tabernacle conference.[18] These meetings in Atlanta help illuminate the introduction of Northern fundamentalism into the South because the conference was not an isolated event devoid of influence outside of Atlanta. The ideas propagated at the Tabernacle filtered throughout the South.

Large crowds attended the conference sessions, so large that at times hundreds, even thousands, were turned away.[19] During the 1906 conference, the police had to be called to control the crowd and an estimated 2,000 people could not enter the Tabernacle.[20] The largest audience attended a special Sunday afternoon lecture in the Armory

---

[18]On Moody's support, see n.a., "Big Conference Is on at Tabernacle," *AC*, 16 March 1907, 7 and n.a., "Tabernacle Cornerstone Is Placed in Position before Immense Crowd," *AC*, 10 March 1910, 4. See also, n.a., "Broughton," *Baptist Biography*, 48.

[19]N.a., "Many Attending the Conference," *AC*, 9 March 1900, 6; n.a., "Six Thousand Heard Speaker," *AC*, 18 March 1901, 5; n.a., Thousands Listen Eagerly on Last Day of Conference," *AC*, 10 March 1902, 7; n.a., "Will Enlarge Big Tabernacle," *AC*, 26 February 1904, 3; n.a., "Lecture Made $1000 for Church," *AJ*, 28 February 1904, 10; and n.a., "Today Is Last of Conference,"*AC*, 18 March 1906, C-5.

[20]N.a., "Two Thousand Turned Away," *AC*, 9 March 1906, 5 and n.a., "Great Crowd Struggled to Gain Admission to Church," *AJ*, 12 March 1906, 4.

Auditorium to hear G. Campbell Morgan, an associate of Moody. A standing room only crowd of 10,000 jammed the hall, while another 3,000 heard Brice Rankin, Morgan's assistant, preach in the lobby, and between 2,000 and 4,000 more people failed to hear either.[21] But what also impressed newspaper reporters was the number of out of town conferees. During the first few conferences, most of them came from Georgia and surrounding states, but the reputation of the conference soon attracted visitors from every state in the South. In later years, delegates came from as far away as Massachusetts, Pennsylvania, Michigan, Missouri, Colorado, and Texas.[22] A number of benefits mitigated the cost of attending the conference. The newspapers did not mention a registration fee or a charge for attending the lectures. The only exceptions were the occasional Friday night lectures given by the main speaker at which 50 cents was charged for admission. The rest of the sessions were free and open to the public.[23] For out-of-town visitors, railroads and boarding houses offered reduced rates, and the women of the Tabernacle provided box lunches.[24] Precisely how the conference was financed is unclear. The Tabernacle seems to have borne most of the burden, though its contribution may have been supplemented by offerings at the meetings. On several occasions, Broughton had to make special appeals for donations to erase the deficit incurred by the conference.[25]

---

[21]N.a., "Morgan Thrills Immense Crowd in Great Sermon," *AC*, 13 March 1911, 1.

[22]N.a., "Big Conference Is on at Tabernacle," *AC*, 16 March 1901, 7; n.a., "Great Audience Hears Dr. Morgan," *AC*, 24 February 1904, 3; n.a., "Today Is Last of Conference," *AC*, 18 March 1906, C-5; n.a., "Campbell Morgan Will Speak at Conference," *AJ*, 7 March 1908, 2; n.a., "Bible Conference to Open Friday," *AC*, 11 March 1909, 9; and n.a., "Campbell Morgan Coming to the Bible Conference," *AC*, 8 March 1911, 9.

[23]N.a., "Will Enlarge Big Tabernacle," *AC*, 26 February 1904, 3; n.a., "Gypsy Smith's Lecture Attracts Attention," *AC*, 28 March 1907, 2; n.a., "Large Crowd at Services," *AC*, 14 March 1908, 3; and n.a., "Faith Superior to the [sic] Reason," *AC*, 15 March 1911, 1.

[24]N.a., "Bible Conference to Begin Tonight," *AC*, 6 March 1899, 4 and n.a., "Great Bible Conference to Open Thursday Night," *AJ*, 7 March 1906, 7.

[25]N.a., "Great Crowd Struggled to Gain Admission to Church," *AJ*, 12 March 1906, 4; n.a., "End Has Come to Conference," *AC*, 16 March 1908, 6; n.a.; "How to Be

Significantly, a sizable portion of the visitors were ministers and other Christian workers.[26] The *Atlanta Journal* estimated that half of the registered conferees to the 1908 conference, about 600 or 700 people, were pastors.[27] Furthermore, Baptist clergy were not the only pastors in attendance. The large number of Methodist ministers at the 1904 conference reminded the *Wesleyan Christian Advocate*'s editor of a Methodist Annual Conference.[28]

The conferences also attracted some participation from Atlanta's black residents. "I don't believe in mixing races," Broughton said, "but I do believe, since we are children of one common Father in the spiritual sense, that there are times when the souls of all should 'mingle together in sweet delight.'"[29] Apparently the conferences were not one of those times. Though the newspapers reported African-Americans attending conference sessions, the more typical report was of conference speakers preaching in special services in black churches.[30] During the later years of the conference, Broughton organized

---

Fishers of Men Told at Conference," *AJ*, 17 March 1909, 8; and n.a., "All Spellbound by Morgan Magic," *AC*, 18 March 1911, 1.

[26]N.a., "Two Denominations Fail of Admission," *AC*, 2 March 1903, 11; n.a., "Crowds Throng at Conference," *AC*, 22 March 1905, 11; and n.a., "Crowd of 15,000 Throng Conference Sessions," *AC*, 27 March 1905, 5.

[27]N.a., "Campbell Morgan Will Speak at Conference," *AJ*, 7 March 1908, 2 and n.a., "Dr. Morgan Tells of Origin of Religion," *AJ*, 10 March 1908, 4.

[28]N.a., Editorial comment, *Wesleyan Christian Advocate*, 18 March 1910, 4 (hereinafter cited as *WCA*). See also, n.a., "Great Sermons at Tabernacle," *AC*, 7 March 1910, 5.

[29]Leonard G. Broughton, *Up from Sin: The Rise and Fall of a Prodigal* (Chicago: Fleming H. Revell, 1909) 117. Discussion of "the race problem" rarely occurred in Broughton's published sermons and never in the newspaper accounts of the sermons delivered at the conference. Broughton preached against lynching, and on one occasion his opposition resulted in the vandalization of the Tabernacle and himself being burned in effigy. Idem., "Tabernacle Tenth Anniversary," *Golden Age*, 11 March 1909, 3.

[30]N.a., "Bible conference Largely Attended," *AJ*, 10 March 1900, 10; n.a., "Street Service Held Yesterday," *AC*, 11 March 1900, 8; n.a., "Thousands Listen to Word of God," *AJ*, 20 March 1901, 5; n.a., "Bible Meetings Closed on Sunday," *AJ*, 25 March 1901, 9; n.a., "Two Visitors to Preach," *AC*, 8 March 1903, 4; n.a., "Don't Kick, Says Gypsy Smith, Evangelist," *AJ*, 22 March 1907, 5; and n.a., "Politics in Pulpit Barred by Dr. Gray," *AC*, 13 March 1913, 2.

separated meetings in black churches that paralleled the main ones in the Tabernacle.[31]

Broughton selected speakers for the conference that represented a sampling of conservative Protestants. Though only about one-fourth of them can be identified with the movements that supplied members for the fundamentalist coalition in the 1920s,[32] Broughton assured them a prominent place in the conference program in two ways. First, he invited certain individuals several times. For example, A. C. Dixon, pastor of Moody Memorial Church in Chicago and editor for part of *The Fundamentals,* and Morgan spoke at seven conferences. William Moody attended six, and James Gray, president of Moody Bible Institute, lectured at four. Moreover, Broughton gave these men and their allies the best attended sessions for their lectures. The conferences averaged ten days, beginning before one weekend and running through the following Sunday.[33] A typical conference day had six sessions: three in the morning, two in the afternoon, and one in the evening. The first session in the morning was a devotional time, given to prayer, singing, and brief meditations on the Bible. The second morning service dealt with one of the themes of the conference or was an exposition of a biblical book. The afternoon meetings were practical, focusing on Sunday school work, missions, church music, or evangelism. Broughton usually reserved the third morning session and the one at night for his fundamentalist friends when they would have the largest audiences.

The messages that the conference speakers delivered embodied the emerging fundamentalist consensus. The four currents that were

---

[31]N.a., "Great Audience Attends Opening of Bible Meeting," *AC,* 2 March 1914, 1.

[32]The determination of whether a conference speaker might be classified as a fundamentalist was based on the comments in a Biographical Index in Dollar, *History,* 299–375, and on their place in Marsden's and Sandeen's analyses of the origins of fundamentalism. They were W. E. Biederwolf, Lewis Sperry Chafer, Solomon Dickey, A. C. Dixon, William J. Eerdman, A. P. Fitt, S. D. Gordon, James Gray, Elmore Harris, Charles Inwood, Sam Jones, H. C. Mabie, Stuart MacArthur, F. B. Meyer, G. Campbell Morgan, Charles Needham, A. T. Pierson, C. I. Scofield, Gypsy Smith, R. A. Torrey, Henry Varley, and Robert Dick Wilson.

[33]For a day by day schedule of one conference, see "Program of the Conference," *Record of Christian Work,* April 1902, 320.

crucial in the development of the theological dimensions of Northern fundamentalism appeared with regularity in the sermons of the conference speakers.[34] The revivalistic heritage appeared in several forms. The cause of world missions was presented to the conferees through the stream of missionaries and rescue mission workers who reported on their work in fields ranging from Bulgaria to the Congo to China to the slums of New York city.[35] Speakers also lectured on "soul-winning," the evangelistic church, evangelism, and personal work. Their purpose was both practical and motivational. Not only did the speakers try to train their audiences in evangelistic techniques, but they also hoped to inspire them to use what they had learned.[36] Finally, the services often resembled revival meetings, with personal testimonies of conversion experiences, evangelistic messages, and invitations to members of the audience to commit their lives to Christ. At the first two conferences, the evening meetings were plainly evangelistic, and the sermons resulted in a large number of conversions.[37] Thereafter, the gospel preaching was limited to special Sunday afternoon meetings held at an Atlanta theater under the auspices of the YMCA, or as a direct application of a regular conference lecture. In 1904, H. W. Pope preached on conversion and

---

[34]The emphasis on these four interests does not mean that they were the only themes that the conferees heard. A fairly regular feature was a discussion of Sunday school work in the afternoon sessions.

[35]N.a., "Bible Conference Today," *AC*, 12 March 1899, 8; n.a., "Hundreds Hear Rescue Work," *AC*, 7 March 1903, 7; n.a., "Bible Conference Schedule," *AC*, 27 February 1904, 7; n.a., "Great Crowds at Meetings of Conference," *AJ*, 31 March 1905, 13; n.a., "No Objection to Miss Stone," *AC*, 11 March 1906, B-2; and n.a., "Phenomenal Crowds Expected at Conference Today," *AC*, 24 March 1907, C-5.

[36]See C. L. Goodell, "The Evangelistic Message," *Record of Christian Work*, May 1907, 387; G. Campbell Morgan, "The Evangel," *Record of Christian Work*, April 1904, 319; John Pullen, "Soul Winning: Our Responsibility," *Record of Christian Work*, May 1905, 288–91; n.a., "Famous Ministers Are Addressing the Tabernacle Bible Conference,: *AC*, 8 March 1900, 5; n.a., Dr. A. C. Dixion Joins Forces," *AC*, 6 March 1902, 11; n.a., "Fine Welcome for Dr. Meyer," *AC*, 24 March 1905, 4; and n.a., "Bustard Lashes New Preachers," *AC*, 6 March 1912, 5.

[37]N.a., "Dr. Dixon Spoke Yesterday," *AC*, 8 March 1899, 3; n.a., "Many Attend the Bible Conference," *AC*, 9 March 1899, 4; and n.a., "Many Attending the Conference," *AC*, 9 March 1900, 6.

then conducted an "after-meeting" in which he explained how to experience the new birth. Scores responded to his invitation.[38]

The fundamentalist holiness teachings were also an important part of the Tabernacle conferences. In fact, Broughton viewed these doctrines as "the main rock on which the conference" stood.[39] The version heard in Atlanta focused on personal holiness explaining how a "complete surrender" of one's life to Christ and how yielding to the direction of the Holy Spirit enabled the Christian to overcome sin and have power for effective evangelism. Broughton secured some of the more noted holiness teachers for these meetings. The major burden for preaching on holiness fell on R. A. Torrey (in 1900 and 1901), F. B. Meyer (in 1901, 1905, and 1912), and S. D. Gordon (in 1905 and 1914), and they were assisted by C. I. Scofield who lectured on the Holy Spirit (1904) and by Charles Inwood, a leader of the Keswick conferences in England, who delivered a series on the surrendered life (1912). These speakers gave considerable attention to the problem of sin undermining a Christian's testimony to the gospel. Frequently, they enumerated and described signs of society's moral decay and warned against the snares that might trap the Christian in sin. F. B. Meyer defined holiness as "separation from sin and common use"[40] and claimed that when a Christian chose the path of holiness certain practices had to be relinquished:

> If you go through that gate, you will have to give up the dance, you will have to give up the ballroom. Of course, you will have to give up the theater. You can not get that through. You will have to give up that girl who is not a Christian, or that young

---

[38]Howard W. Pope, "The New Birth—What It Is—How It Is Brought About—Its Results," *Record of Christian Work*, April 1904, 256–58; n.a., "Bible Conference Attracts Much Attention," *AJ*, 1 March 1904, 9. For other similar instances, see n.a., "Lecture Tonight on Spurgeon's Life," *AC*, 8 March 1902, 12 and n.a., "New Men Come to Conference," *AC*, 13 March 1906, 7. For the theater meetings, see n.a., "Bible Meetings Closed on Sunday," *AJ*, 25 March 1901, 9; n.a., "Thousands Listen Eagerly on Last Day of Conference," *AC*, 10 March 1902, 7; n.a., "Scores Ask Prayer in the Bijou Theatre [sic]," *AJ*, 9 March 1903, 3; *AC*, 20 March 1909, 1.

[39]N.a., "Spend-the-Day at the Conference," *AC*, 11 March 1910, 7.

[40]N.a., "Six Thousand Heard Speaking," *AC*, 18 March 1901, 5.

man who is not a Christian, but you will thank God for it. If you are having things in your life which Christ prohibits, it will damn you. I pray you man and woman tonight to give it up.[41]

For Broughton and the conference speakers, the crux of the problem was that trivial, but worldly pleasures sapped the spiritual vitality of the church and hindered the preaching of the gospel. "Our churches lose their spiritual life," complained Broughton, "because of a failure to insist upon a rigid maintenance of their covenant vows of separation from the world."[42] A. C. Dixon was more blunt: "A card-playing, theater-going, dancing, wine-guzzling Christian for soul-winning is not worth a penny a hundred. The great weakening force of the church is worldliness."[43]

The Tabernacle conference also became a platform for premillennialism but not of the dispensational variety. It is significant that Broughton had Scofield, a leading dispensationalist teacher, lecture on the Holy Spirit not prophecy. The speakers on prophecy frequently tied their teaching to the other conference themes. In 1905, R. V. Miller used prophecy to explain why problems existed in the church. He suggested that one sign of Christ's return was an enfeebled church and that prophecy foretold of a great falling away from the church. Looking at the church's condition in his day, particularly the sin and growing acceptance of liberal theology, Miller concluded that "the mass of church members have apostatized and are allied with the world."[44] Premillennial teaching also motivated Christians to fulfill their obligation to evangelize the world. Though the message would be rejected, the Christian's duty was to proclaim the gospel, not convert people. Moreover, the more rapidly the gospel was

---

[41]N.a., "Large Audience at Tabernacle," *AC*, 19 March 1901, 9.

[42]N.a., "Countess Tells of Foreign Work," *AC*, 13 March 1900, 10.

[43]N.a., "Dr. Dixon Makes Impulsive Talk," *AC*, 14 March 1900, 5.

[44]R. V. Miller, "Studies in Prophecy," *Record of Christian Work*, April 1905, 263; cf., W. E. Blackstone, "The Blessed Hope," *Record of Christian Work*, May 1905, 303.

preached to every nation, the sooner Jesus would return.[45] Finally, because these speakers believed that premillennialism expressed the verities of what an infallible Bible taught concerning the end times, they attacked other eschatological schemes as erroneous. James Gray bluntly labeled as false the postmillennial view that the world would gradually be Christianized before Christ's return.[46] George Needham appealed to history to refute postmillennialism: "The one great lesson of the ages is that man, with all the advancement and progress, with all the light of nature around them, and the light of conscience, man, in his alienation from God, is deteriorating and growing worse."[47]

Discussions of the authority and inspiration of the Bible appeared regularly on the conference schedule. Generally, the speakers did not spend much time replying to challenges of liberal critics and science but rather lectured on Bible study methods and the doctrine of inspiration. A. P. Fitt (1903), James Gray (1907), and Broughton (1909) spoke on the former while Henry Varley (1902), A. C. Dixon (1908), and Elmore Harris (1908) delivered messages on the latter.[48] Nevertheless, audiences also heard traditional conservative defenses of the supernatural character of the Bible. Probably some of the material in Camden Cobern's lectures on New Testament archeology in 1912 and 1914 dealt with the veracity and authenticity of the Bible. One headline in the *Constitution* over a story on Cobern's presentations proclaimed, "Science Proves Truth of the Bible."[49] A series of lectures given by Robert Dick Wilson, an Old Testament professor at Princeton seminary, was the most sustained and scholarly rebuttal to liberal critics heard at the conferences. Though he dealt with such complicated topics as the Babylonian influence on Hebrew

---

[45]Leonard G. Broughton, "The 'New Religion' v. Christianity," *Golden Age*, 28 October 1909, 2; cf., Timothy P. Weber, *Living in the Shadow of the Second Coming: American Premillennialism, 1875–1925* (New York: Oxford University Press, 1979) 66–73.

[46]N.a., "Nashville Seeking Atlanta Conference," *AC*, 12 March 1913, 2.

[47]N.a., "Many Hear Sermons at Bible Conference," *AJ*, 16 March 1901, 3.

[48]N.a., "Campbell Morgan Will Speak at Conference," *AJ*, 7 March 1908, 2; Elmore Harris, "The Inspiration of the Bible," *Record of Christian Work*, May 1908, 291.

[49]N.a., "Science Proves Truth of Bible," *AC*, 3 March 1914, 2.

religion—presenting them in so technical a fashion that Broughton confessed he had trouble following the nuances of Wilson's arguments—Wilson was popular with the audiences. At the conclusion of his lecture on "The Follies of the Critics," the congregation broke into spontaneous applause and sang the doxology.[50]

Reception of all facets of the conference teaching was not universally enthusiastic, and criticisms of Broughton and his conference foreshadowed those leveled at fundamentalists after 1920. The specific element that aroused the most opposition was premillennialism. In assessing the first conference, the *Atlanta Constitution* noted that W. A. Nelson's sermons of the second coming of Christ "have created intense interest in the city."[51] The paper did not explain the nature of that interest, but editorials in the *Christian Index* provide a few clues. The editors of this Southern Baptist newspaper criticized Broughton for failing to use local Baptist preachers as speakers and accused him of establishing doctrinal tests of fellowship that created divisions among Baptists.[52] They also complained about the peculiarity of the doctrines. Commenting on the conference teachings concerning the surrendered life, the endowment of power from the Holy Spirit, missions, and premillennialism, they claimed that "these four doctrines are thus interwoven into a system which is common to the Keswick, Northfield, and Gordon schools, but very uncommon among Baptists."[53] Their concern extended beyond warning Southern Baptists to making sure that the people of Atlanta understood that the conference teachings were not standard Baptist theology: "It is our place as servants of the denomination to let the character of the teaching be known to the churches, and to see it, as

---

[50]N.a., "Attacks on Higher Critics Make Tabernacle Shout," *AC*, 15 March 1906, 9; n.a., "Attendance Shows Daily Increase," *AJ*, 16 March 1906, 9; and n.a., "All Day Service for Conference," *AC*, 17 March 1906, 13.

[51]N.a., "Dr. Dixon Spoke Last Night," *AC*, 10 March 1899, 7.

[52]N.a., Editorial, *Christian Index* (Atlanta GA), 16 March 1899, 6.

[53]N.a., Editorial, *Christian Index*, 30 March 1899, 6. Not to belabor the point, but it is worth noting that these remarks indicate that some Southern Baptists were uncomfortable with the developing fundamentalist formulation of Protestant doctrine and thus simply equating Southern Protestantism with fundamentalism is misleading.

best we can that the community at large is led to recognize that the doctrines presented are peculiar, and do not generally prevail among Baptists."[54]

They soon focused their attention on premillennialism. First, they published an article by W. W. Landrum, pastor of Atlanta's First Baptist Church, in which he faulted premillennial exegesis as "a 'crazy-quilt' style of handling the Word of God…too common with many Sunday school teachers, evangelists, and highly emotional and spiritualizing preachers." According to Landrum, the Bible taught that Christ's second coming was to judge the world, not to inaugurate the millennium. He concluded with a brief defense of postmillennialism, emphasizing the ease with which it allowed Scripture to be interpreted and the many centuries that it had remained the accepted understanding in the church of Christ's return.[55] Broughton replied by claiming that Scripture clearly supported the premillennialists and cited several passages to bolster his contention. He pointed to Matthew 24:37-42 to show that the world would not gradually be converted, as postmillennialists believed. He suggested that 1 Thessalonians 4:13-18 demonstrated that a separate resurrection and transformation of the saints preceded the tribulation. He concluded by explaining how Revelation 20:1-6 revealed that the last judgement *followed* the thousand-year reign of Christ on earth.[56] The editors had the last word in this round. They questioned Broughton's interpretation of each passage and pleaded for moderation: "About the details of that coming there is much of mystery that may indeed lead to blessed conjecture and anticipation, but to a modest avoidance of dogmatism, and much caution in presentation."[57]

---

[54]Editorial, *Christian Index*, 23 March 1899, 6.

[55]W. W. Landrum, "The Second Coming of Christ," *Christian Index*, 30 March 1899, 3.

[56]Leonard G. Broughton, "The Return of Our Lord," *Christian Index*, 27 April 1899, 6.

[57]N.a., Editorial comment, *Christian Index*, 27 April 1899, 6. The editors fired one more salvo in 1902 when they published a series of articles by S. M. Provence, an Alabama minister who made similar remarks about the "unbaptistic" character of Broughton's theology and disliked Broughton's attitude that suggested that other churches should fall into line with his doctrines. S. M. Provence, "Tabernaclism,"

To be sure, changes occurred in the conference, but they indicate the importance of Broughton to maintaining the conference as a fundamentalist institution. In 1909, under Broughton's leadership, the Tabernacle's Board of Deacons approved a plan to enlarge the sanctuary, in part to accommodate the crowds at the conferences. The cornerstone was laid in 1910, and the building completed the following year. During this time Broughton received several invitations from other churches to become their pastor but refused them all, even though acceptance would have meant a larger salary and a broader ministry. In 1912, however, the prestige of a call from Christ Church in London was too great to resist. After the 1912 conference, Broughton left the Tabernacle. Over the next several years, the church went through several pastors, declined in membership, and struggled to keep current on its debt for the new building.[58] The conference continued for two years after Broughton left, led by a committee of Atlanta pastors and businessmen. Its leadership broadened to include Presbyterians, Methodists, Congregationalists, Episcopalians, and Lutherans.[59] In effect, the direction of the conference passed from Broughton and the Tabernacle, for his successors did not participate in the committee and he could not give effective leadership from London.[60]

With Broughton gone, the conference lost its distinctiveness, a loss reflected in the revision of the conference themes. At a meeting in 1912 called to plan the future of the conference after Broughton's departure, William Moody suggested that the essential planks in the

---

Christian Index, 23 January 1902, 1; and 27 February 1902, 2. Criticism of the conference disappeared from the pages of the Index.

[58]Perkins and Doverspike, "The Baptist Tabernacle," in History of Atlanta Baptist Churches, ed. James L. Baggott (Atlanta: privately published, no date) 5; n.a., "Brooklyn after Broughton," Golden Age, 28 October 1910, 4–5; Baptist Biography, s.v., "Broughton, Leonard Gaston," n.a., "Tabernacle Church Will Go for Debt unless City Helps," AC, 6 March 1916, 1.

[59]N.a., "Theory of Evolution Is True, Says Morgan," AC, 16 March 1913 16 and n.a., "Bible Conference Attendance Proves Remarkable Influence of Annual Meeting in Atlanta," AC, 8 March 1914, A-4.

[60]N.a., "Theory of Evolution Is True, Says Morgan," AC, 16 March 1913, 16 and "Bible Conference Will Open Today," AC, 1 March 1914, 1.

conference platform should be the deity of Christ, his death as the only means of salvation, and the Bible as the revelation of God's will. Others felt that the conference should emphasize social service and work with boys and young men.[61] In 1913, Broughton tried to recall the conference to its original purposes with a statement that it should serve as "an inspiration in the main work of the church—the salvation of the lost.... Everything else is secondary to the work of saving souls."[62] The confusion was reflected in the speakers and topics of the last two conferences. James Vance, a Presbyterian minister from Nashville, provided the most notable illustration. He used the conference platform to advocate a postmillennial view of the return of Christ.[63] Finally, Atlanta's churches began turning their attention to other activities. In the spring of 1915 during the usual time of the conference, most of the churches supported a revival led by J. Wilbur Chapman. Some thought was given to conducting a conference concurrently with the revival with Chapman presiding in Broughton's place, but the conference never took place.[64] During the 1920s, the Tabernacle made an effort to revive the conference under the leadership of Will Houghton, who later became president of Moody Bible Institute. Despite having speakers who reflected the fundamentalist character of earlier conferences, those in the 1920s did not have the notoriety or popularity.[65] Meanwhile Broughton returned to the states in 1916 to pastor First Baptist Church of Knoxville,

---

[61]N.a., "$5,500 Pledged for Conference," AC, 10 March 1912, B-7.

[62]N.a., "Bible Conference Draws Thousands," AC, 8 March 1913, 1.

[63]N.a., "No Double Standard in the Eyes of Jehovah," AC, 12 March 1913, 9.

[64]N.a., "Revival to Open this Afternoon," AC, 14 March 1915, 1.

[65]See announcements in Moody Bible Institute Monthly, March 1927, 356 and March 1928, 344. Into the 1940s, the conference tradition continued. The Christian Index carried ads announcing the conference schedule. See for example, n.a., n.t., Christian Index, 28 February 1946, 7. Speakers for this conference included several associated with post-war fundamentalism like Paul Beckwith of the Inter-Varsity Christian Fellowship, Bob Jones, Jr., Robert A. Forrest, president of Toccoa Falls College, Lee Roberson of Chattanooga, and Homer Hammontree of Philadelphia.

Tennessee. He filled the pulpits of several other Southern churches, including the Tabernacle in 1929–1931, before he died in 1936.[66]

Assessing the significance of the Tabernacle conferences is difficult. One measure is to recognize that they inspired interest in imitation in other parts of the South. With the formation of the committee in 1912 to direct the Atlanta conference, pastors from other cities—Nashville, Raleigh, and Little Rock—sought to arrange conferences with the aid of Atlanta's committee. The goal was to create a chain of Bible conferences across the South.[67] The plan saw success only in conducting "auxiliary" conferences in the Georgia cities of Rome, Athens, and Macon in conjunction with the 1914 conference.[68] With the collapse of the Tabernacle meetings after 1914, this project also died. More notable was the effort to establish a Bible conference in Florida. In 1904, at the invitation of Clarence Strouse, a Southern evangelist, Broughton with two Tabernacle conference participants, W. E. Blackstone and S. H. Hadley, spoke at the first Gainesville Winter Bible Conference.[69] The dates of the Gainesville meetings did not conflict with those of the Tabernacle, and occasionally speakers in Atlanta appeared on the Gainesville platform. Though Broughton was "no stranger to the conference" and was announced as a speaker for the 1907 conference, he did not participate in that year or in any of the following years.[70] By 1909 when Strouse no longer directed the conference, it lost its fundamentalist flavor and became an appendage to the Chatauqua meetings that followed.[71]

---

[66]James L. Baggott, *Meet 1000 Atlanta Baptist Ministers, 1843–1973* (Atlanta: James L. Baggott, 1973) 33–34.

[67]N.a., "Bible Meeting Ends Tonight," *AC*, 21 March 1909, 1; n.a., "Nashville Seeking Atlanta Conference," *AC*, 12 March 1913, 2; and n.a., "Bible Conference Ends," *AC*, 16 March 1913, 16.

[68]N.a., "Great Interest in Macon," *AC*, 4 March 1914, 5; n.a., "Conference Leaders Heard at Covington," AC, 8 March 1914, 4.

[69]N.a., "Evangelistic Field," *Record of Christian Work*, February 1904, 127.

[70]N.a., "Announcements," *Alabama Christian Advocate*, 7 February 1907, 16; n.a., "Bible Conference Begins," *Gainesville* (FL) *Daily Sun*, 8 February 1907, 2.

[71]N.a., "Speakers Announced for Bible Conference," *Gainesville Daily Sun*, 26 January 1909, 3 and n.a., "Chautaugua Meetings Open," 12 February 1909, 8.

The same Northfield conferences that inspired Broughton also
sparked the creation of the Southfield Bible Conference in Crescent
City, Florida, but the success of the Tabernacle meetings may have
been the element to encourage the Southfield leaders to start their
conference. In 1904, Lewis Sperry Chafer and his brother Rollin led
the first conference in Crescent City, a small town a few miles South
of St. Augustine on Florida's east coast.[72] Working as an agent of the
Northfield extension service, Lewis spoke at the Tabernacle conference
and knew of Broughton's involvement in Northfield's Christian
Worker's Conference. Southfield's program, though, was more limited
than both its namesake and the Tabernacle meetings, concentrating
on biblical exposition by the Chafers, C. I. Scofield, and A. C.
Gaebelein.[73] But Southfield outlasted the Atlanta and Gainesville
conferences and held to its fundamentalist origins longer than
Northfield. The conference continued meeting into the 1940s in part
because of income received from a trust established by Edwin Gilbert
to perpetuate its existence.[74] The Chafers' involvement also meant that
the conference maintained its fundamentalist character. Its impact on
the development of a fundamentalist movement in the South was
limited, though, as the conference appeared aimed at ministering to
northerners wintering in Florida than attracting southerners to its
meetings. In 1920 an advertisement in the *Sunday School Times*
enticed Northerners to "combine pleasure with spiritual profit by
attending the extended Bible study lectures at Crescent City."[75] By the
1940s, though, the conference was in decline. Crescent City was no

---

[72]L. S. Chafer, "A New Bible Conference," *Record of Christian Work*, February
1904, 131.

[73]*Record of Christian Work*, March 1905, 168; March 1907, 216; February 1908,
106; March 1909, 183; February 1910, 85; *Christian Worker's Magazine*, February
1917, 484; March 1918, 593; March 1920, 582; March 1921, 342.

[74]Lewis Sperry Chafer, LSC to George W. Reily, 23 November 1949, (Lewis Sperry
Chafer Papers, Mosher Library, Dallas Theological Seminary, Dallas, TX) (hereinafter
cited as LSC Papers).

[75]*Sunday School Times*, 18 September 1920, 512; see also, *Sunday School Times*, 19
November 1921, 670; 9 December 1922, 760; and 8 December 1923, 770; cf., *Our
Hope*, November 1904, 272; September 1905, 131; January 1906, 384; and April 1906,
574.

longer a popular tourist destination, support from the local churches disappeared as the clergy became modernists, income from the trust disappeared during the 30s, and a fire destroyed the conference facilities.[76]

The creation of a chain of Bible conferences across the South was realized in a modest way through the efforts of J. B. Phillips, a Southern Baptist pastor who spent a significant part of his career in Chattanooga. While pastor of the Baptist Tabernacle in South Chattanooga, Phillips organized the first Chattanooga Bible Conference in the early spring of 1914. Initially conducted for the benefit of his congregation, the presence of noted bible teachers attracted participation from other churches.[77] Phillips's conferences usually lasted for two weeks, but unlike the Tabernacle conference the evening meetings were not held in a central location. During the first week each of the conference speakers led services in churches in different parts of the city. During the second week, after creating interest in the speakers, the meetings moved to a central auditorium.[78] In the late teens, Phillips left the pastorate to devote full time to organizing Bible conferences and city-wide campaigns for evangelists like Billy Sunday.[79] In 1920 he began conducting conferences in other Southern cities. Macon, Georgia, and Memphis, Tennessee, joined Chattanooga in hosting fundamentalist speakers like R. A. Torrey, Charles Blanchard, and James Gray. In each city, Phillips enjoyed the support not just of Baptists but also of Presbyterians and Methodists.[80] The newspapers indicated that the

---

[76]LSC to George C. Stebbins, 29 January 1944 and LSC to George W. Reily, 23 November 1949 in LSC Papers.

[77]N.a., "Bible Meeting Opens Today," Chattanooga (TN) Daily Times, 3 March 1923, 10.

[78]N.a., "Bible Conference Will Bring Noted Speakers to City," Macon (GA) News, 2 January 1920, 1; n.a., "Plans Mass Meeting," Memphis (TN) Commercial-Appeal, 2 October 1920, 7; n.a., "Bible Meeting Opens Today," Chattanooga Daily Times, 3 March 1923.

[79]N.a., "Billy Sunday Man Praises Phillips," Macon News, 4 January 1920, 8.

[80]In Memphis in 1920, participating churches included Central Baptist, First Presbyterian, Idlewild Presbyterian, Court Avenue Presbyterian, Madison Heights Methodist, St. John's Methodist, and McLemore Christian. N.a., "Plans Mass Meeting," Memphis Commercial-Appeal, 2 October 1920, 7. Macon churches in 1920 were Tatnall Square Baptist, Mabel White Baptist, East Side Presbyterian, and

speakers preached on the same themes evident at the Tabernacle conferences and reported that large crowds attended the meetings attracted in part by paid publicity that included handbills and advertisements.[81] Interest in the conferences remained strong in Macon through the mid-twenties while it faded in Memphis. In 1922 Phillips accepted a call from Highland Park Baptist Church in Chattanooga, and pastoral duties restricted his supervision of conferences in other cities though he continued leading the Chattanooga Bible conference.[82] The importance of the Gainesville conferences, Southfield, and Phillips' work in introducing southerners to fundamentalism was not only that they attended the conferences but also that the conferences brought fundamentalists South where they added other Southern destinations to their itinerary.

One such fundamentalist was A. C. Gaebelein.[83] He immigrated to America from Germany in 1879 and two years later began work as an assistant pastor in a German Methodist church in New York city. While serving as pastor for a Methodist church in Hoboken, New Jersey, he developed a deep and abiding interest in immigrant Jews and eventually became a missionary for the Methodist church to the Jews in New York city. He grew so fluent in Yiddish that Jews did not

---

Vineville Presbyterian. N.a., "Bible Conference Will Bring Noted Speakers to City," *Macon News*, 2 January 1920, 1. In 1924 First Baptist, Tabernacle Baptist, Tatnall Square Baptist, First Presbyterian, Mulberry Methodist, Vineland Methodist, Centenary Methodist, and First Christian participated in Phillips' Macon conference. N.a., "Bible School Opens Sunday," *Macon News*, 4 January 1924, 12. Chattanooga churches in 1923 included First Baptist, Baptist Tabernacle, Highland Park Baptist, First Presbyterian, Cumberland Presbyterian, and Centenary Methodist. Advertisement, *Chattanooga Daily Times*, 3 March 1923.

[81]On advertising, see *Macon News*, 3 January 1920, 3; 4 January 1920, 1; 2 January 1921 13; and *Chattanooga Daily Times*, 3 March 1920. On crowds, see *Macon News*, 10 January 1920, 1; 13 January 1920, 1; 19 January 1920, 14; 17 January 1921, 10; *Memphis Commercial-Appeal*, 5 October 1920, 17; 11 October 1920, 5.

[82]N.a., "Bible Conference Comes to a Close; Many Attend," *Macon News*, 21 January 1924, 10.

[83]This biographical sketch is drawn from David A. Rausch, *Arno C. Gaebelein, 1861–1954, Irenic Fundamentalist and Scholar*, Studies in American Religion, vol. 10 (New York: Edwin Mellen Press, 1983) 1–17, 53–106.

believe he was a Gentile.[84] This part of his ministry led Gaebelein to revise his eschatology, and he became a leading dispensationalist. His reputation as an interpreter of prophecy was such that C. I. Scofield confessed to Gaebelein, "I sit at your feet when it comes to prophecy."[85] Gaebelein gave his ministry a dual focus, one of evangelization of Jews and the other of education of Gentiles. The latter often occurred in a prophetic context. Gaebelein followed the usual dispensational interpretation that events surrounding the Jews were an important guide to the progress of God's prophetic plans. During the late 1890s, Gaebelein became a popular Bible conference speaker on prophecy and on Jewish life and culture. In 1897 he stopped working for the Methodist Church and became an independent preacher and evangelist.[86]

Gaebelein was no stranger to the South before speaking at the first Southfield conference in 1904.[87] On his way to Florida, he stopped in Savannah, Georgia, the fourth time by his count. Previously, in 1901, he had visited Charlotte, North Carolina, and several towns in the Chattanooga, Tennessee area. From 1904 through 1907, Gaebelein was on the Southfield program, and during those years he developed a circuit of engagements that included towns in central Florida such as Orlando, Apopka, and Plymouth. In addition to the 1907 trip to Southfield, Gaebelein made his first trip to East Texas, and in each year from 1910 through 1920 he made at least one

---

[84]Ibid., 8.

[85]Quoted in ibid., 242.

[86]Additional biographical information can be found in David A. Rausch, "Arno C. Gaebelein (1861–1945): Fundamentalist Protestant Zionist," *American Jewish History* 68 (September 1978): 43–56. For Gaebelein's role in the prophecy conferences that popularized dispensationalism, see idem, *Zionism within Early American Fundamentalism, 1878–1918: a Convergence of Two Traditions* (New York: Edwin Mellen Press, 1979) passim.

[87]This analysis of Gaebelein's southern tours is based what he reported to the readers of *Our Hope* in a monthly section describing previous speaking engagements and announcing upcoming ones. The cities and towns mentioned did not represent every place Gaebelein preached on these tours. For example, in *Our Hope*, May 1903, 609, he said he visited several places in Georgia in association with his trip to Savannah. See for example, *Our Hope*, November 1901, 253; December 1901, 300; April 1905, 575; February 1906, 444.

trip through the region.[88] Galveston was his primary base of operations. He preached there twelve times, usually in conjunction with the Gulf Bible Conference in the late fall, and from there he ventured out to several other Texas cities like Houston, Dallas, Ft. Worth, and Austin as well as visiting smaller towns like Bay City, Kirbyville, Gonzales, and Palestine. Sometimes his meetings were held in secular buildings like Lawton Memorial Hall in Savannah or the opera house in Ft. Worth. Occasionally Gaebelein spoke under the auspices of the YMCA or as a participant in a Bible conference,[89] but more frequently a local church hosted him and opened the meetings for all in the city to attend. Finally, Gaebelein's popularity suggested that he had a message southerners wanted to hear. In 1901, he reported that he turned down fifty invitations to other Southern towns that were offered during his Chattanooga engagement while in 1919 he claimed, "So many calls have come from the state of Texas that we could spend six months there."[90]

Another fundamentalist active in the South before the 1920's was George Guille, but Guille represented different element of fundamentalist activity. Guille was a native Southerner working for a Northern institution conducting Bible conferences and supplying speakers for churches across the South. Born in Zanesville, Ohio, but raised on a farm in East Tennessee, Guille graduated from Southwestern Presbyterian College and was ordained in 1897 by the Knoxville Presbytery. For the next seven years he pastored small churches in East Tennessee. In 1905 he accepted a call from Greene Street Presbyterian Church in Augusta, Georgia, and stayed there seven years until he left pastoral work in 1912 to preach under the

---

[88]Gaebelein went out of the east Texas region only three times to speak in Amarillo in 1912, Ballinger in 1916, and El Paso in 1919. *Our Hope*, May 1912, 687; October 1916, 204; and March 1919, 527.

[89]In addition to Southfield and Gulf, Gaebelein spoke at Bible conferences in Asheville in 1909 and 1910 and in Ft. Worth in 1917. *Our Hope*, September 1909, 139; May 1910, 678; and July 1917, 14.

[90]*Our Hope*, August 1919, 82; cf., ibid., December 1901, 300.

auspices of the Moody Bible Institute (MBI) Extension Department.[91] Organized in 1897 for the purpose of taking the Institute's distinctive teaching and training for laymen to those unable to come to Chicago, the Extension Department not only coordinated speaking engagements for MBI's faculty but also by 1917 employed "a permanent staff of experienced Bible teachers, evangelists, singers and organizers" to "conduct Bible conferences, circuit of weekly Union Bible Classes, Christian work institutes, classes in gospel music, evangelistic campaigns and consecration work following the meetings, inspirational services for the deepening of spiritual life, etc."[92] Guille's specialty was Bible teaching in which he would concentrate on one book or follow a particular theme through several books. Lewis Chafer, founder of the first fundamentalist seminary, admired Guille's ability so much that Chafer employed Guille as one of the visiting lecturers on the English Bible at the Evangelical Theological College.[93] Guille's engagements took him across the South with most of them in Georgia, Tennessee, and Florida. He usually conducted conferences for one church, most often Presbyterian, but occasionally other denominations participated.[94] His meetings usually lasted a week with services in the morning and evening each weekday, and through them he carried fundamentalist teaching to southerners. In Cape Charles, Virginia, Guille taught the "fundamentals of the faith" while giving expositions of Romans and Hebrews.[95] In Augusta at his former church, he lectured on prophecy using Daniel as the basis of his

---

[91]Obituary clipping from *Chattanooga Times*, no date, in LSC papers and PC-US, *Ministerial Directory of the Presbyterian Church, US*, 1861–1941, E. C. Scott, compiler, 181.

[92]*Catalog of the Moody Bible Institute* (1917–1918) quoted in Gene A. Getz, *MBI: the Story of the Moody Bible Institute* (Chicago: Moody Press, 1969) 269. For more details on the Extension Department, see ibid., 267–276.

[93]See Evangelical Theological College, *Bulletin*, November 1925, 20; November 1926, 8; January 1930, 16; and January 1931, 16.

[94]This analysis of Guille's itineraries and meetings is based on the description of Guille's activities in the "Extension Department" section of the *Christian Worker's Magazine* for the years 1914–1925. See for example, March 1917, 588; April 1919, 597; May 1920, 749; May 1921, 419; September 1922, 37; June 1923, 500; April 1924, 441; and October 1925, 86.

[95]"Extension Department," *Christian Worker's Magazine*, December 1919, 236.

talks.[96] William Bell Riley found Guille's teaching appropriate to include at Riley's 1920 Fundamentals Conference in Charlotte, North Carolina.[97] Guille's preaching won him a following among southerners. The churches in Cape Charles invited him back the next year while First Presbyterian of Meridian, Mississippi, and Floyd Street Presbyterian of Lynchburg, Virginia, each hosted Guille's conferences on three different occasions.[98]

Guille was only one of several individuals that toured the South for the Extension Department. While Southern locales were not absent from their itineraries during the 1910s, engagements in the South became a regular feature of some MBI teachers during the 1920s. In fact, the Bible Institute developed a rather extensive network of conferences and extension work in the South during these years. In addition to Guille, Henry Ostrom, C. E. Putnam, Virginia Williams, Margaret Russell, and James Sutherland spent several months of each year teaching in Southern churches. Like Guille, and sometimes in association with him or each other, Ostrom, Sutherland, and Putnam conducted week-long Bible conferences in individual churches. Putnam's specialty was lectures on dispensationalism illustrated by a series of charts, while Ostrom concentrated on exposition of the Bible. Sutherland was noted for his work with children and for meetings with students in public schools.[99] Williams and Russell taught special Bible classes for women in churches and occasionally under the sponsorship of the YWCA. They spoke in all Southern states but had the most engagements in Florida and Texas, the fewest in Arkansas, Louisiana, Kentucky, and Virginia. Their Bible conferences and Bible classes tended to be in smaller towns, but Charlotte, Atlanta,

[96]N.a., "Dr. Guille Attracts Crowds," *Augusta* (GA) *Chronicle*, 27 February 1919, 10.

[97]N.a., "Never Another World Empire," *Charlotte* (NC) *Observer*, 20 February 1920, 4; n.a., "Spiritualism Is Denounced," 21 February 1920, 2.

[98]"Extension Department," *Christian Worker's Magazine*, May 1920, 749; November 1920, 138; March 1921, 342; March 1923, 319; April 1923, 396; May 1924, 488; October 1925, 86.

[99]N.a., "Summer Bible Conferences," *Moody Bible Institute Monthly*, October 1921, 65.

Jacksonville, Miami, Birmingham, Memphis, Baton Rouge, Houston, and Ft. Worth were regular stops on their itineraries.

In format, these conferences were much like the Tabernacle conference and covered much the same theological ground, but instead of several teachers covering the topics one individual might focus on a particular theme or lecture on them all. For example, in 1921, James Gray, the president of Moody Bible Institute, conducted a Bible conference in Tenth Avenue Presbyterian Church in Charlotte, North Carolina. During the afternoons, Gray delivered an exposition of Romans while he devoted the evenings to a series entitled "Great Gospel Themes." Gray began the series with a sermon on the divinity of Christ followed by one on salvation by grace. The third night Gray explained how the Christian could have victory over sin through yielding to the Holy Spirit. "The Reward of Service" was Gray's effort to encourage Christians to become "soul-winners," and the series concluded with a sermon on the second coming of Christ.[100] Sometimes these conferences were evangelistic services, as when Sutherland preached in Wilmington, North Carolina, in November, 1924. Calvary Baptist Church hosted Sutherland's preaching, and its members made an effort to involve the entire community by calling their neighbors on the phone. The nearly 4,000 calls had an effect as the newspaper reported "large crowds" attending the services.[101] Sutherland preached every evening for two weeks, and during the

---

[100]The conference began the day before Gray arrived with a sermon on the inspiration of Scripture by Albert S. Johnson of First Presbyterian of Charlotte. N.a., "Large Crowd Hears Dr. Johnson," *Charlotte Observer*, 15 November 1921, 6. For coverage of the conference, n.a., "Dr. Gray Leads Bible Studies," *Charlotte Observer*, 16 November 1921, 13; n.a., "Dr. Gray Gives 'Way' of Life,'" *Charlotte Observer*, 17 November 1921, 5; n.a., "Believer Has Two Natures," *Charlotte Observer*, 18 November 1921, 20; n.a., "Dr. Gray Ends Bible Series," *Charlotte Observer*, 19 November 1921, 11; n.a., "2nd Coming Closing Theme," *Charlotte Observer*, 21 November 1921, 8. Gray also spent one evening attacking Christian Science. n.a., "Is Not Religion Though it Heals," *Charlotte Observer*, 21 November 1921, 6.

[101]N.a., "Special Meetings at Calvary Baptist," *Wilmington* (NC) *Morning Star*, 5 November 1924, 8.

afternoons on weekdays he conducted services for children.[102] Despite
the newspaper's remark that Sutherland's meeting created "much
interest" in the town and produced "several conversions."[103] Calvary
Baptist did not see tangible results in converts added to the church
role. In fact, Calvary's net increase in membership for that year was
lower than any in the previous ten.[104]

In addition to organizing itineraries of Bible conferences for
individuals, the Extension Department supplied speakers for established conferences. Southfield was a regular stop on Guille's schedule
while MBI workers participated in the conferences of J. B. Phillips.[105]
Finally, the Extension Department created conferences that drew
together several of its speakers. Several such conferences were held in
Florida during the winter of 1924 and the summer of 1925.[106] These
Florida conferences may have been like Southfield in attracting vacationing northerners, but in 1924 the Extension Department began
holding conferences for vacationing southerners in the mountains of
North Carolina. In that summer and continuing through the late
twenties, the Baptist and Presbyterian churches in Hendersonville
hosted a Bible conference staffed by MBI speakers. In describing the
location to its readers, *Moody Bible Institute Monthly* emphasized that

---

[102]N.a., "Sutherland Services Continue," *Charlotte Observer*, 8 November 1924.
Sutherland's talks to children were scheduled for only one week, but they proved so
popular that he continued them for a second week.

[103]N.a., "Meetings Come to an End," *Charlotte Observer*, 15 November 1924, 4.

[104]Calvary received a total of 47 new members, but its net increase was only two.
Wilmington Baptist Association, *Minutes of the Annual Meeting*, 17. The remark
concerning lowest net increase is based on figures contained in the statistical report of
these *Minutes* for the years 1914–1925.

[105]"Extension Department," *Christian Worker's Magazine*, February 1917, 484;
November 1917, 223; March 1918, 593; March 1920, 582; January 1921, 244; and
March 1921, 342.

[106]In addition to Florida in the winter of 1924, Extension Department speakers
and MBI faculty spoke at conferences in Quitman, Georgia, and Birmingham,
Alabama. "Extension Department," *Christian Worker's Magazine*, January 1924,
273. The Extension Department conducted a more ambitious conference in the
summer of 1925 holding meetings in many of the same Florida towns plus Alcolu and
Sumter, South Carolina, Birmingham, Alabama, Laurel, Mississippi, and Galveston,
Texas. "Extension Department," *Christian Worker's Magazine*, June 1925, 479.

the area's natural beauty attracted over 50,000 visitors, most of whom were southerners.[107] The first conference attracted over 600 registrants from fifteen states and ten different denominations and had the standard conference topics on its schedule. Guille interpreted Exodus for the conferees. The work of Sutherland "greatly blessed" the children. Williams gave suggestions for organizing women's Bible classes. Pastors learned how to promote men's evangelistic clubs and lead gospel singing. Gray explained "How to Master the English Bible" and "What Is Meant by the Second Coming of Christ" and closed the conference with a warning to southerners about the threat theological liberalism posed to their faith in "Modernism: A Revolt against Christianity."[108] The financial difficulties resulting from the depression reduced the scope of this conference and severely curtailed Extension Department work in the South.

Evaluating the impact of the itinerants' activities is difficult. Apart from the exception of J. Frank Norris, no Southern minister who built his career in the South played a prominent role in the denominational controversies of the 1920s. Indeed, efforts to recruit southerners to the organized fundamentalist cause failed. One of the largest and most active organizations was the World's Christian Fundamentals Association (WCFA).[109] Immediately after the 1919 conference at which the WCFA was organized, its leaders launched a nationwide series of conferences to recruit members. By 1924, they had conducted over 250 meetings with conferences in the Southern states accounting for approximately one-third of this total.[110] The first wave of conferences included Southern cities like Charlotte, Columbia, Macon, Jacksonville, Houston, and Ft. Worth,[111] but the

---

[107]*Moody Bible Institute Monthly*, September 1924, 24–25.

[108]Ibid.

[109]For a good discussion of the WCFA, see William Vance Trollinger, Jr., *God's Empire: William Bell Riley and Midwestern Fundamentalism* (Madison: University of Wisconsin Press, 1990) 33–61.

[110]N.a., "Report of the Ex-Chairman of the Conference," *Christian Fundamentals in Church and School*, October 1924, 9.

[111]N.a., "Fundamentals Conferences Moving Southward" *Sunday School Times*, 31 January 1920, 66 ; and "A Southern Fundamentals Conference," ibid., 2 October 1920, 538.

effort eventually reached the hinterlands as evangelists associated with the WCFA conducted revivals in towns like Danville, Kentucky, Bonham, Texas, and Petersburg, Virginia.[112] This first series of conferences was little more than a traveling Bible conference. In Charlotte at the First Baptist Church, Riley, Guille, A. C. Dixon, and W. P. White delivered the usual Bible conference fare with no reports of direct solicitation of southerners to join the WCFA. Riley simply mentioned that this conference was one of many being held "to fight the wave of skepticism" sweeping the country.[113] The recruitment became more direct when the WCFA took its annual convention to Southern cities in 1923, 1925, and 1927. An announcement for the 1925 meeting in Memphis, Tennessee, explained the reason for choosing a Southern site. Noting that the South was "the stronghold of orthodoxy" and that the Southern denominations were not "as yet badly infected with modernism," the announcement asserted:

> Many of the lesser denominational bodies of the South are in practically absolute line with the convictions of Fundamentalism. It is a good thing, therefore, for the national convention to lend these great bodies its help against the surreptitious methods of the modernists, for it is an open secret that they are just as determined to enter the South as they have been to capture the North. Our convention should mean the

---

[112]N.a., "Conferences During the Past Quarter," *Christian Fundamentals in Church and School*, January 1923, 19.

[113]N.a., "Spiritualism Is Denounced," *Charlotte Observer*, 21 February 1920, 2. The *Observer* gave fairly good coverage to the meetings, at times reproducing substantial portions of the sermons. It seems likely, therefore, that had Riley discussed and promoted the WCFA, the paper would have mentioned it. For a description of the conference topics, see n.a., "Big Conference to Begin Today," ibid., 15 February 1920, 4. The conference did attract large crowds, at times filling the auditorium, and the paper reported that many of the county's ministers attended the sessions. N.a., "3 Lectures at Conference" Ibid., 17 February 1920, 5; n.a., "Man Made League Won't Stop War," ibid., 19 February 1920, 7; n.a., "Dr. Dixon Preaches on Heaven and Hell," ibid., 23 February 1920, 2; n.a., "Dixon Tells of City of Horror," ibid., 25 February 1920, 4.

strengthening of all those schools and churches in the South that stand steadfastly for the Christian faith.[114]

By 1927, though, the WCFA was in decline, and Riley recognized that southerners were not enlisting in it. The 1927 Atlanta convention held its main sessions in Tabernacle Baptist while its speakers filled the pulpits of several Atlanta churches for their Sunday services.[115] In Atlanta, he complained that "some Atlanta churches and religious bodies are withholding their support of this movement" and acknowledged that "our audiences in the Tabernacle have not been at all what we expected."[116]

Even when fundamentalists tried to unite conservatives in denominations from the same broad tradition, southerners resisted fundamentalist efforts at recruitment. For example, the Baptist Bible Union (BBU) formed in the 1920s to unite American (both Northern and Southern) and Canadian Baptists in their battle against liberals in their respective denominations. Led by Riley and T. T. Shields of Toronto, one of the BBU's Southern contacts was J. Frank Norris. He used his newspaper to explain that the BBU was not a separatist organization calling for the creation of a new denomination, but rather its main purpose was the promotion of cooperation and fellowship among fundamental Baptists to help them combat modernism and evolution in their denominations.[117] In an effort to explain the BBU, Riley sent to all Southern Baptist newspaper editors a copy of the BBU's statement of faith. It was essentially a slightly

---

[114]N.a., "Seventh Annual Convention of the World's Christian Fundamentals Association," *Christian Fundamentals in Church and School,* April 1925, 4–5.

[115]N.a., "Fundamentalists to Convene Here," *AC,* 1 May 1927, 1, 12; and n.a., "Literalist Urges Union of Churches into 3 Groups," *AC,* 2 May 1927, 1, 12. It is worth noting that Will Houghton, a Northerner, was pastor of the Tabernacle at this time.

[116]N.a., "Literalists Meet in Philadelphia," *AC,* 7 May 1927, 12; cf., C. Allyn Russell, "William Bell Riley—Organizational Fundamentalist," in *Voices of Fundamentalism: Seven Biographical Studies* (Philadelphia: Westminster Press, 1976) 99.

[117]J. Frank Norris, "Baptist Bible Union—What It Is Not," *The Searchlight,* 23 March 1923, 1; cf., William Bell Riley, "The Baptist Bible Union of America," *The Searchlight,* 27 April 1923, 6.

modified version of the historic New Hampshire Confession of Faith with one significant addition, a premillennialist interpretation of biblical prophecy.[118] The extent of the desire of the BBU's leaders to bring Southern Baptists onto their side was seen in their decision to hold their first meeting in the same town and just prior to the 1923 annual meeting of the Southern Baptist Convention (SBC).[119] But the BBU had no more success than the WCFA in rallying Southern Baptists to the fundamentalist cause. Apart from Norris and his allies, few SBC ministers participated, and in the late 1920s the Union fell apart over Shields's alleged affair with a BBU secretary and over the administration of an effort to create a fundamentalist Baptist University in Des Moines, Iowa.[120]

The failure of the WCFA and the BBU resulted from a number of factors. First, the WCFA leaders seemed to be insensitive to the activities of Southern denominations. For example, they scheduled their national conventions at the same time as the annual meeting of the Southern Baptist Convention. Such timing seriously restricted the participation of members from the South's largest denomination. Moreover, it denied the dissemination of the WCFA's message through the press as Southern papers gave greater coverage to the Baptist conference. Even in the Southern cities where the WCFA met, the newspapers shifted their attention from the fundamentalists to the Baptists.[121] The BBU's decision to meet prior to the SBC meeting was not an adequate solution, as the added expense and time away from their congregations restricted ministers from attending both gatherings.

The problem was not simply a matter of tactics but the message Northern fundamentalists preached. Southerners were in general

[118]N.a., "Confession of Faith," *The Searchlight*, 6 April 1923, 1–2.
[119]Riley, "Baptist Bible Union," 6.
[120]Dollar, *History*, 109–112.
[121]See for example, n.a., "Fundamentalists to Gather Here Today," *Memphis Commercial-Appeal*, 3 May 1925, 13 and n.a., "Southern Baptist Convention Convenes," *Memphis Commerical-Appeal,* 8 May 1925, 1; and n.a., "Baptists Begin Convention Today," *AC*, 5 May 1927, 1.

theological agreement with the fundamentalists.[122] Most Southern clergy acknowledged the authority and inspiration of the Bible. They accepted a supernatural characterization of Christianity that affirmed the deity of Jesus Christ and the reality of miracles. They preached with fervor the necessity of conversion and the perils of rejecting the gospel message. They questioned the confidence some fundamentalists had in a premillennial interpretation of Christ's second coming, but they believed he was coming again.[123] They agreed with fundamentalists that current modern thought—especially evolution, social trends, and liberal theology—menaced this interpretation of Christianity, but southerners denied that their denominations were infected to the same extent as the Northern ones. As southerners looked at the divisions in the Northern denominations, though, many saw that their theological sympathies lay with the fundamentalists. While studying at Columbia University in New York at the height of controversy among Northern Baptists and questioned about his stand in the fight, W. C. Boone, a pastor from

---

[122]This assertion is not to deny differences among southern clergy and between denominations but rather to suggest the general evangelical character of southern Protestantism. The homogeneity of southern theology across denominational lines is a theme in the writings of Samuel S. Hill. See for example, his *Southern Churches in Crisis* (New York: Holt, Rinehart, and Winston, 1967) xvii, 14–18, 90–102. See also, Wayne Flynt, "One in the Spirit, Many in the Flesh: Southern Evangelicals," in *Varieties of Southern Evangelicalism*, ed. David Edwin Harrell (Macon GA: Mercer University Press, 1981) 23–44. In *Fundamentalism*, 103, George Marsden argued, "This theological conservatism, often combined with the warm revivalist evangelicalism inherited from the early nineteenth century, created in southern religion many characteristics that resembled later fundamentalism."

[123]The inclusion of premillennialism as a theological tenet of fundamentalism is not to elevate this doctrine over others. As noted in the previous chapter, the battle against modernism in northern denominations attracted to the fundamentalist cause many who were not premillennialists. Nevertheless, conservative southern clergy saw premillennialism as a fundamentalist doctrine. See James J. Thompson, *Tried as by Fire: Southern Baptists and the Religious Controversies of the 1920s* (Macon GA: Mercer University Press, 1982) 148–151.

Owensboro, Kentucky, replied, perhaps overstating the case, "I am a Southern Baptist. Practically all of us are Fundamentalists."[124]

Southern Baptist reaction to the Baptist Bible Union is particularly instructive on this point. A few editors of Baptist newspapers expressed approval of some of the purposes of the BBU. The editor of Kentucky's *Western Recorder* liked the potential the BBU had in providing an "inspirational platform" for Northern and Southern Baptists to join in fighting the "downgrade movement of modernism."[125] In Texas's *Baptist Standard*, E. C. Routh wrote that he was in "hearty agreement" with many parts of the BBU's Confession of Faith and acknowledged the necessity of resisting "teachings... which discredit the Word of God."[126] But a variety of factors compelled Southern Baptist leaders to spurn the BBU's overtures. They questioned the BBU's assumption that the Convention was so racked with strife over modernism and evolution that it needed the BBU's help to withstand these challenges to its doctrinal heritage. Louie Newton, editor of Georgia's *The Christian Index*, pointed out that in Virginia "there is no strife, alienation, or serious division of any kind on these matters" nor was he aware of any in other parts of the South.[127] Not only were Southern Baptists undisturbed by doctrinal divisions, they were, according to Routh, "already united on the great doctrines of the Bible, more so that any other great body of Baptists on earth and...[did] not need any new organization."[128] A more troubling element was the inclusion of premillennialism in the BBU's doctrinal statement. The *Western Recorder* bluntly refused to endorse

---

[124]W. C. Boone, "Rationalistic Savants Frightened at Growing Influence of Fundamentalists," *Western Recorder* reprinted in *Christian Fundamentals in Church and School*, January 1923, 24.

[125]Editorial, "Concerning the Still Unborn Baby Baptist Bible Union," *Western Recorder*, 3 May 1923, 2–3; cf., a similar endorsement the previous week in "American Bible Union at Kansas City," *Western Recorder*, 26 April 1923, 13.

[126]E. C. Routh, "The Baptist Bible Union of America," *Baptist Standard* (Dallas TX), 12 April 1923, 9.

[127]Louie D. Newton, "Uniting by Dividing," *Christian Index*, 12 April 1923, 13; cf., Routh, "Baptist Bible Union," 9; and L. R. Scarborough, "Is the Baptist Bible Union Needed in the South?" *Western Recorder*, 3 May 1923, 5.

[128]Routh, "Baptist Bible Union," 9.

any movement that made acceptance of premillennialism a condition for participation, while Routh believed that the BBU's premillennialism would be a source of division rather than union.[129] L. R. Scarborough, President of the SBC's seminary in Ft. Worth, argued that the Bible's lack of clarity on the end times necessitated caution in composing confessions of faith and offered this warning to the BBU: "Any movement that comes in to disturb the peace of Southern Baptists and makes it a test of fellowship what view one holds of the Second Coming of Christ is in itself detrimental to the peace and progress of the cause among Southern Baptists, and I think will find scant following in the South."[130]

Perhaps most damaging to the BBU's efforts was its main Southern advocate. Texas Baptists in particular were sensitive to the prominent role J. Frank Norris played in promoting the BBU, and Scarborough minced no words in reminding his readers that Norris did not cooperate with Convention programs and must be "regarded as a destructionist making false issues and misrepresenting almost everything about which he writes or speaks."[131] Writing in the *Baptist Standard*, F. S. Groner predicted that Norris's purpose in sponsoring this "cult" was to create a "new denomination" that he and his fellow "reactionaries...could boss till their heart's content."[132]

One consequence of fundamentalist recruiting efforts and the fights and divisions in the North was to alert southerners to the dangers and to call "the South to a renewed consciousness of its distinctive religious position."[133] One measure of fundamentalist

---

[129]N.a., "American Bible Union," 13; and Routh, "Baptist Bible Union," 9. See also, Newton, "Uniting," 12–13.

[130]Scarborough, "Is the Baptist Bible Union Needed," 4. In one a rare instance of fairness, Norris printed an edited version of this article in *The Searchlight*, 4 May 1923, 1. Norris did not distort Scarborough's position, but he did leave out Scarborough's attacks on Norris and references that praised the SBC.

[131]Ibid. In "Uniting by Dividing," 13, Newton has a veiled reference to Norris's activities.

[132]F. S. Groner, "Editor Norris Promotes a New Sect," *Baptist Standard*, 26 April 1923, 7.

[133]Ferenc Morton Szasz, *The Divided Mind of Protestant America, 1880–1930* (University: University of Alabama Press, 1982) 104.

influence on Southern denominations was the speed with which they affirmed their orthodoxy and then moved to purge suspected liberals. For example, Southern Methodists heard William Bell Riley charge that their denomination was "already so far swamped by skepticism that little or no hope of its salvation can be intelligently entertained."[134] W. E. Hawkins, a Methodist evangelist based in Fort Worth, repeated similar accusations at the 1923 WCFA convention.[135] Such criticisms gave conservative Methodists the leverage to force the resignation of John A. Rice from the theology school at Southern Methodist University.[136]

A more complex and interesting Methodist controversy developed over the effort to reunite Northern and Southern Methodist denominations.[137] Southern opponents of reunion employed a variety of arguments to defeat the plan, but one of the more prominent had a characteristically fundamentalist perspective. The more radical opponents charged that liberalism already infected the Methodist Episcopal Church, South (MECS), thus reunion with the theologically suspected Northern Methodists would destroy what little hope there was for restoring the orthodoxy of the MECS. For example, in the 1920s, Robert Meek, editor of the independent *Southern Methodist*,

---

[134]William Bell Riley, "Darwinism—the Devil's Wedge," *Christian Fundamentals in Church and School*, January 1923, 8.

[135]N.a., "War upon Evolution Studies Opened," *Fort Worth* (TX) *Star-Telegram*, 1 May 1923, 1.

[136]Szasz, *Divided Mind*, 104 and Kenneth K. Bailey, *Southern White Protestantism in the Twentieth Century* (New York: Harper and Row, 1964) 54.

[137]General discussions of Methodist efforts at reunion can be found in Frederick E. Maser, "The Story of Unification, 1874–1939," in *The History of American Methodism*, ed. Emory Stevens Bucke, 3 vols. (New York: Abingdon Press, 1964) 3:407–78 and in Robert Watson Sledge, "A History of the Methodist Episcopal Church, South, 1914–1939" (Ph.D. diss., University of Texas at Austin, 1972) 97–132, 261–273. The role of race has been considered by Paul A. Carter in "The Negro and Methodist Union," *Church History* 21 (March 1952): 55–70 and by Kirk Mariner in "The Negro's Place: Virginia Methodists Debate Unification, 1924–1925," *Methodist History* 18 (April 1980): 155–170. For regionalism in the Methodist story, see William R. Glass, "Religion in Southern Culture: Southern Methodists and Reunion, 1920–1940," (paper presented at the annual meeting of the Popular Culture Association, New Orleans LA, 22 April 2000.

made the case that theological liberalism had infected almost every aspect of the MECS, from its pulpits, to its schools, to its publications and literature, to the missionaries in foreign countries, to its leaders.[138] S. A. Steel, a lay contributor to the *SM* explained that should this trend continue, the result would be the end of Southern "Methodism as an evangelical agency."[139] The source of this infection was not hard to trace according to an unnamed Mississippi contributor: the liberalism in the MECS resulted from the fact that teachers in Southern Methodist schools have been educated in the North "where rationalism is unblushingly propagated."[140] Meek and his contributors detailed the extent of liberalism among Northern Methodists,[141] and thus a grave danger threatened Southern Methodism. In apocalyptic terms, Meek challenged his readers with these questions:

---

[138]A comprehensive article detailing the evidence is Robert A. Meek, "Can Southern Methodism Be Saved from the Menace of Rationalism?" *Southern Methodist*, August 1922, 1–5 hereinafter cited as *SM*). The following is a sampling of articles on specific issues. Pulpit: Ruby Burgess, "A Plea for Doctrinal Preaching," *SM*, 5 December 1923, 2; n.a., "Some Sputterings of a North Carolina Preacher," *SM*, 30 January 1924, 6; schools: n.a., "A Brave Texan Protests," *SM*, August 1922, 7; Bob Shuler, "The Wrong Way," *SM*, 16 January 1924, 6; n.a., "A Protest against Dr. Rall as Lecturer and Teacher," *SM* 17 December 1924, 8; Methodist literature: Robert A. Meek, "There Are Things Worse Than Failure," *SM*, April 1922, 6; Maurice Johnson, "Henry Hunting in the S. S. Literature," *SM*, 13 February 1924, 6–7; missions: J. F. Corbin, "Modernism in the Foreign Field," *SM*, April 1922, 1; n.a., "The China Christian Advocate, the Official Organ of Our Church in the Orient, Is Boldly Advocating Modernism," *SM*, 9 January 1924, 6–7; leadership: Bob Shuler, "Mouzon and Channing," *SM*, 12 March 1924, 1.

[139]S. A. Steel, "From the Pelican Pines," *SM*, April 1922, 8.

[140] N.a., "Why the Surprise," *SM*, April 1922, 10.

[141] See for example, n.a., "The Address of the Bishops on the Unification Commissions," *SM*, 28 November 1923, 4; n.a., "Southern Methodists, Are You Ready for This?" *SM*, 7 May 1924; L. W. Munhall, "Conditions in the Methodist Episcopal Church (North)" from *Breakers: Methodism Adrift*, reprinted in *SM*, 18 May 1924, 8; n.a., "Against Union with Modernism," *SM*, 8 October 1924, 7; and n.a., "Bishop Berry Declares Modernism Dominant in the Methodist Episcopal Church," *SM*, 31 December 1924, 1.

Southern Methodists, are you willing to commit the
superintendence of the affairs of our beloved Church to such a
body of men–a body in which the Rationalists would be in
complete control? ... Will you thus pave the way for the
wrecking of the faith of the Southern people, the ruin of our
noble denomination, and the destruction of all the ideals and
traditions of the South? *We do not believe that any greater
calamity could befall the Christianity of America and the
World.*[142]

Even mainstream leaders like Bishop Warren A. Candler agreed.
He called the reunion plan "a Trojan horse" that would undermine
the evangelical faith of Southern Methodists by admitting modernists
into their pulpits.[143]

Perhaps a more compelling factor was the way in which
fundamentalist opponents appealed to regional pride and Southern
identity to rally southerners to their side. One of the most common
justifications for reunion was that it would end the problem of "altar
versus altar," or the competition between the two denominations in
which each church had congregations in the same community. The
Methodist Episcopal Church (MEC, the Northern denomination) had
several hundred thousand members in congregations scattered across
the South. Opponents of reunion charged this circumstance resulted
from the MEC's violation of the antebellum agreements concerning
the division of church's resources and territory. Furthermore, they
alleged that this plan of reunion should be rejected because it did
nothing to stop Northern annual conferences from continuing to
establish congregations where Southern conferences already had
churches. Opponents of reunion most frequently described the
presence of MEC churches in the South as a result of an "invasion."
According to Bishop Candler, this plan "legalizes and legitimizes the

---

[142]Robert A. Meek, editorial comment on L. W. Munhall, "Conditions in the
Methodist Episcopal Church (North)," From *Breakers: Methodism Adrift*, reprinted in
SM 18 May 1924, 1.

[143]Quoted in Bailey, *Southern White Protestantism*, 57.

invasion of our territory by the Northern Church."[144] Furthermore, Candler saw an anti-Southern bias at work in the MEC's actions: "it is pertinent to note that the Northern Church invades no other Church but ours, and invades ours nowhere but in the South."[145] Similarly Bishop W. N. Ainsworth argued that the plan left in place all the Northern conferences and congregations, thus they "will penetrate the heart" of the South and "will perpetuate the Northern Church in the South and legalize their occupancy of territory where they are now trespassers."[146] In this regard, J. N. Peacock noted that, while Northern Methodists claimed to be brothers in Christ with southerners, some of these "brothers" should "get to acting more like it and stop Brother Sherman's ecclesiastical 'march through Georgia.'"[147]

Reunion's opponents also appealed to another aspect of Southern identity, racial solidarity, to win support for their cause. Southern Methodists in the 1920s faced the prospect of uniting with a Northern church that had two African-American bishops and about 300,000 black members, most in congregations in the South. The plan would not permit any bishop to preside over a district or annual conference without the conference's invitation nor could a church transfer membership from one conference to another without both conference's permission. Moreover, each congregation remained free to accept or reject a person's application for membership whether by profession of faith or transfer of letter. Opponents to reunion seemed to prefer an explicit statement that the reunited denomination would maintain a policy of racial separation. In the *Wesleyan Christian Advocate*, Reverend J. N. Peacock of Albany, Georgia, noted that the MEC has "two Negro Bishops who sit on perfect equality with the white bishops. To be sure, they preside at present only over conferences of their own color, but how long this will last no one can tell, and the plan fails to specify."[148] But even if no violation of the

---

[144]Warren A. Candler, "Some Objections to the Proposed Plan of Reunion," *WCA*, 6 June 1924, 3.

[145]Warren A. Candler, "At One with My Church," *WCA*, 13 June 1924, 6.

[146]W. N. Ainsworth, "Methodist Union–Which Way?" *WCA*, 13 June 1924, 4.

[147]J. N. Peacock, "Unification, Some Things to Consider," *WCA*, 27 June 1924, 5.

[148]Ibid.

South's racial code occurred, the mere symbolism of an integrated denomination demanded rejection of the plan. While MECS Bishop W. N. Ainsworth pointed out that African American bishops would continue to preside at sessions of the college of Bishops and General Conference,[149] Colonel E. C. Reeves described what he believed was the logical consequences, even to the point of invoking the need to protect Southern white women from association with African-American men:

> The plan not only does not provide against the tendency to social equality, but on the contrary encourages it by providing for equality in the Church. The Negro member is just as eligible to any position in the proposed Church as is the white member.... He is eligible to the Episcopacy. He is eligible to a seat on the Judicial Council...which will have finally determine the church rights of white members of the Church. He is eligible to be elected, or appointed, to the head of any bureau, or organization of the Church where the whites will have to serve as equals, or as inferiors by appointment of a Negro; and if our Southern daughters are under the necessity to work in some department of the Church they would have to work beside a Negro, or under one as the head of a department.[150]

Methodist opponents in the 1920s affirmed that they wished no disrespect to African-Americans. They confessed that they had grown up with African-Americans, that they could enjoy all the privileges appropriate to their place in Southern society, including education, opportunity, and protection from lawlessness. But a fundamental principle of Southern society was at stake, the violation of which would lead to its destruction with serious consequences for the entire nation. Furthermore the Bible mandated racial separation. The editor of the *Southern Methodist* argued that "because Christ died for all

---

[149]W. N. Ainsworth, "Methodist Reunion—Which Way?" *WCA*, 13 June 1924, 4.
[150]C. E. Reeves, "A Negro Equality Church," *SM*, 3 September 1924, 2.

men, it does not follow that it is the Divine Will that all barriers of every kind should be broken down and that they should all be gathered promiscuously into one ecclesiasticism."[151] Meek was quite blunt about the nature of the MECS: "It is a white man's church, and is going to continue as such."[152] And since the plan under consideration to reunite Methodists threatened that purity, it must be rejected. Colonel Reeves went further. He saw the plan as a "scheme to revolutionize the social relations of the Southland" and believed that it was "conceived in iniquity and born in sin."[153] Therefore reunion had to be rejected. After a bitter two-year struggle, Southern Methodists rejected the plan in 1925.

On the other hand, Southern Presbyterians clearly were concerned about the presence of evolution and liberalism but in general did not engage in extended hunts for heretics within their ranks. John Wells, president of Columbia Theological Seminary, cautioned that modernism was "the greatest danger that menaces the world today."[154] In 1923, the General Assembly warned its schools not to employ teachers whose beliefs varied from the "evangelical doctrines of our faith."[155] For some, words were not enough, and the controversy among Northern Presbyterians demanded Southern Presbyterians take action. Eugene Bell, a retired Southern Presbyterian missionary to Korea, criticized Southern Presbyterian newspapers for not mobilizing to support the theological conservatives in the North. "It seems to me," Bell wrote to the editors of Charlotte's *Presbyterian Standard*, "here is an opportunity to rally around the fundamentals of the faith, in the identical position assumed and steadfastly maintained by our own Southern Assembly."[156] James R.

---

[151]R. A. Meek, "A CME Editor Attacks Bishops Candler and Ainsworth," *SM*, 6 August 1924, 7.

[152]R. A. Meek, "A Group of Six Matters," *SM*, 10 December 1924, 8.

[153]Reeves, 4.

[154]Quoted in Szasz, *Divided Mind*, 104.

[155]Quoted in Bailey, *Southern White Protestantism*, 52.

[156]Eugene Bell to the Editors of the *Presbyterian Standard*, 12 November 1923 (James R. Bridges Papers, Presbyterian Historical Society, Montreat NC) (hereinafter cited as Bridges Papers).

Bridges, editor of the *Standard*, offered a few observations on the Northern conflict, plainly siding with the fundamentalist faction but not the sustained commentary necessary to rouse Southern Presbyterians to the cause.[157] During the 1920s, Bridges' editorial policy was to explain the nature of the Northern debate while reassuring his Southern readers of their church's orthodoxy. For example, after attending commencement at Union Seminary in Richmond, he thanked "God that amid the many changes in doctrine prevalent now among theological schools, this school of our church still holds to the old faith. Theological degeneracy has not yet reached them [sic]."[158] At the same time, Bridges recognized that his ordination vows required him and all Southern Presbyterian ministers to maintain the doctrinal standards of its Confession of Faith. Therefore, the church had a duty "to hold all its officers to a strict doctrinal accountability."[159]

The extent to which Southern Presbyterians would uphold this policy was tested at the end of the decade in the controversy surrounding Hay Watson Smith, pastor of Second Presbyterian Church in Little Rock, Arkansas.[160] Born and raised in North Carolina, Smith attended Davidson College and Union Seminary in Richmond and then spent a year at Union Seminary in New York.[161] Ordained in 1901 in the Congregational Church, he served a church in Brooklyn until 1911 when he accepted a call to the Little Rock church, a pulpit he held until his death in January, 1940.[162] In moving to the Southern Presbyterian church, Smith had to appear before the

---

[157]See the following editorials, n.a., "Fundamentalists and Modernists," *Presbyterian Standard*, 2 January 1924, 1–2; R. W. Jopling, "Thoughts on Modernism," *Presbyterian Standard*, 27 February 1924, 3; "The Belief of Modernism," *Presbyterian Standard*, 14 May 1924, 1–2; "The Recent Assembly of the Northern Church," *Presbyterian Standard*, 18 June 1925, 2; and Albert Sidney Johnson, "The Menace of Modernism," *Presbyterian Standard*, 23 September 1925, 1.

[158]Editorial, "The Union Seminary Commencement," *Presbyterian Standard*, 14 May 1924, 2.

[159]Editorial, "Some Characteristics of the Presbyterian Church," *Presbyterian Standard*, 14 May 1924, 1.

[160]See Bailey, *Southern White Protestantism*, 52–53; cf., Ernest Trice Thompson, *Presbyterians in the South*, 3 vols. (Richmond VA: John Knox Press, 1973) 3:329–31.

[161]PC-US, *Ministerial Directory*, 1941, 660.

[162]Ibid.

Arkansas Presbytery for an examination to see if his doctrinal views agreed with the denomination's Confession of Faith. In a thoughtful and carefully phrased statement, he explained where he differed with the Confession. Because he accepted some of the results of higher criticism concerning the authorship and origin of various books of the Bible, he rejected inerrancy as "rigid and unprovable" but nevertheless affirmed the Bible as "the inspired revelation of God's will."[163] He believed that the Genesis account of creation was true "in substance" but that the "method of creative work was...evolutionary."[164] The point of his "sharpest disaccord" was on the doctrine of the total depravity of human nature. He rejected it as unreasonable, a distortion of the Bible, and contrary to the "attitude and teaching of Christ."[165] With his views known, the Presbytery voted 18-1 with one abstention to receive Smith into the ministry of the Southern Presbyterian church.[166]

What precipitated a controversy was Smith's public statements concerning evolution in the mid-1920s. J. F. Lawson of Little Rock's Central Presbyterian Church and Fred Z. Browne of Texarkana's First Church sent various clippings of Smith's statements to James Bridges. Lawson complained that Little Rock Presbyterians were "growing impatient with [Smith's] insolence and his attacks on the doctrines of our beloved Church," while Browne believed Smith was "dishonest" in retaining membership in a denomination whose doctrines he disbelieved.[167] But Bridges knew of Smith's views from Smith himself. In 1925, the pastor bragged to the editor, "So far as I know the Second Church is the only Church in the Southern Assembly

---

[163]"Statement by Dr. Smith before the Presbytery of Arkansas, April 12, 1912," 2–3 (typed copy in Marion A. Boggs Papers, Presbyterian Historical Center, Montreat NC). Boggs was Smith's successor in Little Rock.

[164]Ibid, 4. He explained that evolution was "to me simply God's method of bringing the world and its life into existence."

[165]Ibid., 5–6.

[166]E. D. Robertson to Fred Z. Browne, 1 March 1929, typed copy in Bridges Papers. Robertson was the sole dissenting vote.

[167]J. F. Lawson to James R. Bridges, 8 October 1925; and Fred Z. Browne to James R. Bridges, 12 March 1927, in Bridges Papers. In Lawson to Bridges, 6 September 1927, Lawson indicated that he had never met Browne.

that has come out against the impossible theory of verbal inerrancy and on the side of the theory of evolution. The story of the fight that I have made here for an intelligent facing of modern problems might prove interesting, but the *Standard* would not publish it if it were written."[168]

But later that summer Bridges did publish an editorial critical of ministers who vowed in their ordinations to uphold the Confession but subsequently and openly repudiated its teachings. Without mentioning Smith by name, Bridges bluntly advised ministers, "If you cannot keep your vow, leave that church whose creed you vowed to accept."[169] The issue came to a head in the early 1930s when a special judicial commission of the Arkansas Presbytery investigated Smith's beliefs. Though the commission found Smith "somewhat liberal in the matter of interpretation" and went "in certain particulars beyond the orthodox views of the church," it concluded that "the points of his divergence" were not "of sufficient character to disqualify him from remaining a minister in good standing in the Southern Presbyterian Church."[170] In part, the commission reached this conclusion because Smith seemed to be an isolated case so that a fundamentalist crusade to root out heresy was not needed. However uncomfortable Southern Presbyterians were with some of Smith's views, his beliefs did not appear to threaten the overall integrity of their church's theology at this time.

Of the three largest Southern denominations, the Southern Baptists experienced the most agitation in a large measure due to the

---

[168]Hay Watson Smith to James R. Bridges, 13 May 1925, in Bridges Papers.

[169]N.a., Editorial, "Ministerial Honesty," *Presbyterian Standard*, 26 August 1925, 2. Someone interpreted these words as being meant for Smith as he received a copy of the editorial marked as though it concerned him. Hay Watson Smith to James R. Bridges, 15 September 1925, in Bridges Papers.

[170]Quoted in W. M. McPheeters, *Facts Revealed by the Records in the So-Called Investigation of the Rumors Abroad Concerning the Soundness in the Faith of Rev. Dr. Hay Watson Smith* (Decatur GA: privately published, 1934) 37, 40. McPheeters' pamphlet was an extended attack on the commission's work, basically alleging that it ignored the evidence.

presence of J. Frank Norris.[171] He regularly assaulted the Southern Baptist Convention and its schools in his newspaper *The Searchlight* (later called *The Fundamentalist*). Norris's most potent issue was not the threat of theological liberalism but the growing bureaucratization of the convention that diminished the autonomy of the local church.[172] His efforts won him a following in the Southwest but also alienated Baptists in other regions who doubted his charges of liberalism in the convention and questioned the dangers he saw in the growth of denominational boards. One measure of the limited range of Norris's appeal was his troubled relations with other Baptists in Texas. As early as 1914, Ft. Worth's Pastor's Conference revoked Norris's membership because of critical attacks on other members. In 1922, the Tarrant County Baptist Association and in 1924 the Texas General Conference refused to seat Norris and delegates from his church at their meetings because of his failure to cooperate with Convention programs and use of non-Baptist speakers in his pulpit.[173] Further undercutting Norris's appeal was a series of scandals that included arson charges and a trial for murder. In 1912, fire destroyed the sanctuary of First Baptist Church, and rumors circulated that Norris set the fire in order to collect insurance to be able finance the construction of a larger building. A district attorney uncovered enough evidence to charge Norris with arson, but a jury found Norris innocent. In 1927, Norris was acquitted of charges that he murdered a man in his study at the church. Norris did not deny killing the man but pleaded self defense even though the man was unarmed. In 1929, another mysterious fire destroyed the church, but no charges were filed this time.[174] By this time, most Southern Baptists had adopted the

---

[171]An excellent biography of the public career of Norris is Barry Hankins's, *God's Rascal: J. Frank Norris and the Beginnings of Southern Fundamentalism* (Athens: University Press of Kentucky, 1996). While Norris is a central figure in the story of fundamentalism in the South, the evidence presented in this chapter suggests that Hankins overstates his case by claiming that Norris "introduced fundamentalism in the South" (2).

[172]In *Tried as by Fire*, 137–165, Thompson discusses Southern Baptist fundamentalism and describes very little fundamentalism outside the orbit of Norris.

[173]C. Allyn Russell, "J. Frank Norris: Violent Fundamentalist," *Voices*, 39–40.

[174]Ibid., 34–37.

attitude articulated earlier in the decade by A. T. Robertson: "We just pay no attention to him and go on with our work."[175]

Historian James J. Thompson argues that Southern Baptists' "acceptance or rejection of fundamentalism often hinged on their attitude toward" Norris.[176] Nevertheless, Norris and those in his orbit were not the only Southern Baptists trying to win a favorable hearing for fundamentalists. An unsigned article in the *Western Recorder*, a Southern Baptist newspaper published in Louisville, Kentucky, suggested that the controversy among Northern Baptists had important lessons for Southern Baptists: "The noble fight of Northern Baptist Fundamentalists puts Southern Baptists under the deepest obligations. Not only are they defending our treasured faith.[sic] They are allowing themselves to be a clinic for our study, so that when this slimy, treacherous, Jekyll-and-Hyde apostasy begins...among Southern Baptists,...we shall be forewarned and forearmed."[177]

For Charles T. Alexander, a pastor from Kansas City, Missouri, the situation in the North was a call to arms. Responding to Southern Baptist criticism of fundamentalists, he denied that the movement's aims included promoting church union or imposing premillennialism as a test of orthodoxy and then asked, "Are Southern Baptists great enough in soul and doctrine to measure up to the call of the hour, and lead the Christian forces of America in the battle to throw back the tides of infidelity that are coming in upon us?"[178] Unlike Norris,

---

[175]A. T. Robertson to Lewis Sperry Chafer, 20 April 1928, in LSC Papers. Robertson was a respected New Testament scholar at Southern Baptist Seminary in Louisville and made this remark in the context of a minor controversy surrounding his appearance at Chafer's school to deliver a series of lectures. On the announcement of Robertson's lectures, Norris wrote Chafer that Robertson was a theistic evolutionist. Chafer cabled Robertson for a response to the charge Robertson emphatically denied. Thereupon Chafer politely told Norris to mind his own business. J. Frank Norris to LSC, 17 April 1928; and LSC to J. Frank Norris, 20 April 1928, in LSC Papers.

[176]Thompson, *Tried as by Fire*, 145.

[177]N.a., "Southern Baptists and Northern Fundamentalists," *Western Recorder*, reprinted in *Christian Fundamentals in Church and School*, January 1923, 32. Note that from the author's perspective modernism was not yet infecting the denomination.

[178]Charles T. Alexander, "Fundamentalism versus Modernism," *Western Recorder*, reprinted in ibid., 43.

neither attacked the Southern Baptist Convention. They saw signs of the disease, but it was not yet pandemic.[179]

In one sense fundamentalists' activity failed. It did not create an active Southern wing of their movement that supported Northern conservatives' efforts to maintain control over their denominations. Nor did the activity establish continuing forums or institutions that facilitated an ongoing dialogue between Northern fundamentalists and Southern conservatives. But apart from the efforts of the WCFA and the BBU in the 1920s, such goals were not a part of the reasons that fundamentalist itinerants toured the South. In most cases they came at the invitation of Southern ministers like Leonard Broughton and J. B. Phillips who wanted their congregations and cities to benefit from fundamentalist Bible teaching that had enriched their lives. Indeed, this aspect may have been the most successful and important part of the itinerants' work. Through their Bible conferences and preaching tours, the itinerants created a Southern constituency for the fundamentalist interpretation of Christianity. The size of this group, the degree to which fundamentalist teaching penetrated all parts of the South, and the extent to which southerners accepted each element cannot be measured with any degree of precision. But the large crowds attending the conferences and the extended tours of MBI Extension Department workers suggest that the itinerants found a receptive and appreciative audience for their message among southerners. Moreover, the significance of the itinerants' work was in not only their impact on Southern Protestantism but also on the fundamentalist movement. Fundamentalists found a region where the cultural values still supported a conservative understanding of Christianity. During the 1920s and 1930s when they began creating separate institutions to replace the denominational ones lost to the control of the modernists, some fundamentalists looked South. Their efforts to build fundamentalist institutions in the South marked a

---

[179]Nor did W. C. Boone. See "Rationalistic Savants," 24–28.

significant departure in the development of Southern fundamentalism, but one dependent on the work of the itinerants.

3

INTERDENOMINATIONAL FUNDAMENTALISTS: EDUCATING THE NEXT GENERATION

Train up a child in the way he should go, even when he is old he will not depart from it.
—Proverbs 22:6

In June 1920 James Gray, president of Moody Bible Institute, spoke in Columbia, South Carolina, about the establishment of a Bible school in the South. Gray told an audience of approximately 200 that Bible schools played an important role in training laypeople to assist the clergy in the church's main task of evangelizing the world. By supporting such a school, the people of Columbia would provide a service that would benefit not only their community and region but also the nation and the cause of Christianity.[1] The next day, Gray offered practical advice on organizing and financing a school and appealed again to the pride of Columbia's citizens. Such a school, according to Gray, would make Columbia, "the center of education" in the South by attracting students from the entire region.[2] Those attending this meeting passed a unanimous resolution supporting the

---

[1] N.a., "Dr. Gray Speaks on Bible School," *The State* (Columbia SC), 29 June 1920, 3.

[2] N.a., "More Discussion on Bible School," *The State*, 30 June 1920, 10.

creation of a Bible institute in Columbia and named a committee of
three pastors and two laymen to direct the effort.[3] The next year, their
work bore fruit when the Southern Bible Institute opened in the fall of
1921 with a limited class schedule.[4] The Institute lacked strong
leadership until Robert C. McQuilkin accepted the position of Dean
and committed himself to begin full time work in the school in the fall
of 1922. McQuilkin was deeply involved in Northern fundamentalist
circles, having served as assistant editor of the *Sunday School Times*
and itinerating as a speaker for Victorious Life Conferences.[5] Those at
the Bible institute knew McQuilkin from the conferences he led in
Columbia in the winters of 1920 and 1921. At McQuilkin's
suggestion, the Board of Trustees changed the name of the school to
Columbia Bible School because to McQuilkin's Northern ears
"Southern" Bible Institute sounded too regional.[6] Under McQuilkin's
direction, Columbia Bible School became solidly established and an
important part of the network of interdenominational institutions
fundamentalists created in the twenties and thirties.

The creation and growth of schools like Columbia Bible College
illustrate a new stage in the development of fundamentalism in the
South and a new direction for the broader fundamentalist movement.
According to a 1924 list in the *Sunday School Times*, of the thirty-one
schools that met fundamentalist standards, only two were in the
South.[7] By 1950, though, the number of Southern schools in the
fundamentalist camp had grown to twenty-six, roughly one-third of
the national total of seventy-five schools.[8] The dramatic increase in

---

[3]Ibid.

[4]See photocopies of articles from n.a., "Carolina Gets Bible Institute," *The State*,
15 September 1921 and n.a., "Columbia's New Bible School to Open Tuesday A.M.," 2
October 1921 reproduced in Alleene Spivey Hehl with John Hehl, *This is the Victory*
(Columbia SC: privately published, 1973) 52–53.

[5]Marguerite McQuilkin, *Always in Triumph: the Life of Robert C. McQuilkin*
(Columbia SC: Columbia Bible College, 1956) 78–81, 88–92.

[6]Hehl, *This is the Victory*, 36.

[7]N.a., "Listing Sound Bible Institutes," *Sunday School Times*, 26 January 1924,
50.

[8]These figures were compiled by studying the list published in "Evangelical Schools
and Colleges, 1950," *United Evangelical Action*, 15 June 1950, 12–16. In "The

the number of schools points to both the growth of Northern fundamentalist traditions in the South and the growing importance of the South to the fundamentalist movement. Moreover, a close study of the establishment and development of fundamentalist educational institutions in the South reveals that religiously conservative southerners were not simply coopted by a Northern movement but used the movement to further their own concerns. At the same time, such a study shows that the variety in the curricular focus of the Southern schools represented an expansion of the educational interests of the interdenominational fundamentalist movement. Particularly in the areas of vocational training, graduate education, and professional preparation for the pastorate, fundamentalist schools in the South extended the range of the movement's educational efforts and represented a significant part of the movement's response to its leaders' calls for institutions free from the stain of modernism. But even when some schools focused on the traditional fundamentalist concern for the training of laypeople, the Southern versions of Bible institutes and colleges should not be dismissed as mere imitations of Northern models but seen as an important step in building a Southern wing of the movement and broadening the movement's coalition.

The appearance of fundamentalist institutions in the South during these years should not be divorced from Northern developments. Fundamentalists in these decades failed to regain control of their denominations in the North and left them to form independent churches, fellowships, associations, mission boards, publishing houses,

---

Development of the Bible College or Institute in the United States and Canada since 1880 and Its Relationship to the Field of Theological Education" (Ph.D. diss., New York University, 1950) 49, Harold W. Boon counted 140 schools in 1946, while S. A. Witmer, in *The Bible College Story: Education with Dimension* (Nanhasset NY: Channel Press, 1962) 39, noted that 73 percent of all Bible schools still in existence in 1962 were started during the years 1931–1960. Neither Boon nor Witmer paid much attention to the geographical location of the schools, and they included denominationally affiliated schools in their tabulation. The figures cited above were schools listed as "independent," "interdenominational," or "undenominational" and located in the states of Alabama, Arkansas, Florida, Georgia, Kentucky, Louisiana, Mississippi, North Carolina, South Carolina, Tennessee, Texas, and Virginia.

and conferences.[9] In other words, they sought to create agencies and structures that they could control to assure a faithful witness to a supernatural Christianity based on an inerrant Bible. Bible institutes and colleges were not the only institutions established in these years, but they were perhaps the most important. These schools formed the hub of networks of churches, functioning in some ways like a denominational headquarters for fundamentalists.[10] The schools supplied pastors "sound in the fundamentals" and recruits for the independent missions. Their magazines replaced denominational periodical literature. Churches supported these schools by sending both their money and their children. Bible colleges and institutes also represented a link between the theological and cultural battles fundamentalists waged. Because of the liberal theological education given in denominational seminaries, fundamentalists needed schools that would prepare men for the ministry without undermining fundamentalist orthodoxy. At the same time, fundamentalists wanted college education that would not destroy their children's faith through the teaching of evolution or expose their children to the immorality at secular universities that challenged the fundamentalist lifestyle. Furthermore, fundamentalists hoped that the graduates would season American society with the values learned at the schools and thus help reverse the social and cultural trends fundamentalists found so disturbing.

In the 1920s and 1930s fundamentalists started a variety of postsecondary educational institutions ranging from Bible institutes to liberal arts colleges to seminaries.[11] Most started small, usually as a

---

[9]Joel A. Carpenter, *Revive Us Again: The Reawakening of American Fundamentalism* (New York: Oxford University Press, 1997) 13–32.

[10]Ernest R. Sandeen, *The Roots of Fundamentalism: British and American Millenarianism, 1800–1930* (Chicago: University of Chicago Press, 1970; reprint, Grand Rapids MI: Baker Book House, 1978) 241–43. For a good case study of the development of one such network, see William Vance Trollinger, Jr., "Riley's Empire: Northwestern Bible School and Fundamentalism in the Upper Midwest," *Church History* 57 (June 1988): 197–212.

[11]For an overview of fundamentalist educational efforts, see Virginia Lieson Brereton, *Training God's Army: The American Bible School, 1880–1940* (Bloomington: Indiana University Press, 1990). Brereton occasionally uses Southern schools for

Bible institute, which was little more than a glorified Sunday school holding weekday evening classes taught by local pastors. They had no academic accreditation and awarded certificates upon the completion of one or two years of courses. The addition of daytime classes and a three year program like that of Moody Bible Institute marked the next stage of development, followed by the inclusion of enough liberal arts courses for four years of classes and to justify awarding students a Bachelor of Arts diploma on graduation. Authority for granting these degrees came not from accreditation associations but from special acts of state legislatures. Columbia Bible College (founded in 1921), Toccoa Falls Institute (1910), Southeastern Bible School (1934), and the Dallas Bible Institute (1940) are Southern representatives of this trend. Another group of schools did not follow this pattern but emphasized liberal arts courses or vocational training. The required Bible courses, strict regulation of students' lives, and the effort to teach all subjects from a biblical point of view created the fundamentalist character of these schools. Southern schools of this type included Bob Jones College (1927), John Brown University (1919), and Bryan College (1930). Graduate education was not a significant part of these initial educational endeavors in the South except for ministerial training. As they grew, some schools (e.g., Columbia Bible College, Bob Jones College) added seminary courses to their curriculum while one independent fundamentalist seminary (Dallas Theological Seminary) began training ministers and missionaries in 1924.

The origins of these schools varied but they all grew out of common fundamentalist concerns that were at the heart of the movement's effort to thwart the liberals' impact on the denominations. According to fundamentalists, the denominational educational institutions had failed in their mission to supply the churches with pastors and lay leaders who believed in a supernatural Christianity. Writing in *Moody Bible Institute Monthly*, Lowell Coate estimated that nine-tenths of the graduates of denominational colleges never returned to serve their church, and the remaining one-tenth were made unfit for

---

illustrative purposes but does not acknowledge the distinctive contribution of Southern schools.

service because the colleges taught "modern philosophy, rationalistic materialism, evolution, destructive criticism, radicalism, and liberalism."[12] In the eyes of Charles Blanchard, president of Wheaton College, college education in the twenties was "becoming distinctly unchristian and antichristian."[13] One conse-quence of this development was a growing apostasy in the churches. "In other words," according to Coate, "the colleges have backslidden the churches."[14] If allowed to continue, this trend could have tragic consequences for the nation. J. Gresham Machen argued that "the widespread ignorance of the Christian religion as that religion is founded on the Word of God" precipitated "a most deplorable and most alarming intellectual decline" in American education.[15] Albert S. Johnson, a prominent Southern Presbyterian minister, believed that "the modernist evolutionary system of education" threatened "the security of our government,...orderly society,...Christian morality,... the sanctity of the home,...[and] the perpetuity of the Church of Jesus Christ."[16] In a similar vein, Charles G. Trumbull, editor of the *Sunday School Times*, apocalyptically warned that if "the insidious injection of poison into the minds of our boys and girls" was not stopped, then "civilization cannot be maintained."[17]

The seminaries as well came under fundamentalist indictment. In William Bell Riley's estimate, not one Northern seminary remain-

---

[12]Lowell H. Coate, "A New Scholarship Needed," *Moody Bible Institute Monthly*, June 1923, 471. Coate's numbers appear to have been pulled out of the air, but the accuracy of his estimate is irrelevant. More significant is his assessment of the utter failure of denominational colleges.

[13]Charles Blanchard to Lewis Sperry Chafer, 18 July 1924 (Lewis Sperry Chafer Papers, Mosher Library, Dallas Theological Seminary, Dallas TX) (hereinafter cited as LSC Papers).

[14]Coate, "A New Scholarship", 470. William Jennings Bryan supported Coate's ideas. See Lowell H. Coate, "Mr. Bryan Endorses Association of Orthodox Colleges," *Moody Bible Institute Monthly*, November 1923, 109–110.

[15]N.a., "Professor J. Gresham Machen, D. D., Declines the Presidency of Bryan University," *Moody Bible Institute Monthly*, September 1927, 16.

[16]Albert S. Johnson, "The Educational Crisis," *Christian Fundamentals in Church and School*, July 1925, 38.

[17]Charles G. Trumbull, "Fundamentalists Expose Modernism in the South," *Sunday School Times*, 26 May 1923, 324.

ed consistently evangelical in its teaching, and "even in the South, the rationalism of evolution...is nibbling into our theological teaching."[18] Graduates of these schools lacked the preparation to be effective pastors. Instead of learning how to teach the Bible, they learned how to criticize it and rationalize the miraculous. They spent too much time acquiring academic tools to become biblical scholars and not enough mastering the practical skills of evangelism needed to preach the gospel to a lost world. The emphasis on intellectual training doused the spiritual fire of the students leaving them without a heartfelt piety.[19] With these kinds of problems in mind, A. C. Gaebelein counseled those seeking training for the ministry "to stay away from the modern theological seminary, for it is a most dangerous institution."[20]

Fundamentalists pursued a variety of solutions. Their efforts to ban the teaching of evolution in public schools was one tactic.[21] Another was forcing college professors in denominational schools to resign by accusing them of teaching evolution or the liberal view of the Bible.[22] Proposed by Lowell Coate and endorsed by William

---

[18]William Bell Riley, "An Orthodox Premillenarian Seminary," *Christian Fundamentals in Church and School*, January 1923, 20.

[19]For examples of these complaints and others, see A. C. Gaebelein, "The Modern Theological Seminary," *Our Hope*, December 1915, 332–33; Albert P. Haupert, "Bible Institutes vs. Theological Seminaries," *The Moravian*, reprinted in *Christian Worker's Magazine*, May 1919, 719–20; Leslie E. Dunkin, "What of the Seminaries," *Christian Worker's Magazine*, January 1920, 382; Robert Clark, "Bible Institutes and Theological Seminaries," *Moody Bible Institute Monthly*, March 1922, 853–54; Riley, "An Orthodox, Premillenarian Seminary," 20; Trumbull, "Fundamentalists Expose Modernism," 324; Albert S. Johnson to Lewis Sperry Chafer, 22 January 1932, in LSC Papers; and Robert C. McQuilkin to J. Oliver Buswell, 26 August 1937 (Robert C. McQuilkin Papers, Buswell File, in Library, Columbia Bible College, Columbia SC) (hereinafter cited as RCM Papers).

[20]Gaebelein, "The Modern Theological Seminary," 333.

[21]See Ferenc Morton Szasz, *The Divided Mind of Protestant America, 1880–1930* (University: University of Alabama Press, 1982) 107–125.

[22]At the 1923 World Christian Fundamentals Association convention in Fort Worth, professors at Methodist schools in Texas were put "on trial" for teaching evolution and casting doubt on the accuracy of the Bible. The star witnesses were their former students. Trumbull, "Fundamentalists Expose Modernism," 323. J. Frank Norris drove G. S. Dow, professor of sociology, out of Baylor University with charges that Dow taught evolution. See "Prof. Dow and Baylor University," *The Searchlight*,

Jennings Bryan, a third route was the creation of an association of orthodox colleges to address problems of mutual concern and to serve as an agency to help maintain their conservative Christian character.[23] After two years of discussion, representatives from a handful of colleges met at Moody Bible Institute in 1924 but failed to form an ongoing organization.[24] Concurrently with these schemes, and almost as an admission that these plans were doomed, fundamentalists called for the creation of new, independent educational institutions under fundamentalist control. In 1923 the convention of the World Christian Fundamentals Association passed a resolution reaffirming its support for an independent, evangelical seminary, which would be "the greatest single agency in meeting the menace of modernism and saving the present day pulpit from future apostasy."[25] In 1925 fundamentalists called for the establishment of an university to memorialize William Jennings Bryan because "America needs a Fundamentalist University as she needs nothing else."[26]

Already in place were the Bible institutes, and the crisis of the twenties brought a new evaluation of their role in the fundamentalist movement. These schools represented the institutionalization of the ideals and theology of the popular Bible conferences. Initially intended to train laypeople to be more diligent students of the Bible and faithful workers in their churches, these schools became acceptable alternatives to liberal seminaries for training pastors for fundamentalist churches and missionaries for fundamentalist mission boards.

---

11 November 1921, 1–2; J. Frank Norris, "The Greatest Convention in Twenty Years," *The Searchlight*, 9 December 1921, 1–3; and idem., "Prof. Dow Resigns," *The Searchlight*, 16 December 1921, 1, 4.

[23]Coate, "Mr. Bryan Endorses," 109–110.

[24]N.a., "A Convention of Orthodox Colleges," *Moody Bible Institute Monthly*, November 1924, 110; and Newton Wray, "Why Orthodox Colleges Should Come Together," *Moody Bible Institute Monthly*, January 1925, 220–22.

[25]N.a., "Resolutions of Fundamentals Convention," *Christian Fundamentals in Church and School*, July 1923, 10. According to n.a., "The Great Objectives of the Fort Worth Convention," *Christian Fundamentals in Church and School*, April 1923, 25–26, the WCFA had been calling for a seminary for five years.

[26] "William Jennings Bryan University," *Moody Bible Institute Monthly*, October 1925, 59. The same article was printed verbatim in *Christian Fundamentals in Church and School*, October 1925, 52–54.

Dwight Moody's influence here is very significant, and one of his more enduring legacies to fundamentalism was the school he founded in Chicago. The Moody Bible Institute (MBI), as it came to be called, was one of several started in the 1870s and 1880s, but it became the largest, and its courses established the pattern upon which others based their curricula.[27] As founded by Dwight Moody, A. B. Simpson, A. J. Gordon, and others, the early institutes provided the opportunity for laymen of all ages to study the English Bible in depth and to be trained in evangelistic techniques. Their purpose in the late nineteenth century was not to become substitutes for seminaries but to offer training to those who might not have the time, money, or ability for formal theological training but who wanted to be of greater service in their churches. In 1914, C. I. Scofield justified Bible institutes by explaining, "The purpose of Bible institutes is to train lay workers. It is not proposed that they shall take the place of the theological seminaries in the training of ministers.... In an age so highly specialized as ours, it is felt necessary that the great host of Sunday school teachers and mission workers shall have clear and competent instruction in the Scripture and in the best methods of Christian work."[28]

Similarly, an early catalog for Gordon's Boston Missionary Training School announced that the school was "designed for young men and women who have heard the call of God to engage in Christian service, but who, from age or other reasons cannot pursue

---

[27]A good account of the history and influence of the school is Gene Getz, *MBI: The Story of the Moody Bible Institute* (Chicago: Moody Press, 1969). In "An Historical Analysis of the Bible College Movement during Its Formative Years" (Ph.D. dissertation, Temple University, 1985), Larry James McKinney compared the development of Moody Bible Institute with three other schools: Nyack Missionary Training Institute started by A. B. Simpson, Boston Missionary Training School founded by A. J. Gordon, and Philadelphia School of the Bible established by C. I. Scofield.

[28]C. I. Scofield, "And Now a Bible School," *Serving and Waiting*, January 1914, quoted in Renald E. Showers, "A History of Philadelphia College of Bible" (Th.M. thesis, Dallas Theological Seminary, 1962) 62.

an academic or college course."[29] Such lay participation was important in the minds of the founders if evangelical churches were to make an effective response to the problems of the late nineteenth century. In his words, Moody created his institute in Chicago to help raise an army of unordained men and women who would stand "in the gap" to stem the tide of the forces assaulting evangelical Christianity through an aggressive campaign of urban evangelism.[30] Simpson's Missionary Training Institute in Nyack, New York, sought to help meet the need for missionaries to serve overseas.[31] In several respects their curricula resembled an expanded program for a Bible conference. The courses in Gordon's school emphasized "a consecrated and victorious Christian life,...a comprehensive and ready knowledge of the Scriptures,...[and] a constant and effective practice in Christian work."[32] By the twenties, the leaders and supporters of these schools touted just such a course of study as a remedy for the problem of evangelical ministerial students losing their fervor and their faith in liberal seminaries. As early as 1915, Arno Gaebelein advised future pastors to attend a Bible institute not a seminary.[33] Moreover, fundamentalists recognized these schools as suitable substitutes for seminaries and attributed their existence to God's favor. According to Robert Clark, "the Bible schools are institutions raised up by God to

---

[29]Quoted in Nathan R. Wood, *A School of Christ* (Boston: Gordon School of Theology and Missions, 1953) 17–18.

[30]For a good discussion of Moody's educational interests, see Donald Austin Wells, "D. L. Moody and His Schools: An Historical Analysis of an Educational Ministry" (Ph.D. diss., Boston University, 1972); in particular, 294–98, with reference to laymen standing in the gap. See also, James Findlay, "Moody, 'Gapmen,' and the Gospel: The Early Days of Moody Bible Institute," *Church History* 31 (September 1962): 322–35.

[31]John H. Cable, "Education," in Robert B. Ekvoll, Harry M. Shuman, Alfred C. Snead, John H. Cable, Howard van Dyck, William Christie, David J. Fant, *After Fifty Years: A Record of God's Working through the Christian and Missionary Alliance* (Harrisburg PA: Christian Publications, 1939) 92.

[32]Quoted in Wood, *A School of Christ*, 18; cf., Cable, "Education," 95–96; and Wells, "Moody and His Schools," 312–14.

[33]Gaebelein, "The Modern Theological Seminary," 333.

take the place of other institutions that have been unfaithful to their call and opportunities to witness to the gospel of truth."[34]

The founding of Southern schools in the 1920s and 1930s was a part of this trend.[35] The general nature and character of these schools were very similar to those in the North because a cluster of fundamentalist concerns linked together these schools with their counterparts in the North. The founders of Southern schools offered their institutions as solutions to the problems fundamentalists saw in religious education. Paramount among these concerns was the effort to ensure that these schools were faithful to and defended fundamentalist orthodoxy. Most of the schools included in their literature brief statements of faith to indicate their loyalty to the doctrines undermined by liberal interpretation of the Bible. While similar to and, in some cases, derivative of statements adopted by other fundamentalist organizations, the creeds of the Southern schools represented part of fundamentalists' efforts to define the theological boundaries of their movement.[36] These statements affirmed that the school taught the inspiration and infallibility of the Bible, the trinity, the virgin birth of Christ, his death as an atonement for sin, his resurrection, the necessity of conversion, the premillennial second coming of Christ, and the reality of heaven and hell.[37] In its first

---

[34]Clark, "Bible Institutes and Theological Seminaries," 853; cf., Haupert, "Bible Institutes vs. Theological Seminaries," 719.

[35]The appearance of fundamentalist schools in the South has not received much scholarly attention. The main exceptions are B. Dwain Waldrep, "Fundamentalism, Interdenominationalism, and the Birmingham School of the Bible, 1927–1941" *The Alabama Review* 49 (January 1996): 29–54; and Mark Taylor Dalhouse, *An Island in the Lake of Fire: Bob Jones University, Fundamentalism, and the Separatist Movement* (Athens: University of Georgia Press, 1996). In his excellent study, Dalhouse chooses to emphasize the national constituency of Bob Jones University and consequently misses the opportunity to explore regional context of the school's development.

[36]See Douglas Edward Herman, "Flooding the Kingdom: The Intellectual Development of Fundamentalism, 1930–1941" (Ph.D. diss., Ohio University, 1980) 118–24, for a discussion of the theological boundaries of fundamentalism, but he rarely used creeds from schools and virtually ignored Southern sources.

[37]For a typical example, see "Statement of Doctrine" from the Southern Bible Institute reproduced in Hehl, *This is the Victory*, 55. The "Doctrinal Standards"

promotional pamphlet, Bob Jones College made its position clear by "unqualifiedly affirming...the inspiration of the Bible" and other characteristically fundamentalist doctrines.[38] Similarly, the *Bulletin* of John Brown University assured prospective students that the Federation Bible College was "sound and sane in the Fundamentals" standing for "the full inspiration of the Holy Scriptures, the Deity of Christ, His Virgin Birth, His Vicarious Death, and the lost condition of every man who had not accepted this atonement for his sins."[39] Most of these statements were brief lists of doctrines, but as the Dallas Theological Seminary came under attack for its dispensationalism, its statement gradually evolved into a lengthy description and scriptural defense of the school's doctrinal position.[40]

Defending the fundamentals of the faith involved first and foremost teaching a fundamentalist interpretation of the Bible, but a secondary and vital part included inculcating a lifestyle that reflected biblical values. Students had not only to affirm fundamentalist orthodoxy but also to live according to fundamentalist norms. R. A. Forrest promoted Toccoa Falls Institute as a school where "character is developed with intellect,"[41] and this motto exemplified the emphasis that these schools put on cultivating a Christian lifestyle in their students. John Brown University proclaimed its objective as graduating students "whose lives reflect the love of Christ," and who

---

changed only in expression under McQuilkin's leadership of Columbia Bible College; see Columbia Bible College, *Catalogue*, 1941–1942, 20; the "College Creed" served as a doctrinal statement for Bob Jones College and was the first item a student found in the *Announcement*, 1938–1939, 3; John Brown did not include a doctrinal statement in his school's catalogue but simply affirmed that it was "definitely evangelical" and held "steadfastly to the 'Faith once delivered.'" John Brown University, *Bulletin*, 1941–1942, 16.

[38]Bob Jones College, "Announcement, 1927–1928" 4.

[39]John Brown University, *Bulletin*, 1925, 70.

[40]Selected parts of the statement were published in "A True Theological Seminary," *Sunday School Times*, 6 September 1924, 526, while the entire eighteen article statement was available in a pamphlet from the school. Evangelical Theological College, "Doctrinal Statement," (Dallas: Evangelical Theological College, 1924); cf., Dallas Theological Seminary, "Doctrinal Statement," *Bulletin*, 1941–1942, 34–38.

[41]Milton John Scripture, "A History of Toccoa Falls Institute Where 'Character Is Developed with Intellect'" (M. A. thesis, University of Georgia, 1955) 28.

participated throughout their lives "in Christian activities, with talent and means, being reverent toward God, and showing tolerance, humility, and helpfulness toward other people."[42] Required chapel services, active participation in local churches, Christian service obligations, school sponsored Bible conferences and evangelistic services, and other similar activities helped the schools fulfill their responsibility for nurturing the spiritual growth and health of their students.[43]

A particularly important aspect of fundamentalist living the schools cultivated was an evangelistic zeal. On a practical level, evangelism for many fundamentalists took a higher priority than defending the fundamentals because it confirmed directly by experience the supernatural character of Christianity. Denying the miracles in the Bible undermined the mystery of conversion while conversion validated fundamentalist claims concerning the nature and authority of the Bible. Most of the schools emphasized this theme in their literature. Columbia Bible College proclaimed its purpose as "to know Him [i.e., Jesus Christ] and to make Him known."[44] Similarly, the "one main objective" of the education at Southeastern Bible School was "to so cultivate the spiritual life of the student that his ministry will be characterized by a faithful teaching of the Word and aggressive soul winning in person or group evangelism."[45] An interest in both home and foreign mission fields was part of this evangelistic enthusiasm, and fundamentalist educators nurtured it in a variety of ways. Schools like the Bible institutes and colleges expected

---

[42]John Brown University, *Bulletin*, 1953–1954, 11. For similar statements about the development of character, see Southeastern Bible School, *Bulletin*, 1948–1949, 10; Columbia Bible College, *Catalogue*, 1941–1942, 14–15; and concerning Bryan College, see Judson A. Rudd to RCM, 17 February 1933, in RCM Papers.

[43]Columbia Bible College, *Catalogue*, 1941–1942, 20; Bob Jones College, *Announcement*, 1939-1940, 16; John Brown University, *Bulletin*, 1953–1954, 11; for Bryan College, see George Guille to LSC, 4 March 1931, in LSC Papers.

[44]Columbia Bible College, *Catalogue*, 1941–1942, 12, 14; cf., Columbia Bible School, *Announcement*, 1923–1924, reprinted in Hehl, *This is the Victory*, 95.

[45]Southeastern Bible School, *Bulletin*, 1948–1949, 10; cf., Southeastern Bible School, *Catalogue*, 1942–1943, 6.

their students to enroll converted,[46] while Bob Jones warned parents
not to "send your son and daughter to Bob Jones College unless you
want them to become a Christian."[47] In 1950, Jones boasted to J.
Frank Norris that he had kept that promise: "As far as I know only
one student ever stayed here a year and went away unconverted....
This is an institution where there is constant revival."[48] Courses in
personal evangelism taught students the techniques of "soul-winning,"
while the chapel services inspired and motivated students to use what
they had learned.[49] Mission conferences and visiting missionaries kept
students informed about developments in evangelistic work overseas.[50]
Finally, student clubs sponsoring evangelistic exercises, prayer groups
for missionaries in different regions around the world, and Christian
service obligations fulfilled through activities like leading a child
evangelism club, street preaching, or working in a rescue mission gave

---

[46]Columbia Bible College, Catalogue, 1941–1942, 16; Southeastern Bible School,
Catalogue, 1942–1943, 7. His biographer recorded that R. A. Forrest would rather see a
student at Toccoa Falls Institute "soundly saved than thoroughly educated—if he
could not be both." Lorene Moothart, Achieving the Impossible...with God: The Life
Story of Dr. R. A. Forrest (Toccoa Falls GA: Toccoa Falls Institute, 1956; reprint,
Harrisburg PA: Christian Publications, 1971) 112.

[47]Bob Jones, "Editor's Page," Bob Jones Magazine, June 1928, 3.

[48]Bob Jones to J. Frank Norris, 15 February 1950 (J. Frank Norris Papers,
Southern Baptist Historical Library and Archives, Nashville TN) (hereinafter cited as
JFN Papers). cf., similar comments in letter dated 16 February 1950, 22–1024.

[49]At Columbia Bible College, the personal evangelism course was required of all
students. See Columbia Bible College, Catalogue, 1941–1942, 57. For other schools, see
Southeastern Bible School, Catalogue, 1942–1943, 17; and John Brown University,
Bulletin, 1941–1942, 61. Bob Jones College did not have a course until 1940–1941
when the Department of Christian Education offered "Church and Society," which
included a discussion of the "methods of the propagation of Christianity." Bob Jones
College, Announcement, 1940–1941, 54. With the expansion of the curriculum to
include the training of ministers, a course in "Practical Projects in Evangelism and
Christian Education" became a regular offering. Bob Jones University, Announcement, 1947–1948, 83.

[50]Robert McQuilkin regularly used missionaries in Columbia Bible College's
chapel services. See "Visiting Missionaries and Speakers," Columbia Bible College,
Catalogue, 1940–1941, 8; 1941–1942, 11, 1946–1947, 9; 1950–1951, 13–14. On the
missionary emphasis at Toccoa Falls Institute, see Moothart, Achieving, 102–103. At
John Brown University, the Volunteer Missionary Band sponsored missionary conferences. John Brown University, Bulletin, 1941–1942, 35.

students the opportunity to apply what they had learned in their classes and chapel services.[51]

Strict rules governing student conduct were common. Schools forbade the use of tobacco and alcohol, carefully chaperoned relations between the sexes, and limited students' ability to leave campus.[52] To focus on restrictions and prohibitions, though, is to misunderstand the purpose of these regulations in relation to the schools' educational goals. The rules were concrete applications of broader principles of Christian conduct and were intended to help the schools develop Christian leadership for the churches and the nation. Also, some of the rules reflected fundamentalist disapproval of developments in college life in the teens and twenties. For example, John Brown and Bob Jones did not field intercollegiate athletic teams and banned fraternities and sororities from their colleges.[53] In their place, fundamentalists substituted a variety of special interest clubs and organizations that served the same purpose as fraternities: to integrate the students into a "peer

---

[51]On the various clubs and organizations, see Columbia Bible College, *Catalogue*, 1940–1941, 16–17; John Brown University, *Bulletin*, 1941–1942, 35–37; Bob Jones College, *Announcement*, 1938–1939, 17–18; and Bob Jones University, *Announcement*, 1947–1948, 28–29. Faithfulness in evangelism became a matter of requirement for ministerial students at Bob Jones. "We do not take any 'preacher boy' back in," wrote Jones, "unless he speaks to an average of at least one person a day in the summer and writes a record of the case." Bob Jones to J. Frank Norris, 15 February 1950, in JFN Papers, 22–1024. On student evangelistic activities at Southeastern Bible College, see Southeastern Bible School, *Bulletin*, 1942–1943, 18 and 1952–1953, 12.

[52]Toccoa Falls Institute, *Catalogue*, 1911, 11–12; Bob Jones College, *Announcement*, 1927–1928, 8; John Brown University, *Bulletin*, 1939–1940, 46–47; Southeastern Bible School, *Catalogue*, 1942–1943, 7–8; and Columbia Bible College, *Catalogue*, 1941–1942, 16.

[53]Alfred J. Crabaugh, "Teaching the Dignity of Labor," *Journal of the National Education Association* (25 February 1926): 41; Bob Jones College, *Announcement*, 1927–1928, 8; Bob Jones College, *Catalogue*, 1939–1940, 17; cf., the exchange of letters between Lewis Chafer and George Guille concerning fraternities at Bryan College where Chafer advised against fraternities because they created divisions among students. George Guille to Lewis Sperry Chafer, 22 August 1931, and LSC to George Guille, 7 September 1931, in LSC Papers.

society" where they learned the norms of the student subculture,[54] and in the case of these schools, a culture governed by fundamentalist values. For example, at Bob Jones College, the Laymen's Club was comprised of male students who had decided to "use all their opportunities to lead the unconverted to their Lord and Savior."[55] Similarly, the Fisherman's Club of John Brown University equipped "its members for leadership in spiritual activities" through personal evangelism and street preaching.[56]

One other concern linking these schools was their founders' belief that their schools had to be kept independent of denominational control. They wanted their schools to be of service to all denominations. Some were almost apologetic and quite defensive about their independence, indicating an awareness of Southern Protestants' intense loyalty to their denominations. The brochure announcing the first classes at Birmingham School of the Bible tried to clarify its relation to the city's churches by stating:

> In order to avoid any possible misunderstanding regarding the aim and purpose of this school, the officers wish it to be distinctly known that the Birmingham School of the Bible does not have the faintest intention of starting a new denomi-

---

[54]At Bob Jones, the heart of the network was literary societies, which ironically adopted Greek letters to distinguish themselves and were governed by a pan-Hellenic council. Bob Jones College, *Announcement*, 1939–1940, 17. Clubs at John Brown gathered around vocational interests like teaching, farming, engineering, business, and aviation while social activities were sponsored by clubs organized by the students' home states. John Brown University, *Bulletin*, 1941–1942, 35–39. At the Bible colleges and institutes, student life centered around nurturing and promoting an interest in evangelism and foreign missions. See Columbia Bible College, *Catalogue*, 1941–1942, 27 and Southeastern Bible School, *Gateway* (Yearbook), 1949, 48–49. The liberal arts colleges had similar organizations. See references cited above. Paula S. Fass, in *The Damned and the Beautiful: American Youth in the 1920s* (New York: Oxford University Press, 1977) 141–49, analyzes the role of fraternities in college life and discusses the significance of "peer societies." Unlike the fraternities and other organizations Fass studied where the norms were developed by the students, the clubs at fundamentalist schools took their values from the fundamentalist movement.

[55]Bob Jones College, *Announcement*, 1939–1940, 18.

[56]John Brown University, *Bulletin*, 1941–1942, 36.

nation or sect in Birmingham....Nor does this school desire to interfere with the organized services of any church in Birmingham. This school hopes to assist the evangelical denominations of this city in their efforts to train and equip their teachers for more useful service.[57]

Reflecting the influence of Dallas Seminary graduates on its staff, the Dallas Bible Institute announced that it was "denominationally unaffiliated" and intended to "work in harmony with all orthodox evangelical churches."[58] Columbia Bible College tried to reassure denominational loyalists that its program did not threaten their programs by asserting that its students were "among the most devoted workers" in denominational churches and that students were required to join a church while enrolled.[59]

In some ways, the development of Southern Bible institutes embodied an effort to enlarge and formalize the work of the itinerants that toured the network of Southern Bible conferences in the early 1900s. Specifically, the institutes provided continuing in-depth Bible study that Southerners learned to appreciate from Bible teachers like James Gray, A. C. Gaebelein, George Guille, and the extension workers of the Moody Bible Institute. The catalog of the Dallas Bible Institute reminded prospective students that it was "neither a seminary nor a college, but a school for intensive Bible study" with the purpose of giving "each student a thorough heart-knowledge of the Word of God and to direct this knowledge into various fields of Christian activity that souls might be saved."[60] According to an

---

[57]Birmingham School of the Bible, "Announcement," 1934. To avoid conflict with churches' traditional Wednesday night prayer meetings, classes began with a Tuesday-Thursday night schedule.

[58]Quoted in Gordon F. Gurney, "A History of the Dallas Bible Institute" (Th.M. thesis, Dallas Theological Seminary, 1964) 26. Lewis Chafer used the phrase "denominationally unrelated" to describe the relationship between his seminary and the denominations.

[59]Columbia Bible College, Catalogue, 1941–1942, 20. The same statement was in the school's first announcement; see Hehl, This is the Victory, 93.

[60]"Statement of Purpose" Catalogue of the Dallas Bible Institute, 1940, quoted in Gurney, "History of the Dallas Bible Institute," 24.

announcement for the Birmingham School of the Bible, such a course of study would fulfill a need that churches and conferences did not meet by appealing to laymen and women "who have been seeking for a training that is extensive enough in the courses taught and long enough in the time required to give one an adequate knowledge of the Bible."[61] This Bible study was not simply gaining knowledge for knowledge's sake but was intended to create a core of committed workers for the churches. The purpose of the Southern Bible Institute was to train "Christian men and women in the knowledge and practical use of the Bible" thus equipping "its students to become pastors assistants, Bible teachers, Sunday school teachers, city mission workers, Christian community workers, [and] home and foreign missionaries."[62] Such statements indicate that the founders and supporters believed their schools met Southerners' demands for fundamentalist teaching that Bible conferences could not fulfill. In other words, the establishment in the South and the support by Southerners of such schools suggest that some Southern Protestants used fundamentalism to satisfy their desire for a particular kind of Bible teaching generally unavailable from their denominations.

Moreover, the specific circumstances leading to the creation of Toccoa Falls Institute and Southern Bible Institute reinforce this conclusion. Both schools grew out of the need for trained lay workers to assist evangelistic efforts among the Southern white working class. R. A. Forrest's tours of the South for the Christian and Missionary Alliance (CMA) took him into the coal camps and mill towns of the region. He discovered that his converts needed not only a continuing program of Bible study to help them grow in their faith but also basic literacy skills simply to read the Bible. Forrest found recruiting qualified Southern workers difficult because they lacked basic education and money to attend school for the necessary training. The circumstances of J. F. Dunn typified the problem. He left school after the third grade to work in a cotton mill. Converted under Forrest's

---

[61]"Announcement, 1934" Birmingham School of the Bible, n. p.

[62]N.a., "Columbia Gets Bible Institute," *The State*, 15 September 1921, n.p., photocopy in Hehl, *This is the Victory*, 52.

preaching, Dunn told Forrest of his desire to become a preacher. Dunn's sincerity and desire convinced Forrest that the South needed a school to help people like Dunn. Recognizing the South's need for such schools and seeing in Forrest's plans an avenue for meeting that need, CMA supporters in Atlanta gave Forrest their encouragement and financial support.[63] In 1910 he began a school in Golden Valley, North Carolina, that was part Bible institute and part high school. Needing a more accessible location, he moved the school to a defunct resort hotel near Toccoa, Georgia. Despite a series of financial crises, not the least of which was the loss of its uninsured main building to a fire, the school survived and began fulfilling its purpose of providing remedial education with fundamentalist theological training. One of its first graduates was J. F. Dunn who later became a minister in Alabama Methodist churches.[64]

Miss Emily Dick of Columbia, South Carolina, faced a similar need for trained workers to assist in her work in the South's cotton mills.[65] Beginning in 1913 she conducted a Sunday school for children at the Palmetto Mill's village near Columbia. Her classes opened opportunities to conduct Bible studies in their parent's homes. She also recruited "uptown" women to teach classes in sewing and cooking to the women of the mill.[66] Feeling inadequate to lead Bible studies, Dick turned to the fundamentalist training offered at MBI in the spring of 1917. By the end of that year, Dick's efforts had come to the attention of H. C. Dresser, executive vice-president of the Martel Mills because he noticed that some workers in the Palmetto Mill were "more alert and faithful to do a conscientious job."[67] He gave her a paid position to establish similar classes in the mill's other villages in the South. Dick returned to MBI for further study and to recruit workers. The need for trained workers was not met from volunteers from MBI, so Dick sought to bring the training to the South where people were already

---

[63]Moothart, *Achieving*, 59–60.

[64]Ibid., 9–12, 58–61; and Troy Damron, *A Tree God Planted* (Toccoa GA: Cross Reference Books, 1982) 31–32, 34–35, 45–47.

[65]See Hehl, *This is the Victory*, 4–13.

[66]Ibid., 7.

[67]Ibid., 10.

interested in the mill work. As early as 1918 Dick expressed a desire to
have a Bible school in the South, but not until James Gray's visit in
1920 were concrete steps taken for the establishment of the Southern
Bible Institute. Columbia's citizens responded to Gray's appeals and
supported Dick's efforts to bring Northern-style fundamentalist lay
training to the South. Some served on the advisory board of the
Southern Bible Institute while H. T. Patterson, a businessman, was
president of the Board of Trustees of Columbia Bible College into the
1950s.[68]

Schools like Toccoa Falls Institute and Columbia Bible College
followed the pattern of MBI in focusing their curriculum on Bible
study and evangelism. Other Southern schools were more ambitious,
seeking to develop a liberal arts program in a region with a strong
tradition of denominationally sponsored colleges and universities.[69]
The distinctive mission of these schools centered around teaching the
liberal arts in a Christian environment from a fundamentalist point
of view.[70] An early promotional pamphlet for Bob Jones College
promised the school would give students "a general education...in the
essentials of culture and in the arts and sciences" while "combating all
atheistic, agnostic, pagan, and so-called scientific adulterations of the
Gospel."[71] John Brown University sought to prevent students from
learning "a wrong sense of values" by giving every student "a
thorough knowledge of the Word of God and faith in its teaching and

---

[68]N.a., "Bible College May Come Here," *The State* (Columbia SC) 5 June 1920, 5,
and N.a., "More Discussion on Bible School," 30 June 1920, 10, lists Columbians
working on committees to start the Bible institute. See also Southern Bible Institute,
"Announcement, 1921," reprinted in Hehl, *This is the Victory*, 55 and Columbia Bible
College, *Catalog*, 1954–1955, 7, for other local supporters.

[69]According to Kenneth K. Bailey in *Southern White Protestantism in the
Twentieth Century* (New York: Harper and Row, 1964) 26, in 1900 out of 26,237
Southern college students, 13,859 were in church sponsored schools.

[70]Such an ideologically controlled curriculum raises the questions of the quality of
education offered and the nature of academic freedom at these schools, but such issues
are not relevant to understanding what the establishment of these schools meant for
fundamentalism or for the creation of a Southern wing of the movement.

[71]"Announcement of Bob Jones College, 1927–1928" (n. p., n. d.), 4.

its person, Jesus Christ."[72] The schools achieved these goals partially through required courses in the Bible. For example, before graduation with a BA or BS, students at John Brown took sixteen hours of Bible courses.[73] In the twenties, all students and faculty members at Bob Jones College were required to attend a Bible class three times a week, and by the thirties students took at least one class per semester in the Bible.[74] Moreover, the content of certain courses reinforced the biblical training. For example, in the ethics course at John Brown, students learned "the fundamental principles underlying moral conduct, with particular reference to the Christian faith as furnishing the most adequate basis for the good life."[75] The comparative religions course at Bob Jones demonstrated "how 'man by wisdom' has not known God, and how the Christian religion is the only one that meets the needs of Adam's fallen race."[76] The liberal arts courses at Bible colleges as well taught the fundamentalist perspective on its subjects. At Columbia Bible College, the "Principles of Sociology" were studied "from the viewpoint of Christian revelation," which agreed "with all the truly scientific conclusions of students of sociology."[77] Somewhat surprisingly, these schools avoided the issue of evolution by not teaching courses in biology that addressed modern science's most serious challenge to Christian revelation. In its 1925 catalog John Brown University listed science courses only in the fields of chemistry and physics, while Bob Jones offered classes in invertebrate zoology and general botany.[78] By the late thirties, John Brown University more forthrightly faced the issue by offering a junior level course in

---

[72]T. Marshall Morsey, "Why John Brown University," John Brown University *Bulletin*, 1925, 13–14.

[73]Brown's requirement reflected a two-hour Bible course each semester at the University. John Brown University *Bulletin*, 1939–1940, 62, 66, 73, 128; John Brown University *Bulletin*, 1948–1949, 53, 58, 99, 104, 120.

[74]N.a., "The Bob Jones College," *Moody Bible Institute Monthly*, November 1927, 114; *Catalogue* of the Bob Jones College, 1938–1939, 25.

[75]John Brown University *Bulletin*, 1939–1940, 126.

[76]Bob Jones College, *Catalogue*, 1938–1939, 29.

[77]Columbia Bible College, *Catalogue*, 1940–1941, 57.

[78]John Brown University, *Bulletin*, 1925, 56–59; and Bob Jones College, *Announcement*, 1927–1928, 9.

"Biological Philosophy" that promised to give the "Christian viewpoint" on the "Spontaneous Generation of Life, Biogenesis, Theory of Evolution, Cell Theory, Organismic Theory and various others" and to consider "the Biblical account of creation."[79]

Training lay workers, defending fundamentalist orthodoxy, and providing a fundamentalist environment to study the liberal arts did not exhaust fundamentalist educational efforts. Several of the fundamentalist schools in the South emphasized vocational training. At Toccoa Falls Institute, the training was not oriented toward preparing the students for career but was used to help students pay for their education and to hold down the costs of running the school. In its early years the Institute required all students to work twelve hours a week at a variety of chores around campus.[80] Even those who could afford to pay all their expenses were not exempt from this rule because "the household and farm work is intended to contribute in some degree to the completeness of the of the student's training."[81] In the late 1930s Bob Jones College added business courses like bookkeeping, typing, and shorthand to give those financially unable to attend college for four years the opportunity to learn skills "in the environment of a Christian college."[82]

A similar concern about vocational training in a fundamentalist atmosphere moved R. G. LeTourneau to start a technical school after World War II in East Texas. LeTourneau was a businessman who made his fortune in designing and building large earthmoving equipment. During a city-wide revival during the 1904 Christmas season the sixteen-year-old boy was converted while his family lived on the west coast.[83] His faith was nurtured through the Plymouth

---

[79]John Brown University *Bulletin*, 1939–1940, 138.

[80]Moothart, *Achieving*, 66; Damron, *Tree God Planted*, 33–34. Some schools used these methods to help cut expenses during the difficult years of the Depression. See for example, Judson A. Rudd to RCM, 17 February 1933, in RCM Papers, Bryan University File, concerning Bryan College.

[81]Quoted in Moothart, *Achieving*, 66.

[82]Bob Jones College, *Announcement*, 1939–1940, 56.

[83]R. G. LeTourneau, *Mover of Men and Mountains: The Autobiography of R. G. LeTourneau* (Chicago: Moody Press, 1967) 32–34.

Brethren movement and the Christian and Missionary Alliance. The latter contact brought him in touch with R. A. Forrest and the Toccoa Falls Institute.[84] During the 1930s, LeTourneau's generosity was perhaps the most important factor in helping the Institute survive the Depression. He made several contributions that enabled the school to meet current expenses and to expand their facilities through the construction of a gymnasium and dormitories.[85] In 1938 the National Youth Administration (NYA) used the Institute for a Residential Project where participants took liberal arts courses from the Institute's staff and received vocational training from the NYA. LeTourneau established a co-op program with the Institute that allowed some of these students to work their way through college by employment at LeTourneau's manufacturing plant in Toccoa.[86] This experience with the Institute seems to have directed LeTourneau's interests toward establishing a school where students earned degrees in technical fields like engineering while taking courses in the Bible. Looking for a place to build a new manufacturing plant, LeTourneau found a closed military hospital complex in Longview, Texas. Though not appropriate for a factory, the buildings could be renovated for a school. LeTourneau bought the hospital and opened the LeTourneau Technical Institute in the fall of 1949 with John Brown participating in the dedication services.[87] Within a few years the school awarded

---

[84]Ibid., 219–20; cf., Moothart, *Achieving*, 135–37.

[85]LeTourneau, *Mover of Men*, 223; Moothart, *Achieving*, 156. Forrest and the work of the Institute so impressed LeTourneau that LeTourneau convinced his eldest son to enroll in the school. LeTourneau, *Mover of Men*, 220.

[86]Moothart, *Achieving*, 153, 156. NYA participants were allowed to take courses from the Bible school curriculum as well. As a site for a plant, North Georgia attracted LeTourneau because he needed hills on which he could test his earth moving equipment. Although fairly isolated, Toccoa was served by the Southern Railway. Construction on the plant began in November 1938, and completed by the following summer. LeTourneau, *Mover of Men*, 220–22.

[87]Ralph C. Kennedy, Jr. and Thomas Rothrock, *John Brown of Arkansas* (Siloam Springs AR: John Brown University Press, 1966) 118, suggest that Brown's school was the main inspiration for LeTourneau, but LeTourneau does not indicate in his autobiography that the example of Brown influenced his thinking. Nevertheless, the presence of Brown at the dedication services does indicate that LeTourneau recognized the similarity of mission between the two schools.

four-year degrees in several technical fields while students learned their skills "in a good Christian environment."[88]

The preeminent place of vocational training in the curriculum of John Brown University was due in part to the experiences of the school's founder. Born in 1879 John Brown was raised in a strict Quaker home in Southeastern Iowa.[89] He learned the value of work when he had to seek employment at age eleven to help support his poor family. In 1896 he moved to Arkansas with an older brother and was converted in a Salvation Army meeting. Brown then devoted his spare time to working for the Army and under its tutelage trained for full-time Christian service. During the next few years, Brown conducted evangelistic campaigns in the small towns of Arkansas, Texas, and Iowa.[90] His reputation from these endeavors open the door in 1900 for him to become president of Scarritt College, a Methodist institution in Neosho, Missouri.[91] The two years he served profoundly affected his views on college education. After seeing the influence of sports over the school's academic program and the haughtiness and prejudice of students whose parents paid for their children's education against those who worked their way through college, Brown determined to open a school where students' labor would be respected and would pay for their education.[92]

Brown's dream came true when the John E. Brown College opened in September 1919, on Brown's farm outside of Siloam Springs, Arkansas. Brown originally intended that only students who could not afford to attend other colleges be admitted to his school. In fact, Brown required letters of reference from a doctor, teacher, and minister attesting to the applicant's financial need.[93] Students took traditional

---

[88]LeTourneau, *Mover of Men*, 240–42. LeTourneau built a steel mill outside of Longview and set up a co-op program where students from the technical school gained practical experience by working in the mill.

[89]Kennedy and Rothrock's *John Brown of Arkansas* is a good introduction to Brown's life. See 1–9 for Brown's early years.

[90]Kennedy and Rothrock, *John Brown of Arkansas*, 11–15, 21–29; Landon Laird, "Evangelist, Editor, and College President," *American Magazine*, February 1923, 64.

[91]Crabaugh, "Teaching the Dignity of Labor," 42.

[92]Ibid.

[93]Laird, "Evangelist," 64.

college courses, along with required courses in the Bible, and learned a trade by working four hours per day on the farm, with the dairy cattle, in a print shop or automobile garage, or in building the school's dormitories and classrooms.[94] Brown's guiding principle was that "education and manual labor can and should go hand in hand."[95] By 1924 the school had 300 students, assets of almost $400,000, and over 3,000 applications.[96] By then, as well, the interest in vocational training was so strong among some parents who could pay for their children's education that in 1925 Brown responded by reorganizing the school into a university with a vocational college, a liberal arts college, a high school, and a Bible school.[97] Within a few years eight to twelve hours of "vocational studies" were a requirement for graduation from each school.[98] While the vocational element in the curriculum was unusual, it was tied to the fundamentalist hope of penetrating and influencing American society. "There is no more urgent need," according to Brown, "than to train Christian leadership for organized labor in industry," and the graduates of the Vocational College were qualified to meet that need.[99]

Lay training, liberal arts, and vocational education laid the foundation of fundamentalist educational efforts in the South, and from that base a few schools expanded their curricula with graduate courses. At Columbia Bible College this addition came partially in response to the demand of college graduates wanting to earn a degree for their work in the Bible school courses. Beginning in 1936 those who held a bachelor's degree could earn credit toward a Master of Arts

---

[94]Crabaugh, "Teaching the Dignity of Labor," 41.

[95]Quoted in ibid.

[96]John E. Brown, "America's only 'Wholly-Pay-by-Work' College," *Moody Bible Institute Monthly*, January 1924, 243.

[97]Morsey, "Why John Brown University?" 14.

[98]John Brown University, *Bulletin*, 1925, 28; cf., John Brown University, *Bulletin*, 1940–1941, 51, 64, 278, 293. By this catalog, though, the commitment to the "pay-by-work" principle was gone. According to Brown, the University "is not a work school where boys and girls are working their way to an education." John E. Brown, "John Brown University—What Is It?," ibid., 17.

[99]Brown, "John Brown University," *Bulletin*, 1940–1941, 15.

in Bible Education.[100] But this new graduate school also included courses for the training of ministers. The creation of this professional program grew out of fundamentalist concern over liberal control of the denominational seminaries and was an effort to put "the great spiritual aim of the Bible institute movement...at the very center of... seminary training."[101] The Bible was the heart of curriculum. Students were required to master its contents in English as well as learn the original languages. The coursework also emphasized "soul winning through personal work, evangelistic preaching, and Bible teaching, a missionary passion, the living of the life in the fullness of the Spirit, [and] carrying on Christian service through prayer and faith."[102] Such courses would restore the "great spiritual principles of God's Word" to the "training of Christian leaders."[103]

The addition of graduate courses at Bob Jones College built on the strengths of its liberal arts program and grew out of a desire to give graduate education in a Christian environment for the purpose of creating leadership for America with fundamentalist values. The Department of Religion offered the first graduate degree when in 1942 students began earning credit toward a Master of Arts in Religion.[104] In 1944, the Graduate School of Fine Arts accepted its first students for courses in speech and music, and a Ph.D. program began to complement the MA in Religion.[105] In 1949 the School of Religion entered the field of ministerial training by offering the graduate-level professional degree of Bachelor of Divinity.[106] These programs constituted the graduate offerings at Bob Jones University through the 1950s.[107] In 1946 the Board of Trustees authorized the reorganization of the college into a university and explained the mission of the school. Indicating their fundamentalist hope that their school's graduates

[100]Columbia Bible College, *Catalogue*, 1940–1941, 31.
[101]Ibid.
[102]Ibid., 31–32.
[103]Ibid., 31.
[104]Bob Jones College, *Announcement*, 1942–1943, 69.
[105]Bob Jones College, *Announcement*, 1944–1945, 82–83, 88.
[106]Bob Jones University, *Announcement*, 1949–1950, 91–92.
[107]Bob Jones University, *Bulletin*, 1959–1960, 11.

would leaven American society, the Trustees believed that the addition of these programs as well as the continuing efforts to strengthen the undergraduate curriculum would make "the university a center of the highest academic standards and Christian culture" and from it would leave "trained Christian leaders" prepared "to render service" in the fields of "the fine arts, the Bible, missions, evangelism, pastoral training, history, journalism, education, Christian education, theology, international relations, the social sciences, and languages."[108]

Unlike these other schools, the founders of Dallas Theological Seminary designed the school from its inception in 1924 to be a graduate professional school for the training of pastors.[109] Fundamentalists saw ministerial education as a crucial battleground in the crisis of the 1920s. They recognized that Bible institutes were only an emergency solution yet were unable to cooperate to establish a seminary of their own. That the first seminary under fundamentalist control started in the South is somewhat serendipitous, yet its Southern location seems to have obscured the importance of Dallas Seminary to fundamentalism and its significance for the movement in the South.[110] As the first

---

[108]Quoted in Bob Jones University, *Announcement*, 1947–1948, 19.

[109]The original name of the seminary was the Evangelical Theological College, reflecting the influence of W. H. Griffith-Thomas, an Oxford trained Anglican minister involved in the Keswick and Victorious Life Conferences in American and Great Britain. The name changed in 1936 in part to end the confusion over the use of college, which suggested an undergraduate school, and to indicate more clearly to American fundamentalists the nature and purpose of the school. See Rollin T. Chafer, "What's in a Name?," *Bibliotheca Sacra* 93 (April 1936): 132.

[110]In *Revive*, 20, Carpenter simply noted the founding of the school as part of the network of institutions fundamentalists created in the 1930s and 1940s and its links to fundamentalists in Presbyterian denominations. Sandeen, *Roots*, ignored the school altogether, as does Louis Gasper in *The Fundamentalist Movement, 1930–1956* (Netherlands: Mouton and Company, 1963; reprint, Grand Rapids MI: Baker Book House, 1981). In *Fundamentalism and American Culture: The Shaping of Twentieth Century Evangelicalism, 1875–1925* (New York: Oxford University Press, 1981) 194, George Marsden acknowledged that Dallas Seminary in the '30s became an important center of the movement but offers little analysis of its role. Stronger, but still very brief, assessments of Dallas's contribution can be found in George W. Dollar, *A History of Fundamentalism in America* (Greenville SC: Bob Jones University Press, 1973) 163; and Timothy P. Weber, *Living in the Shadow of the Second Coming: American Premillennialism, 1875–1982* (Grand Rapids MI: Zondervan Publishing

school offering graduate ministerial training under fundamentalist auspices, this seminary took fundamentalist education into a new field, and a careful analysis of its founder's rationale of the school's mission reveals a distinctive approach to winning the battle with liberalism.

While others participated in planning the creation of the seminary, the energy and vision of Lewis Sperry Chafer determined the shape of the school's mission.[111] Born and raised in Ohio, Chafer trained at the Oberlin College conservatory and worked on leaving the school as musical director and soloist for itinerating evangelists in the 1890s.[112] Despite the absence of formal theological training, Chafer was ordained to the Congregational ministry in 1900 and pastored a church in a small town near Buffalo, New York. In 1901 Chafer returned to the sawdust trail as a preacher associated the evangelist J. Wilbur Chapman. Disillusioned with what he believed were the manipulative methods of mass evangelism,[113] Chafer joined the staff of Moody's schools in Northfield, Massachusetts, as music director for the summer conferences and music teacher at the school for boys. Students' questions about training for the pastorate alerted Chafer to the growing problem of modernist influence in seminaries. He found he was unable to recommend any school that was consistently evangelical in its theological training.

These years at Northfield (1903–1910) were crucial to Chafer's development because they brought him into contact with many itinerants who taught in the Bible conferences, most notably C. I.

Corp., 1983) 238. An excellent and thorough analysis of the early years of the school is John David Hannah's "The Social and Intellectual History of the Origins of the Evangelical Theological College" (Ph.D. diss., University of Texas at Dallas, 1988).

[111]Biographical information on Chafer is incomplete and limited to brief sketches in discussions of the history of the school. See Rudolf A. Renfer, "A History of the Dallas Theological Seminary" (Ph.D. diss., University of Texas, 1959) 83–97; and John A. Witmer, "'What Hath God Wrought'—Fifty Years of Dallas Theological Seminary; Part I: God's Man and His Dream," *Bibliotheca Sacra* 130 (October 1973): 292–95.

[112]In "Social and Intellectual History," 88–89, Hannah reports that Chafer did not graduate.

[113]For his criticisms, see Lewis Sperry Chafer, *True Evangelism* (New York: Gospel Publishing House, 1911).

Scofield. Scofield encouraged Chafer to hone his skills as a preacher in the mold of a Bible conference teacher.[114] The Southfield Conferences in Florida were but one part of an itinerating ministry that took Chafer across the country in the 1910s.[115] In these travels, Chafer discussed with pastors their seminary training and found that they felt unprepared to teach the Bible to their congregations. These conversations planted the seeds of an idea to build a seminary devoted to producing pastors trained to preach the Bible expositionally in the style of Bible conference teachers. The growing theological warfare between liberal and conservative factions in the denominations reinforced Chafer's conviction that fundamentalists needed a seminary under their control.

Specific steps toward starting a seminary began in the early '20s when Chafer solicited advice from A. B. Winchester, B. B. Sutcliffe, and W. H. Griffith-Thomas, fellow itinerants.[116] They committed themselves to support Chafer's endeavors but left the burden of organizing and administrating the school to Chafer. The most important task facing Chafer was finding a place for the school. Chafer and his advisors gave some thought to opening a branch of the school on both coasts, but they discarded that idea in favor of one central location.[117] Chicago was one city given serious consideration because of an opportunity to use the campus of Wheaton College. Chafer learned that Charles Blanchard, president of Wheaton, was offering to turn the college's facilities over to anyone "willing to run

---

[114]According to Chafer in "What I Learned from Dr. Scofield," *Sunday School Times*, 4 March 1923, 120, Scofield also was instrumental in Chafer adopting a dispensational framework for interpreting Scripture.

[115]See chapter 2 for a discussion of the Southfield Conferences.

[116]A. B. Winchester served as a missionary in China and in the 1910s and 1920s as pastor of the Knox Presbyterian Church in Toronto. In the '20s, B. B. Sutcliffe organized and taught a city-wide Bible study class in Portland, Oregon and later pastored an independent church that grew out of the class. W. H. Griffith-Thomas was an Oxford trained Anglican minister who based an itinerant ministry out of Philadelphia. He died the summer before the school opened. He was to teach the systematic theology courses, but that burden fell to Chafer. Renfer, "A History," 52–68, 109; and Witmer, "God's Man," 294–96.

[117]On the selection of a location for the school, see Renfer, "A History," 125–36; and Witmer, "God's Man," 296–97.

it for the glory of God" because of financial difficulties. Chafer arranged to meet with Blanchard to discuss the possibility of the seminary taking over the campus, but on the morning of the meeting, Blanchard received a substantial monetary gift enabling him to keep the college open.[118] Chafer spent much of 1922 in Dallas conducting a Bible conference in First Presbyterian Church and then as pastoral supply for the Scofield Memorial Church. In both churches, he found enthusiastic lay support and financial backing for the project. Moreover, he gained a respected ministerial ally in William Anderson, pastor of First Presbyterian Church, who insisted that the school be established in Dallas.[119] Chafer accepted the proposal and turned his attention to recruiting faculty and students while a committee of laymen and pastors from Dallas arranged for facilities and raised money. In part, Chafer accepted because of the evident enthusiasm of the local support, but also because he wanted to distance the school from the controversies swirling in the Northern denominations.[120] In 1924 classes began with thirteen students, and the fundamentalist movement had a seminary of its own.

Chafer's thoughtful exposition of the school's purpose described what this development meant for fundamentalism. In his analysis an essential ingredient in fundamentalist efforts to reverse liberal control of the denominations was the development of a seminary dedicated to training ministers committed to defending the fundamentals through

---

[118]Lewis Sperry Chafer, "The Founding of Dallas Theological Seminary," Chapel Message, no date, recording in Mosher Library, Dallas Theological Seminary, Dallas, Texas. In 1926 Chafer received an offer to move the school to Wheaton as the college's graduate program. He refused in part because of commitments to supporters in Dallas. S. J. Bole to LSC, 22 May 1926; and LSC to S. J. Bole, 4 June 1926, in LSC Papers. Another factor was Chafer's desire to keep the school independent of outside control and influence, even from fundamentalists of a similar moderate temperament.

[119]Other local pastors involved at this time included William Galbraith, Anderson's assistant, T. O. Perrin of Westminster Presbyterian, Robert Hill of First Presbyterian of Tyler, Texas, W. I. Carroll of First Presbyterian of Marshall, Texas, and Luther Rees of First Presbyterian of Paris, Texas. Renfer, "History," 135–36.

[120]Witmer, "God's Man," 295.

expository preaching of the Bible.[121] Most seminaries doused the evangelical fire and undermined the faith of their students because of their emphasis on scholarship that questioned accuracy and authenticity of the Bible. The result was "a floodtide of educated unbelief coming out of" the seminaries denying laypeople the biblical teaching needed for their spiritual health.[122] Bible colleges and institutes had the right spirit and creed but did not have the rigorous curriculum necessary for training a new generation of pastors capable of teaching the Bible with authority. The school in Dallas would combine the best of both traditions. According to Chafer:

> Theological seminaries are teaching certain subjects which are vitally important to the minister's training but woefully neglecting the introduction to the Bible itself. The Bible Institutes are giving an elementary course in the Bible, but omitting those ministerial subjects which are of great importance. This institution proposes to give ministerial training on the highest possible plain, combining an introduction to the Bible which is advanced and intensified beyond the courses given at the Institutes.[123]

While students took sixteen hours of systematic theology and eight of church history, the heart of the three-year course of study was the Bible, "the *sine qua non* of the preacher's preparation."[124] Students took twenty-four hours in the English Bible providing an introduction to every book in the Bible as well as twenty hours in learning Greek and Hebrew.[125] An admissions requirement of a bachelor's

---

[121]For a general discussion of Chafer's views on theological education, see Lewis Sperry Chafer, "Effective Ministerial Training" in Evangelical Theological College, *Bulletin*, May 1925, 7–11.

[122]LSC to James Bowron, 30 April 1926, in LSC Papers.

[123]LSC to Fred Z. Browne, 12 February 1925, in LSC Papers.

[124]Evangelical Theological College, *Bulletin*, January 1931. 23.

[125]If survey introductions to the Old and New Testaments (4 hours) and the exegetical courses (12 hours) were included with the language and English Bible courses, 60 of the 98 semester hours required for graduation were in biblical studies. Ibid., 23–24. A similar distribution of hours was used in earlier years. See Evangelical

degree and the denial of transfer credit for courses taken at a Bible college or institute reinforced the school's graduate curriculum.[126] But Chafer found that three years was not enough time to cover the material necessary to reach his educational goals. In 1935, in a move that remains unique in theological education, Chafer added a fourth year of courses, replacing the Bachelor of Theology degree with a Masters of Theology as the standard degree received on graduation.[127]

Even while calling for the creation of new schools, fundamentalists harbored suspicions of education, and Chafer's ambitious program ran the risk of appearing to sacrifice piety for scholarship. At the new seminary, though, neither the intensity nor the length of the course of study would sap the evangelical enthusiasm of the students. Chafer employed a several strategies to prevent the loss of spiritual fervor.[128] Within the curriculum itself, courses in "The Realization of the Spiritual Life" and "Personal Evangelism" invigorated students'

Theological College, *Bulletin*, June 1926, 8. According to Chafer, this curriculum included the standard courses offered at other seminaries plus "50 percent more material." LSC to William A. Anderson, 20 June 1928, in LSC Papers; cf., LSC to R. T. Cudmore, 23 August 1929 and LSC to Robert J. Alderman, 6 October 1926, in LSC Papers.

[126]Only in "exceptional cases" was the requirement of a college degree waived. Evangelical Theological College, *Annual Announcement*, September 1924, 12; cf., LSC to R. T. Cudmore, 23 August 1929, in LSC Papers. Regarding Bible institute students, Chafer found that they did poorer than college graduates in the seminary's classes. LSC to William T. Strong, 7 June 1926 and RTC to L. C. Stumpf, 16 June 1925, in LSC Papers.

[127]Rollin T. Chafer explained the change in "The Four-year Course Plan," *Bulletin*, February 1935, 2–3. Out of 140 hours required for graduation, Bible courses accounted for 32 hours (including introductory surveys), languages for 38 hours (with the possible requirement of an additional 8 hours if a student entered deficient in Greek), and systematic theology for 24. Students also had to write a Master's thesis. Dallas Theological Seminary, *Bulletin*, October 1936, 8–9. According to Renfer, in "A History," 210, biblical languages and English Bible courses comprised over 49 percent of the hours required for graduation.

[128]In describing this aspect of seminary life, the early catalogs become rather defensive, as though Chafer had to convince applicants and supporters alike that this school, in the words of a critic of a later school, would not "worship the goddess of scholarship." Erling C. Olsen to LSC, 12 June 1949, in LSC Papers. See Evangelical Theological College, *Bulletin*, January 1925, 4; May 1925, 10–11; November 1925, 12–13.

piety.[129] In the early years of the school some of the leading itinerants like George Guille and A. C. Gaebelein taught the English Bible courses giving the flavor of a Bible conference to the instruction.[130] Chapel services and requirements of Christian service helped "to develop that evangelistic spirit and true spiritual enthusiasm which should dominate the life of every true minister of Jesus Christ."[131] Also, careful selection of students helped maintain the desired spiritual climate. "We have never run a school for all comers," boasted Rollin Chafer, the registrar. "We proceed upon the truth that only a saved and surrendered man can be taught the truth, therefore, we cannot waste our time with men who have not had a real experience in the saving knowledge of Christ."[132] At the same time Lewis Chafer assured supporters that these aspects of the program did not turn the seminary into a "glorified Bible institute"[133] and defended his school's program: "The impression is abroad that education is the enemy of spirituality, and that one must choose between the two. This institution is a live protest against that modernistic notion and we believe that, far beyond any expectation that we ever had, we are now proving these things to be true."[134]

Providing ministerial training that was academically rigorous and spiritually uplifting did not exhaust Chafer's vision of the service

---

[129]Evangelical Theological College, *Bulletin*, September 1924, 12.

[130]Ibid., 4.

[131]LSC to Mrs. William P. Craig, 20 July 1929, in LSC Papers. Activities included pastoring churches, preaching in church services, leading Sunday school classes, directing music in worship services, and directing young people's programs. See "College Notes," Evangelical Theological College, *Bulletin*, November 1926, 3; and "Student Activities," Evangelical Theological College, *Bulletin*, March 1929, 6–9.

[132]RTC to J. P. Epp, 9 July 1938, in LSC Papers. In the first *Annual Announcement* of the Evangelical Theological College, 12, the "Terms of Admission" included a letter certifying that the applicant was "born again, yielded to the will of God, and...endowed with ministry gifts."

[133]According to an unspecified critic quoted in Rollin T. Chafer, "'They Say—What They Say? Let Them Say,'" *Bulletin*, March 1930, 3. See also, Lewis Chafer's replies to suggestions that the school was not much better than a Bible college, LSC to Fred Z. Browne, 12 February 1925 and LSC to Robert W. Dixon, undated (c. September 1929) and 11 October 1929, in LSC Papers.

[134]LSC to George H. Dowkontt, 10 March 1931, in LSC Papers.

the seminary would render to fundamentalism. To achieve his dream that graduates would take positions in evangelical churches of all denominations, Chafer believed that the seminary had to be free from outside control, especially that of denominations and even that of other fundamentalists. Chafer adopted the awkward but accurate phrase "denominationally unrelated" to describe the relationship of the school to the denominations.[135] Like other fundamentalists, Chafer recognized that the crisis of the 1920s meant that the significant divisions in American Protestantism were no longer along denominational lines. In Chafer's eyes, most of the major denominations were divided between fundamentalists and modernists and between premillennialists, postmillennialists, and amillennialists. A denominational seminary might have representatives from all of these factions on its faculty resulting in a lack of doctrinal unity in the teaching. Without denominational control and support Chafer's seminary was free to focus its teaching in a specific theological tradition and thus serve the fundamentalist-premillennialist factions of all denominations.[136]

Chafer also kept the seminary independent of organized fundamentalism. While plans for the school were being made in the early 1920s, the World Christian Fundamentals Association (WCFA) called for the creation of a fundamentalist seminary. "It is the greatest single need of the hour," according to William Bell Riley, president of

---

[135]Lewis Sperry Chafer, "Why a Denominationally Unrelated Theological College?" *Bulletin*, February 1926, 3–7. Chafer rejected the terms "interdenominational" because it implied uniting all denominations and "undenominational" because it implied rejection of denominations.

[136]Ibid. Responding to an inquiry, Chafer elaborated his position, "We are not a denominational school...[because] there is such a division as to doctrinal views among the men of each of the denominations that wherever a denominational school exists today these two elements are found warring with each other on the faculty and injuring the effectiveness of the course of study. Our teachers are taken from various denominations, but are unified around one system of interpretation so that there is no conflict in the student's mind....We are in hearty sympathy with the work being done by the denominations, we are not opposed to them, and they are glad to receive our students into important pastorates after their training here." LSC to L. S. Bird, 19 February 1928, in LSC Papers.

the WCFA.[137] Perhaps indicating an awareness of Chafer's plans and an effort to co-opt Chafer's work, Riley wanted the faculty to include W. H. Griffith-Thomas, A. B. Winchester, and A. C. Gaebelein, among others.[138] For Chafer and the new school, ties to the WCFA could mean substantial financial and organizational support, yet no evidence suggests that Chafer and his supporters seriously considered connecting their school to the WCFA. One factor was differing perspectives on the size of the school that suggested different views on education. Riley dreamed of a school beginning with 500 students the first year growing to 1,000 in the second.[139] Because of the nature of the curriculum and the desire to ensure students received high quality education, Chafer envisioned a school of no more than 100 men.[140] Also Chafer's educational philosophy implied a different strategy for fighting modernism. Where the WCFA's basic tactic was confrontation and criticism, Chafer's goal was for the graduates to act as a fifth column to reform the denominations from within.[141] Responding to criticism from J. Frank Norris, Chafer explained, "Our policy...is not one of controversy and rebuttal, nor do we desire to make ourselves responsible for the correction of evil that others may do. We are organized to maintain a constructive testimony, and to give out the vital truth."[142] Association with the controversial WCFA might jeopardize Chafer's efforts to place graduates in denominational

---

[137]Riley, "An Orthodox, Premillenarian Seminary," 20.

[138]Ibid.

[139]Ibid.

[140]LSC to Rev. Brank, 3 July 1929, in LSC Papers; cf., Rollin T. Chafer, "Personal Direction Necessary in Efficient Educational Training," *Bulletin*, January 1928, 1–3.

[141]By 1930, Chafer recognized that such a strategy might not work. He wrote, "We are moving very rapidly up to a consummation of a united church.... Naturally there is going to be a withholding on the part of many individual churches and the forming of what will be called, probably, the continuing church. The opportunity for ministry at that time, will be beyond all comparison, for the continuing church will be standing for the most positive doctrine and aggressive evangelism, and yet, there will be few men, probably, to undertake the full requirement of the ministry." LSC to Jack Withow, 11 October 1930, in LSC Papers. In Chafer's eyes, Dallas graduates would be well equipped to serve these independent congregations.

[142]LSC to J. Frank Norris, 20 April 1928, in LSC Papers.

churches. Yet independence of denominations created other problems
that restricted Chafer's ability to realize this goal.

   While Chafer foresaw graduates serving in fundamentalist
churches of all denominations, he hoped they would play a special role
in influencing Presbyterian denominations. "The Dallas Theological
Seminary is thoroughly Presbyterian in all its theology and outlook,"
asserted Chafer,[143] and with its fundamentalist orientation would
supply ministers to help wrest the Northern Presbyterian church from
liberal control and maintain the conservative character of the
Southern denomination. Chafer pursued a variety of strategies to give
the seminary a Presbyterian flavor and to place graduates in
Presbyterian churches. First, Presbyterians dominated the faculty. In
1926 five Southern Presbyterians taught at the school, and by 1944
seven professors represented three different Presbyterian denominations.[144] During the 1920s Chafer tried to recruit students from
Southern Presbyterian colleges, but no graduate of these schools
enrolled in the seminary during the 1920s.[145] With the ouster of J.
Gresham Machen and other conservative professors from Princeton
Theological Seminary in 1929, Chafer promoted his seminary as the
school of choice for conservatives studying to become Presbyterian

---

[143]LSC to S. Carson Wasson, 18 May 1944, in LSC Papers. Elsewhere he explained,
"When we use the word 'Presbyterian' I do not merely mean the denomination but
the Calvinistic doctrine which the reformed churches have defended from the
beginning." LSC to Miss Sidney E. Boyle, 11 October 1930; cf., LSC to William T.
Strong, 7 June 1926; LSC to William P. White, 7 April 1928; LSC to J. Gresham
Machen, 3 July 1929; RTC to Chairman, Pulpit Supply Committee, 8 August 1938;
and LSC to George Vorsheim, 24 January 1945, in LSC Papers.

   [144]LSC to R. W. Crain, 10 April 1926, and LSC to S. Carson Wasson, 25 May
1944, in LSC Papers.

   [145]In the spring of 1926, Chafer traveled to Maryville College, Davidson College,
and Hampden-Sydney College. LSC to A. J. Crowell, 15 May 1926, in LSC Papers. No
other trips can be documented. The most prominent characteristic of the educational
background of the students listed in the "Register of Students" in the seminary's
Bulletin was their connection with a fundamentalist school. For example, the 1930
Register recorded that of the forty-five students working for a certificate or Th.B.,
eighteen had attended a Bible institute or Wheaton College. See the "Register of
Students" in Evangelical Theological College, *Bulletin*, November 1929, 21–22; June
1926, 6–7; April 1927, 10–12; January 1928, 12–15; and January 1930, 17–21.

ministers.[146] This tactic was undermined in part by Machen's establishment of Westminster Theological Seminary outside of Philadelphia and the continued presence of a strong conservative faction at Princeton.[147] Chafer also used his ties to conservative Northern Presbyterians to try to find pastorates for graduates, but rarely was he successful.[148] Finally, in the 1940s Chafer tried and failed to have the Philadelphia Presbytery include Dallas Seminary on its list of approved schools for Presbyterian ministerial training.[149] Part of the reason for Chafer's failure was that Presbyterians simply did not believe Chafer's protestations of his seminary's orthodoxy and Presbyterian character. Presbyterians criticized, in particular, the dispensationalism taught in the theology classes. First in the 1930s with professors in Machen's school and then in the 1940s with leaders of the Southern Presbyterian denomination, controversies over dispensationalism undermined Chafer's efforts to send graduates into Presbyterian churches.[150]

---

[146]LSC to Adam H. Davidson, 7 January 1928, 24 June 1929, and LSC to W. Irving Carroll, 28 June 1929, in LSC Papers.

[147]On Westminster, see C. Allyn Russell, "J. Gresham Machen: Scholarly Fundamentalist," in *Voices of Fundamentalism: Seven Biographical Studies* (Philadelphia: Westminster Press, 1976) 155–56. On the continuing importance of Princeton to conservatives, see George M. Marsden, *Reforming Fundamentalism: Fuller Seminary and the New Evangelicalism*, (Grand Rapids MI: Eerdmans, 1987) 21–22.

[148]See for example, the correspondence between LSC and Donald Grey Barnhouse, pastor of Tenth Presbyterian Church in Philadelphia. LSC to Donald Grey Barnhouse, 29 December 1928, 7 January 1929, 16 January 1931, and 31 October 1932 in LSC Papers.

[149]LSC to Alexander Mackie, 27 April 1944, 1 May 1944, 8 May 1944, and 16 May 1944; LSC to S. Carson Wasson, 18 May 1944 and 25 May 1944. Graduate of Dallas Seminary and pastor of Philadelphia's Westminster Presbyterian Church, George Vorsheim reported that the presbytery declined to include Chafer's school on its list because of the dispensationalism in the seminary's theology courses. H. George Vorsheim to LSC, 12 January 1945, in LSC Papers.

[150]See chapter 4 for details of the controversy in the Southern Presbyterian church. Even after this denomination declared dispensationalism to be inconsistent with its doctrinal standards, Chafer still maintained that his school was "as Presbyterian as any seminary in the United States" and its theology as "Calvinistic." LSC to George Vorsheim, 24 January 1945, in LSC Papers. These controversies over dispensationalism seriously weakened Chafer's ability to place graduates in Presbyterian churches. For example, thirty graduates in the classes 1935–1939 served in

These Southern schools not only contributed to and were an integral part of the expansion of fundamentalist educational efforts but also represented the basis for building and maintaining fundamentalism in the South. In the effort to create a Southern constituency to support the schools, fundamentalists were also building a Southern wing of their movement. The central person in developing a network of support for these schools was the founder or the president who used a variety of means to promote their schools. Most of these men were itinerant evangelists or Bible teachers before becoming involved with a school and continued their touring after starting their schools. Their tours were perhaps the most important method of bringing the needs of their schools to the public's attention, but they were not as frequent or as long because of the administrative duties involved in running a school. While the main focus remained the Bible teaching or evangelism, they took on secondary purposes of recruiting students and soliciting financial support. The press occasionally took notice of the preacher's educational work while reporting on the revival or Bible conference. Both Bob Jones and John Brown had notable reputations in the South as evangelists before becoming educators, and both continued their campaigns while

---

Presbyterian churches over the course of their careers while only three served in independent churches. In the classes of 1950–1954, only four pastored Presbyterian churches while twenty-five went into independent churches. DTS Alumni Records. Adding to the difficulty was the complicated procedure that led to ordination in Presbyterian denominations. A candidate for ministry came "under the care" of a presbytery, which was responsible for supervising the candidate's education. Presbyteries expected, but did not require, a candidate to attend a Presbyterian seminary or spend at least one year there. It was not rare for Presbyterian students at DTS to take a year or two of training at DTS and then transfer to and graduate from a Presbyterian seminary. For example, J. Vernon McGee took one year of courses at Dallas then transferred to and graduated from Columbia Theological Seminary of the Southern Presbyterian church. He returned to Dallas and earned a Th.M. and Th.D. LSC to E. Schuyler English, 27 June 1940, in LSC Papers. Others, like Herbert E. Kahn (class of 1938), James G. Spencer (class of 1939), and Philip Austin (class of 1940), earned Bachelor of Divinity degrees at Presbyterian seminaries like Columbia or Princeton, Masters at Dallas, and served Presbyterian churches throughout their careers. DTS Alumni Records.

building their schools.[151] In 1925 Brown preached for a month in Birmingham, Alabama, and the newspaper gave daily coverage of the meetings. In its biographical sketch of the evangelist, though, the paper highlighted Brown's work in establishing his university.[152] Robert Forrest of Toccoa Falls Institute was the first CMA worker for the South and was responsible for a region that stretched from Virginia to Florida to Texas. His tours in the early 1900s established CMA groups in several Southern towns, most notably Atlanta and Orlando, which in turn became important supporters for his work at the Institute. Moreover, his biographer records that not only were "hundreds and hundreds won to Christ," but also "the work of Toccoa Falls Institute [was made] known to thousands."[153] Robert McQuilkin continued touring after accepting the presidency of Columbia Bible Institute and tried to accept engagements that would bring him in touch with potential students. For example, during the late 1920s McQuilkin was a regular speaker at a Presbyterian youth conference held in Winter Park, Florida, while also preaching in similar conferences in Clinton, South Carolina, Montreat, North Carolina, and Slocomb Springs, Alabama.[154]

Sometimes the press of administrative and teaching duties restricted opportunities for off-campus engagements. During his first seven weeks in Birmingham at the Southeastern Bible School, James Mooney received numerous requests for Bible conferences as well as

---

[151]On Jones's evangelistic endeavors, see R. K. Johnson, *Builder of Bridges: The Biography of Dr. Bob Jones, Sr.* (Murfreesboro TN: Sword of the Lord, 1969) 65–167; particularly, 83–85, 151, for indication that Jones used the contacts developed in these campaigns to build support for the school. In *John Brown of Arkansas*, 79–89, 97–100, Kennedy and Rothrock record how Brown conducted revivals throughout the 1920s and 1930s mostly in California and in the South. The contacts in California provided the money for the construction of a girls' dormitory, according to Crabaugh, "Teaching the Dignity of Labor," 41.

[152]Dolly Dalryple, "Salvation Army Seen as 'Covered Wagon' Blazing Spiritual Trail," *Birmingham* (AL) *News*, 11 January 1925, 7.

[153]Moothart, *Achieving*, 47.

[154]Appointment Calendar, 1921–1936, RCM Papers. The Winter Park meetings were held in the month of June for the years, 1926–1929; Montreat in July 1927; Clinton in June 1930 and 1933; and Slocom Springs in June 1929.

filling in for vacationing pastors in various area churches.[155] His mentor, Lewis Chafer, warned, "Try to conserve your strength. You must not overdo and get set back in your health."[156] By spring semester Mooney found that school responsibilities overwhelmed the work off-campus and consequently hindered his ability to publicize the school through this work.[157] Apparently the frustration of these circumstances and the lack of cooperation from the Board of Trustees in finding help became too much. Mooney left at the end of the academic year to accept the pastorate of a church in Mora, Minnesota.[158]

Most of the schools and their founders maintained or sought to establish ties with Northern fundamentalists. McQuilkin continued his contacts with fundamentalists in the North through his association with the *Sunday School Times*, the Victorious Life conferences held in Keswick, New Jersey, and various Bible conferences in Eastern Pennsylvania,[159] and those efforts paid dividends in recruiting

---

[155]James S. Mooney to LSC, 5 September 1944, in LSC Papers. According to this letter, Mooney's duties included teaching thirteen classes at the school, an extensive weekend ministry in area churches, overseeing the school's bookstore, administrating the school, and counseling the students. The load did not lighten over the course of the year. In March he wrote to Chafer that "most of the teaching in the Day School has fallen to my lot and I am obligated for two classes in the Evening School.... In addition, there are Extension classes, throughout the city, a pulpit ministry on Sunday's, the preparation of the Monthly Bulletin, and an endless stream of requests for...pastoral visits." James S. Mooney to LSC, 15 March 1945, in LSC Papers.

[156]LSC to James S. Mooney, 28 September 1944, in LSC Papers.

[157]James S. Mooney to LSC, 15 March 1945, in LSC Papers.

[158]The frustration is plainly evident in the tone of the letter cited in the previous note. Adding to Mooney's disenchantment with his situation in Birmingham was the refusal of the Birmingham Presbytery to ordain him because of his education at Dallas and his dispensational beliefs. James S. Mooney to LSC, 24 April 1945, in LSC Papers. Tragically, in January 1946, Mooney died of complications from the flu after only a few months in his new position. Dallas Theological Seminary, "Alumni Newsletter," 20 April 1946, in LSC Papers.

[159]In *To Know Him and to Make Him Known: The Leadership and Philosophy of Columbia Bible College* (Columbia SC: Columbia Bible College, 1978) 20, Marjorie A. Collins reports that McQuilkin preached at Keswick at least twice a year and during 1931–1936 wrote the weekly Sunday lesson for the *Sunday School Times*. His Appointment Calendar, 1921–1936, in RCM Papers, confirm the regular visits to Keswick (usually at the young people's conferences) as well recording an average of two other engagements a year in the middle Atlantic states.

students. During the 1930s and 1940s nearly one quarter (22.9 percent) of the students came from Pennsylvania, New York, and New Jersey.[160] Robert Forrest's ties with the CMA represented an important connection with Northern fundamentalist traditions that not only introduced the program and needs of the school to Northerners but also provided contacts with wealthy fundamentalists. In 1919 the National Council of the CMA met on the Institute's campus advertising in a most direct and effective way the school's existence to the 400 delegates from around the country.[161] Forrest's tours on behalf of the CMA took him around the country and introduced him to several fundamentalists of means who helped the school out of a variety of financial crises. In 1913 fire destroyed the uninsured main building of Institute, leaving the fledgling school with a $20,000 mortgage. Forrest retired that debt later that year when in California the needs of the school became known to Lyman and Milton Stewart, fundamentalist philanthropists who financed the publication and distribution of *The Fundamentals*.[162] On another occasion while preaching at the Gospel Tabernacle in New York city, the church started by the CMA's founder A. B. Simpson, Forrest so impressed Mrs. William Borden, wife of the heir to the inventor of condensed milk, that she became a regular donor to the school.[163] As noted earlier, while on a tour of CMA mission work, Forrest met R. G. LeTourneau, and his support sustained the Institute through the Depression.

---

[160]Overall, 57 percent of the students in these years came from Southern states and 43 percent from other states and overseas, but significantly, students from these three Northern states account for over half (53.1 percent) of the non-Southern students. Students from North Carolina, South Carolina, and Tennessee made up almost two-thirds of those from Southern states (64.8 percent). Together students from these six states represented 59.8 percent of all students attending CBC in the 1930s and 1940s. Data based on CBC Applications File.

[161]Moothart, *Achieving*, 104–107.

[162]Lyman became a regular contributor to the school giving $4,500 toward the construction of girls dormitory in 1917 and lesser sums for general expenses into the early 1920s. Ibid., 79–87.

[163]Ibid., 119–22.

The Southern school that most vigorously sought to exploit the Northern fundamentalist network, but found its wooing rebuffed, was Bryan College in Dayton, Tennessee. Its efforts produced few concrete rewards forcing the school's leaders to develop a regional network for support. Moreover, their efforts reflected a continuation of the efforts of Daytonians to use fundamentalism to bring notoriety and hopefully return prosperity to their town. Dayton's economy was in decline in the 1920s but still had the manpower and natural resources necessary for development.[164] Its leading citizens looked in vain for ways to advertise the advantages Dayton had to offer business until George Rappleyea, an employee of the troubled Cumberland Coal and Iron Company, suggested prosecuting a teacher under the provisions of the Butler Bill which forbade the teaching of evolution in the public schools.[165] These men got the publicity they wanted for the town, but unfortunately it was not the kind to inspire businesses to come to Dayton.[166]

Soon after the death of William Jennings Bryan fundamentalists called for the creation of a university to memorialize their fallen leader, but a dispute developed over its location. Dayton's civic boosters claimed that Bryan agreed to establishing a preparatory school in their town, while prominent fundamentalists argued that it should be a

---

[164]Warren Allem, "Background of the Scopes Trial at Dayton Tennessee" (MA thesis, University of Tennessee, 1959) 25.

[165]Ibid., 56–61. On the Butler Bill, see Ray Ginger, *Six Days or Forever? Tennessee v. John T. Scopes* (New York: Oxford University Press, 1958) 1–21.

[166]Allem, "Backgrounds," 97–98, reports that Dayton did prosper during the trial with some restaurants and hotels making over $3,000 and one taxi company earning $4,200 ferrying people back and forth to Chattanooga. On the press, see ibid., 90–93, and Martin Olansky, "When World Views Collide: Journalists and the Great Monkey Trial" (paper presented at the Annual Meeting of the Association for Education in Journalism and Mass Communication, Norman, OK, 3–6 August 1986). It is worthy of note that in his delightful *Only Yesterday: An Informal History of the 1920s* (New York: Harper and Row, 1931; reprint, New York: Perennial Library, 1964) 167–71, Frederick Lewis Allen placed his discussion of the Scopes Trial in the context of describing the "ballyhoo" technique by which the press excited great interest in events of minor significance.

university in a metropolitan area.[167] Perhaps seeking to claim Bryan's mantle for himself or to be in a position to influence the university's development, William Bell Riley suggested Chicago because of its central location, its prominence as an educational center, and the presence of fundamentalist organizations, not the least of which was Riley's WCFA.[168] Daytonians, though, had the support of Bryan's widow, and their own desire for a university rather than a prep school meshed with fundamentalist dreams of a school to combat modernism.[169] Moreover, such an endeavor would bring more prestige, notice, and prosperity to their community than a prep school. They formed the Bryan Memorial University Association, which in turn recruited a national committee to raise money to build the school. Composed of politicians, businessmen, and fundamentalists (Riley was not a member), this committee had the task of raising five million dollars to build the campus,[170] but individuals apparently took their committee membership as little more than an endorsement of the dream to build a Christian university because the committee never came close to reaching its goal. Nevertheless, enough money came in to begin construction on the administration building in 1927,[171] but financial

---

[167]Written as an undergraduate senior thesis, David Noel Zopfi's "Forward through Faith: The Founding of William Jennings Bryan Memorial University" (Senior thesis, Bryan College, Spring 1979) is nonetheless a solid narrative of the origins of the school, consistently more accurate in details than Jess Willard Lasley's "The History of Bryan College" (Ph.D. dissertation, Baylor University, 1960). Zopfi notes, 9, others suggested Washington, DC, and Miami, Florida, as appropriate places for establishing the university.

[168]William Bell Riley, "William Jennings Bryan University," *Christian Fundamentals in Church and School*, October 1925, 53–54.

[169]N.a., "Mrs. Bryan Writes," *Christian Fundamentals in Church and School*, October 1925, 54; Zopfi, "Forward through Faith," 4–10.

[170]"Bryan Memorial University: Campaign for Five Million Dollars," pamphlet in Bryan College Archives, Bryan College, Dayton, TN. Among the fundamentalists listed as committee members were John Roach Straton, pastor of Calvary Baptist Church in New York City; T. C. Horton of the Bible Institute of Los Angeles; evangelists Paul Rader and L. W. Munhall; and Bible teacher W. E. Biederwolf.

[171]In ibid., The artist's depiction of the proposed campus reveals the grandiose dreams of the Association. Dominating a hill overlooking the town, the Administration Building was surrounded by buildings housing various academic disciplines

difficulties halted progress after only the basement was dug and the foundation poured.[172]

Fundamentalist priorities seemed to be shifting, but recognizing that the natural constituency for supporting the university was fundamentalists, the Association sought to renew interest by recruiting a prominent member of their ranks as President of the school. J. Gresham Machen declined the offer,[173] and the Association convinced George Guille to accept the position despite his lack of educational credentials for such a post.[174] He did have two qualifications that made him an attractive candidate. Though hardly a household name in fundamentalist circles, Guille did have strong connections to fundamentalist circles through his work for the Extension Department of MBI and as a Bible lecturer at the Dallas Theological Seminary.[175] Moreover, he lived just twenty miles to the east in Athens, Tennessee. Guille's selection suggests that the Association was trying to maintain ties to and draw support from the broader fundamentalist movement while creating a stronger regional base for their endeavors. By the time Guille took office in 1930, the school was suffering from the economic effects of the Depression that dimmed prospects for resuming construction. Thus the school opened its doors in September 1930, with students drawn primarily from the local area and without its own building, holding classes, ironically, in the old high school where John Scopes taught evolution.[176] Among the enrolled was Harry Shelton, a high school student who testified for the prosecution at Scopes's trial.[177]

---

and schools. According to Zopfi, "Forward through Faith," 15, the Administration Building was longer than a football field, 428 feet to be exact.

[172]Zopfi, "Forward through Faith," 15–16.

[173]N.a., "Professor J. Gresham Machen," 16.

[174]George Guille to Rollin T. Chafer, 20 June 1930 and 9 July 1930, in LSC Papers.

[175]See chapter 2 for a discussion of Guille's background and work with the Extension Department.

[176]Zopfi, "Forward through Faith," 16, 19.

[177]George Guille to LSC, 13 October 1930, in LSC Papers. According to Zopfi, "Forward through Faith," 20, enrollment for the first year was seventy-four people including many adult Daytonians. Guille's letter indicates that they probably were admitted as special students to take the Bible classes taught by Guille.

In the long run, support from Northern fundamentalists would be of limited value without help from Southern churches. One method that some presidents used to establish and maintain good relations with Southern churches was to serve as a pastor. During his first year at Columbia Bible Institute and despite being a Presbyterian, Robert McQuilkin pastored a Baptist church in a lumber mill village in Alcolu, South Carolina. Not only did that work provide income to meet his living expenses, but also it introduced McQuilkin to Alderman family who owned the mill and who became supporters of the institute.[178] In a similar manner, William Bennett supplemented his income from Southeastern Bible Institute by pastoring the Porter (Alabama) Baptist Church.[179] In 1925 Robert Forrest curtailed his travels on behalf of the CMA to become the minister of the First Presbyterian Church of Toccoa, Georgia, a position he held for twenty-five years. This connection also introduced Forrest and his school to a broader audience as the church broadcasted his sermons over the local radio station. Moreover, that Forrest won the respect of other Presbyterian ministers in North Georgia was indicated by their selection of him to serve a term as Moderator of the Athens Presbytery.[180]

Another avenue of securing support from local churches was to recruit their pastors to teach in the schools, and they were particularly important to the Bible institutes. Before they developed a day program most Bible institutes relied heavily on local pastors as instructors in their evening classes. For the schools the ministers represented a cost-saving measure by not having to pay for a full time instructor. Occasionally, these ministers were the ones who wanted the institution for their community. At Dallas Bible Institute ministers from Galilean Baptist Church, Scofield Memorial Church, and Westminster Presbyterian Church carried the teaching responsibilities for its first year.[181] Moreover, these pastors provided access to

---

[178]Hehl, *This Is the Victory*, 86–87.
[179]Southeastern Bible School, *Catalogue*, 1942–1943, 3.
[180]Moothart, *Achieving*, 112–13.
[181]Gurney, "History," 23, 30.

resources that were just as important to the schools as their teaching skills. Sunday school rooms became classrooms during the week or offices for the school. Church secretaries became the school's staff. Most significantly, members of their congregations enrolled as students, served on the Board of Trustees, and contributed financial support.

Pastors were important to the development of other kinds of schools that fundamentalists founded in the South. John Brown recruited Merwin A. Stone, pastor of First Presbyterian Church of Siloam Springs, to establish a survey of biblical history and doctrines.[182] Lewis Chafer recruited Presbyterian pastors as adjunct instructors and administrators. Fred Z. Browne, pastor of First Presbyterian in Texarkana, Texas, taught church history in the late 1920s, while W. Irving Carroll of the Presbyterian Church of Marshall, Texas, served as lecturer on the English Bible, and his successor in the Marshall pulpit, Charles A. Nash, taught theology and homiletics and became Registrar in 1945.[183] Such involvement, though, did not always endear the school to the congregation. Fred Browne believed that opposition to his ministry from within his congregation developed because he "dared to be connected with the DTS"[184] Some parishioners resented the neglect of church duties resulting from faculty responsibilities. A member of Nash's congregation wrote to Robert McQuilkin complaining that Nash devoted too much energy to the work in the seminary.[185]

Another important method of carrying the institutes' work beyond its local area was the development of an extension program. While not appropriate for seminary or liberal arts curricula and though no Southern school developed a program as extensive as Moody

---

[182]Merwin A. Stone to LSC, 8 July 1932 and 5 January 1933, in LSC Papers.

[183]Evangelical Theological College, *Bulletin*, November 1925, 20; Dallas Theological Seminary, *Bulletin*, 1942–1943, 7; *Bulletin*, 1949, 8–9; DTS Alumni Records.

[184]Fred Z. Browne to Dewey Duncan, 1 May 1943, in LSC Papers.

[185]Mrs. G. B. Scheer to RCM, 22 May 1944, pastorate recommendations file, in RCM Papers. It is interesting to note that from 1953 to 1964, William Benchoff, a graduate of Columbia Bible College, served in Nash's church. Presbyterian Church in America, *Yearbook*, 1984–1985, 144.

Bible Institute's, this work carried the distinctive emphasis on lay training and fundamentalist doctrines of these schools to those unable to attend the school. Additionally, such itinerating representatives kept the news and needs of the school before sympathetic churches and laymen. In some cases, like at Southeastern Bible Institute, these programs were little more than offering brief courses in other churches in the school's town.[186] In many instances, though, the extension program had the effect of advertising the school to a broader region. For example, Evelyn Forrest, wife of the President of Toccoa Falls Institute, taught Bible classes in churches in Asheville, North Carolina, and in Greenville and Spartanburg, South Carolina. In Atlanta her class at the CMA's Gospel Tabernacle attracted up to 750 students during its four-year term followed by another two years of classes at the city's First Presbyterian Church.[187] Columbia Bible College perhaps had the most extensive program regularly employing three to six women teachers. During the 1930s and 1940s they conducted classes and conferences in a variety of locations including chapel services in public schools, weekly devotional programs in boarding houses for nurses, Bible studies in Columbia's black neighborhoods, and evangelistic work on Charleston's beaches during the summer. The Extension Department also arranged Bible conferences in churches in surrounding states for the school's faculty.[188]

A few schools found ways of bringing constituencies to themselves. In 1943 Dallas Bible Institute and Dallas Theological Seminary sponsored a prophecy conference that attracted pastors and laymen from most parts of Texas. Held at the Scofield Memorial Church, most of the speakers were faculty members from the seminary, but a few prominently featured participants from outside

---

[186]James S. Mooney to LSC, 15 March 1945, in LSC Papers; and Southeastern Bible School, *Bulletin*, 1948–1949, 10.

[187]Moothart, *Achieving*, 141–42.

[188]Columbia Bible College, *Catalogue*, 1930–1931, 7; 1936–1937, 5; 1940–1941, 16–17; 1943–1944, 22–23; 1946–1947, 20. During the 1930s the women were usually single and recent graduates of the college. Mention of the work in the black community and on the beaches disappeared from the post-war catalogs.

the Dallas network included Bob Jones, Sr., and Presbyterian pastors Wil R. Johnson of Galveston and Albert Sidney Johnson of Charlotte.[189] With its location in the scenic mountains of North Georgia, Toccoa Falls Institute opened its grounds for conferences sponsored by several Southern denominations, including the Baptists, Presbyterians, Episcopalians, and Christians.[190] In the early 1930s McQuilkin started an interdenominational conference center called Ben Lippen outside of Asheville, North Carolina, where he led Bible conferences during the summer months. While having programs and speakers catering to all ages, the Ben Lippen conferences also became fruitful source of students for the Bible College.[191]

Finally, the most important aspect of the schools' work in developing a Southern wing of fundamentalism was the careers of their graduates. Consider, for example, the alumni of Dallas Theological Seminary.[192] One area where the graduates made important contributions to the fundamentalist cause was through their work in education.[193] Several Dallas graduates significantly

---

[189]Gurney, "History of Dallas Bible Institute," 46–49. Efforts to make the conference annual failed. See also the list of pastors who attended contained in a letter to Lewis Chafer: Harlin J. Roper to LSC, 9 April 1943, in LSC Papers.

[190]Moothart, *Achieving*, 110–11.

[191]On Ben Lippen, see Columbia Bible College, *Catalogue*, 1940–1941, 36. Of those indicating on their applications how they learned of CBC, 9.1 percent indicated hearing of the school at Ben Lippen in the 1930s. In the 1940s Ben Lippen dropped to 6.8 percent Similarly, McQuilkin was more effective in the 1930s than in the 1940s (18.2 percent to 7.7 percent). In both decades, though, CBC's students, staff, and alumni were the busiest recruiters. In the 1930s 22.7 percent and for the 1940s 29.1 percent of the graduates indicated on their applications learning of CBC through people associated with the college. Data based on CBC Applications File. In the late 1930s the conference buildings began to be used during the winter months as a Christian preparatory school catering particularly to the sons of missionaries. Financial difficulties and wartime shortages hindered its development until the early 1950s when it became coeducational and gained effective administrative leadership in J. Robertson McQuilkin. McQuilkin, *Always in Triumph*, 185–91; and R. Arthur Mathews, *Towers Pointing Upward*, classroom edition (Columbia SC: Columbia Bible College, 1982) 51–53.

[192]This analysis is based on analysis of DTS Alumni Records.

[193]Ranging from seminaries like Princeton and universities like Purdue to struggling Bible institutes like those in Birmingham, Dallas, and Atlanta, 192

influenced the development of some Southern schools by serving as their presidents or by starting a school while serving as a pastor.[194] But more critical to growth of grassroots fundamentalism was their work as pastors in Southern churches. Though most graduates served churches outside the South, a little more than one-quarter of the graduates pastored a Southern church at some point during their careers.[195] Their churches were located in communities of all sizes, from cities like Richmond, Miami, Birmingham, New Orleans, and Houston to small towns like Roanoke, Virginia, Covington, Kentucky, and Texarkana, Texas.[196] Most frequently, Dallas graduates were

---

graduates served as faculty or administrators in 110 post-secondary schools of all shapes and sizes. Over three-quarters of the schools were a part of the fundamentalist-evangelical network and half were Bible colleges or institutes. Cullen Story, class of 1940, was an associate professor at Princeton Theological Seminary from 1967 to and Donald Waite, class of 1952, was an instructor at Purdue University from 1954 to 1956. DTS Alumni Records. These figures include all graduates from 1935–1955 who worked in any capacity at a post-secondary educational institution for at least one academic year. Seventeen of the schools were seminaries (15.4 percent), nineteen were liberal art colleges (17.3 percent), fifty-six were Bible schools (50.9 percent), and eighteen fell into no category (16.4 percent). Twenty-six did not have clear ties to fundamentalism (23.6 percent). Only seventeen had Southern addresses, but with the exception of Dallas Seminary, Reformed Theological Seminary, Bryan College, John Brown University, and Bob Jones College, the rest were Bible institutes. DTS Alumni Records.

[194]The central person in the growth of Dallas Bible Institute was Martin O. Massinger, class of 1940, who served president and dean from 1943–1974. Gurney, "History of Dallas Bible Institute," 31–40. Nineteen different graduates of the seminary taught at the school, most while they pursued their graduate degree. DTS Alumni Records. William C. Bennett from the same class went to Southeastern Bible School to supervise the establishment of day school curriculum. William C. Bennett to LSC, 23 May 1941, in LSC papers. During his ministry at First Presbyterian Church of Miami Beach, Willis Garrett founded Miami Bible College in 1949. David E. Wiles, "Miami Christian College: Thirty Years of History, 1949–1979," *Communicare*, Fall 1979, 8–9.

[195]142 of 512 (27 percent) of those in the DTS Alumni Records.

[196]Churches in many smaller communities had Dallas graduates for their ministers. Overall, the graduates of the 1935–1955 classes served 144 Southern communities. The state with the most was Texas (sixty-five) followed by Florida (fourteen), while Mississippi, Georgia, and South Carolina had the fewest (two each). The large number of communities in Texas is primarily a result of the school's

found in Presbyterian churches, but those who served Southern churches after World War II gravitated away from Southern denominations into independent churches.[197] This seminary not only supplied pastors to established Southern independent churches, but also its graduates contributed to the growth of independent churches in the South either by creating a new church from scratch or by splitting an existing congregation and leading the fundamentalist faction into its own church.[198]

Through their careers, the graduates of Columbia Bible College also contributed to the growth of fundamentalism in the South. According to the 1940-1941 *Catalogue*, the curriculum was designed to train students for a variety of Christian service occupations ranging from pastors and missionaries to youth and children's workers, Sunday school directors, and Bible teachers.[199] Holding such positions

---

location and the decision of the Alumni Office to include churches served while a student. DTS Alumni Records.

[197]This pattern was more pronounced when all the graduates are considered. For example, thirty graduates in the classes 1935–1939 served in Presbyterian churches (of the thirty, eighteen pastored Presbyterian churches in the South) over the course of their careers while only three served in independent churches (all in the South). In the classes of 1951–1955 eighteen pastored Presbyterian churches (only two served Southern churches) while sixty-one served an independent churches (twenty-one in the South). DTS Alumni Records.

[198]Reinhardt Bible Church in Dallas is a good example of a congregation started under the influence of the seminary and then served by its graduates throughout most of its history. Willis Garrett in Miami Beach and William P. Jones in Greensboro, North Carolina, both pastored Presbyterian churches and took fundamentalist factions out their congregations to form independent churches in the same cities. DTS Alumni Records.

[199]Columbia Bible College, *Catalogue*, 1940–1941, 13. The catalog listed the following vocations: "Foreign missionary service; the ministry; Christian community or settlement work in industrial centers; Christian education in Sunday Schools, daily vacation Bible schools, summer camps. etc.; home missionary work in mountain or rural districts, and in city missions; the teach ing of Bible in connection with the public schools; the directing of young people's work and assisting of pastors in churches; church visitation, and other types of Christian work." Such a frank suggestion of the adequacy of the curriculum's preparation for vocational Christian service reflected both the maturation of educational efforts of the Bible college movement and the growing acceptance by the fundamentalist movement of Bible college education as an alternative to seminary training.

offered the alumni the means of introducing the fundamentalist interpretations of the Bible and fundamentalist perspective on religious and social issues to the uninformed and thus broaden the movement's Southern constituency.[200] Listing 1,846 graduates, their vocation, and their place of residence, the 1956 Alumni Directory provides evidence for evaluating the contribution of the college's graduates to the development of Southern fundamentalism. Over one-third (38.5 percent) were engaged in vocational Christian service with over 80 percent of those employed as pastors or missionaries. About one-quarter (23.5 percent) lived overseas, with over half (54.1 percent) of those in the states living in the South. Alumni in South Carolina, North Carolina, Florida, Texas, and Virginia accounted for nearly three quarters (74.3 percent) of the graduates in the South. Graduates ministered as pastors and religious workers in towns and cities of all sizes but worked more frequently in the smaller communities of these states.

Moreover, the contribution of those not working in a professional capacity to the spread of fundamentalism should not be ignored. Some worked in secular fields (4.7 percent), taught school (5 percent), or had not reported their vocational status (10.4 percent).

---

[200]The assumption that alumni maintained their fundamentalism throughout their careers is open to challenge. It is not to be denied that some graduates may have modified their fundamentalism after graduation, but a 1980 study of Columbia Bible College's graduates revealed the persistence of fundamentalist interpretations. The study asked a sample of alumni to agree or disagree with a series of statements concerning doctrinal issues. The responses were rated (agree = +1, unsure = 0, disagree = -1), totaled, averaged, and classified according to groups of graduating classes (pre-1956, 1956–1970, and 1971–1980). On all statements and in all classes, average rate of agreement was over .9. For example, the pre-1956 classes averaged .94 for the inerrancy of the Bible, .99 for the necessity of repentance for conversion, .99 for the reality of hell, and .96 for the creation of the world by a special act of God. The rate of agreement for the pre-1956 classes for the statement, "My doctrinal stand is basically the same as CBC's," was a strong .93. The area of greatest variation was on the interpretation of prophecy, but even on this controversial issue, 84 percent the respondents from the pre-1956 classes identified themselves as premillennialists. Robert Kallgren, *Alumnview '80* (Columbia SC: Columbia Bible College, 1980) 71–73. Furthermore, given this high rate of agreement with the fundamentalist creed of the college, it is not unreasonable to assume that the alumni taught this perspective when in positions of leadership.

The largest group of nonprofessionals was those who appeared in the directory as wives. More than half (57.7 percent) of the graduates in the directory were women, and over one-quarter (28.7 percent) of the women married men who served as pastors or missionaries. One-fifth (20.2 percent) of the alumnae were employed in vocational Christian service most frequently as missionaries or children's workers, never as a pastor. Another one-quarter (28.3 percent) of the women were listed in the directory as wives, with no indication of their husbands occupations.[201] Geographically, the women spread in approximately the same pattern as the men. Over half (55.6 percent) of the women lived in the South. The directory did not indicate their volunteer religious work, but it is not unlikely that some served as Sunday school teachers or leaders in their churches' women organizations. At the very least many joined fundamentalist churches or identified with fundamentalist factions in denominational churches. In short if they were not leaders in Southern fundamentalism, they helped make up its rank and file.[202]

These schools and their graduates are not the complete story of Southern fundamentalism, but they are a central feature of the story. They represented the establishment of Northern interdenominational fundamentalist traditions in continuing institutional forms in the

---

[201]The directory fairly consistently indicated if a woman married a pastor, missionary, or other religious worker even if he did graduate from the college. Thus it is likely that most of these women married men engaged in some kind of secular occupation. For a general analysis of female graduates of fundamentalist schools and their career opportunities, see Margaret Lamberts Bendroth, *Fundamentalism and Gender, 1875 to the Present* (New Haven: Yale University Press, 1996) 73–96.

[202]Support for the maintenance of fundamentalist beliefs after graduation can be found in the study of the college's alumni. The responses were classified according to gender and occupation. Women indicated stronger agreement than men to the statement concerning the continued acceptance of the college's creed (95 percent to 89 percent) while alumni engaged in secular work showed only slightly weaker agreement with the statement than those in vocational Christian service (87 percent to 92 percent). Kallgren, *Alumnview*, 71–73. Nearly half of the respondents (45.4 percent) indicated that their affiliation in 1980 was with a church in the fundamentalist wing of American Protestantism. Ibid., 91–92. Unfortunately, the study did not refine the consideration of these issues by addressing regional variations or by classifying these responses according to graduation classes.

South, and they significantly expanded fundamentalist educational efforts by sponsoring vocational training and graduate professional training for the pastorate. The Bible institutes gave some Southerners the opportunity to hear the style of Bible teaching and to continue the training they experienced in Bible conferences. Extension departments carried the distinctive educational efforts of the institutes into communities without schools. Moreover, churches disposed to this kind of teaching hired graduates of these schools to serve as pastors, youth workers, song leaders, and Christian education directors. In short, both the establishment and growth of these schools and the careers of their graduates represent important elements in the creation of a Southern wing of the fundamentalist movement. This development, though, was not welcomed by Southern denominations. Instead of reinforcing and strengthening their conservative character, Southern interdenominational fundamentalists divided the loyalties of conservatives and played central roles in introducing Northern patterns of fundamentalist controversy into Southern denominations.

4

DENOMINATIONAL FUNDAMENTALISTS:

THE PRESBYTERIANS

If you continue in my word, then you are truly disciples of mine.
—John 8:31

William P. Jones, graduate of Dallas Theological Seminary in 1936, represented the contribution Lewis Chafer hoped his seminary could make to the Southern denominations. Chafer had a special dream that graduates of Dallas Seminary would help the Southern Presbyterian church (the Presbyterian Church in the United States or PCUS) maintain its traditional theological standards despite growing liberal tendencies in the denomination, and Jones was in the vanguard of graduates to enter the denomination.[1] Born in rural Northwestern Pennsylvania and raised in Lynchburg, Virginia, Jones came to the seminary with strong connections to the Southern Presbyterian

---

[1]On Chafers's hopes, see chapter 3. Chafer's remark in his recommendation of Jones to fill the vacancy in the Presbyterian Church in Charlottesville, Virginia, is one measure of his respect of Jones's abilities. Calling Jones "a man of unusual judgement and force of character," Chafer believed that the church "would have gained a real victory [if it] could secure" Jones as its pastor. LSC to H. A. Dinwiddie, 13 March 1944 (Lewis Sperry Chafer Papers, Mosher Library, Dallas Theological Seminary, Dallas, TX).

church. He was a member of Rivermont Presbyterian, pastored by Chafer's friend Graham Gilmer, and attended Lynchburg College and the Presbyterian-sponsored Hamden-Sydney College during his undergraduate career.[2] On graduation from seminary Jones accepted a call from Westminster Presbyterian Church in Greensboro, North Carolina. The Orange Presbytery was reluctant to ordain Jones because he attended a non-Presbyterian seminary despite the fact that his home presbytery of Montgomery had approved his educational plans. Respecting the wishes of the congregation, though, the Presbytery licensed Jones to supply Westminster's pulpit with a view to ordination upon completion of a course of study in Presbyterian history, doctrine, and polity directed by Orange Presbytery ministers.[3] Jones satisfied these requirements and was ordained in April 1937.[4]

Jones also represented what some leaders in Southern denominations feared about allowing the graduates of the interdenominational Bible schools and seminaries to serve in their churches. Eleven years later the Orange Presbytery accused Jones of creating discord among his church's members and not supporting the denomination's program. According to a report given to the Presbytery by a Special Judicial Commission, Jones stopped using the denomination's Sunday school literature, encouraged the members to divert money from supporting Presbyterian missionaries to independent missionaries, and sent the church's children to non-Presbyterian summer youth camps. Moreover, disaffected members left the church resulting in precipitous decline in membership and reported to the Commission that their main reason for leaving was the "intolerable conditions"

---

[2]Biographical information gleaned from PCUS, *Ministerial Directory of the Presbyterian Church in the United States*, 1861–1941, revised and supplemented, 1942–1950, E. C. Scott, compiler, 346, and Orange Presbytery of the PCUS, *Minutes of the Orange Presbytery*, September 1936, 89. Jones did not graduate from college. The *Directory* recorded that he received a BA from Hampden-Sydney, but he left Dallas Seminary with a certificate indicating that he did not have a college degree. Alumni Records, Dallas Theological Seminary. Moreover, the *Minutes*, 90, showed that Jones had to explain to the Presbytery why he did not finish his undergraduate course.

[3]*Minutes of Orange Presbytery*, September 1936, 90–92.

[4]*Minutes of the Orange Presbytery*, April 1937, 117–18.

created by Jones's actions.[5] Convinced by the report and other testimony heard before a special meeting of the Presbytery, it accepted the Commission's recommendation that Jones be removed from the pastorate of Westminster by a thirty-seven to sixteen vote.[6] Jones responded by splitting the church, leading his supporters out of the Presbyterian denomination, and starting an independent church.[7]

Jones was a part of the first generation of Southerners trained in Southern interdenominational fundamentalist schools to minister in Southern denominations. He joined with other pastors to form fundamentalist factions in these churches. The creation of these factions in Southern denominations in the 1930s and 1940s is one of the more important ways in which Northern patterns of fundamentalist controversy appeared in the South. While the Southern denominational feuds of the 1940s and 1950s did not concern precisely the same issues as in the North during the 1920s, they were marked with a fundamentalist passion for maintaining traditional interpretations of the denomination's doctrinal heritage against its liberalization and for preventing the denomination's affairs from being directed by those who deviated from the traditional standard. Rarely did Southern conservatives forge formal institutional ties with Northern fundamentalists, but Southerners did rely on fundamentalist analysis of Northern denominations in their own battles with liberals. As in the North Presbyterians and Baptists experienced the most turmoil. The story of these developments begins with the response of Southern churchmen to the interdenominational fundamentalists and their schools and ends with mobilization of theologically conservative elements in a fundamentalistic crusade to block liberal control of their traditions. Ironically its leaders had to distance themselves from the interdenominational fundamentalists in the South and in so doing alienated their strongest supporters.

---

[5]*Minutes of the Orange Presbytery*, April 1948, 72–73.

[6]Ibid., 74–76.

[7]*Minutes of the Orange Presbytery*, May 1948, 79–80. At Jones's request, the Presbytery agreed to divest Jones of his office of pastor in the Presbyterian Church.

The reaction of denominational leaders to the establishment and growth of interdenominational fundamentalist institutions in their region was generally unfavorable, but the reasons for their negative evaluation varied from denomination to denomination and from liberal to conservative factions within the Southern churches. As graduates moved into Southern congregations as ministers or members, fundamentalists actively pointed out what they perceived to be support of liberal policies among denominational leaders and liberal teachings in the denominational schools. They hoped to prevent Southern denominations from going the way of their Northern counterparts and becoming dominated by liberal factions. They criticized the liberal tone of denominational literature and supported parachurch organizations and interdenominational missionaries over liberal-tainted denominational programs. Thus Southern liberals feared that fundamentalist accusations concerning the liberals' activities and theology might energize a reaction that would weaken the liberals' standing in the denomination. Indeed, the expression in the 1940s of fundamentalistic complaints concerning the liberal agenda in several parts of Southern denominations seemed to justify liberal fears. But these pastors and editors also worried about fundamentalists' presence. Though awakening some ministers to the threat liberals posed to Southern denominational traditions, fundamentalist agitation alienated more because it occasionally resulted in churches splitting or withdrawing from Southern denominations. Moreover, most Southern clergy rejected fundamentalist assertions that their Bible colleges and institutes needed to be independent in order to serve all Southern denominations and to complement the work of denominationally sponsored educational institutions. Seeing growing enrollment and expanding facilities in fundamentalist schools, Southerners believed that fundamentalists took students and money away from their schools. Also, rather than producing committed lay workers for Southern churches, these schools sapped the loyalty to Southern denominations by introducing their students to opportunities for service in interdenominational faith missions and independent churches. Additionally, the interest of some fundamentalists in dispensationalism made them appear to be theological innovators like the liberals.

While Southern Baptists and Southern Presbyterians moved to lessen the impact of the interdenominational fundamentalist presence in their region, some ministers began to be troubled by changes occurring within both denominations and by the accusations fundamentalists made concerning liberals' activities. The issues of theological liberalism and cooperative Protestantism were the most important in sparking the creation of factions among Baptists and Presbyterians, and both factions used concerns peculiar to their traditions to aid their efforts in recruiting a following. Presbyterians mobilized support from those alarmed at the prospect of reunion with Northern Presbyterians, while Baptists continued capitalizing on the fears of the growing bureaucratization of the Southern Baptist Convention. Controversies over these issues were not new in the 1930s and 1940s, but the difference and the significance of these years is that these battles resulted in the creation of ongoing factions with their own organizations and publications committed to resisting changes and to influencing the policies and theology within their denominations. While neither faction adopted the designation and both resisted the application of the label, their activities, nevertheless, can be described accurately as fundamentalist. Because of their decision to remain within their churches in order to stop if not reverse liberal trends, they can be called denominational fundamentalists.

Concern over the teaching of modernist theology in denominationally-sponsored colleges and seminaries and the publication of modernist views by denominationally-supported presses was the crucial element that led to action. Southern Baptists and Presbyterians were not unaware of the liberal trends in theology that sparked the Northern denominational wars of the 1920s and even had exponents within their ranks. Yet, unlike their Northern brethren, conservatives successfully ignored, isolated, or expelled what liberals there were without splitting their denominations.[8] During the 1930s and 1940s, though, groups in each denomination realized that the work of

---

[8]See chapter 2, 67-79.

protecting their traditions from modernism was not done. In fact, if their rhetoric is taken into account, they believed that both denominations were about to succumb to liberal domination. The avenue of liberal infiltration was through the denominational schools and publications, and during the 1930s and 1940s denominational fundamentalists mustered evidence to prove their allegations, rally allies to the cause, and "wake up" the complacent orthodox. Significantly, to find success in this endeavor, they first had to distance themselves from the interdenominational fundamentalists.

With their hierarchy of church courts and elaborate rules governing the affairs of the denomination, the Southern Presbyterian church had effective institutional means for resisting fundamentalist penetration and disciplining its dissidents.[9] Concern over fundamentalism revolved around the graduates of Dallas Theological Seminary and their dispensational theology and eventually led to the condemnation of dispensationalism as inconsistent with the denomination's Confession of Faith. This controversy was fairly simple on one level. In response to several overtures, the General Assembly of the Presbyterian Church appointed a committee to investigate dispensationalism to see if this eschatology was consistent with the denomination's Confession of Faith. Its first report was an emphatic condemnation of dispensationalism so broad that it seemed to include historic premillennialism. The Assembly expanded the committee to include premillennialists and asked it to reconsider the report. The committee's second report pointed out specific dispensational teachings that were contrary to the Confession of Faith and concluded with a paragraph that the report was not to be understood as an attack on premillennialists.

The controversy arose because dispensationalists were in the forefront of offering a caustic, fundamentalist critique of what they saw to be the growing liberal tendencies in the Southern Presbyterian church. Occasionally the discord they caused in congregations led to

---

[9]A variety of Presbyterian denominations organized churches in the South, but the largest was the PCUS and will be the focus of this discussion of fundamentalism among Southern Presbyterians.

schisms, as was the result in Greensboro. Viewed as outsiders, they usually came from non-Presbyterian seminaries, and their support of interdenominational missions and activities called into question their loyalty to denominational programs. Thus the attack on dispensationalists was an effort to silence the troublemakers in the denominations.

But the controversy had another layer. More broadly it should be seen as a liberal attack on the conservative wing of the church. Liberals lumped together all who criticized the church and labeled them heretics. This strategy diverted attention away from complaints concerning liberals' deviation from the church's Confession of Faith. But conservative Southern Presbyterians were divided. While agreeing with dispensationalists in general terms concerning conditions in their church, they recognized that defending dispensationalism, a theology clearly at odds with the church's confession, might undermine their efforts to oust liberals or at least control and restrain liberal influence on the denomination. On the other hand, to let liberals attack dispensationalists while clearly distinguishing their conservative faction from this interpretation of prophecy would eliminate one avenue through which liberals could influence church opinion against them. In other words, if liberals wanted to discredit their opponents, it would have to be on some other basis than theological heterodoxy. But this strategy would mean alienating, if not driving from the church, the staunchest opponents of liberalism. For some the result seemed worth the price because the dispensational controversy diverted energy and attention away from the more serious liberal threat to the theological integrity of the Southern Presbyterian church.

That the controversy swirled around the graduates of Dallas Theological Seminary resulted from Lewis Chafer's hopes that its graduates would play a significant role in countering liberal influence in the Southern Presbyterian church. Early in the school's development, J. D. Eggleston, Chafer's friend and President of Hamden-Sydney College, warned him of the difficulty of recruiting Southern Presbyterian students. "Most of them," Eggleston explained, "come here under the care of the Presbytery; they have to report to the Presbytery every year; and they act under the advice of the Presbytery.

Many of them borrow money through the endorsement of the Presbytery and cannot continue to get more unless they are further endorsed by the Presbytery."[10] Nevertheless, by 1930 Chafer boasted that "we have a number of Southern Presbyterian boys this year" and felt confident that "as they are graduated and sent out, our Southern churches will begin to appreciate this training."[11] Unfortunately, the seeds had already been sown that would undermine the realization of Chafer's hopes, and the activities of a few of the graduates in Southern Presbyterian churches did little to improve the reputation of the seminary. In its first few years the seminary had fairly good relations with the Dallas presbyteries of both the Northern and Southern denominations. The support of William Anderson of Dallas's First Presbyterian Church helped with the Southern presbytery while the absence of a Northern Presbyterian seminary in the region made the Northern presbytery receptive to ordaining Dallas graduates.[12] As the seminary students began working in Southern Presbyterian churches in the Dallas-Ft. Worth area, laypeople became enamored of their teaching and in a few instances wanted the students to serve as their pastors. In 1928 Southern Presbyterians resisted the efforts of the members of Ft. Worth's Westminster Presbyterian Church to call Manfred Gutzke as their pastor because he attended a non-Presbyterian seminary. The laypeople had their way, and Westminster was regularly served by Dallas students, but the affair left more than a taste of resentment among Southern Presbyterians in Dallas.[13]

The thorn in the side of Lewis Chafer was Floyd Poe of Dallas's City Temple Presbyterian Church. Poe objected to the seminary's dispensationalism and fought to keep its students and graduates out of

---

[10]J. D. Eggleston to LSC, 3 March 1927, in LSC Papers.

[11]LSC to A. J. Crowell, 2 October 1930, in LSC Papers.

[12]RTC to Mrs. W. H. Osborne, 1 August 1924; LSC to J. D. Eggleston, 16 May 1927; LSC to J. D. Eggleston, 15 June 1928; and LSC to W. M. Baker, 22 February 1930, in LSC Papers.

[13]LSC to J. D. Eggleston, 15 June 1928; LSC to F. Z. Browne, 21 June 1928; RTC to Jacob W. Limkemann, 2 February 1938, in LSC Papers. Other Dallas students and graduates serving Westminster included Archer Anderson from 1931–1933, L. P. McClenny from 1943–1948, and Herbert E. Kann from 1954–1974. DTS Alumni Records.

Southern Presbyterian churches by urging presbyteries to require candidates for ordination to spend a year in a Southern Presbyterian seminary.[14] The result, though, was no consistent policy across the South. The General Assembly refused to impose standards, leaving the presbyteries to determine educational requirements for ordination.[15] The experience of Dallas graduates varied from presbytery to presbytery. For example, Ray Fortna had an easy ordination examination from the New Orleans Presbytery while Fred Stroud found the laypeople of two rural Central Georgia Presbyterian churches enthusiastic about his sermons on prophecy.[16] On the other hand, Alfred Dodds's effort to be installed as pastor of the Presbyterian church in Tonkawa, Oklahoma, produced a "dog fight" between the church's session and presbytery officials over his education at Dallas Seminary and association with Young Life.[17] Lewis Chafer made a vigorous effort to find a Southern Presbyterian church for Warwick Aiken, but to no avail.[18] A few Dallas students avoided some

---

[14]LSC to Alexander Mackie, 16 May 1944; and LSC to George Vorsheim, 24 January 1945, in LSC Papers.

[15]PCUS, General Assembly, *Minutes of the General Assembly of the Presbyterian Church in the United States, 1934*, (Augusta GA: Constitutionalist Job Office, 1934) 102–110; and idem., *Minutes of the General Assembly, 1941* (Augusta GA: Constitutionalist Job Office, 1941) 60.

[16]Ray D. Fortna to LSC, 3 November 1932; and Fred Stroud to LSC and RTC, 30 August 1933, in LSC Papers.

[17]Alfred Dodds to LSC, 27 September 1943, in LSC Papers. Young Life was an interdenominational organization started by James Rayburn, a Dallas graduate, for the purpose of evangelizing teenagers. Bruce Shelly, "The Rise of Evangelical Youth Movements," *Fides et Historia* 18 (January 1986): 52–55.

[18]Chafer wrote at least nine letters of recommendation for Aiken for Southern Presbyterian churches, and no evidence remains that he went to such lengths for any other graduate. See LSC to William Anderson, 28 January 1928; to Clerk of the Session, First Presbyterian Church, Augusta, Georgia, 15 April 1932; to Clerk of the Session, South Highland Presbyterian Church, Birmingham, Alabama, 15 April 1932; to Clerk of the Session, First Presbyterian Church, Big Springs, Texas, 2 May 1932; to Ray D. Fortna, 10 June 1932; to Clerk of the Session, First Presbyterian Church, Ft. Smith, Arkansas, 13 July 1932; to W. I. Carroll, 20 March 1933; to S. J. Sutterlin, 8 May 1933; and to Clerk of the Session, Maxwell Street Presbyterian Church, Lexington, Kentucky, 8 May 1933, in LSC Papers. In addition to his education at Dallas, Aiken's Episcopal background was a stumbling block to Presbyterian ordination. He

difficulties by transferring to and graduating from Southern Presbyterian seminaries, but that option became more difficult to pursue when three Southern Presbyterian seminaries ceased accepting credit for courses taken at Dallas Seminary.[19] A prospective Presbyterian pastor wishing to take advantage of Dallas's strengths, the training in the biblical languages and expository preaching, might forego the opportunity if the courses did not count toward graduation when he transferred.[20]

Moreover, beginning in the late 1920s and continuing into the 1940s several churches and presbyteries across the South experienced trouble from dispensational fundamentalists that disrupted local congregations, sometimes leading to schisms. Occasionally, graduates and faculty of Dallas Seminary were involved. In the late 1920s Fred Z. Browne, adjunct instructor of church history at the seminary, played a central role in the controversy over the liberalism of H. Watson Smith and the failure of the denomination to discipline Smith.[21] In 1938 the Nashville Presbytery removed Fred Stroud, a former student of Dallas Seminary, from the pulpit of Second Presbyterian, even though its investigation concluded that "it is probable that a majority [of the church's members] would favor his continuing as pastor."[22] Stroud criticized what he believed to be the

---

eventually secured a small Episcopal church in Plainview, Texas. Warwick Aiken to LSC, 15 October 1933, in LSC Papers.

[19]According to Rollin T. Chafer in a letter to Charles C. Sterrett, 28 June 1938 (Rollin T. Chafer Papers, Mosher Library, Dallas Theological Seminary, Dallas, TX) (hereinafter cited as RTC Papers), the seminaries, which were not named in the correspondence and which had once accepted courses from Dallas Seminary, stopped the practice because the transferred courses took the place of classes necessary for the preparation of a *Presbyterian* minister. RTC wrote to J. M. Richards, President of Columbia Seminary, on 13 April 1938, questioning him about this point, but Richards's reply, referred to in the Sterrett correspondence, was not found.

[20]Such considerations influenced the decision of P. G. Crosby and Graham Gilmer, Jr. to transfer after one year at Dallas to the Presbyterian seminary in Richmond, Virginia. P. G. Crosby to RTC, 13 July 1938, in RTC Papers.

[21]See chapter 2, 75-76.

[22]Nashville Presbytery of the PCUS, *Minutes of the Nashville Presbytery*, November 1938, 6. The *Ministerial Directory*, revised and supplemented, 658, indicated that Stroud earned his BD at Columbia Theological Seminary in 1933. The *Bulletins* of the

liberal tendencies of the Women's Auxiliary and the Young People's work and did not seek the approval of the church's session in arranging for dispensationalists to lead Bible conferences in the church.[23] In the early 1940s in Reidsville, North Carolina, a group of laypeople influenced by Dallas Seminary dispensationalism disrupted the peace of the First Presbyterian Church.[24]

The battle lines, though, were not drawn over loyalty to and support of the denomination's program but over the troublemakers' dispensationalism. The first salvo came in 1938 from James Bear, a professor at Richmond's Union Theological Seminary, in an article that compared dispensationalism with the creeds adopted by the denomination to define its doctrinal position.[25] Using C. I. Scofield and Lewis Chafer as representatives of dispensationalism, Bear argued that their rigid distinction between the law of the Old Testament and the grace of the New and their denial that the Old Testament prophets foresaw the creation of the Church undermined the "covenant of grace," the foundation of the denomination's doctrinal system.[26] In short, dispensationalists preached an un-Presbyterian theology.

Evangelical Theological College of January 1931 (19) and March 1932 (19) showed that Stroud was an "undergraduate" student taking courses for a Masters of Theology.

[23]Nashville Presbytery, *Minutes*, 4–5. Lewis Chafer was one of the speakers. Stroud did not allow the church's children to attend the Presbyterian sponsored youth camp but sent them to an unspecified camp in North Carolina. It may be speculation only, but it is not unlikely that the camp was Ben Lippen, the one founded by Robert McQuilkin of Columbia Bible College.

[24]Marion S. Huske to RCM, 6 February 1942, in Dispensationalism—Southern Church file (Robert C. McQuilkin Papers, Library, Columbia Bible College, Columbia, Sc) (hereinafter cited as RCM Papers). Huske, pastor of the church, asked McQuilkin to recommend books that would helped Huske refute the dispensational teachings. Huske did not indicate the specific source of these laymen's views, but it may have been William Jones as Reidsville is about twenty-five miles northeast of Greensboro. DTS Alumni Records indicate that no other graduate served a church in this area for these years.

[25]James E. Bear, "Dispensationalism and the Covenant of Grace," *Union Seminary Review* 49 (July 1938): 285–307.

[26]Ibid., 305. In Bear's analysis the dispensationalists' description of law and grace implied two different methods of salvation while their discussion of the prophets contradicted the covenantal theologians' assertion that Old Testament prophetic passages were fulfilled in the Church.

Walter Lingle, a colleague of Bear's, voiced a similar conclusion but reached a wider audience with the publication of his criticisms in the *Christian Observer*, a religious newspaper that circulated primarily among Southern Presbyterians. Lingle suggested that the essence of Presbyterianism was a particular kind of church government and doctrine.[27] Ordination vows required that Presbyterian ministers support both, but Lingle charged that dispensationalists disregarded their promises through their criticisms of the actions of the General Assembly and their espousal of doctrines inconsistent with the denomination's Confession of Faith.[28] Lingle did not mention dispensationalism by name, but his examples of un-Presbyterian teachings abroad in the denomination came from dispensational interpretations of the Bible. Both Bear and Lingle acknowledged that dispensationalism had a popular following among Southern Presbyterians, while Bear indicated its sources in itinerant Bible teachers, interdenominational newspapers, and Bible schools.[29] The professors stopped short of advocating that dispensationalists be driven from the denomination, but both clearly believed that dispensationalism was not an acceptable theology for Presbyterian ministers and laypeople.

---

[27]Walter L. Lingle, "What Does Presbyterianism Stand For?" *Christian Observer*, 10 May 1939, 3, 7.

[28]Ibid.

[29]Bear, "Dispensationalism," 285–86. He specifically mentioned Dallas Theological Seminary, but he incorrectly included Columbia Bible College in his list of institutions that taught dispensationalism. H. Waddell Pratt, theology professor at the college, and Robert McQuilkin, its president, wrote Bear that they did not teach dispensationalism and explained to their students the errors of dispensationalists. Heading a school that attracted a large number of students from Presbyterian churches and running a campground that Presbyterian ministers and laypeople patronized, McQuilkin was concerned that this support not be compromised by misleading information and asked Bear to publish a retraction. H. Waddell Pratt to James E. Bear, 19 July 1938, and RCM to James E. Bear, 27 July 1938, in RCM Papers, Dispensationalism—Southern Church file. Bear replied that he would issue a statement in the *Christian Observer* and *Presbyterian of the South*, but no evidence of the retraction has been found. James E. Bear to RCM, 4 August 1938, in RCM Papers, Dispensationalism, Southern Church file. Earnest Trice Thompson perpetuated Bear's mistake by relying on Bear's article, who identified the college as introducing dispensationalism to Southern Presbyterians. Earnest Trice Thompson, *Presbyterians in the South*, 3 vols. (Richmond VA: John Knox Press, 1973) 3:487.

The next stage of the controversy came when several presbyteries sent overtures to the General Assembly in the late 1930s and early 1940s requesting an investigation of dispensationalism.[30] The 1940 overture from the North Alabama Presbytery indicated that it needed guidance in evaluating an ordination candidate's training if he graduated from a seminary that taught dispensationalism.[31] Since Chafer's school was the only seminary with this doctrine in its curriculum, the overture reflected concern over the growing number of Dallas' graduates seeking ordination in the Southern Presbyterian church. Responding to the overtures, the 1941 Assembly referred the issue to a Committee on Revising the Confession of Faith that appointed an ad interim committee composed primarily of seminary professors to answer the question of "whether the type of Bible Interpretation known as 'Dispensationalism' is in harmony with the Confession of Faith."[32] Citing many of the objections Bear raised, the committee condemned dispensationalism in a manner that seemed to censure all premillennial interpretations of prophecy. The 1943 Assembly recommitted the report to a committee enlarged to include premillennialists. Significantly, the committee remained weighted in favor of trained theologians with four professors from Presbyterian schools while three laymen represented premillennialists.[33] One layman on the committee, Judge Samuel Sibley of Atlanta, confessed that he did not realize he was a premillennialist until he read the literature sent to him by the committee and was "surprised to learn" that

---

[30]Thompson, *Presbyterians*, 3:488; PCUS, *Minutes of the General Assembly*, 1940, 33.

[31]Ibid.

[32]PCUS, *Minutes of the General Assembly*, 1941, 60.

[33]PCUS, *Minutes of the General Assembly*, 1943, 46, 123–29. The professors were James Bear of Union Seminary, F. B. Gear of Southwestern College, James Green of Columbia Seminary, and Eugene McLaurin of Austin Seminary. Premillennialist representatives were Samuel H. Sibley, a judge from Atlanta, Georgia; L. Nelson Bell, a doctor from North Carolina and former missionary to China; and J. P. McCallie, founder of a preparatory school in Chattanooga, Tennessee. Green, McLaurin, and Sibley were members of the committee that wrote the 1943 report that Sibley refused to sign it.

premillennialists were "theologically suspect."[34] Another, apparently feeling out of his league in the theological discussions in the committee's meetings, turned to an interdenominational fundamentalist for advice. J. P. McCallie, the headmaster of a preparatory school in Chattanooga and member of the committee, consulted Robert McQuilkin of Columbia Bible College concerning theology and the tactics premillennialists should pursue in their deliberations.[35] McQuilkin coached McCallie in the fine points of eschatology while urging him to have the committee protect the place of premillennialists among Southern Presbyterians. "I believe," wrote McQuilkin, "it would be a great victory for Premillennialism if the General Assembly would recognize that a man may be a loyal Presbyterian and be a Premillennialist. At the same time, you will have to make clear that this Premillennialism does not carry with it the doctrines [i.e.,

---

[34]Samuel H. Sibley to the Committee on Dispensationalism, 2 December 1943, typed copy in RCM Papers, Dispensationalism—Southern Church file.

[35]McQuilkin's participation needs explanation. First he believed that dispensationalism represented a distortion of the Bible. He had played a similar role in 1937–1938 in educating Charles G. Trumbull, editor of the *Sunday School Times*, about dispensationalism while Chafer debated professors of Westminster Seminary. See RCM to Charles G. Trumball, 20 February 1937, 6 May 1938, and 3 August 1938, in Dispensationalism File, in RCM Papers. Furthermore, he believed that through influencing McCallie he could protect the relationships with Southern Presbyterian churches he had carefully cultivated to support his college and campground. He explained that Presbyterian leaders had criticized his endeavors as "contrary to the denominational scheme of things" and for "drawing support away from the church work.... Now it confuses matters greatly to link these things with the discussion of dispensationalism and the Confession of Faith." RCM to J. P. McCallie, 28 June 1943, in Dispensationalism—Southern Church file in RCM Papers. McQuilkin may have had in mind James Bear's article identifying Columbia Bible College as teaching dispensationalism. See Note 29. Finally McQuilkin believed that liberals were using the dispensational controversy to discredit all conservatives thus opening the way for liberal domination of the Southern church. In McQuilkin's analysis "back of all this discussion looms another ominous fact. The interest of some of the strongest enemies of premillennialism is to bring into the Southern Presbyterian Church that new religion called 'modernism.'" RCM to J. P. McCallie, 21 December 1943, in RCM Papers, Dispensationalism, Southern Church file. In short McQuilkin saw himself as helping preserve the conservative character of the denomination.

dispensationalism] that dear Dr. Chafer has set forth."[36] He recommended that the Committee reaffirm the denomination's historic position of liberty of interpretation in matters of eschatology while condemning certain dispensational teachings as contrary to the Confession of Faith.[37] McQuilkin also encouraged McCallie to use this situation to turn the tables of the liberals. If the Committee's seminary professors insisted "on giving a Premillennialism a black eye," McQuilkin suggested that the laymen issue a minority report "to open up the whole question honestly. Why should we not have a Committee of the Assembly investing whether the system of interpretation called liberalism or modernism is in harmony with the Confession of Faith?"[38]

The premillennialists did not pursue this last suggestion but did succeed in having the Committee adopt the others. Its final report pointed out specific dispensational doctrines that contradicted the church's confession, but its overall evaluation was no less unequivocal: "It is the unanimous opinion of your Committee that Dispensationalism...is out of accord with...the Confession of Faith."[39] Both reports made extensive use of Lewis Chafer's works and the Scofield Reference Bible in defining dispensationalism and condemned both for teaching that God had two different plans of salvation.[40] The concluding paragraph of the second report revealed the influence of the premillennialists. It emphasized that while all dispensationalists were premillennialists not all premillennialists were dispensationalists and that "this report should not be considered as in any sense a criticism of Premillennialism."[41]

Lewis Chafer viewed these developments as an attack not only on himself and his theology but also on his school, one that grew out of jealousy. Writing to Graham Gilmer, Chafer suggested, "Lying back of

[36]RCM to J. P. McCallie, 2 August 1943, in Dispensationalism—Southern Church file in RCM Papers.

[37]Ibid.

[38]RCM to J. P. McCallie, 7 December 1943, in ibid.

[39]PCUS, *Minutes of the General Assembly*, 1944, 126.

[40]Ibid., 125; cf., PCUS, *Minutes of the General Assembly*, 1943, 124.

[41]PCUS, *Minutes of the General Assembly*, 1944, 127.

this whole issue is the resentment on the part of our [i.e., the Southern Presbyterian] seminaries as the character of the work being done by the Dallas Seminary." That the majority of the committee came from Presbyterian schools confirmed his suspicions.[42] From the time of Bear's article, Chafer and his colleagues in Dallas worked diligently to counter what he believed was the misrepresentation of dispensational teachings. First, in an editorial in *Bibliotheca Sacra*, the seminary's theological journal, Rollin Chafer defended the distinction between law and grace and suggested that those who claimed to be premillennial but not dispensational had failed to understand the full implications of their beliefs.[43] This strategy of linking premillennialists to the dispensational cause was one Lewis Chafer used throughout the controversy. On the one hand he tried to subsume dispensationalism under the more acceptable label of premillennialism while on the other he sought to force premillennialists into accepting a dispensational interpretation of their eschatology.[44] If successful in the latter, each convert represented a potential ally in the denominational battle.

---

[42]LSC to Graham Gilmer, 24 May 1944; cf., LSC to Dewey Duncan, 10 July 1943; LSC to David A. Martin, 6 June 1950, in LSC Papers.

[43]Rollin T. Chafer, "Dispensationally-colored Premillennialism," *Bibliotheca Sacra* 95 (July 1938): 257–58. That Lewis did not respond and give a more detailed rebuttal to Bear's criticisms may attributed to the fact that the Chafers were already involved in a similar dispute with Northern Presbyterians. To respond fully to Bear would mean repeating points already made. See Lewis Sperry Chafer, "Dispensationalism," *Bibliotheca Sacra* 93 (October 1936): 390–449; and the editorials by Rollin Chafer, "'Modern' Dispensationalism," *Bibliotheca Sacra* 93 (April 1936): 129–30; and "Of the Same Opinion Still," *Bibliotheca Sacra* 94 (July 1937): 262–63. Lewis Chafer's article was Bear's main source for his critique of dispensationalism. See Bear, "Dispensationalism," 293. For details of the controversy with Northern Presbyterians, see John David Hannah, "The Social and Intellectual History of the Evangelical Theological College" (Ph.D. diss., University of Texas at Dallas, 1988) 353–60.

[44]Chafer often used the term premillennialism when clearly he was discussing dispensationalism. See for example, "Is Premillennialism A Fundamental?" typescript copy; LSC to Paul W. Rood, 23 March 1943; LSC to Donald Grey Barnhouse, 7 January 1929; and LSC to J Gresham Machen, 3 July 1929, in LSC papers. He was not being intentionally devious because he believed that premillennialists had not been instructed accurately in the logical implications of their belief in a millennial kingdom. In Chafer's eyes such a tenet made all premillennialists, by definition,

Whether they became dispensationalists or not, Chafer attempted to rally premillennialists to his side. He appealed to Albert S. Johnson, the widely respected minister of Charlotte's First Presbyterian Church, to organize a fellowship of Southern Presbyterian premillennialists, but Johnson did nothing.[45] Moreover, he carried his case directly to Southern Presbyterian pastors by mailing to each his rebuttal to the ad interim committee's first report.[46] In it Chafer shifted the focus of the debate from dispensationalism's agreement with the denomination's Confession of Faith to its scriptural basis and bluntly called for a revision of the church's theological position to accept dispensationalism as suitable theology for Presbyterian pastors.[47] Behind the scenes he pleaded with the committee for an opportunity to appear before it to defend his writings, but the committee refused his request.[48] F. B.

---

dispensationalists. In "Of the Same Opinion," 262–63, Rollin Chafer argued the point most succinctly: "The moment we employ the term *millennium* or its various grammatical variations, we commit ourselves to the idea a future millennial dispensation. For assuredly we are not witnessing millennial conditions in the earth today. We cannot rightly speak of a *before the millennium* event without accepting the fact of a period of time which will be characterized by millennial conditions following the mentioned event. Such a period is a dispensation in the Scriptural sense. Hence a premillennialist must be a dispensationalist." Cf. comments by Lewis in LSC to J. H. Viser, 3 February 1943; LSC to Charles A. Rowland, 13 March 1944; and LSC to George Vorsheim, 24 January 1945, in LSC papers. Thus Lewis freely interchanged the terms. The effect of this substitution, and it became more deliberate as the controversy became more heated, was as noted above.

[45]According to Chafer in a letter to Graham Gilmer, 4 March 1941, in LSC papers. No correspondence between Chafer and Johnson on this issue has survived.

[46]His reply was in the form of a reprint of an editorial he published in *Bibliotheca Sacra* according to LSC to General Assembly of the Presbyterian Church in the United States, May 1944; and LSC to J. D. Eggleston, 16 May 1944, in LSC papers.

[47]LSC, "Dispensational Distinctions Challenged," *Bibliotheca Sacra* 100 (July 1943): 337–45.

[48]He wrote twice to J. P. McCallie who replied to the first letter that such a meeting might be useful and then ignored the second letter. According to LSC to David A. Martin, 6 June 1950, in LSC Papers. McCallie was indeed troubled that Chafer was not receiving fair consideration of his views. Writing to Robert McQuilkin, McCallie remarked, "My only feeling of incompetence in this matter is that we are trying Dr. Chafer without a hearing on his part." J. P. McCallie to RCM, 5 November 1943, in RCM Papers, Dispensationalism—Southern church file. The committee offered Chafer the opportunity to reply in writing to seven dispensational propositions it believed contradicted the Confession of Faith. Chafer complained such a format was

Gear, chair of the committee, believed Chafer's appearance would serve no useful purpose because Chafer's writings were "so clear and numerous...that, without any unfairness, his views may be ascertained."[49] Failing to influence the committee and forewarned about its conclusions, Chafer tried to take his case directly to the 1944 General Assembly. Sending a letter to Graham Gilmer to read to the Assembly, he reasserted that the main issue should be dispensationalism's biblical basis not its agreement with the denomination's creed and emphatically denied that he taught that God had two ways of salvation. "I surrender second place to no man," Chafer wrote, "in my insistence that salvation is always through Christ alone."[50] The Assembly accepted the report without significant debate nor hearing Chafer's appeal. On the advice of other dispensationalists at the meeting, Gilmer withheld Chafer's letter. He explained, "I showed your letter to several of the brethren who agree with us, but they thought it best not to read it to the Assembly and felt that the whole matter would quiet down more quickly if it were let alone."[51] In another letter he added, "I really do not think that anything much is going to be done about it. Dr. Bear and Dr. Gear have had their way and I feel that this will be the end of the matter."[52]

The Assembly's action laid the foundation for purging dispensationalists, but in accepting the report, the Assembly recommended no specific action, leaving open the door for presbyteries to use the report as they saw fit. Chafer believed the report was an personal attack on him that the Dallas Presbytery would use to excommunicate

---

inadequate because dispensationalism was too complex and interrelated to be encompassed in disconnected commentaries on specific issues. LSC to J. P. McCallie, 10 November 1943, typed copy in RCM Papers, Dispensationalism, Southern Church file.

[49]Quoted in J. P. McCallie to RCM, 31 January 1944, in RCM Papers, Dispensationalism, Southern Church file.

[50]LSC to the General Assembly of the Presbyterian Church, US, May 1944, in LSC Papers. Chafer learned of the committee's report from Graham Gilmer. See Graham Gilmer to LSC, 17 May 1944 and 22 May 1944, in LSC Papers.

[51]Graham Gilmer to LSC, 1 June 1944, in LSC Papers.

[52]Graham Gilmer to LSC, 9 June 1944, in LSC Papers.

him.[53] The presbytery took no action, but Chafer became a pariah at its meetings.[54] It does not appear other presbyteries used the report against dispensationalists already in Presbyterian churches.[55] Rather presbyteries used it to prevent others from holding Presbyterian pulpits. The situation of James Mooney, a Dallas graduate, was a case in point. While serving as Dean of Southeastern Bible School, Mooney applied for ordination from the Birmingham Presbytery. Citing his position at an interdenominational school as service outside the bounds of the Presbytery, his attendance at a denominationally unapproved seminary, and his dispensationalism, the Presbytery rejected his application without examining him. Writing to his mentor, Mooney described the presbytery meeting where his opponents characterized his "entire course of training in the Dallas Seminary as a 'mistake' and extend[ed] condolences to me for being 'misguided.' I have never experienced such an insulting, discourteous, bitter and vindictive attitude anywhere or at any time."[56] Other

---

[53]LSC to Graham Gilmer, 20 May 1944, in LSC Papers. Gilmer concurred with Chafer that the report was a personal attack (Graham Gilmer to LSC, 22 May 1944, in LSC Papers) as did Fred Z Browne (Fred Z. Browne to LSC, 16 September 1944, in LSC Papers).

[54]LSC to Graham Gilmer, 31 March 1949, in LSC Papers. While the presbytery did not move against Chafer, neither did Chafer leave the denomination; he remained a Southern Presbyterian until his death in 1952. This letter, though, indicated Chafer's desire to move his affiliation elsewhere, but he "had not been able to take any action in that respect because of my relation to the Seminary." This comment suggests that Chafer believed that continuing his membership in the Southern Presbyterian church would benefit graduates of the seminary. In short he still dreamed of supplying conservative pastors to the denomination to help maintain its orthodoxy.

[55]Dispensationalism did not appear in the official records as a factor in the dismissal by the Orange Presbytery of William Jones from the pastorate Westminster Church in Greensboro, North Carolina, but it is probable that Jones substituted dispensationally oriented Sunday school literature for the denomination's publications. See *Minutes of the Orange Presbytery*, 27 April 1948, 71–74.

[56]James S. Mooney to LSC, 24 April 1945, in LSC Papers. Mooney was particularly bitter over the fact that a mutual friend, John F. Elliot of Wylam Presbyterian Church, voted against Mooney despite the fact that Mooney preached in Wylam's pulpit on four occasion and that Elliot taught from Scofield leaflets and had Scofield Reference Bibles in his church's pews. To Mooney, Elliot's action was example of "sacrificing of principle for the expediency of political preferment." Ibid.

presbyteries tried to avoid confrontations. One announced its un-willingness to accept graduates from Dallas Seminary while another screened applicants by asking references to indicate if the candidate was premillennial or dispensational.[57]

While theologically conservative Southern Presbyterians used the dispensational controversy to distinguish themselves from the funda-mentalists, they mobilized to address the issues raised by the funda-mentalists regarding liberalism in the Southern church. Ironically, in these efforts to preserve their doctrinal heritage, they engaged in a fundamentalistic crusade but one moderate in tone and not resulting in schism. Significantly, while they relied on fundamentalist analysis of the Northern Presbyterian church, they did not establish direct associational or institutional links to Northern Presbyterian conser-vatives who battled liberals in the 1920s and 1930s. They concentrated their support on one paper, the *Southern Presbyterian Journal*. To label this faction of Southern Presbyterians as fundamentalists is not to suggest that they identified with all the theological parameters of fundamentalism as defined by George Marsden. Nevertheless, two elements in their program mark them as fundamentalists, and in fact, their efforts mark the appearance in the Southern church of a controversy similar to what had troubled the Northern church in the 1920s. First, they sought to maintain what they believed to be their tradition's heritage, particularly its affirmation of a Reformed view of the Bible's authority and its mission in terms of a spiritual duty to win the lost to Christ. Second, they organized a coalition of like-minded laity and clergy for the purpose of wresting control from the liberals of the denomination's institutions and policies.[58]

---

[57]Thompson, *Presbyterians*, 3:488, did not record which presbytery issued a blanket refusal to Dallas graduates nor does he cite a source for this observation. The El Paso Presbytery included on its recommendation form questions concerning the eschatological views of candidates for ordination. Copy of form included in correspondence, George Westberg to LSC, 19 December 1950, in LSC Papers.

[58]In "Fundamentalism and the Neo-Evangelicals," *Fides et Historia* 24 (Winter-Spring 1992): 81–96, Douglas A. Sweeny described the lingering fundamentalist ideological commitments of the post-World War II evangelicals. The argument is that the evidence presented here concerning the activities of those trying to stop reunion

A series of liberal victories in the 1930s and early 1940s was the occasion for starting the *Journal*. During the late 1930s, liberal efforts to modify the strict Calvinism of Southern Presbyterians' Confession of Faith failed only because the by-laws required a three-fourths vote at a General Assembly to revise the Confession, but a majority favored change.[59] Even what appeared to be a liberal defeat in 1939 when the Assembly voted to require the affirmation of certain fundamental doctrines at ordination was weakened by the Assembly's failure to make clear the purpose of the declaration.[60] Moreover, efforts to unite Northern and Southern Presbyterians gained momentum in 1937 when the Assembly created the Permanent Committee on Cooperation and Union, and the presbyteries voted in 1940 to continue its existence. An attempt to limit its activities to cooperation failed in 1942.[61] Then in 1941 the General Assembly appeared to endorse cooperative Protestantism by voting to join the Federal Council of Churches.[62] The same assembly rejected a call for an investigation of unorthodox teaching at the denomination's seminaries.[63] In the eyes of

---

reflects a similar commitment to a fundamentalist program in denominational politics.

[59]Thompson, *Presbyterians*, 3:492. The 1939 General Assembly adopted some minor modifications in language and punctuation, but a conservative partisan interpreter saw these revisions "watering down" the Confession's doctrines. See Morton H. Smith, *"How is the Gold Become Dim:" The Decline of the Presbyterian Church, US, as Reflected in Its Assembly Actions*, 2nd ed. (Jackson MS: The Steering Committee for the Continuing Presbyterian Church, 1973) 49–51.

[60]The doctrines included the infallibility and authority of the Bible, the deity of Christ, the virgin birth, substitutionary atonement, the resurrection, and a future judgement of mankind. The 1947 Assembly interpreted it as an *in thesi* statement, not binding the presbyteries to enforce. Thompson, *Presbyterians*, 3:492; and Smith, *How is the Gold*, 41.

[61]Smith, *How is the Gold*, 119–20.

[62]Southern Presbyterians actually voted to rejoin the Council having been a member from 1912 to 1931. Smith, *How is the Gold*, 130; and Thompson, *Presbyterians*, 3:266–72, 553.

[63]In particular, conservatives were concerned with the activities of Ernest Trice Thompson, professor of church history at Union Theological Seminary and editor of the *Presbyterian Outlook*. During the 1930s Thompson used the columns of the paper to introduce his readers to liberal biblical interpretations based on higher critical methods. Tom Glasgow, an elder in a Charlotte church, led the conservative assault,

some, liberals appeared to be controlling the direction of the Southern Presbyterian church.

In the *Journal*'s first issue of May 1942, the editors made plain their analysis of the "underlying and fundamental issue" causing the problems in their denomination: a failure to uphold the "integrity of Scripture."[64] This issue manifested itself in two symptoms, the analysis of which became the main themes of articles and editorials appearing throughout the 1940s and into the 1950s. First, the editors condemned participation in cooperative Protestantism, particularly affiliation with the Federal Council of Churches, because of its "constant meddling...in economic, political, social, and racial matters."[65] The more serious symptom was the effort to reunite Southern Presbyterians with the Northern denomination, and the editors of the *Journal* were blunt about the consequences. "Union with the Northern church," they warned, "would not be union, it would be *absorption*, with our individual testimony as a church gone, with our agencies disrupted, with the control of our church destiny taken from our hands, and in the long run, certain grievous heartache and disunity."[66] A third symptom became apparent in the pages of subsequent issues. A number of articles dealt with liberalism in the denomination's seminaries and publications, and the editors linked these symptoms by emphasizing that those who held a liberal

---

publishing several pamphlets describing Thompson as the most notorious example of liberalism among Southern Presbyterians. The institutional structure of the denomination prevented Glasgow from directly challenging Thompson because presbyteries had the primary responsibility for investigating charges of heterodoxy. Being members of different presbyteries, Glasgow's accusations had no standing in Thompson's presbytery, but Thompson asked for an investigation and his presbytery affirmed his orthodoxy. Conservatives then launched in 1940 and 1941 a broader effort to root out liberalism by asking the General Assembly to investigate all its seminaries. This effort failed. Thompson, *Presbyterians*, 3:333–38; and Smith, *How is the Gold*, 85–86.

[64]N.a., Editorial, "Why?" *Southern Presbyterian Journal*, May 1942, 3. Hereinafter cited as *SPJ*.

[65]Ibid.

[66]Ibid.

interpretation of Christianity were the ones who urged cooperation with the Federal Council and promoted reunion.[67]

Significantly, these issues were the ones fundamentalists and dispensationalists had raised in the previous decade, and one of the contributing editors of the *Journal* acknowledged the affinity. L. Nelson Bell, one of the lay members of the dispensational committee, explained to F. B. Gear, the committee's chair, that dispensationalism was not the cause of the criticisms of the denomination. "The real issue facing the church," Bell argued, "has been ignored and Dispensationalism blamed for a dissatisfaction which goes far deeper than any question of eschatology."[68] Bell's position as committee member and editor of the *Journal* was central to the efforts of the faction emerging in support of the *Journal* to distance itself from the troublesome dispensationalists. As a committee member, Bell played a key role with McCallie in moderating the report, while as a contributing editor he helped delineate conservative Presbyterian concerns. Interestingly, the *Journal* had little to say about the dispensational controversy. It published one article obliquely critical of dispensationalists' definition of dispensation,[69] but it did not comment on, much less endorse, the General Assembly's approval of the committee's report. This silence suggests that the editors recognized their constituency included some dispensationalists and hoped to maintain their participation in the coalition of denominational fundamentalists forming around the *Journal*.[70]

---

[67]For an example of how the three issues were linked, see Chalmers W. Alexander, "A Little Band of Determined Liberals," *SPJ*, 15 August 1950, 13.

[68]L. Nelson Bell to Felix B. Gear, 18 October 1943, typed copy in RCM Papers, Dispensationalism—Southern Church file.

[69]W. G. Foster, "Scriptural Dispensationalism," *SPJ*, May 1943, 12–15. Foster was pastor of Westminster Presbyterian Church in his hometown of Chattanooga, Tennessee. He spent the first two years of his seminary training at Dallas Seminary and graduated from the Presbyterian Columbia Theological Seminary because, in his words, "I did not feel led to leave my denomination and I felt that I should make friends and contacts within my church." W. G. Foster to LSC, 9 November 1940, in LSC Papers. Foster made clear that though he respected Chafer's spirituality and ability as a teacher he could not accept Chafer's system of dispensationalism.

[70]The difficulty in realizing this goal is reflected in a letter to W. G. Foster from Coleman Luck, a Dallas graduate and pastor of Mahota Memorial a Southern

The man behind the organization of the *Journal* was L. Nelson Bell, who recruited Henry B. Dendy for its editor.[71] Jointly, they were responsible for its editorial policies. Dendy was the pastor of the Presbyterian church in Weaverville, North Carolina, a small town near Asheville. Born in Northeast Georgia in 1895, Dendy was educated in Presbyterian schools, graduating from Davidson College in 1919. After earning his divinity degree from Columbia Theological Seminary in 1922, he accepted the pastorate of the Weaverville church where he stayed until his retirement in 1967.[72] As secretary-treasurer of the *Journal*'s Board of Directors in 1942, Bell became its associate editor by 1944, contributing some of the most pointed editorials criticizing denominational developments. After spending twenty-five years as a Southern Presbyterian medical missionary in China, Bell established his home in Montreat, North Carolina, at the Southern Presbyterian conference center and in the same county as Dendy's church.[73] Bell actively participated in the governance of the Presbyterian church, serving as an elder on the local level, a representative of the Asheville Presbytery to the General Assembly, a premillennialist on the dispensationalism committee, and moderator

---

Presbyterian church in Marietta, Oklahoma. After taking Foster to task for his theology, Luck concluded his letter, "Your article has weakened the enthusiasm which I had for the 'Southern Presbyterian Journal.' I had thought that the purpose of the magazine was to unite all of our ministers who believe in the great fundamentals of the faith, and not make an issue of the Lord's return.... Just as I was intending to write an enthusiastic letter to the editor, with my renewal, I came across your article." Luck did not say if he renewed his subscription. Coleman Luck to W. G. Foster, 23 June 1943, typed copy in LSC Papers. It is worth noting that Luck left the Presbyterian church in 1947 to become an instructor at the Moody Bible Institute, a position he held for the rest of his career. DTS Alumni Records.

[71]John C. Pollock, *A Foreign Devil in China: The Story of Dr. L. Nelson Bell, an American Surgeon in China*, crusade edition (Minneapolis MN: World Wide Publications, 1971) 227–29.

[72]While serving Weaverville, Dendy also pastored churches in Dillingham (1922–1934), Red Oak (1923–1925), and Ivy Park (1925–1926, 1932–1939). PCUS, *Ministerial Directory of the Presbyterian Church in the United States, 1861–1967*, E. D. Witherspoon, compiler, 141.

[73]Bell arrived in China in 1916 after graduating from the Medical College of Virginia and returned to the states in 1941. Ruth Bell Graham, *It's My Turn* (Old Tappan NJ: Fleming H. Revell Co., 1982) 22, 60, and 62.

of the General Assembly in 1972.[74] Moreover, Bell developed significant ties to the broader fundamentalist movement through his son-in-law, Billy Graham, and his work in helping to establish *Christianity Today* as the voice of American evangelicals.[75]

Dendy and Bell rallied the support of their generation of Southern Presbyterians to the *Journal*'s cause. Representing the leaders of the emerging faction of denominational fundamentalists, thirty-five ministers served as contributing editors or as members of the *Journal*'s Board of Directors and Advisory Committee.[76] Many were like Dendy in background and career. Nearly half (sixteen) were born in the deep South with almost all in the nineteenth century (thirty-one).[77] Nearly two-thirds (twenty-two) earned bachelor's degrees at Southern Presbyterian colleges and only two lacked theological degrees from Presbyterian seminaries.[78] In 1945 over three-quarters (twenty-seven)

---

[74]Patricia Daniels Cromwell, *A Time for Remembering: The Story of Ruth Bell Graham* (New York: Harper and Row, 1983) 212.

[75]Pollock, *Foreign Devil*, 235–40.

[76]Eleven laymen joined with the ministers, but they only lent their names to the advisory committee; Bell was the only laymen in a position to influence the editorial policies of the *Journal*. Demographic information of these men was difficult to find because the Presbyterians had no record comparable to their *Ministerial Directory* of their lay leaders. Some had been involved ·in other controversies like Tom Glasgow, an elder from Charlotte who spearheaded the attack on E. T. Thompson in the late 1930s, and J. P. McCallie, who served with Bell on the dispensational committee.

[77]This information on the pastors is gleaned from the *Ministerial Directory*. The analysis is based on the list of editors, board members, and advisory committee published in SPJ, May 1945, 2. Their average age was 56. The upper South (the states of Virginia, North Carolina, Kentucky, and Tennessee) was the birthplace for seven, the Southwest (the states of Arkansas, Texas, and Oklahoma) for five, while three were born outside the South and two overseas (two did not have their birthplace recorded). The deep South includes South Carolina, Georgia, Florida, Alabama, Mississippi, and Louisiana.

[78]Davidson College was the most frequently attended college (eleven). Interestingly, three listed the fundamentalist Moody Bible Institute for their undergraduate education. One had no seminary degree, and the other attended Dallas Theological Seminary. Union Seminary in Richmond graduated fourteen while Columbia graduated ten.

filled a pulpit with nearly two-thirds of those churches (seventeen) in towns with populations under 50,000.[79]

By contrast, the *Presbyterian Outlook*, edited by Ernest Trice Thompson, voiced the liberal perspective among Southern Presbyterians. The twenty-three clergymen among its contributing editors formed a key element of the liberal leadership and an interesting contrast to the clergy associated with the *Journal*.[80] The birthplace of one-third (eight) was the deep South, one-fifth (five) in the upper South, and another fifth (five) outside the South, but significantly over half (thirteen) were born in the twentieth century.[81] Nearly all graduated from a Presbyterian school at some point in their education, but over 80 percent (nineteen) earned a graduate degree beyond the Masters of Divinity compared to only 20 percent (seven) of the *Journal's* editors and committee members.[82] Slightly more than half (twelve) of the *Outlook's* contributing editors were pastors but

---

[79]Three were seminary professors, one was an Army chaplain, one was an evangelist, and three were retired. Nine of the twenty-seven pastors were in towns under 10,000. Population analysis is based figures from the 1940 census recorded in US, Department of Commerce, Bureau of the Census, *Seventeenth Census: U. S. Summary, Number of Inhabitants*, 1950.

[80]This analysis is based on the list of contributing editors published in *The Presbyterian Outlook*, 31 December 1945, 8. Totaling thirty-nine, it included twenty-three ministers and sixteen laypeople, two of whom were women. The *Journal* had no women on its list.

[81]Four were born in the Southwest, one overseas, and one did not have his birthplace listed. Their average age was forty-eight, eight years younger than the clergy associated with the *Journal*.

[82]Only one editor attended neither a Presbyterian college or seminary. Davidson College had the most alumni among the editors with, six while fourteen earned their M.Div. at Union Seminary in Richmond. This large number from Union probably reflects Thompson's position as editor and professor at Union. Only one of the fourteen was not at Union when Thompson was there either as a student or instructor. Of the advanced degrees, seven were MAs, eight Ph.D.'s, eight Th.M.'s, and three Th.D.'s. They were earned at Union Seminary (seven), University of Edinburgh (three), Columbia University (two), and one each at University of Chicago, Princeton Seminary, University of Virginia, University of Berlin, Illinois Wesleyan University, Yale, and Stanford. The *Journal's* clergy earned four MAs, two Ph.D.'s, three Th.M.'s, and two Th.D.'s. They graduated from Union Seminary (two), University of South Carolina (two), Davidson College (two), and one each from University of Cincinnati, Princeton Seminary, Harvard University, and Illinois Wesleyan University.

nearly 40 percent (nine) were employed in education.[83] Moreover, during the course of their careers, over half (thirteen) left the pastorate to serve their denomination as educators and administrators.[84] Slightly more than one-third (twelve) of the *Journal*'s editors held positions other than as a minister, but their careers were solidly identified with the pastorate.[85] These men averaged 42.8 years of work with 26.7 years as a pastor. *Outlook*'s editors who served outside the pastorate had slightly shorter careers (41.6 years), but only spent 12.1 years in the pulpit. One last point of comparison is worthy of note. The *Outlook* editors worked in the urban areas of the South. In 1945 almost two-thirds (fifteen) worked in towns with more than 50,000 people, over half (twelve) in cities of over 100,000.

An analysis of how Southern Presbyterian ministers voted on the Plan of Union shows a similar pattern of division in the 1950s.[86] Antiunion ministers tended to be older pastors of smaller churches in more rural areas. Their pro-union brethren had more education and worked in churches located in areas of greater economic vitality. For example, comparing the five presbyteries where antiunion sentiment was the strongest with the five strongest pro-union presbyteries reveals that nearly half (47.4 percent) of the ministers in the former were born before 1900 while almost two-thirds (65.2 percent) of the clergy in the latter had birthdays in the twentieth century.[87] Educationally,

---

[83]Seven were professors (four in seminaries, three in colleges), and two were presidents (Davidson College and Louisville Seminary). Two editors were retired, and one was a chaplain in the army.

[84]Four never held a position as a pastor while ten others left the pastorate to become professors or direct agencies like the Presbyterian Foundation of Georgia, the Board of Church Extension, or the Executive Committee on Religious Education.

[85]Among the *Journal*'s editors, only one never pastored a church. Five were professors during their careers, one was President of Columbia Seminary, and the rest served as supervisors of home missionaries and as secretaries of presbyteries or synods. None headed a denominational agency or board.

[86]See the "Note on Method" at the end of this chapter for a discussion of how this analysis was made.

[87]These trends became more pronounced in certain presbyteries. In the three where it could be determined how each member voted, over half (53.6 percent) of those who voted against union were born before 1900 while 70 percent of the pro-union pastors were born after 1900.

both groups had about the same number of ministers who had only the basic seminary degree (56.1 percent of the antiunion to 53.9 percent of the pro-union), but more of the antiunion group had no seminary degree (24.3 percent to 18 percent) while pro-union clergy more frequently had training beyond the standard seminary course (28.1 percent to 19.6 percent).[88] Antiunion pastors led churches with an average membership of 269, while churches with pro-union pastors averaged 348 members.[89] The communities where these ministers worked showed significant differences in terms of size and economic life. The average size of towns where antiunion pastors worked was about 17,000 versus an average population of slightly more than 40,000 for the towns of pro-union clergy. Unemployment was slightly higher where antiunion pastors worked (5.1 percent to 3.7 percent), but the communities of pro-union pastors had a smaller percentage of their populations earning what the Census Bureau defined as low incomes (36.4 percent to 49.1).

Thus, both the leadership of the pro-union and antiunion forces and the ministerial rank and file indicates that the battle lines among Southern Presbyterians were drawn during the 1940s and 1950s between an older generation of rural pastors and a slightly younger one, more educated and more urban. In short, Presbyterians divided between the traditional South and the new South.

An analysis of the themes in the *Journal's* articles supports this conclusion. The criticisms of the liberals' theological innovations and the opposition to reunion reflect a desire on the part of the *Journal's* editors and writers to preserve a portion of the South's religious heritage and, more broadly, Southern society. D. Maurice Allan, a

---

[88]To note that some ministers had no seminary degree does not mean they lacked all training. Most spent some time in a seminary, only a handful had no course work. In the three presbyteries where the vote of each member could be determined, the most significant difference from the numbers cited in the text was that 40 percent of the pro-union ministers had additional training beyond the standard seminary course compared to 21.4 percent of the antiunion pastors.

[89]In Concord Presbytery the difference in average membership between the antiunion and pro-union churches was the most dramatic (266 to 383) while in the group of three presbyteries the difference was much smaller (269 to 299) but still showed the same general tendency.

liberal elder in the Hamden-Sydney Presbyterian Church, perceptively made this point to explain opposition to reunion:

> This alarm at the passing of the old South is transforming itself into a desperate determination to find in the church a stronghold of purity and fidelity to the old order in which to take refuge. The reasoning, whether conscious or unconscious, seems to be as follows: We are in the midst of a shifting population, confused standards, changing school curricula, radical universities, unpredictable politics, headstrong young people, a declining Sabbath, a menacing Negro problem, a rising crime rate, a mounting divorce rate, vanishing loyalties. Here is one institution—the Southern Presbyterian Church—which we may hope to keep pure, unchanging, and loyal to the faith of our fathers.[90]

Significantly, the articles and editorials in the *Journal* employed a fundamentalist rhetoric to defend Southern culture.

As the writers for the *Journal* surveyed the condition of their denomination in the 1940s, they believed that the most serious threat to its doctrinal integrity was liberalism in its seminaries and colleges. In fundamentalist fashion they attacked schools for inviting noted liberals to address their students because these lectures gave the impression that the schools endorsed the speakers' views.[91] More dangerous than an occasional lecture, though, was the presentation of liberalism in the classrooms by the schools' professors, particularly in the seminaries. Theological education from a liberal perspective meant liberal ministers for the pulpits. Showing a distinctly fundamentalist analysis of the consequences, one editorial explained, "A low view of inspiration on the part of the professor will inevitably

---

[90]D. Maurice Allan, "The Real Issues that Divide Us; Part II," *The Presbyterian Outlook*, 1 March 1948, 6.

[91]See for example, R. William Cousar, "Van Dusen at Union Seminary," *SPJ*, February 1945, 5; and H. B. Dendy, Editorial, "Anent Dr. Buttrick," *SPJ*, 1 June 1950, 2–3.

bring many of his students to the same position. This, in turn, must affect the ministers of the Church."[92]

The most direct evidence for what professors taught was their publications, and Samuel Cartledge's *A Conservative Introduction to the Old Testament* created a storm of controversy in the 1940s. Teaching at Columbia Theological Seminary, Cartledge did not affirm the Mosaic authorship of the Pentateuch but suggested that the higher critical view, that its creation was the result of the work of several redactors, might have some merit. He also implied that Jesus' comments on the Old Testament reflected the misconceptions of his times.[93] The *Journal's* reviewer denied that the book represented a "conservative" perspective on these issues because such an interpretation denied the Bible's inerrancy while an editorial suggested that the seminary's Trustees demand a retraction of the views expressed in the book.[94] Columbia's Board of Directors approved a resolution affirming Cartledge's orthodoxy but mildly rebuking him for the position taken in his book.[95] This action did not prevent Cartledge

---

[92]N.a., Editorial, "Needed—A Clear Distinction," *SPJ*, August 1943, 2; cf., n.a., Editorial, "A Sacred Trust," *SPJ*, September 1943, 2–3; and R. E. Hough, "The Hersey of Silence," *SPJ*, February 1945, 11–12.

[93]Samuel A. Cartledge, *A Conservative Introduction to the Old Testament* (Grand Rapids MI: Zondervan Publishing House, 1943) 47, 60–63. Cartledge's main sin seems to have his willingness to explain the conclusions of the critics while failing to offer a forthright refutation or denunciation. See also his comments on the unity of Isaiah (125–30) and on the date and author ship of Daniel (220–24).

[94]John E. Richardson, review of *A Conservative Introduction to the Old Testament*, by Samuel A. Cartledge, *SPJ*, (July 1943): 6–7; and L. Nelson Bell, Editorial, "A Bent Sword," *SPJ*, July 1943, 5. Seemingly in an effort to confirm its analysis, the *Journal* reprinted reviews from other papers. In September 1943, 3–4, it ran Montgomery J. Shoger's positive review from the *Christian Century* of 2 June 1943. The editors reminded their readers of the liberal character of the *Century* and doubted that Cartledge could be considered conservative in light of such liberal approval. Northern conservative criticism included William Hendriksen's review from *The Banner*, 8 October 1943, reprinted *SPJ*, November 1943, 4; and Martin J. Wyngaarden's review in *Calvin Forum*, December 1943, reprinted *SPJ*, January 1944, 3–5.

[95]Copy of Resolution in R. E. Hough to Charles J. Woodbridge, 27 November 1945, typed copy in RCM Papers, Southern Presbyterian Church file.

from issuing a second edition with no changes in his position,[96] and this time one of the *Journal*'s Board of Directors, R. E. Hough, sent a protest to the seminary demanding Cartledge's resignation. Hough warned that retaining Cartledge on the faculty implicitly approved his book and "thus will begin a vicious circle wherein the seminary will forfeit the confidence and support of the conservative element in its constituency and will gradually but surely forced into the liberal camp."[97] Cartledge remained on the faculty, but denominational fundamentalists believed that his presence and others with similar views on the seminaries' faculties signified a retreat from the doctrinal standards in the denomination's Confession of Faith.[98]

While a similar fundamentalistic concern over doctrinal compromise was an important element in the *Journal*'s criticism of the Federal Council of Churches (FCC),[99] equally disturbing was the Council's social, economic, and political pronouncements. And though couching its criticisms of these statements in a traditional Southern Presbyterian analysis of the church's mission, the *Journal*'s contri-

---

[96]Samuel A. Cartledge, *A Conservative Introduction to the New Testament*, 2nd ed. (Athens: University of Georgia Press, 1944). Cartledge included a Preface (7–10) in which he answered some of the fundamentalist complaints and affirmed his belief in the Bible's inspiration in matters of faith and practice but not its inerrancy in all matters.

[97]Typed copy in RCM Papers, Southern Presbyterian Church file. Savannah's Independent Presbyterian Church, pastored by Charles Woodbridge, voted to discontinue support of the seminary because Cartledge's presence on the faculty. Robert C. McQuilkin to S. C. Byrd, 12 January 1946, in RCM Papers, Southern Presbyterian Church file.

[98]See the general comments on seminaries in Richardson Ayers, "A Challenge to Our Church," *SPJ*, 1 November 1946, 7–8; and John R. Richardson, "Proceedings of the 87th General Assembly of the Presbyterian Church in the United States," *SPJ*, 16 June 1947, 5–6. In *Presbyterians*, 3:493–97, Thompson offered a similar interpretation of the broadening of the church's doctrinal position in the 1940s through the teaching of liberals in the denomination's seminaries.

[99]The main complaint was the FCC was dominated by liberals. See comments in Daniel Iverson, "The Aims and Purposes of the Federal Council," *SPJ*, May 1942, 21–23; Robert L. Vining, "Is the Federal Council Evangelical?" *SPJ*, May 1945, 22–25; Vernon W. Patterson, "The Federal Council Speaks for the Churches," *SPJ*, 1 July 1946, 6–8; and L. Nelson Bell, Editorial, "Come Let Us Reason Together," *SPJ*, 15 May 1947, 4–6.

butors displayed a fundamentalist understanding of the church's primary purpose as a basis for attacking their denomination's membership in the Council. According to editorials and articles in the *Journal*, membership in the FCC meant that the organization spoke for Southern Presbyterians when it took positions on various issues facing America, positions few Southern Presbyterians supported.[100] For example, Robert Vining described the FCC as a "foe of capitalism" and, if not a friend of communism, sympathetic to its defense of the rights of workers.[101] Its pacifism in the early 1940s was out of step with America's battle to defend democracy.[102] Its support of racial integration showed the shallowness of its analysis of Southern racial problems and its ignorance of Southern race relations.[103] Furthermore, such efforts contradicted the traditional Southern Presbyterians' understanding the relationship of their church to the world. The FCC's activities misdirected the denomination's energy by representing a social gospel understanding the church's mission in society. For writers in the *Journal*, the church had first and foremost a spiritual mission to evangelize the world and nurture its members, not one influencing politics or reforming society. According to Tom Glasgow, in words most fundamentalists would heartily approve, "the *primary objectives* of the Church are *neither moral nor social uplift nor the improvement of individual or community ethics and economic standards....* The *primary objective* of the Church is *SALVATION!*"[104] Not surprisingly, the *Journal*'s editors called for

---

[100]This point is central to the criticisms in Patterson, "Federal Council Speaks," 6–8; and L. E. Faulkner, "The Voice of the Federal Council of Churches of Christ in America Speaks for Your Church and for You," *SPJ*, 15 October 1946, 7–8.

[101]Robert L. Vining, "The Federal Council: Foe of Capitalism," *SPJ*, August 1943, 5–7; and idem., "The Federal Council and Communism," *SPJ*, September 1943, 21–23.

[102]Iverson, "Aim and Purpose," 21–23; and Vernon W. Patterson, "The Principles and Objectives of the Federal Council," *SPJ*, October 1944, 15–18.

[103]L. Nelson Bell, Editorial, "Race Relations: Whither?" *SPJ*, March 1944, 4–5; Patterson, "Principles," 16; idem., "Federal Council," 7; and L. E. Faulkner, "The Federal Council of Churches of Christ in America," *SPJ*, 15 April 1947, 13.

[104]Tom Glasgow, "Lest We Forget," *SPJ*, October 1943, 10; cf., L. Nelson Bell, Editorial, "The Mission of the Church, *SPJ*, June 1945, 5–6; and D. S. George, "Characteristics of the Presbyterian Church in the United States," *SPJ*, 1 March 1948, 11–12. On the widespread belief in the church's spiritual mission among Southern

their denomination to withdraw from the FCC. In August 1945 editor H. B. Dendy reminded the General Assembly of its promise to submit the question of membership to the presbyteries.[105] In 1947 the Assembly instructed each presbytery to vote on the issue, and the result was a decisive victory for cooperation. Sixty-two presbyteries supported membership in the FCC, only twenty-four opposed, and one presbytery split on the issue.[106] The *Journal's* message about the dangers of membership had not been believed, but perhaps some of its criticisms of the FCC's social and political activities had been accepted. In 1950 the delegates to the General Assembly over-whelmingly affirmed the 1947 presbytery decision by voting 243 to 120 to keep their church a member of the FCC but then passed a resolution (214-114) disassociating Southern Presbyterians from its social and economic statements.[107]

While concern over liberalism in the seminaries and over membership in the FCC reveal the emergence of a fundamentalist sentiment among some Southern Presbyterians, the issue that transformed this sentiment and mobilized conservatives into an organized faction ready to do battle with liberals was reunion with Northern Presbyterians. The editors rarely published an issue of the *Journal* without attacking some aspect of the efforts at reunion. Writers in the *Journal* raised a variety of objections that became more specific over time as details of a plan for implementing reunion were negotiated.[108] For example, they argued that reunion would hurt the

Presbyterians, see Ernest Trice Thompson, *The Spirituality of Church: A Distinctive Doctrine of the Presbyterian Church in the United States* (Richmond VA: John Knox Press, 1961).

[105]H. B. Dendy, "Do not Trifle with the Truth," *SPJ*, August 1945, 2–3.

[106]N.a., Editorial, "The Presbyteries and the Council," *The Presbyterian Outlook*, 3 May 1948, 8. L. Nelson Bell call the decision "a disappointment" in "The General Assembly: One Laymen's Appraisal," *SPJ*, 15 June 1948, 4–7.

[107]John R. Richardson, "The Mid-Century General Assembly," *SPJ*, 1 July 1950, 10.

[108]Comprehensive articles explaining objections to reunion include W. Calvin Wells, "Church Union," *SPJ*, April 1944, 7–18; Melton Clark, "Church Union," *SPJ*, June 1944, 8–10; R. B. Woodworth, "The 1943 Plan of Reunion: Comments and Criticism," *SPJ*, June 1945, 24–25; Daniel Iverson, "Unionitis," *SPJ*, 1 March 1946, 12–15; R. Wilbur Cousar, "Reasons Why It is Unwise to Unite with the Northern

growth and vitality of the Southern church. One series of articles showed that the PCUS was growing faster and gave more money per capita than the Northern denomination. Reunion would stall this growth.[109] Because Northerners would have a numerical superiority, they warned that Southern influence on policies and direction of the new denomination would be negligible. Southerners would lose control of their property at both the denominational and congregational levels.[110] The most important objection, though, was the character of the Northern church. Here, the *Journal's* contributors showed a fundamentalist consciousness and their dependence on a fundamentalist analysis of the Northern Presbyterian church. In brief, the problem was that the Northern denomination was an "inclusive" church that tolerated a variety of theological perspectives, including liberalism, and did not maintain strict theological standards.[111]

Presbyterian Church," *SPJ*, 15 January 1948, 8–9. Doctrinal laxity in the Northern church was common in all. The loss of Southern control over church property and agencies was the next most prominent objection. Woodworth, and to a lesser extent Clark and Cousar, suggested that government of the new denomination would be less democratic while Well, Clark, and Woodworth believed the plan devalued the role of elders in the spiritual life of a congregation. Iverson and Cousar bluntly warned that reunion would cause schism. Cf., Thompson's analysis in *Presbyterians*, 3:570–71.

[109]Kenneth S. Keyes, "Shall We Merge with the Northern Church?" *SPJ*, 1 January 1947, 30; 15 January 1947, 13; 15 February 1947, 15; 1 March 1947, 9; 1 April 1947, 21; 15 April 1947, 9; cf., J. E. Flow, "How Will Union with the Northern Presbyterian Church Affect Our Mission Work?" *SPJ*, 1 February 1947, 9–10.

[110]Randolph B. Lee, "Comments on the Proposed Plan of Re-union between the Presbyterian Church in the USA and the Presbyterian Church in the US," *SPJ*, 2 December 1946, 6–7; and 1 January 1947, 11–12. See also, Daniel J. Currie, "Was It Right?" *SPJ*, 15 September 1945, 7–8; B. W. Crouch, "The Proposed Plan of Union," *SPJ*, September 1944, 9; C. Ellis Ott, "Why Precipitate More Lawsuits?" *SPJ*, 1 November 1945, 3–5; and William Childs Robinson, "Presbyterian Doctrine of Church Property," *SPJ*, 1 June 1950, 3–4.

[111]The editors showed their debt to Northern fundamentalists by reprinting in their first issue an article describing the theological character of the Northern church. See Edwin Paulson, "The Triumph of Inclusivism," *Christianity Today*, Fall 1941, reprinted in *SPJ*, May 1942, 7–10; cf., D. J. Woods, "An Inspection of the Plan of Union Presented by the Joint Committees of USA and US Presbyterian Churches," *SPJ*, July 1945, 10–11. In "Reunion with the Presbyterian Church, USA: Con," *The Presbyterian Outlook*, 26 February 1945, 5–6, Charles W. McNutt cited a survey of Northern Presbyterian ministers that revealed that 66 percent believe that inspiration

Reunion would thus entail weakening the doctrinal position of the PCUS. Signs of doctrinal laxity in the Northern church included the election of Henry Sloan Coffin, a noted liberal, as its moderator, its Sunday school literature that suggested that the Bible was historically inaccurate, and its failure to discipline ministers who denied fundamental doctrines like the deity of Christ while attacking orthodox leaders like J. Gresham Machen.[112] Another sign was the Northern church's misplaced emphasis on the social gospel that minimized the church's spiritual mission.[113] But nearly every discussion of theological compromise in the Northern church mentioned the 1924 Auburn Affirmation. Called the "root of Presbyterian apostasy"[114] and the origin of the Northern church's inclusivism,[115] it remained an "obstacle" to reunion unless the Northern General Assembly passed a resolution repudiating it and reaffirmed as "essential to faith" the infallibility of the Bible, the virgin birth, the resurrection, the miracles, and substitutionary atonement.[116]

---

made the Bible different form other literature, 69 percent believe in the virgin birth, 50 percent in the resurrection of the body, and 47 percent in a day of judgement.

[112]Robert L. Vining, "Church Union," *SPJ*, February 1943, 18–20; H. B. Dendy, Editorial, "The Moderator of the USA Church," *SPJ*, July 1943, 4; Gordon H. Clark, "The Auburn Heresy," *SPJ*, 15 July 1946, 7–9; Oswald T. Allis, "The New Presbyterian USA Curriculum for Sunday Schools," *Sunday School Times*, 26 June 1948, reprinted in *SPJ*, 15 November 1948, 6–9; and Charles Alexander, "Dr. Anderson Please Explain," *SPJ*, 18 July 1951, 5–8.

[113]Tom Glasgow, "The USA Church and the Labor Unions," *SPJ*, October 1944, 5–6; and J. E. Cousar, "'Eye to Eye in Church,'" *SPJ*, 15 April 1948, 8–10. In "Some Things to Think About as We Face Reunion with the USA Church," *SPJ*, 1 July 1947, 14–15, J. J. Hill showed that some issues never die. He reminded the readers that the Northern denomination had not repudiated the Springs Resolutions of 1861 that demanded loyalty to the federal government as a condition of membership. This meddling in political affairs, according to Hill, provoked the split that established the Southern church on the principle of the spirituality of the church's mission.

[114]Clark, "Auburn Heresy," 7.

[115]Daniel S. Gage, "The Auburn Affirmation," *SPJ*, August 1942, 16–19; cf., L. Nelson Bell, Editorial, "An Open Letter," *SPJ*, 27 June 1951, 3–5.

[116]In 1910 conservative Presbyterians in the North won approval in the General Assembly for certain doctrines being cardinal principles of faith in the Presbyterian church. Reaffirmed in 1916 and 1923, this declaration stated that the Bible's

Underlying this characteristically fundamentalist concern for doctrine was a series of objections that reflected these Southerners' desire to maintain their church as a central part of their region's identity. Consider the issue of liberalism in the Southern Presbyterian schools. From the discussions of the necessity to reject reunion because of the Northern church's liberalism and the complaints concerning liberal professors in Southern seminaries, a perceptive reader might conclude that Southern Presbyterian schools were being run by a group of theological scalawags whose teachings undermined the distinctive character of the Southern church. For example, one layman blamed the turmoil over reunion on these seminary professors. Writing to the Moderator of the General Assembly after the plan had been defeated, he claimed, "Those in our ranks...[who] started this idea were *not of us*, they came in to us in the Trojan horse. They had the idea instilled in them in our USA dominated Seminaries. Why can't these preachers go North, if they dislike the South so much and let the US [Church] alone. You would see God prosper the Southern Church as never before."[117]

One theme frequently mentioned was that reunion would mean the loss of the Southern church's distinctive mission and the disappearance of the Southern church altogether. In an editorial, R. Wilbur Cousar feared the result of reunion would be that "our Southern Church would not really be merged, but absorbed, since it is

---

inerrancy, the Virgin Birth, the propitiatory sacrifice of Christ on the cross, the resurrection of Jesus, and his ability to work miracles were "essential doctrine[s] of the Word of God and our Standards." Presbyterian Church in the United States of America, *Minutes of the General Assembly*, 1910, 272–73. In a sense, Southern Presbyterians were calling on their Northern brethren to affirm a more conservative theology. The resolution was the suggestion of Richardson Ayers, "The Real Issue in Union," *SPJ*, 15 March 1946, 8–9. In "In—But—Not of," *SPJ*, January 1943, 3, L. Nelson Bell described virtually the same list of doctrines as "essential." Others criticizing the Affirmation include D. B. Gregory, "Remaining Obstacles to Union," *SPJ*, 1 June 1946, 6–7; L. Nelson Bell, Editorial, "Why Is It?" *SPJ*, April 1943, 5–6; and Mark K. Poole, "Union or Old Time Religion, *SPJ*, 1 December 1945, 9–10.

[117]W. P. Dickson to Wade H. Boggs, 27 April 1955 (Wade H. Boggs Papers, Extremists File, Department of History, Presbyterian Church in the United States of America, Montreat NC) (hereinafter cited as Boggs Papers).

less than one third the size of the Northern body."[118] Randolph E. Lee, an elder, charged that a "vote for this Plan of Union means a vote for the destruction of our Southern Presbyterian Church."[119] Cousar also appealed to pride in the Southern church's work. "We do not like comparison," wrote Cousar, "but the Southern Presbyterian Church is already one of the leading churches in the world in Stewardship, Women's Work, Home Missions and in other phases. We see no reason for abandoning these programs that have proven themselves so highly efficient and useful in the Master's service."[120] If Cousar was embarrassed by comparisons, Kenneth S. Keyes, a South Florida real estate developer, positively gloried in this appeal to regional pride. He toured the South with a series of charts and graphs showing that the PCUS was growing faster and gave more money per capita than the Northern denomination. Thus, according to Keyes, reunion should be rejected because it would stop this growth.[121] Finally, reunion not only threatened the Southern church's theological traditions but also its broader mission as a voice of evangelical Protestantism crying in the Babel of theological liberalism. Randolph Lee believed that the Southern Presbyterian "testimony for the Lord Jesus Christ would never be heard in the concerted din of Modernism and the Social Gospel which is so loudly preached by those two Northern churches."[122]

But *Journal* contributors suggested that something more sinister existed in the drive for reunion. They argued that the structure of the new denomination would give Northerners control over its policies

---

[118]R. Wilbur Cousar, "Beamed at Our Northern Brethren," *SPJ*, 4 March 1953, 4.

[119]Randolph E. Lee, "Analysis of the Concurrent Declarations," *SPJ*, 27 May 1953, 8.

[120]Cousar, "Beamed," 4.

[121]Some of this material is reproduced in Kenneth S. Keyes, "Shall We Merge with the Northern Church?" *SPJ*, 1 January 1947, 30; 15 January 1947, 13; 15 February 1947, 15; 1 March 1947, 9; 1 April 1947, 21; 15 April 1947, 9; cf., J. E. Flow, "How Will Union with the Northern Presbyterian Church Affect Our Mission Work?" *SPJ*, 1 February 1947, 9–10. According to Robert McFerran Crowe, President of Belhaven College, Keyes's efforts were one of the more effective means of mobilizing opposition to reunion. See Robert McFerran Crowe to Kenneth S. Keyes, 5 March 1955 (Robert McFerran Crowe Papers, History Department, Presbyterian Church in the United States of America, Montreat NC) (hereinafter cited as Crowe Papers).

[122]Lee, "Analysis," 8.

and property. For example, articles and editorials pointed out the actual consolidation of church institutions would be left up to a committee in which Southern representatives had only one-third of the votes. Thus the fate of Southern seminaries, mission boards, publishing houses, and the rest would be determined by Northerners. Some comments almost sounded as though the authors believed reunion would unleash predatory theological carpetbaggers to pillage the Southern church's institutions. William Child Robinson pointed out that:

> The adoption of the Plan of Union means that our home missions will be directed from New York, not conducted by each local Presbytery. It means that our world missions will be directed also from New York by consultation with other New York denominational boards but with little left to the discretion of the missions that are on the foreign field. It means that our educational institutions will be supported by gifts to a National Board of Education rather than by local interested constituencies. Whether all of these institutions will survive such a program only time can tell.[123]

Moreover, the reorganization of synods and presbyteries would decrease Southern representation in the new General Assembly. Thus it could, if it wanted, pass a new Confession of Faith altering the Southern church's stand to a Reformed interpretation of church doctrine. Southerners could do nothing to stop such an action.[124]

But the most emotional issue was church property, particularly control of congregational buildings and land. *Journal* contributors suggested that the Plan of Union prevented local congregations from selling property without approval of the presbytery. Significantly, they argued that such a policy imposed a Northern practice on Southerners. Furthermore, the purpose of this provision, according to Randolph E.

---

[123]William Childs Robinson, "The Plan of Union Lacks Those Tokens Which Have Evidenced God's Presence with and Favor upon Our Church," *SPJ*, 7 October 1953, 9.

[124]Lee, "Analysis," 4.

Lee, was to "secure denominational control of the physical property of an individual church, in order to make it easier to whip the church in line." [125] For proof of such allegations and as a warning of what might befall the PCUS, several authors pointed to the fate of another Southern denomination, the Cumberland Presbyterian Church, when it merged with the USA church in 1905. They alleged that the Northern denomination closed Cumberland churches rather than allow congregations who did not want union to continue using the property. [126] According J. E. Flow, "This so-called union was a *wreck*" and represented "the latest model of union with the USA Church." [127]

One objection to reunion needs separate consideration, and it perhaps most clearly reveals the *Journal's* defense of Southern traditions. Rarely mentioned, and in some ways significant for the reticence, the disturbing prospect of uniting with a racially integrated denomination hovered in the background of these other issues. Southern Presbyterians maintained a separate synod embracing the entire South with four presbyteries for its black members, [128] and the negotiations on reunion considered eliminating this synod,

---

[125] Ibid., 7. See also Henry E. Davis, "The Ownership of Local Church Property," *SPJ*, 29 July 1953, 4–8; William Childs Robinson, Editorial: "Denominational Ownership of Local Presbyteries—But Doctrinal Soundness Measured Exclusively by Presbyteries," *SPJ*, 17 February 1954, 3–4; and W. C. Tenney, "The Plan of Union," *SPJ*, 3 March 1954, 7–8.

[126] Tenney, "Plan," 7–8. See also L. Nelson Bell, Editorial, "The Dilemma," *SPJ*, 12 August 1953, 3; N.a., Editorial: "Who Shall Govern the Church? A Majority or the Lord Jesus Christ?" *SPJ*, 28 October 1953, 3; L. Nelson Bell, Editorial: "On Being a 'Good Presbyterian,'" *SPJ*, 28 April 1954; and Thomas H. Campbell, "Studies in Cumberland Presbyterian History" (no bibliographic information provided), reprinted in "The Cumberland-U. S. A. Presbyterian Dis-Union," *SPJ*, 19 May 1954, 5.

[127] J. E. Flow, Editorial: "'Traditional Presbyterian Church Policy,'" *SPJ*, 19 August 1953, 4.

[128] In 1948 the synod of Snedecor Memorial had forty-seven churches with only 2,410 members, with slightly more than one-third (958) in the presbytery of North and South Carolina. Southern Presbyterians maintained the principle of racial separation by segregating Indians in Oklahoma and Mexican-Americans in Texas into their own presbyteries. The Indian Presbytery had thirteen churches with 534 members while the Texas-Mexican had twenty-nine churches with 2,798 members. PCUS, *Minutes of the General Assembly*, 1948, 336.

incorporating its churches into white presbyteries, and including black Northern Presbyterian churches in Southern presbyteries along the border between the two regions. Only one article addressed this suggestion, condemning it because, according to the author, the Bible required racial segregation, and because the consequence of allowing black churches in white presbyteries eventually would mean allowing African-Americans membership in white churches.[129] Though no other contributor quite so directly rejected reunion because it might lead to racial integration, the *Journal* consistently carried articles commenting on Southern race relations.[130] It reassured readers that segregation was scriptural.[131] It attacked the FCC for supporting a permanent Fair Employment Practices Committee and the elimination of poll taxes, for declaring segregation contrary to the gospel, and for promoting

---

[129]William Childs Robinson, "Are the USA Liberals to Determine the Terms of Union?" *SPJ*, 15 March 1946, 5–6.

[130]It is worth noting explicitly that these articles and editorials commenting on race began in mid-1945, at the height of the changes being wrought by World War II in the region and in race relations. Thus they may also be read more broadly as part of conservative Southern reaction to these developments. Some liberal Southern Presbyterians also were troubled by developments in post-war race relations. In "The Real Issues, Part II," 5, D. Maurice Allan, commented, "In the deep South the feeling is intense on this issue. The conviction has been growing that the Negro is been encouraged to aspirations and demands that *we* [emphasis added] are not yet ready to grant. Many feel that the liberals in our church are hardly less guilty than Mrs. Roosevelt and the protagonists of the FEPC in fomenting Negro ambition and rushing this impressionable race headlong towards total equality.... Many others who feel that we have not yet rendered Christian justice to the Negro are nevertheless honest in thinking that in this realm so full of hidden explosives we must hasten slowly."

[131]Primarily on the basis of Acts 17:26 that says that God has set "the bounds of habitation for the nations." Also mentioned was Noah's curse on Canaan to explain the inferior status of blacks and God's commands to the Jews to maintain their racial separation. B. W. Crouch, "Dr. Palmer on Racial Barriers," *SPJ*, 2 December 1946, 5–6; W. A. Plecker, "'Interracial Brotherhood Movement,' Is It Scriptural?" *SPJ*, 1 January 1947, 9–10; J. David Simpson, "Non-Segregation Means Eventual Inter-Marriage," *SPJ*, 15 March 1948, 6–7; William H. Frazer, "The Social Separation of the Races," *SPJ*, 15 July 1950, 6–7; and J. E. Flow, Editorial, "Is Segregation Unchristian?" *SPJ*, 29 August 1951, 4–5.

interracial brotherhood.[132] It criticized their denomination for permitting black and white young people to mix at summer camps and apocalyptically warned that this practice might lead to intermarriage and "racial amalgamation."[133] Along with acknowledging that the South had racial problems, it offered several recommendations for solving them. Most prominent among them were conversion, Christian charity, and a kinder, gentler system of Jim Crow that maintained the separation of the races while ending lynching and providing education and jobs for blacks.[134] On one other point the *Journal*'s contributors were clear: the South should not have solutions for its racial problems imposed upon it by Northern outsiders.[135] Race was not exploited as a reason for opposing reunion. Nevertheless, this line of commentary kept the issue before the *Journal*'s subscribers, and when read in conjunction with articles on the liberalism of the Northern denomination and about the Northern dominated FCC, it became, perhaps only subliminally, part of the mosaic of factors that

---

[132]William Childs Robinson, "Christ Our Peace in Race Relations," *SPJ*, July 1945, 7–8; J. E. Flow, "The Federal Council and 'Race Relations,'" *SPJ*, 15 May 1946, 9–10; and Plecker, "'Interracial Brotherhood Movement,'" 9–10.

[133]William Childs Robinson, Editorial, "Distinguishing Things that Differ," *SPJ*, 15 January 1947, 3–4; and L. Nelson Bell, "Race Relations: Whither?" *SPJ*, 15 November 1947, 4–5. In 1950 Bell served on a committee to establish policies for meetings at Montreat, the Presbyterian campground in the North Carolina mountains. It recommended the integration of all adult meetings, including the General Assembly, but the continuation of segregated youth meetings. As an aside in this editorial, Bell suggested establishing the black synod as a separate Presbyterian denomination. L. Nelson Bell, Editorial, "Race Relations and Montreat," *SPJ*, 15 June 1950, 2–3.

[134]William C. Robinson, Editorial, "Georgia and the Slain Negroes," *SPJ*, 15 August 1946, 2–3; L. Nelson Bell, Editorial, "Racial Tension, Let Us Decrease—Not Increase Them!" *SPJ*, 15 February 1947, 2–3; idem., Editorial, "Some Little Things Which Help," *SPJ*, 2 June 1947, 3–4; idem., Editorial, "Murder," *SPJ*, 16 June 1947, 2; Simpson, "Non-Segregation," 6; and W. G. Foster, Young People's Department, "The White Faction," *SPJ*, 1 July 1948, 14–15.

[135]Crouch, "Dr. Palmer," 6; Bell, "Murder," 2; and Simpson, "Non-Segregation," 6. In "Real Issues," 5–6, Allan noted that this kind of "holier-than-thou meddling in Southern affairs by Northern and Western politicians" had sparked a "rebirth of Southern sectionalism" among conservative opponents to reunion.

demanded resistance to reunion and the continuation of a separate Southern Presbyterian denomination.

Two actions taken by the General Assembly in the early 1950s kept the issue of race relations within the denomination on the minds of Southern Presbyterians and heightened concerns over how reunion would affect the PCUS's racial policies. First, the General Assembly took a step toward integration by approving a plan to consolidate the African-American presbyteries into three, to eliminate the separate synod, and to incorporate the presbyteries into existing white synods. The presbyteries ratified the plan.[136] Then in 1954 the same General Assembly that approved the Plan for Union also endorsed a report from the General Assembly's Council of Christian Relations that urged the desegregation of Southern Presbyterian churches and recommended that local churches receive people into membership "on the Scriptural basis of faith in the Lord Jesus Christ without reference to race."[137] The Council made these recommendations out of the conviction that "enforced segregation of the races is discrimination which is out of harmony with Christian theology and ethics and that the Church, in its relationship to cultural patterns, should lead rather than follow."[138] Reaction to the Assembly's actions took a variety of forms. For example, the session of the First Presbyterian Church in Jackson, Mississippi, adopted a resolution that it would not follow the report's advice but would "maintain its traditional policy and practice of distinct separation of the races."[139] The Association for the Preservation and Continuation of the Southern Presbyterian Church (APCSPC), an antiunion organization, called for "patience" and noted that "changes in the social pattern are of slow growth if they are

---

[136]David M. Reimers, "The Race Problem and Presbyterian Union," *Church History* 31 (June 1962): 208–209. During these years the Oklahoma Synod reorganized and eliminated the separate Indian presbytery, and at the end of 1954, the Mexican-American presbytery was dissolved with its churches incorporated in Anglo presbyteries.

[137]PCUS, *Minutes of the General Assembly*, 1954, 194; the entire report can be found on 187–97.

[138]Ibid., 193.

[139]N.a., "First Church of Jackson, Miss., Declares Itself on Segregation," *SPJ*, 7 July 1954, 8.

to endure, and that happy and lasting benefits are not produced by either ecclesiastical resolution or civil edict."[140] Contributors to the *Journal* reaffirmed their beliefs that segregation of the races was scriptural and natural, that separation benefited African-Americans, that desegregation would lead to intermarriage and racial amalgamation, and that this "agitation" disturbed the peaceful pattern of Southern race relations.[141] For L. Nelson Bell the key to good race relations was to apply the Golden Rule and to see each person regardless of race as "a person for whom Christ died and who is loved by Him."[142] This belief led Bell to modify slightly his views on segregation. He argued that insofar as Jim Crow laws denied black citizens their rights as Americans they should be struck down. But he continued to believe that mandated integration "un-Christian, unrealistic, and utterly foolish" because it denied a person the "the inherent right...to chose his or her own intimate friends."[143] J. S. Robinson perhaps best summarized the *Journal*'s post-*Brown* view of race relations: "Certainly we should be kind and gracious to all races of people, seeking to give them the Gospel that they might be saved. But evidently the Lord never intended a union of the races in domestic life. 'Physical separation and spiritual union' is the best formula for race relations."[144]

But this commentary was made while the presbyteries debated the Plan for Union. Though the antiunion forces rarely mentioned race as a reason for rejecting reunion, the connection was nonetheless apparent in a variety of ways.[145] For example, when it voted to reject

[140]N.a., "Resolutions Adopted," *SPJ*, 1 September 1954, 4–5.

[141]L. Nelson Bell, "Montreat and Desegregation," *SPJ*, 15 September 1954, 3; "Segregation," *SPJ*, 7 July 1954, 7; William Childs Robinson, "Pluralism," *SPJ*, 7 July 1954, 6–7; "They Don't Want It," *SPJ*, 7 July 1954, 8; and J. S. Robinson, "'Determining the Bounds of Their Habitation,'" *SPJ*, 6 October 1954.

[142]L. Nelson Bell, "Christian Race Relations Must Be Natural, Not Forced," *SPJ*, 17 August 1955, 5.

[143]Ibid., 4. Bell offered only slim concessions that these ideas might create circumstances where African-Americans might join white churches.

[144]Robinson, "Determining the Bounds," 4.

[145]Sanford M. Dornbusch and Roger D. Irle, "The Failure of Presbyterian Union," *American Journal of Sociology* 64 (January 1959): 353; Reimers, "The Race Problem,"

the plan, the Tuscaloosa Presbytery also approved a resolution rejecting the General Assembly's 1954 action "on race relations as being ill-advised and thus in error."[146] F. A. Mathes, pastor of Birmingham's South Highland Church, told his congregation that he supported the principle of reunion but opposed this plan citing, among other reasons, its centralization of church government, its limitations on congregational control of church property, and its failure to address "social questions, and in particular the racial problem."[147] The APCSPC's comments on maintaining the racial status quo came at the conclusion of a series of resolutions opposing reunion adopted at its August 1954 meeting.[148] The *Journal* reminded its readers of both the social activism of the Northern church and its views on race relations by pointing out that the PCUSA's Stated Clerk testified before a congressional committee in favor of the FEPC.[149] The most extreme comment from a contributor to the *Journal* came from the pen of J. E. Flow, a retired minister in North Carolina. Flow mentioned several reasons why the PCUS had a right to maintain a separate existence but his final reason was that "Our church stands for the purity and integrity of the white man of North America upon whose shoulders are laid the burdens of the world. He cannot fulfill his destiny nor meet the fearful responsibilities except by remaining white as God made him and intended him to be."[150] Comments such as these were quite rare, but they do indicate that for some Southern Presbyterians reunion would mean not only the loss of a distinctive Southern institution but also represented a threat to the South's racial arrangements.

212–13; and Thompson, *Presbyterians*, 3:570–571 all note the thin commentary on race in antiunion propaganda.

[146]Tuscaloosa Presbytery, *Minutes*, 20 July 1954, 465.

[147]F. A. Mathes, "Church Union," in church bulletin, South Highland Presbyterian Church, 12 September 1954, in Crowe Papers.

[148]N.a., "Resolutions Adopted," 3–5; see also, Henry B. Dendy, "meeting of the Association for the Preservation and Continuation of the Southern Presbyterian Church, Weaverville, N. C., August 18, 1954," *SPJ*, 1 September 1954, 2–3.

[149]N.a., "Disturbing," *SPJ*, 10 March 1954, 1.

[150]J. E. Flow, "Positive or Negative?" *SPJ*, 29 September 1954, 9.

The effort to stop reunion was more than a war of words; it also involved creating organizations that could be effective in the political battles over reunion within the denomination. The first and most important of these was the Continuing Church Committee. John R. Richardson explained that its name was based on the advice Jesus gave to his followers in John 8:31: "If you continue in my word, then you are my disciples indeed." In other words, the purpose of the Committee was to continue the tradition of the Southern Presbyterian church's loyalty to God's Word. According to Richardson, reunion would mean absorption into a denomination that was unfaithful to the Bible.[151] The primary functions of the Committee were to disseminate information on why reunion would be a mistake and to mobilize support for its position on both the presbyterial and denominational level where the voting on reunion would occur.[152] The *Journal* played a critical role as the propaganda arm of the Committee while its editors and supporters supplied the core of its leadership. Organized in 1945 at a summer meeting *Journal* supporters, the Committee hardly varied from the *Journal's* analysis of the problems with reunion.[153] It differed in that laymen held the leadership positions

---

[151]John R. Richardson, "How the Continuing Committee Got Its Name," *SPJ*, 15 January 1948, 2–3.

[152]The Committee was not the only group with a conservative agenda to form. In 1948 supporters of the *Journal* created the "Southern Presbyterian Evangelical Fellowship" for the purpose of holding the denomination's schools to teaching a conservative theology that included the infallibility of the Bible, the deity of Christ, and the Westminster Confession of Faith as a "faithful systemization" of Bible doctrine. H. B. Dendy, "Southern Presbyterian Evangelical Fellowship," *SPJ*, 1 November 1948, 2. As the *Journal* mentioned it on only two other occasions, it is probable that the Fellowship members concentrated their energies on reunion and let their organization collapse. In the early 1950s another group, based in Memphis, Tennessee, organized "The Association for the Preservation of the Southern Presbyterian Church" with the similar goal of blocking reunion. In 1952 it joined forces with the Committee to form "The Association for the Preservation and Continuation of the Southern Presbyterian Church," but the Board of Directors of the *Journal* formed the overall supervisory committee of the new organization. N.a., "Meeting of the Association for the Preservation and Continuation of the Southern Presbyterian Church," *SPJ*, 3 September 1952, 1.

[153]See for example n.a., "Meeting at Montreat: Report of Committee on Findings," *SPJ*, 1 September 1945, 2; n.a., "Continuing Church Committee Holds Meeting in

while pastors dominated the *Journal*'s editors, Board of Directors, and Advisory Committee. Some overlap existed. The clergy that served on the Committee's executive committee usually had a connection with the *Journal*, but the Committee's officers were elders from Presbyterian churches. The only exception was H. B. Dendy who was the secretary for the Committee.[154]

The Committee focused its activities in support of L. Nelson Bell's efforts to have the General Assembly direct the Committee on Cooperation and Union (COCU) to suspend negotiations on reunion. In 1948 the Assembly approved Bell's motion for a five-year review of the plans for union during which time no vote would be taken on reunion. Believing he had succeeded in stopping reunion, Bell announced to the Assembly that the Continuing Church Committee would disband.[155] Bell's motion, though, had been amended by liberals to have the Assembly also direct COCU to explore "avenues of acquaintance and cooperation."[156] In the spring of 1949 COCU's report to the Assembly recommended a variety of activities including greater combination of efforts in home and foreign missions, joint meetings of overlapping or contiguous synods and presbyteries, pastors exchanging pulpits for a Sunday with one from the other denomination, and the federation of Northern and Southern churches in small communities.[157] To Bell these suggestions violated the spirit of

---

Atlanta," *SPJ*, 15 December 1945, 5–7; and H. B. Dendy, "The Findings of the Annual Meeting of the Continuing Church Committee," *SPJ*, 1 September 1947, 3–4.

[154]See the lists of leaders for the Committee in n.a., Editorial, "Meeting of the Southern Presbyterian Journal Supporters and the Continuing Church Committee," *SPJ*, 2 September 1946, 2; and H. B. Dendy, "Meeting of the Southern Presbyterian Journal Supporters and the Continuing Church Committee," *SPJ*, 1 September 1947, 2. For the *Journal*, see the publication data list on *SPJ*, May 1944, 2.

[155]L. Nelson Bell, Editorial, "The Continuing Church Committee," *SPJ*, 15 June 1948, 3.

[156]N.a., Editorial, "On Presbyterian Reunion," *The Presbyterian Outlook*, 21 June 1948, 8. The liberal editors of the *Outlook* welcomed this moratorium with "unrestrained enthusiasm" because it would allow time for the flaws to be worked out of the plans for union.

[157]Committee on Cooperation and Union, "Report to the General Assembly, May 1949," reprinted in *SPJ*, 1 March 1949, 3–4.

his motion, and to others they represented steps toward union.[158] Bell
tried to have the 1949 Assembly define the meaning of the motion
more in line with his restrictive purpose, to kill all reunion activity
and discussion for five years. The effort failed, and the Continuing
Church Committee resumed its activity, turning its energy from
parliamentary maneuvers in the General Assembly to defeating
reunion at the grassroots.[159] Concentrating its appeals to the laity, in
particular the ruling elders, the Committee held public meetings in
sympathetic churches and used the *Journal* to spread its message.[160] The
paper and Committee still based their opposition on the theological
character of the Northern Presbyterian church, but before the
effectiveness of this strategy could be tested an unforeseen event
intervened. In the same month that the General Assembly over-
whelmingly approved a plan for reunion and sent it to the presbyteries
for their evaluation, the Supreme Court handed down its landmark
decision in *Brown v. Board of Education* undermining the legal basis
of Jim Crow.[161] During the following year the presbyteries voted 43-42
against accepting the reunion plan.[162]

In the spring of 1955 Wade H. Boggs, the Moderator of the PCUS,
appeared before the General Assembly of the Northern denomination
and apologized for the vote, suggesting that had the vote been left to the

---

[158]L. Nelson Bell, Editorial, "Unthinkable," *SPJ*, 1 March 1949, 2–3; and William
Childs Robinson, Editorial, "Reconciliation Then Thy Gifts," *SPJ*, 2 May 1949, 2.

[159]Having some indication of what COCU might recommend as early as July 1948,
Bell warned that his Committee would resume lobbying in opposition to union. L.
Nelson Bell, Editorial, "Restrictive—Not Directive," *SPJ*, 15 July 1948, 2. See also
idem., Editorial, "Breakers Ahead," *SPJ*, 15 June 1949, 2–3; John R. Richardson, "The
89th General Assembly of the Presbyterian Church in the United States," *SPJ*, 15 June
1949, 18; and n.a., "Continuing Church Committee Meets in Atlanta," *SPJ*, 15 July
1949, 12a–12d.

[160]For an account of one gathering, see n.a., "Enthusiastic Meeting at
Birmingham," *SPJ*, 15 November 1949, 3. That elders might be receptive to the
Committee's message may be seen in a letter that a group of Mississippi elders sent to
COCU which was sharply critical of its suggestions. N.a., "Mississippi Elders Write to
Committee on Cooperation and Union," *SPJ*, 15 March 1949, 21.

[161]In *Presbyterians*, 3:574, Thompson recorded the General Assembly vote as
283–169 in favor of the plan.

[162]PCUS, *Minutes of the General Assembly*, 1955.

ministers the outcome would have been different. Disturbed by these remarks, W. A. Burgess, a seventy-seven-year-old elder from St. Albans, West Virginia, rebuked Boggs that his remarks were out of place given the results. Burgess nevertheless concluded his letter with "sincere regards from an old Ruling Elder to a younger Teaching Elder."[163] While the rejection of reunion did not result simply from generational differences and a split between the lay leaders and clergy, Burgess's remarks do point to factors generally overlooked in explanations of why the plan for union failed in the Southern Presbyterian church. Most scholarly observers point to Southern racism as a crucial element. Among the first to suggest a connection between the vote and Southern reaction to *Brown* were Sanford Dornbusch and Roger Irle, sociologists working under the auspices of the Laboratory of Social Relations at Harvard University. They discovered that the presbyteries rejecting the plan tended to have a higher percentage of African-Americans in their populations and to be less urban. They concluded that the specter for forced desegregation resulted in the defeat of reunion.[164] David M. Reimers provided another perspective. After a careful survey of the racial policies of Northern and Southern Presbyterians and those policies' role in previous negotiations for reunion, he concluded that the 1955 plan was doomed but that race "helped account for the decisive nature of the defeat."[165] The most comprehensive discussion of reunion is in the third volume of Ernest Trice Thompson's *Presbyterians of the South*. Thompson described the mechanics of negotiating a merger, the politics of moving the proposal through the denomination's courts, and the various arguments for and against both the principle of union and the specific plan to implement it. In telling this story Thompson created the impression that reunion would be approved, and thus to explain the plan's defeat, he resorted to race as the issue that was "decisive."[166] Using racism, though, as the central component of their

---

[163]W. A. Burgess to Wade H. Boggs, 20 June 1955, in Boggs Papers.

[164]Dornbusch and Irle, "Failure," 353–54.

[165]Reimers, "The Race Problem," 213.

[166]Thompson, *Presbyterians*, 3:558–75; quote on 574. Thompson cited Dornbusch and Irle's study to support his conclusion about the role of race in the reunion vote.

analysis forced these authors to ignore or at best minimize internal factors such as those suggested in the exchange between Boggs and Burgess. A close reading of the *Southern Presbyterian Journal* and a careful evaluation of the demographics of the vote within the presbyteries suggests that race was an important factor in defeating the plan, but that issue needs to be placed in the broader context of concern over the loss of regional identity. The most significant internal ingredient was the rise of a fundamentalist faction that mobilized a coalition of laymen and older clergy to defeat the plan.[167]

Whether the vote derived from the reaction to broader social changes or represented a victory for their strategy and a vindication of their position, denominational fundamentalists approved the outcome of this battle, but the war was not over. The issues of theological liberalism and reunion continued to be the center of controversy among Southern Presbyterians, and the organizations and institutions created in the 1940s by the denominational fundamentalists continued to play major roles. By the early 1970s, though, the ability of denominational fundamentalists to influence the denomination had diminished to the point that some leaders believed that the liberalization of the denomination could not be reversed and that the only means of "continuing" the traditions and theology of the Southern Presbyterian church was to separate from it and start a new denomination. During these same years that denominational fundamentalists mobilized among Southern Presbyterians, similar groups began emerging in the Southern Baptist Convention. Their story has several parallels with the Presbyterian tale but differs in specific issues and has a much different outcome: Southern Baptist fundamentalists won.

---

[167]In *Religion and Race: Southern Presbyterians, 1946 to 1983* (Tuscaloosa: University of Alabama Press, 1994), Joel L. Alvis places the role of racism reunion vote in the context of the PCUSs ongoing effort to reform its racial policies.

THE PRESBYTERIANS 183

A NOTE ON METHOD

In 1955, the Presbyterian Church in the United States had 780,853 members and 3,197 ministers. They were organized into 3,806 churches, eighty-six presbyteries, and sixteen synods.

The statistical analysis of the presbytery vote on reunion was developed in the following manner. I inspected the meeting minutes of all the presbyteries when the vote was cast. The minutes recorded the total number of votes for and against the Plan of Union, but only three noted how each member voted (Piedmont in Northwestern South Carolina, North Mississippi in Northwestern Mississippi, and Birmingham). In one presbytery (Concord in Central Western North Carolina) the minutes recorded the names of whose who voted against a resolution to disband the Committee on Cooperation and Union. I interpreted their vote as favoring the principle of reunion though some may have voted against the 1954 plan.

I calculated the percentage of antiunion vote for each presbytery and used for more detailed analysis the five presbyteries where antiunion sentiment was the weakest (Upper Missouri in the Kansas City area, El Paso in Western Texas, Louisville, Missouri in central part of the state, and Guerrant in Southeastern Kentucky; combined only one percent of the votes was cast against reunion) and the five presbyteries where antiunion sentiment was the strongest (North Alabama, Florida in the panhandle, Congaree in the Columbia, South Carolina area, Meridian in Southeastern Mississippi, and Harmony in East Central South Carolina; combined 90.4 percent against). These fourteen presbyteries had 104,944 members and 453 ministers in 541 churches and formed the basis of my discussion of how ministers divided on the reunion vote. I did not combine the information into one sample, rather I maintain three distinct groups: Concord Presbytery, the three where I determined how each member voted, and the 10 where antiunion sentiment was the weakest and the strongest. The general pattern I described in the chapter was the same for all three groups.

I gathered information from the following sources. For church membership, I consulted the *Minutes of the General Assembly of the Presbyterian Church in the United States*, 1955. The *Ministerial Directory of the Presbyterian Church, US, 1861-1941*, revised and supplemented, 1950, was the most useful source for biographical information about the ministers. It listed the birth date, birthplace, and education (schools attended and degrees earned) and described their careers by including the churches served and positions held. For demographic information about the cities, towns, and counties where the churches were located, I used the *1950 Census of the Population*, vol. 2: *Characteristics of the Population*.

5

Denominational Fundamentalists:

The Baptists

Contend earnestly for the faith which was once for all delivered to the saints.
—Jude 3

In the late 1940s and early 1950s E. P. Alldredge issued a series of broadsides aimed at the Southern Baptist Convention (SBC). His story illustrates some of the obstacles denominational fundamentalists faced among Southern Baptists as well as revealing a fundamentalistic critique of doctrinal developments within the Convention. Thus his attacks represented an expansion of the patterns of fundamentalist controversy because he offered the first sustained fundamentalistic critique of the Convention in the post-World War II era from someone apart from the orbit of J. Frank Norris.

In 1948 Alldredge published *Unionizing Southern Baptists*, a pamphlet that combined a description of the efforts of some Southern Baptists to encourage Convention participation in cooperative Protestantism with a fundamentalist critique of that endeavor, particularly that such cooperation entailed doctrinal compromise.[1] The following year Alldredge tried to force Southern Baptists who participated in the Federal Council of Churches (FCC) either to end their affiliation with the organization or to leave the denomination.[2] At the 1949 meeting of the Convention he introduced an amendment to the denomination's constitution forbidding Southern Baptists who were members of local, state, or national councils of churches from serving on any of the Convention's Boards or at an institution supported by the Convention.[3] After a heated debate the Convention voted to table the amendment.[4] Later that year he distributed *While Southern Baptists Sleep*, another scathing indictment of Southern Baptists who supported Convention cooperation with the FCC, particularly the leaders of the Foreign Mission Board in Richmond, Virginia.[5] Unable to reach the Southern Baptist rank and file because the Convention bookstores refused to sell his pamphlets and because the editors of Southern Baptist newspapers erected an "iron curtain" denying him access to their pages, Alldredge started his own paper, *The Baptist Challenge*, in February 1950.[6] Lacking the resources to sustain

---

[1]E. P. Alldredge, *Unionizing Southern Baptists: A Survey of the Past and Present Efforts to Bring Southern Baptists into "Cooperative Christianity" and the "United Church of America,"* rev. ed. (Nashville TN: privately published, 1948) 72–73, 76–79, 81. Alldredge did not adopt the badge fundamentalist and portrayed the threat as being to distinctive Baptist doctrines. Yet this concern for doctrine makes appropriate the characterization of his criticisms as fundamentalist.

[2]That the intention of the amendment was to purge FCC supporters from the Convention is evident in E. P. Alldredge, "Dr. Taylor's Interpretation of My Proposed Amendment," *Baptist and Reflector*, (Nashville TN), 21 July 1949, 2 (hereinafter cited as *BAR*).

[3]Typed copy of amendment in the Records of the Executive Committee of the Southern Baptist Convention, Box 4, Southern Baptist Historical Commission, Southern Baptist Historical Library and Archive, Nashville, Tennessee.

[4]N.a., "Baptists Block Bid to Blacklist Church Council," *Arkansas Gazette*, 20 May 1949, 1, clipping in ibid.

[5]E. P. Alldredge, *While Southern Baptists Sleep* (Nashville: privately published, 1949).

[6]N.a., Untitled article, *The Faith* (Mayfield KY), February 1950, 3; cf., I. W. Rogers, "The Southern Baptist Iron Curtain," *The Faith*, May 1950, 1, 3–4; Alldredge, *While Southern Baptists Sleep*, 5, 10, 57–59; and E. P. Alldredge to J. Frank Norris,

the paper, he merged it with an independent Baptist paper published in Western Kentucky to form *The Faith and Southern Baptists*.[7] In its pages until his death in 1953 he continued his efforts to awaken Southern Baptists to the menace the Convention faced from cooperative Christianity while enlarging his analysis to include the dangers of liberal professors in the Convention's seminaries, liberal pastors in its pulpits, and the Cooperative Program, its method of financing its activities.[8]

What is noteworthy about Alldredge's activities is not his message but the messenger. For most of the 1930s and 1940s Southern Baptists heard similar criticisms from J. Frank Norris who continued attacking the trends toward liberalism he believed he saw in the Convention. But Alldredge was not an ally of Norris nor a spokesperson for Norris's brand of fundamentalism.[9] Rather Alldredge called himself a "cooperating Southern Baptist" and cited as proof his fifty-six years of service to the Convention.[10] Licensed to preach in 1896 he supplied pulpits while earning bachelor's and master's degrees at

---

fall, 1949 (E. P. Alldredge Papers, Southern Baptist Historical Library and Archives, Nashville TN) Box 1, Folder 30 (hereinafter cited as Alldredge Papers).

[7]N.a., "Two Magazines Become One," *The Faith and Southern Baptists* (Mayfield KY), August 1950, 1 (hereinafter cited as *FSB*). Alldredge's paper joined with *The Faith*, edited by I. W. Rogers of Hickory, Kentucky. Rogers was the editor and Alldredge, a contributing editor. Both the title and the editing arrangement suggest that Alldredge's paper was the one having difficulties. Before the first issue of the *Challenge* appeared, Alldredge confessed that he had problems with finding the finances. E. P. Alldredge to J. Frank Norris, fall, 1949, in Alldredge Papers, 1–30.

[8]E. P. Alldredge, "Dr. E. M. Poteat's New Position," *FSB*, October 1950, 11; idem., "Shall We Continue to Support the Co-operative Program?" *FSB*, November 1950, 11; idem., "Professor Clyde T. Fransisco's New Book—*Introducing the Old Testament*," *FSB*, December 1950, 5–6; idem., "Dr. E. A. McDowell's New Book on Revelation," *FSB*, June 1951, 3–5; idem., "Five Major Defects in the Cooperative Program," *FSB*, October 1952, 1–2.

[9]Correspondence from the 1920s clearly showed Alldredge's opposition to Norris and his activities. See for example, E. P. Alldredge to L. R. Scarborough, 1 March 1921, in Alldredge Papers, 13-8; E. P. Alldredge to F. S. Groner, 18 October 1922, Alldredge Papers, 13-4; E. P. Alldredge to L. L. Gwaltney, 21 November 1922, Alldredge Papers, 13-4; and E. P. Alldredge to Z. T. Cody, 30 July 1926, in Alldredge Papers, 15-4.

[10]E. P. Alldredge, "When One Discovers Termites in His House," *FSB*, July 1952, 2.

Baylor University. Graduating from Southern Seminary in Louisville in 1904 with a Masters of Theology, he pastored churches for seventeen years and then served as secretary of the state conventions in New Mexico and Arkansas. His most important contribution to the denomination was his work in establishing and directing for twenty-five years the Department of Survey, Statistics, and Information. Directing this agency from the offices of the Sunday School Board in Nashville, Alldredge also worked with the American Baptist Theological Seminary, a school for black ministerial students jointly run by the Southern Baptist and National Baptist Conventions.[11] Despite the record of loyal service Alldredge found himself accused of conspiring with Norris to destroy the Convention after the appearance of his first pamphlet and the events at the 1949 Convention.[12] Moreover, because two letters were missing, Alldredge believed that his correspondence files had been searched surreptitiously for evidence of collusion with Norris. He later found the letters misfiled but still believed that his files had been rifled.[13] Calling the

---

[11]Ibid. In *While Southern Baptists Sleep*, 65–66, Alldredge recounted how he chaired the committee charged with writing the seminary's statement of faith and served on the Southern Baptist Commission on the Negro Seminary.

[12]Alldredge, *While Southern Baptists Sleep*, 4–5.

[13]E. P. Alldredge to J. Frank Norris, early June 1949, and 6 June 1949 in Alldredge Papers, 1-30. But some evidence possibly supporting Alldredge's concerns can be found in Box 4 of the Records of the Executive Committee of the Southern Baptist Convention, Southern Baptist Historical Library and Archives, Nashville, Tennessee. It contained typed copies of correspondence between Alldredge and Noel Smith, editor of Norris's newspaper, and of one letter between Alldredge and Norris. The material did not contain the letters Alldredge believed were taken, but it did have letters not found in the Alldredge files. The extant correspondence from both collections showed that Norris initiated contact after Alldredge published *Unionizing Southern Baptists* and was clearly pleased that "a new voice from the inside should sound the tocsin of war." Norris asked Alldredge to deliver a week's worth of lectures at his seminary, an invitation Alldredge declined primarily because he did not have the time but also because he doubted the propriety of such a visit. J. Frank Norris to E. P. Alldredge, 3 and 16 August 1948 and E. P. Alldredge to J. Frank Norris, summer, 1948, in Alldredge Papers, 1–30. The material in the Records of the Executive Committee indicated some sharing of information between Smith and Alldredge but primarily concerned reprinting material from *Unionizing* in *The Fundamentalist*, Norris's newspaper. The Records collection contains no explanation of how or when copies of Alldredge's

charges "Satanic" and "false," Alldredge denied any connection with the Ft. Worth pastor: "Neither Dr. Norris nor any member of his staff had ever seen my proposed amendment or had known anything about it until we presented it to the Convention."[14] But such accusations dogged Alldredge the rest of his days, in part because the Southern Baptist leaders who were the objects of his criticisms found them to be an effective means of undermining Alldredge's credibility.[15] Unlike Norris, who by the 1930s had given up hope of reversing the trends he believed threatened the theological and ecclesiological heritage of Southern Baptists and had established a separate denomination, Alldredge committed himself to preventing the Convention from being dominated and directed by a liberal faction. "I am now 73," he wrote Norris in 1948, "but I am not going to stand on the sidelines...and see everything that Southern Baptists have stood for thrown to the wolves of pacifism, modernism, and unionism.... I have dedicated my remaining days and strength to this one task. God help me!"[16]

---

letters became a part of its files. One possibility is that Alldredge sent them to Executive Committee to show he was not acting for Norris in introducing the amendment, but it seems odd that no cover letter could be found nor any reply from the Committee.

[14]Alldredge, *While Southern Baptists Sleep*, 5. In "Why Don't They Get Out," *The Faith*, July 1949, 2, I. W. Rogers called the accusation that Alldredge introduced his amendment at the behest of Norris "a red herring" to divert attention away from its substance.

[15]See E. P. Alldredge, "Dr. R. G. Lee and the Modernists and Unionists," *FSB*, December 1950, 3–4; and idem., "When One Discovers," 1–2. The tone and content of both of these articles suggest that Alldredge felt the sting of being criticized as an ally of Norris and tried to dissociate himself from Norris. In both, Alldredge admitted that Norris and *The Fundamentalist* editor Smith supplied some information and that Alldredge allowed parts of his pamphlets to be reprinted in Norris's newspaper, but Alldredge also asserted that his own careful examination of the evidence led him to the analysis and conclusions he published.

[16]E. P. Alldredge to J. Frank Norris, 20 August 1948, in Alldredge Papers, 1-30. The difference in perspective is revealed in Alldredge's rebuke of Norris in this letter: "You are very far wrong in supposing that 'a very large percentage' of Southern Baptist leaders 'have gone over boot, bag, and baggage to the Federal Council of Churches.' I know personally nine tenths of the leading unionizers in the South.... Not over 250 to 300 preachers, out of 23,000, belong to any subsidiary organizations of the Federal Council; and not over 1200 of our preachers are sympathetic to the union movement.

Alldredge needed divine aid in this mission because he and other denominational fundamentalists had to overcome several formidable hurdles. First, they had to break the identification of their efforts from those of the rancorous, divisive tactics of J. Frank Norris. To a lesser extent they also needed to distance themselves from the interdenominational fundamentalists because such associations called into question their loyalty to the Convention. Second, they lacked a dramatic issue to galvanize support for their position. Cooperative Protestantism and liberal theology did not raise alarms among Southern Baptists as reunion did among Southern Presbyterians. These issues required educating the rank and file to the dangers they posed, and most Southern Baptists were not convinced by the propaganda. Exploiting fears of the growth of the Convention's boards, resentment over the intrusion of these agencies into the affairs of local congregations, and disaffection from demands to uphold the Convention's program were more effective in recruiting supporters for the cause of the denominational fundamentalists. But this tactic raised a third hurdle that weakened the ability of denominational fundamentalists to create organizations that mobilized their followers into a functioning coalition ready to do battle in denominational politics. Wishing to maintain the cherished Baptist principle concerning the independence of local congregations those pastors attracted to the fundamentalist cause through concern over the bureaucratization of the Convention proved to be equally leery of a fundamentalist "machine" that demanded unquestioning loyalty to its program. Furthermore, the structure of the Convention hampered the ability of denominational fundamentalists to find a line of attack. It lacked the institutional means for disciplining dissidents that Presbyterian fundamentalists tried to employ to achieve their goals.

That Baptist fundamentalists were not entirely successful in redirecting the drift of the Convention in the post-war years was not for the lack of trying. They did manage to put some distance between themselves and J. Frank Norris and have their perspective gain a

---

That is about 5 percent. If your estimate was even approximately correct, the battle would be lost already."

broader hearing within the Convention. Moreover, they took some tentative steps toward creating institutions outside the denominational structure. Like Southern Presbyterians they did not support the interdenominational fundamentalist ones established in the 1920s and 1930s.

Baptists institutions were more diverse than the Presbyterians' and included newspapers, fellowships, and schools. The most significant of these institutions were the newspapers. As early as 1932 V. I. Masters saw the need for an "independent Southwide Baptist paper" that was not dependent upon support from state conventions and thus could speak freely about developments in the Southern Baptist Convention.[17] The importance of the papers to the denominational fundamentalist cause is not surprising given their complaints about being excluded from access to the people by the denominational presses. E. P. Alldredge's efforts in starting *The Baptist Challenge* were a part of this pattern as were several other papers. Moreover, these new Baptist institutions of the 1940s and 1950s had a slightly different cast than the interdenominational ones. Rather than creating a fundamentalist subculture they sought to preserve their founders' vision of a denominational heritage that the founders believed was being undermined from within the denomination by liberal elements. In other words these newspapers, schools, and fellowships did not have, at least in their early years, quite the same cultural attributes as similar ones created by the inter-

---

[17]V. I. Masters to J. Frank Norris, 6 April 1932 (J. Frank Norris Papers, Southern Baptist Historical Commission, Southern Baptist Historical Library and Archives, Nashville TN) box 27, file 1228, (hereinafter cited as JFN Papers). Masters's comment is interesting in two ways. First, he was editor of the *Western Recorder*, the official newspaper of the Kentucky state convention; thus his words suggest that he knew first hand the pressures brought to bear on editors who wished to criticize, or at least question and comment on denominational policies. Second, he was writing to Norris whose independent newspaper already had a wide distribution in the South; thus the need was for a paper more moderate in tone, or, as he wrote, one that "brings a flavor of conservatism, age, regularity, and restraint." This comment suggests the difficulty that denominational fundamentalists had in winning a fair hearing of their complaints and concerns as long their opponents could accuse them of being in league with the renegade Norris.

denominational fundamentalists after the 1920s' controversies. In this respect they perhaps remained more Southern than fundamentalist. Nevertheless these developments reshaped the conflict among Southern Baptists. While the specific issues that divided Southern Baptists were not identical to those that produced fundamentalist controversy among Northern Baptists, a strong element of restoring and defending the doctrinal integrity of the SBC coursed through the debates and marked them as fundamentalistic.

The first step denominational fundamentalists among Baptists took in building their coalition was to distinguish themselves from the interdenominational fundamentalists. The attitude of Southern Baptists leaders toward interdenominational schools made this move necessary. For example, typifying their response to these schools, O. W. Taylor, editor of the *Baptist and Reflector*, the newspaper of the Tennessee Baptist Convention, praised an article by T. T. Shields, a Canadian Baptist, as "a true and common sense discussion of the subject that we reproduce it here in a condensed form as our editorial expression on the subject."[18] Shields began by lashing out at the excessive attention "undenominational" Bible teachers paid to weaving intricate and esoteric dispensational interpretations of the Scriptures while ignoring the simple truths of the Gospel in their preaching. But he reserved his harshest criticism for the schools, saying:

> *Undenominationalism* is perhaps especially obnoxious *in its institutional manifestations*....This is particularly true of so-called educational or training institutes. They prey upon all denominations, and sometimes even exhibit themselves as examples of church unity. But what are the facts? Their representatives seek admission to the pulpits of all denominations. They plead the cause of their institution and

---

[18]O. W. Taylor, Editorial comment before T. T. Shields, "Undenominationalism," *BAR*, 23 May 1940, 3. Taylor did not cite his source of the article. Talyor's use of Shields is somewhat ironic because Shields was a leader of the militant and separatist Baptist Bible Union.

solicit funds for its support, while inviting young people to enroll as students. And when they get there, they effectively undermine and destroy the distinctive denominational principles in which their students have been trained in their respective churches.[19]

The dissemination of such complaints made Southern congregations hesitant to hire graduates from the interdenominational schools. For example Southern Presbyterians were not alone in their reluctance to accept graduates of the Dallas Theological Seminary into their churches. Baptists had similar objections. As early as 1928 Lewis Chafer noted that "the hand of [Southern Baptists] is somewhat against our men because they are being trained in an undenominational seminary."[20] According to a Dallas graduate a decisive factor in the rejection of his candidacy for the pastorate of a Baptist church was "what they [the church members] termed my 'non-baptistic background' and my 'unfortunate' choice of Dallas Theological Seminary as the medium of my ministerial preparation."[21] Baptist ministerial students at Bob Jones University suffered intimidation to take their training at a denominationally sponsored seminary rather than at the interdenominational school. According to Bob Jones the harassment came from "some of the modernistic leaders who holler 'church loyalty'" and who "put pressure on these young preachers because they are enrolled in our school, which they say they are against because of its interdenominational approach."[22]

Fundamentalist schools were not the only aspect of fundamentalist activities that came under criticism. Taylor's complaints in

---

[19]Ibid.

[20]LSC to Donald Grey Barnhouse, 29 December 1928 (Lewis Sperry Chafer Papers, Mosher Library, Dallas Theological Seminary, Dallas TX).

[21]James H. Comstock to Dewey Duncan, 10 November 1945, in ibid. Out of 512 graduates from the seminary in the years 1935–1955, 142 served Southern churches. Of the 142, twenty-five over the course of their careers pastored thirty-five different Baptist churches in twenty-eight different Southern cities. The records did not reveal if the churches were members of the Convention. Alumni Records, Alumni Office, Dallas Theological Seminary, Dallas, Texas.

[22]Bob Jones, Sr. to JFN, 3 February 1949, JFN Papers, 22-1023.

these areas reflected a broader concern among Southern Baptists over Norris's style of fundamentalism. For example Taylor attacked what he perceived to be fundamentalist efforts to undermine loyalty to the denomination and build their movement not by evangelism but by raiding established congregations. The work of itinerant evangelists was especially pernicious in Taylor's analysis, particularly their practice of discrediting Convention activities and programs. Moreover, he believed that their claims to be Baptist deliberately misled congregations as to their identity and purpose. "Thus the churches swayed by [them]," according to Taylor, "are divided and disaffected and weaned away from their Baptist conviction and denominationally loyalty and become prejudiced against it. Accordingly, they cease to be loyal, strong Baptist missionary agencies."[23] Additionally, fundamentalist arrogance troubled Taylor. His complaint here was the name and its implications. If used simply to distinguish between churches that accept the infallibility of the Bible and its teachings and those that follow liberal teachings, then "multiplied thousands" of fundamentalist churches were members of the Convention.[24] But most fundamentalists appropriated the name for themselves "with a subtle sense of superiority" thus monopolizing "the term exclusively for themselves" and thereby implicitly characterizing churches cooperating with the Convention "as unorthodox."[25]

Taylor also attacked fundamentalist theology. Calling it an "Unfair Test of Fellowship" Taylor criticized fundamentalist Baptists requiring acceptance of premillennialism as a basis for cooperation and association.[26] His main objection was that he doubted the Bible

---

[23]O. W. Taylor, "Let Churches Know Their Man," *BAR*, 28 September 1944, 2; cf., idem., "Evangelism under Church Auspices," *BAR*, 4 January 1940, 3.

[24]O. W. Taylor, "'A Fundamentalist Baptist Church,'" *BAR*, 14 March 1940, 2.

[25]Ibid.; cf., idem., "'I Drop 'Em,'" *BAR*, 18 May 1944, 2.

[26]O. W. Taylor, "An Unfair Test of Fellowship," *BAR*, 8 February 1940, 2–3; cf., idem., "Disagreeing Agreeably on the Millennial Question," *BAR*, 17 February 1949, 2. Interestingly, Taylor was a premillennialist, and his objections were directed more toward the dispensational variety. See idem., "The Intent of a Motion," *BAR*, 28 April 1949, 2; and the articles cited in note 27.

was as clear in matters of eschatology as fundamentalists insisted. Occasionally he pointed out errors of interpretation and disagreements among premillennialists over the meaning of certain prophetic passages.[27] But he was more concerned that such a policy would provoke dissension and division within the Convention.[28] Furthermore, the effect on congregations of rabid premillennial preaching was the same as fundamentalist criticisms of the Convention: to "wean away" members "from the historic Baptist position and from denominational loyalty" thus creating divisions "which harmed these churches for years, if not permanently."[29]

But fundamentalism in the 1930s and 1940s among Southern Baptists remained associated primarily with J. Frank Norris, not with the interdenominational fundamentalist schools in the region, and denominational fundamentalists had to break this identification for their concerns to be heard. Having failed in the 1920s to build a Southern Baptist constituency under his leadership for the Northern interdenominational fundamentalist movement, he continued his assault on the Convention by shifting his criticisms to new targets. The teaching of evolution in Southern Baptist schools faded as an issue as he turned his attention to financial mismanagement and cooperative Protestantism while maintaining his attacks on modernism and on the growth of Convention agencies as a threat to the independence of local congregations.[30] He gloated over failure of

---

[27]O. W. Taylor, "The Future of Russia and Germany?" *BAR*, 18 January 1940, 3. While generally approving of the notes, Taylor warned against an uncritical acceptance of Scofield's comments on prophetic passages. See idem., "An Artificial Definition," *BAR*, 15 February 1940, 2; "Did Rashness Launch a Dispensation?" *BAR*, 3 February 1944, 2; and "When Orthodoxy Dispenses Heresy," *BAR*, 26 May 1949, 2.

[28]O. W. Taylor, "The Brother Is Exactly Right," *BAR*, 7 March 1940, 2; and idem., "Disagreeing Agreeably on Millennial Question," 2.

[29]O. W. Taylor, "Postmillennial and Premillennial Ramming," *BAR*, 12 May 1949, 2.

[30]J. Frank Norris, "What Has Been The Record of the Machine in Texas," in *Inside History of First Baptist Church, Fort Worth and Temple Baptist Church, Detroit: Life Story of Dr. J. Frank Norris* (Ft. Worth: privately published, 1938) 173–75, 186–89. The best evaluation of Norris's career is Barry Hankins, *God's Rascal: J. Frank Norris and the Beginnings of Southern Fundamentalism* (Lexington: University Press of Kentucky, 1996).

the $75 Million Campaign, an ambitious 1920s Convention-sponsored project to retire its debt and finance its activities.[31] Privately he believed that the financial problems caused by the Great Depression for the Texas Baptist Convention vindicated his charges of mismanagement.[32] In addition to using his newspaper, radio program, and speaking engagements to publicize his views, he conducted meetings at the same time in the same city as the annual gathering of the Southern Baptist Convention.[33] But Norris invested more of his time and energy in the 1930s into trying to expand his fundamentalist constituency by developing a Northern base and into building an organization that avoided the faults he found with the Convention. His first step in enlarging his following was taken in 1935 when he assumed the pastorate of Temple Baptist Church in Detroit while continuing to lead his Texas congregation.[34] Then in 1938 he reorganized the Premillennial Baptist Missionary Fellowship into the World Fundamental Baptist Missionary Fellowship. The former organization had begun in 1933 as an agency for the support of overseas missionaries, and its disappointingly slow growth over the next five years forced Norris to take action. He moved the Fellowship's offices to Chicago and broadened the scope of the Fellowship's activities to include promoting evangelistic efforts in North America, educating pastors, and opposing liberalism. Within a few months over two hundred churches joined the Fellowship, and Norris was well on his way to giving his opposition to the Convention a permanent institutional structure.[35]

With his influence among Southern Baptists already weakened by the scandals of the late 1920s, his activities and tactics in the 1930s

---

[31]J. Frank Norris, "The Triple Major Operation in Detroit," in ibid., 159–61.

[32]J. Frank Norris to Victor I. Masters, 5 March 1932 and letter with no date (internal evidence suggests summer, 1932) in JFN Papers, 27-1228.

[33]Billy Vick Barlett, The Beginnings: A Pictorial History of the Baptist Bible Fellowship (Springfield MO: Baptist Bible College, 1975) 3.

[34]On his ministry in Detroit see C. Allyn Russell, "J. Frank Norris: Violent Fundamentalist," in Voices of Fundamentalism: Seven Biographical Studies (Philadelphia: Westminster Press, 1976) 30, 40; cf., J. Frank Norris, "How the Dual Pastorate Was Brought About," in Inside History, 269–71.

[35]Bartlett, Beginnings, 19–21.

probably did more to alienate than win followers to his cause. Nevertheless, Norris continued to find some new supporters among a younger generation of Southern Baptist pastors. Luther Peak was one of these men, and his story suggests some of the reasons for Norris's appeal as well as some of the problems within Norris's style of fundamentalism. Peak fell under the spell of J. Frank Norris at the 1932 Southern Baptist Convention in St Petersburg, Florida. Ordained at seventeen to preach and a recent graduate of Georgetown College, a Baptist school in Kentucky, Peak pastored a church in Owenton, Kentucky, a small town about fifty miles northeast of Louisville. Although he believed that Norris was "too harsh" in his attacks on the Convention, Peak came to see that Norris was "right," that "there is only one thing that the church was established to do and that is to preach salvation by grace to a lost world."[36] In addition to discontinuing the use of Convention-published Sunday school lessons, Peak wrote Norris that "I am through with man made programs, drives, unscriptural institutionalism and all the rest of the scheme that modernism has adopted to paralyze the work of the true N[ew] T[estament] Church."[37] Peak's dream "to become the pastor of a true New Testament Church"[38] became reality in 1940 when Norris encouraged the people of Central Baptist Church in Dallas, an independent church, to call Peak as their pastor.[39] By the late 1940s the church outgrew its facilities and began construction on 2,000 seat sanctuary and 41,000 square foot Sunday school building.[40] In

---

[36]Luther C. Peak to J. Frank Norris, 31 May 1932, in JFN Papers, 34–1507. An insightful analysis of the relationship between Peak and Norris can be found in Hankins, *God's Rascal*, 120–26.

[37]Ibid.

[38]Ibid.

[39]Luther C. Peak, "Central Baptist Church of Dallas to Build Modern Two Story Building at Cost of $100,000," typed copy of news release, no date (c. spring, 1947); and J. Frank Norris to Luther C. Peak, 19 April 1947; in JFN Papers, 34-1508. Norris claimed in this letter that he "put in a lot of time and money in buying that fine property over there" and that he "was glad to step aside" when the congregation took Peak as its pastor. These comments suggest that the church started from a group of Norris's supporters and was not associated with the Southern Baptist Convention.

[40]Peak, "Central Baptist."

addition to the traditional programs the church supported Peak's radio ministry and a newspaper.[41] Peak also identified himself and his church with Norris by teaching in Norris's seminary, working with his Fellowship, and supporting him in his battles with the Southern Baptist Convention and factions within the Fellowship.[42] Peak contributed to *The Fundamentalist*'s attacks on the Convention, and one article in which he characterized the Convention newspapers as "kept women" particularly delighted Norris's old ally, V. I. Masters, a former editor of Kentucky Baptists' *Western Recorder*.[43]

In 1947 after one particularly bruising fight in which his opponents charged Peak with "going 'interdenominational,'" Peak curtailed his teaching and Fellowship activities to concentrate on raising the money for the new buildings.[44] Two and one half years later, though, Peak reconsidered and told Norris to "count me in more than ever."[45] Peak remained loyal to Norris during the bloody battle over Norris's control of the seminary and the Fellowship and was rewarded in 1951 with the Presidency of the seminary.[46] Later that year as Norris's health failed, Peak donned his mentor's mantle when he became pastor of First Baptist Church of Fort Worth.[47] Continuing as pastor of the Dallas church, Peak found the work too taxing and resigned from the

---

[41]Peak's stationery shows that his radio program, called "The Bible Broadcast Hour," aired daily over KSKY. See Luther C. Peak to J. Frank Norris, 18 April 1947, in JFN Papers, 34-1508. No copies of the paper could be found, though in 1951 Norris suggested that *The Fundamentalist* combine with Peak's newspaper with Peak as editor. Peak rejected the offer saying that the combination would dilute *The Fundamentalist*'s distinctive voice. J. Frank Norris to Luther C. Peak, 12 March 1951, and Luther C. Peak to J. Frank Norris, 13 March 1951, in JFN Papers, 34-1512.

[42]Luther C. Peak to J. Frank Norris, 18 April 1947, in JFN Papers, 34-1508; and T. H. Masters to Luther C. Peak, 28 June 1950, typed copy in JFN Papers, 34-1511.

[43]V. I. Masters to J. Frank Norris, 14 March 1948, in JFN Papers, 27-1229.

[44]Luther C. Peak to J. Frank Norris, 18 April 1947, in JFN Papers, 34-1508.

[45]Luther C. Peak to J. Frank Norris, 27 July 1949, in JFN Papers, 34-1510.

[46]Luther C. Peak to whom it may concern, 29 May 1950, and Luther C. Peak to Dallas Billington, 3 June 1950, typed copy in JFN Papers, 34-1511; J. Frank Norris to Luther C. Peak, 12 March 1951, and n.a., "Peak Installed by Seminary," *Fort Worth Star-Telegram*, no date, clipping in JFN Papers, 34-1512; and Luther C. Peak to the membership of First Baptist Church, 8 June 1952, in JFN Papers, 34-1513.

[47]N.a., "Norris Turns First Baptist over to Peak," *Fort Worth Star-Telegram*, 19 November 1951, clipping in JFN Papers, 34-1512.

pulpit of First Baptist in June 1952, and the seminary soon thereafter. In his letter to the congregation of First Baptist Peak assured the people that "no person or persons, no circumstance or circumstances" forced him to leave; rather he believed that "God has called me to Dallas and He has not released me from that responsibility. A joint pastorate is not fair to either church."[48]

Over the next three years Peak and his congregation became so disillusioned with Norris-brand fundamentalism that in May 1955, the church voted unanimously to cooperate with the Southern Baptist Convention.[49] The following spring Peak explained the reasons for the change of allegiance in a series of scathing articles published in the *Baptist Standard*, the newspaper of the Texas Baptist Convention. Peak's attacks on his former fundamentalist allies echoed the complaints that O. W. Taylor voiced in the previous decade, but Peak's had the sharper focus born of an insider's familiarity with the movement. Moreover, with their publication in the *Standard*, they represented a part of the continuing efforts of Southern Baptist leaders to discredit fundamentalism. With a fervor once reserved for attacks on the denomination, Peak unleashed his rhetoric on fundamentalists. The focus of Peak's criticisms was the contentious nature of the movement. According to Peak participation in fundamentalism meant that "we were usually in a fight of some kind. If we were not fighting Southern Baptists, Northern Baptists, the National Council of Churches, the Catholics, or Modernism, we fought each other."[50] The consequence was to undermine the efforts of pastors trying to help their churches' members to grow in their faith. Not only did these

---

[48]Peak also said that he had the utmost cooperation from Norris, the church's staff, and its deacons. Luther C. Peak to the membership of First Baptist Church, 8 June 1952, in JFN Papers, 34-1513. Letters from Norris to Peak suggest that Norris appreciated Peak's work and that they maintained a friendly relationship after Peak resigned. See J. Frank Norris to Luther C. Peak, 16 December 1951, in JFN Papers, 34-1512; 18 January 1952, 14 February 1952, 30 May 1952, and 5 July 1952 in JFN Papers, 34-1513.

[49]Luther C. Peak, "Why We Left Fundamentalism to Work with Southern Baptists," *Baptist Standard* (Dallas TX), 14 April 1956, 6–7.

[50]Peak, "Why We Left Fundamentalism to Work with Southern Baptists," *Baptist Standard*, 7 April 1956, 6.

conflicts consume time and energy a pastor might devote to nurturing spiritually his congregation, but also the back-biting and name-calling that fundamentalists hurled at each other in their press damaged the reputation and standing of a pastor within his congregation and community.[51] Rejecting fundamentalists' assertions that the purpose of these accusations was to expose error, Peak believed their intention was more base: to "gather disciples out from under the banner of others and assemble them under...[their] own banner."[52] In Peak's eyes the attacks also had roots in the personal ambitions of fundamentalist leaders. Frustrated in achieving their goals within the denomination, these men created large personal followings by vilifying its programs and leaders and by imposing autocratic control over their congregations. The fundamentalists thus created what they alleged the Southern Baptist Convention had become: a "dictatorial machine" enforcing conformity with its programs and not tolerating criticism or dissent.[53]

The decision to leave fundamentalism meant a reevaluation of cooperation with the Convention. Peak now saw the Convention as a "democratic institution" that respected the decisions and affairs of the local congregation.[54] Moreover, the Cooperative Program efficiently supported the work of foreign missionaries whereas "the fundamentalism with which we were associated had a mission work in name only."[55] According to Peak only three cents of each fundamentalist dollar given to missions went overseas with the rest used to send fundamentalist leaders on world tours and trips to the Holy Land.[56] Finally, the post-war growth in membership and contributions to the Convention was the determinative factor in Peak's decision to

---

[51]Peak, "Why We Left Fundamentalism to Join Southern Baptists," *Baptist Standard*, 21 April 1956, 6–7.

[52]Ibid; cf., comments in Peak, "Why We Left," 7 April 1956, 6.

[53]Peak, "Why We Left," 14 April 1956, 6–7.

[54]Ibid.

[55]Ibid., 7.

[56]Ibid., 17.

affiliate with the denomination. In his eyes it demonstrated "the evident blessing of God upon the Southern Baptists."[57]

Peak's criticisms only confirmed what denominational leaders had said about fundamentalism and probably convinced few to leave the movement. But by the mid-1940s other Southern Baptist pastors and leaders were concerned about the issues that Norris had made the focus of his attacks on the Convention. In other words they came to agree with Norris's diagnosis of the Convention's problems but not with his means of treating the disease with character assassination and destruction of the Convention. Their goal was to find a means of arresting denominational developments that they believed were taking it away from its theological heritage and undermining its distinctive traditions. To be successful, though, these denominational fundamentalists had to break the identification of their efforts with Norris. Their main tactic was to wage a propaganda campaign that made no reference to Norris and vigorously denied any connection to Norris's movement, while affirming their loyalty to the convention. Over the late 1940s and early 1950s they gradually built a loose network of newspapers, churches, fellowships, and schools that gave an ongoing institutional form to their endeavors.

One of the leaders in these developments was I. W. Rogers, a Southern Baptist pastor in Western Kentucky. In April 1945, he began publishing an independent newspaper, and in its pages one can trace the transformation of a Southern Baptist into a denominational fundamentalist.[58] With a Masters of Theology from Southwestern Seminary and two years study at Southern Seminary, Rogers had the pedigree for a loyal Southern Baptist pastor. He worked for the Convention as a field representative of the *Western Recorder*, Kentucky's Baptist newspaper, and as a district missionary in Western Kentucky

---

[57]Peak, "Why We Left Fundamentalism to Join Southern Baptists," *Baptist Standard*, 28 April 1956, 6.

[58]Material from this section has been published in William R. Glass "From Southern Baptist to Fundamentalist: The Case of I. W. Rogers and *The Faith*, 1945–1957, "American Baptist Quarterly" (September 1995): 241–59. Reprinted here with the permission of American Baptist Historical Society, Valley Forge, PA 19482.

for eight years.[59] Then in 1945, Rogers's fifteenth year of serving as a pastor, he joined with two other pastors in Western Kentucky to start "The Faith Enterprises," a bookstore and newspaper. Their purpose was to "teach our people the vital truths of the Word, and help them—especially our young people—to counteract the flood of vile, immoral papers, magazines, and books that are coming into their homes."[60] Rogers edited the paper while the others ran the store, but within a few years, Rogers left the pastorate to devote full time to managing the store and publishing the paper.

In the early years of the paper a steady stream of articles and editorials denouncing dancing, movies, tobacco, and alcohol filled the spaces between lengthier pieces about trends and developments among Southern Baptists in Kentucky.[61] After 1950 television joined the pantheon of vices condemned by Rogers.[62] For a popular religious newspaper, very little devotional material appeared, and the doctrinal exposition focused more on justifying distinctive Southern Baptist practices like immersion and closed communion or condemning activities deemed inappropriate by Rogers for Baptist churches, like union meetings or women preaching.[63] Prior to the summer of 1948

---

[59]E. P. Alldredge, "Editor I. W. Rogers," *FSB*, September 1950, 5.

[60]I. W. Rogers, "How THE FAITH Enterprises Began," *The Faith*, April 1945, 1.

[61]See for example, n.a., "Resolutions against Dancing in Murray State Teachers College," *The Faith*, April 1945, 3; n.a., "Reasons for Not Dancing," *The Faith*, September 1946, 4. In "Bible Institutes," *The Faith*, January 1946, 1, Rogers blames the "backslidden" condition of most Baptist churches on the movies; cf., W. K. Wood, "The Filthy Movies," *The Faith*, July 1946, 4. N.a., "Why Smoke, Anyway?" *The Faith*, October 1945, 3; cf., R. T. Wood, "Cigarettes and Liquor," *National Voice*, reprinted in *The Faith*, December 1946, 2. Millard A. Jenkins, "A Saloonkeeper Goes to Heaven," *The Faith*, November 1945, 2.

[62]As early as 1948 Rogers warned his readers that "press reports indicate that already television is presenting liquor-drinking in a very favorable and attractive manner. We have never seen a television set in operation, but it is easy to see how this new invention can become a most powerful instrument for promoting the works of the devil." Untitled comment, *The Faith*, October 1948, 2.

[63]Rogers believed that Southern Baptists should hold "closed communion," or not allow anyone to partake of the Lord's Supper who had not been baptized in a Baptist church. He also criticized those churches that did not rebaptize new members joining from other denominations. See "Unionism," *The Faith*, September 1945, 1. On women preaching, see n.a., "Women's Work in Baptist Churches, " *The Faith*,

Rogers concentrated more on issues involving the state convention or local, Western Kentucky associations. In particular he attacked what he believed to be the threat of state convention programs to the independence of the local congregation. He objected to the way in which decisions on these projects bypassed the churches and to the expectation by state leaders that churches support their projects. The efforts to consolidate two Kentucky Baptist orphanages into one near Louisville and to build a Baptist hospital in Paducah were the two endeavors that received the most attention from Rogers. Regarding the former Rogers saw it as an attempt by "the Louisville brethren to concentrate everything in Louisville where it will be under their thumbs."[64] Rogers also disliked the way the chairman of the drive to raise money for the hospital sent sermon outlines to Western Kentucky Baptists that ended with an appeal for money. Furthermore, Rogers questioned the need for the hospital and saw the solicitation of money from other denominations as unscriptural cooperation.[65] Describing these efforts as examples of "bossism" and "fascism," Rogers accused the Baptist state "machine" of being more interested in maintaining its program than in helping churches fulfill their duty to evangelize their communities.[66] The agents of its influence and control were home missionaries supported by state convention funds. In Rogers's eyes, they became "program promoters" whose main mission was to insure continued financial support from the churches for the projects of the "machine."[67]

January 1946, 1; n.a., "Women Prophets," *The Faith*, March 1946, 1; n.a., "Resolutions Against Unionism and Feminism," *The Faith*, April 1946, 1.

[64]I. W. Rogers, untitled comment, *The Faith*, October 1946, 1; cf., idem., "An Example of the Cover-up Policy," *The Faith*, October 1947, 3.

[65]Rogers, "Open Letter to Brother Geo. Phillips," *The Faith*, December 1945, 1–2; and idem., "Largest Baptist Hospital in the World," *The Faith*, September 1947, 1.

[66]Rogers, "Fascism among Baptists," *The Faith*, December 1945, 1, 4; idem., "More Fascism," *The Faith*, January 1946, 4; idem., untitled comment, *The Faith*, January 1947, 2; and idem., "'A Baptist Universal Church,'" *The Faith*, June 1947, 1.

[67]Rogers, "Fascism," 4; idem., "Why All the Fuming?" *The Faith*, February 1946, 2–3; idem., "Program Promoters," *The Faith*, November 1947, 1; and idem., "Lording It over God's Heritage," *The Faith*, February 1948, 1, 4.

What is significant about Rogers' criticisms and complaints is that they are not fundamentalist but reflect resentment for the intrusion of the denomination into the affairs of local congregations and a fear that the growing bureaucratization of the Convention would undermine the autonomy of the local church. Rogers argued that "a Baptist church is an independent, self-governing body. It is the highest ecclesiastical body in the world," and therefore, "no association or convention can direct [its] work."[68] Moreover, in drawing attention to these developments, Rogers found himself the object of attacks concerning his loyalty to the Convention and defended himself by appealing to populist imagery. He portrayed himself as the humble rural pastor fighting the sophisticated preachers in the cities:

A plain country Baptist preacher (his initials are I. W. R.) had the audacity to use his God-given right to offer a few words of criticism about the methods of the State Mission Board.... Some of the dear brethren threw up their hands in holy horror at the impudence of anybody (especially a country pastor) who would publish one word of criticism against the methods of said sacred, immaculate, holy Board in Louisville.[69]

In using such rhetoric Rogers hoped to tap for his defense the resentment of rural pastors against the influence of the large congregations in the cities over the Convention. In short, prior to 1948 Rogers represented one segment of Southern Baptists who were alarmed by the denomination's growth and feared diversity would undermine its distinctive characteristics.

After 1948 Rogers turned his attention to broader issues confronting the denomination and did so with a fundamentalist perspective. What altered his outlook was E. P. Alldredge's pamphlet

---

[68]Rogers, "A New Testament Church: An Independent Body," *The Faith*, May 1947, 1–2; cf., idem., "'A Baptist Universal Church,'" 1.

[69]Rogers, "More Fascism," *The Faith*, January 1946, 4.

Unionizing Southern Baptists.[70] Rogers's conversion to Alldredge's perspective was not the sudden alienation of a loyal Southern Baptist, rather his concerns over the independence of local congregations, distinctive Baptist practices, and the growth of the Convention had preconditioned Rogers to be receptive to Alldredge's analysis. In effect *Unionizing Southern Baptists* widened Rogers's perspective by showing him how his concerns were a part of serious threat to the doctrinal orthodoxy of the Southern Baptist Convention. He recognized that those who held union meetings tended to support Southern Baptist participation in cooperative Protestantism, that the "machine" could use its power to compel support not only of its projects but also those of cooperative Protestantism, and that cooperative Protestantism posed a more serious threat to the independence of local Baptist churches than the Convention "machine." In adopting this framework, Rogers became a fundamentalist.

The change in Rogers's perspective, and his evolution into a fundamentalist, is seen most clearly in his discussion of two issues: unionism and support of the Cooperative Program. Unionism covered a multitude of sins, and before 1948 Rogers occasionally wrote concerning unionism in terms more characteristic of a fundamentalist by identifying unionism with cooperative Protestantism.[71] But in these articles, he usually used unionism to refer to occasions when churches from different denominations joined together for special services. Rogers condemned it because it implied toleration if not approval of nonbaptist doctrines and practices.[72] Unionism also became the rubric under which Rogers criticized some Southern Baptists for conducting open communion services and accepting alien immersion as a basis

---

[70]Rogers did not acknowledge explicitly that this booklet influenced him, but the conclusion is almost inescapable given the change in tone and content of articles and editorials in *The Faith*. See the discussion below of unionism and the Cooperative Program.

[71]See for example, Rogers, "Modernism Moving Southward," *The Faith*, June 1946, 1; and idem., "Unionism Again," *The Faith*, February 1947, 1.

[72]See Rogers, "Unionism," 1; n.a., "Resolutions against Unionism and Feminism," *The Faith*, April 1946, 1; n.a., "A Protest Against Unionism," *The Faith*, March 1947, 1; and n.a., "Is Unionism Scriptural," *The Faith*, April 1947, 1; cf., Buell H. Kazee. "Why Baptists Cannot Unionize with Others," *The Faith*, March 1947, 1–2.

for membership in their churches.[73] Churches that allowed open communion permitted any believer present to partake of the Lord's Supper even if they were not members of the church or its denomination. Rogers held that Southern Baptist churches should restrict communion to members of its denomination. Alien immersion referred to the practice of accepting baptisms done in other denominations provided the individual was immersed. Rogers believed the Bible required that new members in Southern Baptist churches had to be rebaptized unless the ceremony had been performed in another Southern Baptist church. Significantly, when Rogers attacked denominational institutions during these years he did so for deviating from Baptist norms in these practices not for teaching theological liberalism or for supporting cooperative Christianity.[74] But Rogers recognized the link between these practices and the threat of modernism. Noting that the Virginia State Convention approved a resolution calling for cooperation with the interdenominational and liberal Virginia Council of Churches, Rogers observed that "a large percent of Virginia Baptist are Open Communionists and Alien Immersionists. This makes these Baptists fertile ground for growing Modernism and Unionism."[75]

After 1948 Rogers discussed unionism almost exclusively in the fundamentalist terms of cooperative Protestantism and doctrinal compromise. For example his attacks on denominational leaders and institutions usually included some comment on their connection to an organization like the Federal Council of Churches. He accused the Foreign Mission Board's Executive Secretary of being an "unionizer" because he was a member of a church associated with the Virginia

---

[73]Rogers, "Unionism," 1; and idem., "Modernism Moving Southward," 1.

[74]In 1945 Rogers queried the President of Southern Seminary regarding what the students learned about open communion and alien immersion. In Rogers' eyes the President avoided directly answering the question by stating that the Seminary's position is the same as when it was founded. Rogers received a similar evasion from the Executive Secretary of the Foreign Mission Board. In both cases Rogers was mildly critical of these leaders for not unequivocally denouncing these practices. See Rogers, "Correspondence with Dr. Fuller," *The Faith*, October 1945, 4; and idem., "Foreign Mission Board Responds," *The Faith*, November 1945, 2.

[75]Rogers, "Modernism Moving Southward," 1.

Council of Churches.[76] He pointed out the "unionistic" affiliations of faculty at Southern Seminary in Louisville.[77] He charged the editors of Convention newspapers with abetting the "unionist" designs of these leaders by not informing Southern Baptists of their connections with cooperative Protestantism.[78] Rogers advised the "unionizers" to leave the denomination and "join the Northern Baptist Convention where they belong" because the "overwhelming majority of Southern Baptists are getting tired of these traitors in our midst."[79] Rogers left unsaid what should be done if they did not leave.

Editorials and articles on the Cooperative Program, the means by which the Southern Baptist Convention financed its activities, also reveal the increasingly fundamentalist cast of Rogers's mind after 1948. Started in 1925, it collected money from the churches and disbursed funds to support home and foreign missionaries, the publication of newspapers, books, and Sunday school literature, the denomination's seminaries and colleges, and a variety of charitable concerns.[80] Resistance to the Program came from several sources, most notably those who saw the Program as a threat to the independence of the local congregation, but by the 1940s it was a well-established part of Convention life. In 1945 Rogers supported the Cooperative Program claiming that "it is the best method we have of doing our mission work," but he was critical of those Southern Baptists who

---

[76]Rogers, "Brother Rankin," 1, 3–4. He published the same material two and one years later in Rogers, "The Unionism of Dr. M. Theron Rankin," *FSB*, August 1951, 5–7.

[77]Rogers, "Dr. Mueller's Record," *The Faith*, June 1949, 3; idem., "The Southern Baptist Convention," *The Faith*, June 1949, 1–2; and idem., "The Source of Our Trouble," *The Faith*, August 1949, 1–2.

[78]Rogers, "Has the *Western Recorder* Lined up with the Unionists?" *The Faith*, April 1949, 1; and idem., "The Southern Baptist Iron Curtain," *The Faith*, May 1950, 1, 3–4.

[79]Rogers, "Why Don't They Get Out?" *The Faith*, July 1949, 2.

[80]On the activities of the Cooperative Program and its place in the Convention, see Robert A. Baker, *The Southern Baptist Convention and Its People, 1607–1972* (Nashville: Broadman Press, 1974) 403–404, 426. In *Tried as by Fire: Southern Baptists and the Religious Controversies of the 1920s* (Macon GA: Mercer University Press, 1982) 200, 204–205, James J. Thompson described the difficult time the Program had in gaining acceptance during its early years.

made support of the Program a test of loyalty to the Convention.[81] His concern, though, reflected the traditional Baptist objections. "A Baptist Church is an independent institution," explained Rogers, and it cooperates with other Baptist churches "on a purely voluntary basis, and not in order that it may become a Baptist Church."[82] Four years later Rogers called the Program "a general policy rotten to the core," and his criticisms became distinctly fundamentalist in tone.[83] He denied that the Program was scriptural. First, the biblical pattern of charity, according to Rogers, was for churches to designate gifts for particular purposes, thus the Cooperative Program failed because churches gave to a general fund from which money was distributed as determined not by the local church but by the Convention and its committees.[84] A more serious problem was that the money went to support unscriptural causes. Rogers minced no words on this point: "There is not any question about it: *the one who supports the Cooperative Program supports Modernism.* And this Modernism is not only unscriptural; it is anti-scriptural, and is a diabolical scheme of the devil to destroy the faith of our young people, especially young preachers, in the Scriptures."[85] By the early 1950s Rogers bluntly advised his readers not to give money blindly to the Program but to "designate our gifts to those boards, agencies, and institutions that are not affiliated with the virus of Unionism and Modernism."[86]

Symbolizing the change in purpose and outlook of the paper from its beginning in 1945, the masthead in 1950 announced in bold letters that:

---

[81]Rogers, "Stabbed by a Friend," *The Faith* June 1945, 2.

[82]Ibid., 1.

[83]Rogers, "Guilty," *The Faith*, February 1949, 4.

[84]Rogers, "Is the Cooperative Program Scriptural?" *FSB*, October 1951, 3–6.

[85]Ibid., 4; cf., comments in Rogers, "Guilty," 4; idem., "Modernist J. M. Dawson Now Supported out of the Cooperative Program," *The Faith*, June 1948, 1; and idem., "Brother Rankin of the Foreign Mission Board 'Categorically' Denies Unionism and Interdenominational ism of the First Church, Richmond, Virginia," *The Faith*, January 1949, 1, 3–4.

[86]Rogers, "The Cure," *FSB*, April 1952, 4.

THE FAITH Earnestly Contends—1. For the great teachings of the word of God, and against false doctrines—especially against modernism and unionism in Baptist ranks; 2. For the freedom and independence of Baptist pastors and churches, and against bossism and political scheming of Baptist denominational officials; 3. For vigorous, Spirit-directed Bible evangelism and missions, both at home and abroad.[87]

Rogers had clearly moved himself and his paper into the fundamentalist camp, but significantly it was not one aligned with J. Frank Norris, rather one committed to reforming the denomination from within.

To be successful in this endeavor, denominational fundamentalists had to broaden their coalition. The editorials of O. W. Taylor in the *Baptist and Reflector* illustrated the effectiveness as well as the limits of the propaganda campaign that denominational fundamentalists waged. Though critical of fundamentalist theology and activities and no friend of denominational fundamentalists, Taylor, nonetheless, came to agree with them that cooperative Protestantism and modernism threatened the distinctive character of the Southern Baptist Convention. Throughout the 1940s Taylor consistently opposed Convention membership in the World Council and Federal Council of Churches, but by the late 1940s he had accepted the fundamentalist perspective that prominent members of the Convention were at work to move Southern Baptists into membership. Two factors account for Taylor's opposition. First, the SBC was a "voluntary association of Baptists" to further missionary and educational activities, thus it did not have ecclesiastical authority over its member churches and could not speak on their behalf.[88] More central to Taylor's objections was the issue of doctrinal compromise, a point prominent in fundamentalist critiques of the FCC. In Taylor's analysis union or cooperation on "the simplest doctrinal basis

---

[87]N.a., Untitled comment, *The Faith*, July 1950, 1.

[88]O. W. Taylor, "An Important Statement Calling for Adoption," *BAR*, 18 April 1940, 3; cf., idem., "In the Interests of Clarity," *BAR*, 21 July 1949, 2.

possible" would result in a "Christianity of minimums" and would "emasculate the rich doctrinal content of New Testament Christianity" accepted among Southern Baptists.[89] Yet Taylor drew the line at efforts to force Southern Baptists who participated in the FCC to either drop their affiliation with the organization or leave the denomination. Commenting on Alldredge's amendment introduced at the 1949 Convention, Taylor showed that he agreed with fundamentalists that some Southern Baptist leaders actively pursued Convention membership in the FCC. In his analysis rather than signaling a victory for this faction, tabling the amendment meant "that the Convention has by implication warned its personnel, agencies, and institutions to clean house.... A period of grace has been given. Southern Baptists are, as a whole, sound in the faith and mean to avoid affiliation with unionizing movements compromising the faith."[90] In short Taylor supported the fundamentalist message of the amendment, that neither the Convention nor individual Southern Baptists should be affiliated with the Federal Council of Churches, but not the fundamentalist tactic of making the Convention the agent to enforce conformity. He did not indicate, though, where he would stand if FCC supporters remained in the Convention and continued trying to influence the direction of the denomination.

Taylor frequently criticized liberal trends in theology, but his complaints usually lacked the pointed criticisms of the fundamentalist attacks. Throughout most of the 1940s his editorials on liberalism were more general and not directed at specific Southern Baptist individuals or institutions.[91] Occasionally Taylor commented on

---

[89]Taylor, "The Christianity of Minimums," *BAR*, 18 May 1944, 2–3' cf., idem., "The Unionist Right Hand of Fellowship," *BAR*, 21 April 1949, 2.

[90]Taylor, "Interpretation of a Motion," *BAR*, 16 June 1949, 2; cf., idem., "In the Interests of Clarity," *BAR*, 21 July 1949, 2.

[91]See for example, Taylor's criticism of the social gospel in "'The Individual Gospel' and 'The Social Gospel,'" *BAR*, 25 April 1940, 2; of liberal's views of the atonement in "Jesus and his Substitutionary Death," *BAR*, 2 May 1946, 2–3; of denying the virgin birth in "Birth of Jesus Not Due to a 'Grave Error,'" *BAR*, 21 March 1946, 2; and of not believing in the resurrection in "The Teaching of Jesus on His Resurrection," *BAR*, 16 May 1946, 2–3. In these articles Taylor did not allege that

reports of liberal Baptists in the South but avoided identifying them as members of the Convention. For example he noted in 1944 that "there appear to be certain brethren and groups wearing the Baptist name in the South who are greatly in love with doctrinal looseness." His recommendation was blunt: "If they feel cramped on orthodox Baptist ground, why do they not go elsewhere? That would be a simple and logical solution and they would be relieved of the onus of their 'narrow' brethren."[92] Two years later Taylor reprinted a letter by Harry Emerson Fosdick, a noted Northern Baptist liberal, to demonstrate Fosdick's "infidelity." In it Fosdick denied the doctrines of the virgin birth and the substitutionary atonement. Indicating Taylor's growing concern about the spread of liberalism in the Convention, his concluding comment was significant: "We wish some Baptists in the South were not so carried away with Dr. Fosdick and his books."[93] Taylor's purpose in both editorials was to alert his readers that claiming to be a Baptist was no guarantee of the individual's orthodoxy. By the end of the decade his warnings became more fundamentalist in tone by including counsel on arresting liberalism's growth among Southern Baptists. He told churches to examine carefully the doctrinal positions of candidates being considered for their pulpits.[94] Taylor also recommended that the Convention adopt a confession of faith and make agreement with it a requirement for admission as representatives to the annual Convention meeting. Taylor denied that such a regulation would led

---

the unorthodox views he criticized were present among Southern Baptists generally or advocated by individual Southern Baptists in particular.

[92]Taylor, "If Cramped on Orthodox Ground, Why Not Go Elsewhere?" *BAR*, 26 October 1944, 2. Taylor's comments referred to a report that a professor in a Baptist school (no names given) said he could speak more freely among Northern liberals than among Southern Baptists.

[93]Taylor, "Unbelief Reaffirmed by Prominent Minister," *BAR*, 21 February 1946, 2. It is also worthy of note that Taylor found the letter in *The Christian Beacon*, a Northern fundamentalist newspaper published by Presbyterian Carl McIntire.

[94]Taylor, "Pre-Pastoral Testing of Ministers," *BAR*, 7 July 1949, 2. Significantly, this advice was the same that Taylor gave in warning churches about taking fundamentalists for their pastors. See idem., "Let Churches Know," 2.

to an inquisition but would help the Convention "keep itself doctrinally pure."[95]

Taylor was not a fundamentalist in 1950, nor did he ever endorse the fundamentalist program. But his editorials suggested a growing affinity with denominational fundamentalists in their analysis of and prescription for remedying problems facing the Southern Baptist Convention. They differed in degree. Where fundamentalists saw the Convention about to be overwhelmed and destroyed by these issues, Taylor believed that most Southern Baptists were orthodox and would not support participation in ecumenical organizations nor tolerate a liberal perspective in the Convention's seminaries and literature. The reasons for Taylor's change are not clear,[96] nor should it be exaggerated, but it does suggest that denominational fundamentalist complaints were beginning to break free of the stain of J. Frank Norris, win an audience beyond their own circle, and gain legitimacy with some Southern Baptist leaders.

In addition to conducting their campaign in newsprint, denominational fundamentalists built new institutions as alternatives to those supported by the Convention. Rogers's efforts with the newspaper and the bookstore were not the only endeavors in this vein. Among Baptists, pastors generally started and edited the papers that may have been little more than newsletters for their congregations in the beginning.[97] In 1954 Rogers noted that when *The Faith* began it was one of the few independent papers circulating among Southern Baptists and in the intervening years had been joined by several others that had similar origins and a common perspective on issues before the Convention.[98] Because they reached all parts of the South these

---

[95]Taylor, "A Convention Confession of Conviction," *BAR*, 10 November 1949, 2.

[96]Taylor's papers are not available.

[97]The *Ashland Avenue Baptist*, edited by Clarence Walker, pastor of Ashland Avenue Baptist Church in Lexington, Kentucky, is an example of this point. It covered primarily activities of the church though Walker commented on denominational developments. See I. W. Rogers, "Rogers' Ramblings," *FSB*, January 1956, 9.

[98]Rogers, "Rogers Ramblings," *FSB*, August 1954, 2. Papers mentioned included *The Harvester* of Louisville, Kentucky, *The Baptist Examiner* of Russell, Kentucky, and *Daybreak* of Winston-Salem, North Carolina. Only information about the last named could be found. Charles Stevens, pastor of Salem Baptist Church, was its editor.

papers, in Rogers's eyes, fulfilled their mission of keeping "the rank and file of the membership of Southern Baptist churches... better informed" about the problems before their denomination.[99]

In the pattern of Northern fundamentalists of the 1920s and 1930s Southern denominational fundamentalists of the 1940s started schools to train pastors because they believed the seminaries infected their students with liberalism thus undermining loyalty to their denominations' distinctive doctrines and practices. Baptists more than Presbyterians pursued this tactic. According to Rogers, "the greatest single need among Southern Baptists...is independent Baptist Bible schools."[100] Anticipating this need, several Southern Baptist pastors began operating schools in the 1940s.[101] I. W. Rogers led one that was designed for men already serving as a pastor and consisted of weekday classes that ran for several weeks. Its purpose was to address the problem that a significant portion of Southern Baptist pastors had

---

The Evangelist, published by Highland Park Baptist Church in Chattanooga, Tennessee, and edited by its pastor, Lee Roberson, would fit into this category. Rogers also acknowledged the contributions that papers like The Sword of the Lord, The Sunday School Times, and The Baptist Bible Tribune made to fundamentalist cause among Southern Baptists. Sword was a paper published in Wheaton, Illinois but edited by a Southerner, John R. Rice; the Times was an interdenominational fundamentalist paper published in Philadelphia; and the Tribune was the official paper of the Baptist Bible Fellowship headquartered in Springfield, Missouri.

[99]Ibid.

[100]Rogers, untitled article, FSB, December 1951, 2. Rogers choice of words ("Baptist Bible") is interesting because a splinter group from J. Frank Norris's used the same phrase to title its fellowship and name its college. Rogers was aware of this school because the previous fall he noted its opening and praised its sponsor suggesting the Baptist Bible Fellowship "bids fair to make a deep impression on the religious life of America." Idem., untitled article, FSB, October 1950, 3. Thus Rogers' words in 1951 may suggest continued approval of the Fellowship's efforts or, more likely, a call for schools that, like the Fellowship's, teach traditional Baptist doctrine but, unlike the Fellowship's, are also more loyal to the heritage of the Southern Baptist Convention. In other words Rogers saw the need for schools that would produce pastors that would help reverse the troubling trends in the Convention.

[101]In "Anti-Conventionism in the Southern Baptist Convention, 1940–1962" (Ph.D. diss., Southwestern Baptist Seminary, 1969) 122–23, Kenneth Cordell Hubbard mentioned the following schools as examples of this trend: Orthodox Baptist Institute in Ardmore, Oklahoma, the Tennessee Temple Schools in Chattanooga, Tennessee, and Piedmont Bible College in Winston-Salem, North Carolina.

no formal training and could not afford the time and money to go to seminary.[102] No detailed description of course content remains for analysis, but Rogers used his allies as teachers, thus the instruction in all likelihood had a fundamentalist flavor.[103]

This endeavor did not endure, but others did, and their founders patterned their efforts after the interdenominational schools but appealed to a Southern Baptist constituency. These schools had to walk the fine line of independence from the Convention in order to maintain doctrinal integrity while not sacrificing Baptist distinctives like the interdenominational schools. In the late 1940s Clarence Walker, pastor of the Ashland Avenue Baptist Church in Lexington, Kentucky, started a Bible institute in his church, which in the early 1950s expanded its work to include a four year college curriculum.[104] With evening classes for students seeking to change careers and a day school for those able to attend full-time, Walker designed the three-year institute course for those who lacked the preparation for college while the college course required 130 semester hours for graduation with a Bachelor of Arts degree in the Bible.[105] Similarly, the Piedmont Bible School in Winston-Salem, North Carolina, combined the interdenominational fundamentalist-style training with a Southern

---

[102]Rogers, "Preachers' Bible School Organized in Mayfield," *The Faith*, October 1945, 1. Rogers estimated that 60 percent of Southern Baptist pastors in western Kentucky had no formal training.

[103]Courses varied from year to year but usually included one in English grammar, one in parliamentary procedure (to help pastors run business meetings), and a couple books of the Bible. See n.a., "Preachers' School Going Fine," *The Faith*, December 1945, 2; n.a., "New Teachers for the Preachers' School," *The Faith*, October 1946, 1; and n.a., "Preachers' Bible School Will Open January 6th," *The Faith*, December 1947, 1. This characterization of teachers is based on their appearance as supporters of Rogers' editorial position in *The Faith*. These included R. G. Aterburn, D. B. Clapp, and Deward Calvin. See n.a., "New Teachers for the Preachers' Bible School," *The Faith*, October 1946, 1; and n.a., "Large Enrollment Expected in the Preachers' Bible School," *The Faith*, October 1948, 1.

[104]N.a., Untitled article, *FSB*, June 1952, 8. In "Rogers' Ramblings," *FSB*, January 1956, 9, I. W. Rogers reported that Walker had been at Ashland Avenue for 40 years and had a membership of 3,000.

[105]I. W. Rogers, "Rogers' Ramblings," *FSB*, January 1954, 12; idem., "Rogers' Ramblings," *FSB*, July 1954, 11; and advertisements for the college in *FSB*, August 1954, 12, and January 1956, 9.

Baptist accent. Founded in 1945 as a Bible institute by Charles Stevens of the Salem Baptist Church, the school came to offer in the early 1950s training in four tracks: two three-year programs, one in Christian Education and another in the Bible; a four-year course of study leading to a Bachelor of Religious Education degree; and a five-year program awarding a Bachelor of Theology upon completion.[106] Its catalog emphasized its distinctive mission: "Although independent in operation, the Piedmont Bible College is Baptist in polity and doctrine, premillennial in interpretation, evangelical in practice, missionary in emphasis, and cooperative in spirit."[107] In short, both the Lexington and Piedmont Colleges offered their training as orthodox alternatives to that of the Southern Baptist seminaries and as a Baptist alternative to the interdenominational institutions for people seeking to serve as pastors, missionaries, and Christian education workers in the Southern Baptist Convention. Moreover, the efforts of both Walker and Stevens won approval for being both fundamentalist and Baptist and thus had critical roles to play in battle to keep the Convention from being controlled by liberals. Walker's schools were ones where "preachers can go and...not become tinctured with either unionism or modernism" and where "Bible-believers can safely invest their money for the training of Baptist young people in the service of the Lord."[108] Stevens's Piedmont Bible College, in the eyes of one supporter, was "a great bulwark against the floods of infidelity that are pouring forth from other Baptist institutions" and against "the attempts of denominational leaders to destroy the freedom and independence of...Baptist churches."[109]

The largest, best supported, and most ambitious of the new Southern fundamentalist Baptist schools was the Tennessee Temple Schools founded by Lee Roberson. When Roberson came to Highland Park Baptist Church in Chattanooga, Tennessee, in 1942 he found a congregation acquainted with interdenominational fundamentalism

---

[106]Quoted by Rogers, "Rogers' Ramblings," *FSB*, August 1954, 5.
[107]Ibid.
[108]Rogers, "Rogers Ramblings," *FSB*, January 1954, 12.
[109]Rogers, "Rogers' Ramblings," *FSB*, August 1954, 12–13; and December 1955, 9.

through the ministry of J. B. Phillips in its pulpit in the 1920s, but he created the schools to serve a narrower Baptist constituency.[110] Roberson's educational efforts began first with a school to train workers for the church's extension chapel program,[111] but its 1946-1947 catalog cast a slightly different perspective on the purpose. Feeling the need "for a distinctively Christian school in this section of the South," members of Highland Park Baptist supported Roberson's endeavor because few of the denominational schools stood "for the faith once for all delivered to the saints. It was stated from the outset that this school was to be EVANGELISTIC, MISSIONARY, FUNDAMENTAL, and PREMILLENNIAL."[112] Not only did this statement reflect a fundamentalist critique of denominational education, but it also revealed a Baptist complaint concerning interdenominational fundamentalism since the fundamentalist Bob Jones College was only fifteen miles away in Cleveland, Tennessee. The problem with Jones's school was not that it failed to meet fundamentalist doctrinal standards but that it was not "distinctively" Baptist to satisfy Roberson and his congregation.

In most other respects the development of Roberson's schools resembled that of the interdenominational institutions. Roberson's efforts began small with a Bible school and a junior college, but their rapid growth in the late 1940s allowed the addition in 1948 of graduate level seminary courses and by 1950 the college granted Bachelor of Arts degrees in Bible and Music.[113] Roberson effectively mobilized the resources of Highland Park to support the establishment

---

[110]See chapter 2, for a discussion of Phillips activities.

[111]Lee Roberson to Roger Carroll Ellison, 31 December 1968, quoted in Roger Carroll Ellison, "A Foundational Study of the Development of Tennessee Temple Schools" (Ph.D. diss., Bob Jones University, 1973) 10–11.

[112]Tennessee Temple College, *Catalog*, 1946–1947, quoted in ibid., 56.

[113]Ibid., 24–28, 60. Ellison reported in ibid., 25, that the schools' combined enrollment in 1946 of 339 grew to 1,326 in 1950. By way of contrast the Lexington and Piedmont schools had only around 150 students each in the mid-1950s. See I. W. Rogers, "Rogers' Ramblings," *FSB*, January 1954, 12; December 1954, 14; and January 1955, 13. Moreover, like Robert Forrest at Toccoa Falls Institute and John Brown, Roberson expanded into primary and secondary education by adding an elementary school in 1951 and a high school in 1971. Ellison, "Foundational Study," 60, 80.

of the Tennessee Temple schools. The church allowed the schools to use its buildings for classes and other activities, supported the schools through monthly contributions, and borrowed money on its credit to finance major construction projects.[114] Like the founders of the interdenominational schools Roberson used his itinerant ministry to recruit students and raise financial support for Tennessee Temple.[115] Some of the cultural concerns of the interdenominational schools also became apparent as conflict between Roberson and the Southern Baptist Convention increased. The school encouraged the development of the "Christian character" of the students through required courses in the Bible, ministry opportunities in Sunday schools, chapels, and rescue missions, and extracurricular activities like missions and premillennial clubs.[116] But Roberson did not weaken his desire to maintain the Baptist character of the schools. He required students and faculty to be members of Highland Park.[117]

---

[114]In "Foundational Study," 17–21, Ellison reports that in 1946 the church gave $500 a month to the schools and by 1949 church support had tripled to $1500 a month. In 1956 the church borrowed $40,000 to give to the school for the construction of a classroom building. By way of comparison, in 1949 Highland Park contributed only an average of $325 a month to the Cooperative Program of the Southern Baptist Convention. N.a., "Contributions," BAR, 17 November 1949, 12.

[115]Ellison, "Foundational Study," 14, called these tours the "most important and most exhaustive method of promotion" of the schools. See ibid., 164–68 on student recruitment. Ellison, 12–15, records that Roberson averaged over fifty such engagements a year. Like his fellow educators, though, Roberson found the press of administrative duties required the curtailment of these trips. He eventually limited himself to Monday through Wednesday revival meetings. Lee Roberson, Double-Breasted (Murfreesboro TN: Sword of the Lord Publishers, 1977) 54–56.

[116]Ellison, "Foundational Study," 49–50, 56–57, 172–83. Fraternities and sororities were forbidden, but the schools fielded athletic teams that competed against other fundamentalist schools and in church leagues in basketball, baseball, soccer, and several other minor sports. Ibid., 183–90. The 1954–1955 catalog for the Piedmont Bible School informed its students that the standards of Christian conduct call for a life of devotion and consistent separation unto God from the things of the world." Quoted in I. W. Rogers, "Rogers' Ramblings," FSB, August 1954, 5.

[117]Ellison, "Foundational Study, 43–46, 174–75. The only exception for faculty was if they were employed by another Baptist church and for students if they lived at home and attended their parents' church.

Newspapers and schools were not the only institutions denominational fundamentalists established in the 1940s. They also created fellowships for mutual support and organizations for coordinating activities in denominational politics. The former was more evident among Baptists and the latter more true of Presbyterian fundamentalists trying to stop reunion. In part, fundamentalist organizational efforts among Baptists were hampered because of Baptist insistence on the independence and autonomy of the local church. If fundamentalist Southern Baptists were alarmed at the prospects of allowing a Convention to direct and dominate affairs in their churches through the Cooperative Program, neither were they going to allow a fundamentalist organization the opportunity for even a reduced measure of influence. Hence they insisted that these fellowships were for little more than mutual encouragement. Further hindering the organizational development of fundamentalists among Southern Baptists was the attitude of Convention leaders. They denounced the formation of and participation in such fellowships as signs of noncooperation to the denomination. Some Southern Baptists were reluctant to join an organization that cast doubt on their loyalty to the denomination.

Fundamentalist Southern Baptists first tried organizing around an important part of their theology, and the Southern Baptist Premillennial Fellowship was a good illustration of the limitations of and difficulties faced by fundamentalist organizations within the Convention. With Lee Roberson playing an active role, the Fellowship was created in the late 1940s to provide a forum for premillennialists to voice their eschatological views among Southern Baptists.[118] They believed they had good reasons for organizing. In their eyes the Convention promoted postmillennialism without permitting alternative views to be expressed. For example, the literature published by the Sunday School Board of the Convention taught postmillennialism.[119] Thus premillennial pastors and churches had to

---

[118]N.a., Untitled article, *The Faith*, June 1948, 1.

[119]Rogers, untitled article, *The Faith*, March 1949, 3. O. W. Taylor, editor of the Tennessee Baptist newspaper, acknowledged the postmillennial perspective of the

use other literature in their Sunday schools when they wanted to teach on prophetic themes and often the only literature that could be found was that published by interdenominational fundamentalists or by Baptists critical of the Convention. The use of such publications created the perception among denominational leaders that premillennial Southern Baptists were not loyal to the denomination.[120] Moreover, premillennialists believed the Convention penalized them by denying them the recognition they deserved. For example, in 1945 Ralph Herring, pastor of First Baptist Church of Winston-Salem, North Carolina, was denied the opportunity to preach the convention sermon at May gathering of Southern Baptists because he was premillennial.[121] I. W. Rogers charged the Convention-sponsored newspapers with ignoring the growth of Highland Park Baptist Church of Chattanooga because its pastor, Lee Roberson, was a premillennialist.[122] To avert criticism that it would divide and weaken the Convention and to demonstrate its loyalty,[123] the Fellowship required its members to support the Cooperative Program, but this stipulation created a "dilemma" for its members. The Sunday School

---

Sunday School Board in "Disagreeing Agreeably with Millennial Editorial," *BAR*, 24 March 1949, 2.

[120]Taylor, "Postmillennial and Premillennial Ramming," *BAR*, 12 May 1949, 2.

[121]Rogers, untitled article, *The Faith*, February 1946, 3. Being a premillennialist, though, did not prevent R. G. Lee, pastor of Bellevue Baptist Church in Memphis, Tennessee, from winning election as the Convention's President in 1950. But Rogers believed he abandoned his views, or at least downplayed them, in order to win the office. According to Rogers, Lee regularly published sermons with a premillennial perspective on prophecy before becoming President. But once in office the publication of such sermons ceased. See idem., "Important Baptist Items," *FSB*, September 1950, 6.

[122]Rogers claimed that Roberson led the Convention in baptisms during the late 1940s with 678 in 1948 and 810 in 1949. He believed that if a denominational leader, like Louis Newton, had reported similar growth the papers would have the news on the front page. See n.a., untitled articles in *The Faith*, June 1948, 1; April 1949, 3; and December 1949, 3.

[123]O. W. Taylor believed that the Fellowship diverted energy from Southern Baptist programs by unnecessarily multiplying denominational machinery, but his greatest fear was that it would divide Southern Baptists by encouraging the more rabid premillennialists to consider themselves more orthodox than those outside the organization. See "Disagreeing Agreeably on Millennial Question," *BAR*, 17 February 1949, 2.

Board drew its budget from funds donated to the Cooperative
Program, thus contributions from Fellowship churches supported the
postmillennial publications of the Board. Fundamentalists outside the
Convention first pointed to the problem,[124] and over time the
Fellowship lost standing among those within the Convention, never
becoming an effective organization for fundamentalists within the
Convention.[125]

A larger, more broadly based fellowship grew out of Lee
Roberson's conflict with the local Southern Baptist association of
churches in Chattanooga. In addition to the schools, a newspaper, and
the Premillennial Fellowship, Roberson used his base at Highland Park
Baptist Church to start a mission board, a rescue mission, and a
church camp. Moreover, the church ran an aggressive bus program
offering rides to church services from all sections of Chattanooga, and
if people did not come to the church then its style of ministry went to
the people in the form of chapels staffed with ministerial students
from Tennessee Temple.[126] The energy and money expended by the
church on these efforts often meant that the Southern Baptist
Convention's concerns fell to second place. Highland Park supported
the Cooperative Program, but not, in the eyes of some, to the degree
that a 12,000 member church could.[127] Some members of the Hamilton

---

[124]J. Frank Norris, "The Dilemma of the Southern Baptist Premillennial
Fellowship," *The Fundamentalist*, 1 April 1949, reprinted in *Information Bulletin of
the Conservative Baptist Fellowship*, March 1949, 6–7. Norris went further: "The
Southern Baptist Convention is Postmillennial from top to bottom.... Its press is a
Postmillennial press.... Its program is a Postmillennial program. Its ambitions, hopes
and aspirations are Postmillennial." Ibid., 6. The editor of the *Bulletin*, a
fundamentalist publication among Northern Baptists, agreed suggesting that this
movement "has not found itself. It is trying to reconcile an staunch Scriptural stand
with the support of an unsound denominational program. Ibid., 7.

[125]In 1956 I. W. Rogers criticized one of its leaders for supporting the Cooperative
Program. See Rogers, "Dr. J. Harold Smith of the Southern Baptist Premillennial
Fellowship Goes All Out for the Cooperative Program," *FSB*, January 1956, 3–4.

[126]Hubbard, "Anti-Conventionism," 140–50. By the mid-1970s Roberson had
seventy-six chapels in operation in Tennessee, Alabama, and Georgia. Roberson,
Double-Breasted, 8.

[127]Membership figure is for 1955 from *Sword of the Lord*, 27 May 1955, quoted in
I. W. Rogers, "Rogers' Ramblings," *FSB*, July 1955, 12. In November of each year the

County Baptist Association interpreted Roberson's promotion of his schools as an alternative to Convention-sponsored colleges and seminaries as implying that they were Southern Baptist schools. Adding to the confusion was that Roberson called the seminary Southeastern Baptist, the same name as Convention seminary on the campus of Wake Forest University.[128] In late 1954 the Executive Committee of the Association issued a statement clarifying the

---

BAR reported the contributions of churches from the Tennessee State Convention to the Cooperative Program, including that given to the general fund and gifts designated to activities supported by the Program. Highland Park's figures show a steady increase over the 1940s, peaking in 1949 with a total of $7492.44 ($3900 undesignated, $3594.44 designated), an increase of 106 percent over the 1940 total. The 1950s show a steady decline, with Highland Park giving only $4980 in 1953, when its membership was pushing 10,000. By way of comparison, First Baptist of Chattanooga gave $10,559.84 in 1940, $30,611.36 in 1949, and $52,386 in 1953. Even allowing for the possibility that First Baptist had a more affluent membership, Highland Park's numbers suggest the extent to which its members channeled their money into Roberson's projects. For example, on support of the schools, see footnote 113, above.

[128]Ellison, in "Foundational Study," 60, recorded that Roberson changed the name to Temple Baptist Theological Seminary in 1953, suggesting that Roberson did not want to mislead his fundamentalist constituency about the character of his school. In part, that analysis may be true. Given the attacks in the Southern Baptist fundamentalist press on the liberalism in Convention seminaries, Roberson did not want his school to be misidentified with the controversy. But another important factor may be the desire of Southern Baptists not to allow Roberson to capitalize on the identification of his school with the Convention seminary and thus draw students and support away from it. Further, Southern Baptists wished to prevent Roberson's graduates from claiming their education was in a Southern Baptist school. Given the reluctance of Southern Baptist churches to hire pastors not educated in denominational seminaries, the possibility existed that churches looking for a pastor might assume that a graduate of Roberson's seminary had his degree from the denominational school in North Carolina. Neither Ellison nor Hubbard, in "Anti-Conventionism," look at the seminary's name change from this angle, but in light of the action that local Baptist association took against Roberson's other schools in 1954, it is not unlikely that both Roberson's desire to distinguish his school and Southern Baptists' concerns account for the name change. Moreover, the new name for the seminary may suggest that a basic shift in Roberson's strategy in combating liberalism in the Southern Baptist convention occurred in the early 1950s. It may be reading too much into the changing of the name, but in light of Roberson's shifting of his activities from the Premillennial Fellowship to the Southern Baptist Fellowship, it seems he gave up the hope of reforming the Convention and moved to creating a new organization without the impurities of liberalism.

relation of Roberson's schools to the Southern Baptist Convention. Not only did the statement explain that his schools were not officially a part of the Convention, but it declared that Roberson and his church were "noncooperating," in other words they did not support fully the Convention's programs and activities.[129] Roberson demanded the Association repudiate the action of its Executive Committee, but the Association sustained it. In 1955 Roberson withdrew from the Association and Convention, and twelve other congregations followed Roberson's example.[130]

In the spring of 1956 Roberson joined with Harold Sightler of the Tabernacle Baptist Church in Greenville, South Carolina, in calling for a meeting of Baptist pastors and workers in the South to discuss the formation of a fellowship.[131] About 100 people from the Southern Baptist Convention, Conservative Baptist Association, World Baptist Association, and independent Baptists attended the meeting held in Roberson's Highland Park church and voted to create the Southern Baptist Fellowship. Its purpose was "to offer fellowship to like minded Baptists," not create a new denomination.[132] No membership fee was assessed nor was the Fellowship to employ any paid workers. Joining the Fellowship did not preclude affiliation with any other convention or association. Only two conditions were imposed: a willingness to be identified with the Fellowship and, most important, agreement with its doctrinal statement. The latter was a blend of fundamentalist and Baptist concerns. It affirmed the inerrancy of the Bible, the trinity, the deity of Christ, and the work of the Holy Spirit in conviction and regeneration. Other articles included traditional Baptist beliefs such as

---

[129]Hubbard, "Anti-Conventionism," 150–54.

[130]Roberson withdrew in two stages: first from the association and then from the Convention. See comments in I. W. Rogers, "Rogers' Ramblings," *FSB*, July 1955, 13; and idem., "The Southern Baptist Fellowship Is Constituted," *FSB*, June 1956, 3. In "Anti-Conventionism," 153, Hubbard listed the twelve churches, all of them in the immediate Chattanooga area.

[131]This account of the origins of this group is based on Rogers, "Southern Baptist Fellowship," 3. See also, Hubbard, "Anti-Conventionism," 252–54; and George Dollar, *A History of Fundamentalism in America* 2nd ed. (Orlando FL: Daniels Publishing Co, 1983) 242–44.

[132]Rogers, "Southern Baptist Fellowship," 3.

immersion and the perseverance of the saints. Significantly, the longest and most strongly worded section concerned the independence of local congregations. Reflecting the concern over bureaucratization of the Southern Baptist Convention, it defined a "New Testament Church" as "a local group of baptized believers" that was "completely independent with no other person, group or body having any authority, right of intervention or control in any form whatsoever over or within a local church."[133] The statement concluded with a brief premillennial statement of the end times and a condemnation of the Revised Standard Translation, modernism, and the National Council of Churches, the successor organization to the FCC. The Fellowship held its first annual meeting in November 1956, at Highland Park with 424 in attendance.[134]

Labeled a "splinter group" by editors of Convention papers, as well as being criticized for including premillennialism in its statement of faith and condemned as a new denomination, the Fellowship had an able defender in Lee Roberson.[135] He emphasized that its members simply met "together for fellowship and for the encouragement which we can give to one another" and that it required no reports from its members nor did it officially sponsor or endorse missions and educational institutions.[136] Roberson may have been technically correct in his claims, but the editors had better insight into the practical consequences of the creation of the Fellowship. It was a denomination in everything but name with Roberson's organizations providing the de facto institutional structure. As George Dollar suggested, Roberson's mission board and schools benefited from the support of pastors and churches joining the fellowship[137]By 1971 the

---

[133]Quoted in ibid.

[134]I. W. Rogers, "First Annual Meeting of the Southern Baptist Fellowship," FSB, January 1957, 7.

[135]According to I. W. Rogers, untitled article, FSB, June 1956, 4, B. H. Duncan called the Fellowship a splinter movement in an editorial in the Arkansas Baptist. The other criticisms came from the editor of the Alabama Baptist in an editorial reprinted in Lee Roberson "The Southern Baptist Fellowship," The Evangelist, copied in FSB, February 1957, 5.

[136]Roberson, "Southern Baptist Fellowship," 5.

[137]Dollar, History, 243.

Fellowship had changed its name to the Southwide Baptist Fellowship and attracted 1,195 pastors from over twenty-one states including some from as far away as California, Pennsylvania, and Michigan.[138]

By the early to mid 1950s, fairly well organized fundamentalist factions had formed among Southern Baptists and Southern Presbyterians. Baptists were more loosely connected, creating their ties through a network of large churches, newspapers, schools, and fellowships. On the other hand, Presbyterians focused their energy to stop reunion with Northern Presbyterians, developing organizations to achieve that goal. Rarely, if at all, did either faction recognize that they were fighting a common battle, much less support the other in their struggles. Yet there were similarities. Both groups believed that many if not most of the ministers and laity subscribed to their conservative theology and needed to be awakened to the dangers facing their denominations. Both saw themselves defending the theological and ecclesiological traditions of their denominational heritage. Thus both had to overcome the negative associations created by the activities of the previous generation of fundamentalists and to distance themselves from the interdenominational fundamentalists active in the South. Both criticized the activities of the organizations of cooperative Christianity and were alarmed by the growth of liberalism in their denominations' schools, seminaries, and publications. But for some denominational fundamentalists, the pace of change was too slow, the prospects for victory too slim. In their analysis the disease of liberalism had so infected their denominations that no cure was possible. In fact, by remaining members of the Southern Baptist Convention and the Southern Presbyterian church, they believed they compromised their stand for orthodox Christianity.

---

[138]Ibid. Slightly more than two-thirds of the membership came from six states: Alabama (72), Florida (109), Georgia (180), North Carolina (180), South Carolina (129), and Tennessee (132).

The proper course of action was not reform, but the path taken by William Jones and Lee Roberson: separation and independence.

6

SEPARATIST FUNDAMENTALISTS

Come out from their midst
And be separate
—2 Corinthians 6:17

In 1942–1943 Robert McQuilkin, founder and president of Columbia Bible College, exchanged a series of heated letters with three pastors of Bible Presbyterian churches in the piedmont of the Carolinas. The letters focused on McQuilkin's decision to remain a minister in the Presbyterian Church in the United States (Southern Presbyterian Church or the PC-US). Several years earlier these pastors had come to the conclusion that certain circumstances revealed the apostasy of their denomination, compelling them to withdraw from the Southern Presbyterian Church. According to one of the three, E. A. Dillard of Charlotte, "The presence and power of modernism has become more apparent" as the denomination rejoined the Federal Council of Churches (FCC), elected as its Moderator a person Dillard believed to be a liberal, and failed to discipline Union Seminary professor E. T. Thompson for his liberal views. In Dillard's eyes these developments "point[ed] to the fact that the Church is under the domination of those who have forsaken the faith of our fathers."[1] Drawing on

---

[1]E. A. Dillard to RCM, 21 January 1942 (Robert C. McQuilkin Papers, Bible Presbyterian File, Library, Columbia Bible College, Columbia SC) (hereinafter cited as RCM Papers).

relationships built over the years as a supporter of McQuilkin's work with the Bible College and displaying the zeal of new converts, they tried to convince McQuilkin that the circumstances that forced them to leave had worsened and that he also should desert the denomination. McQuilkin agreed that many of the signs of apostasy Dillard described were evident in the church, but for him the question was one of degree; the Southern Presbyterian Church might be ailing, but the illness was not yet terminal. He also argued that they needed to be more tolerant of his position and give him the benefit of the doubt that he was obeying God's will for his life. Finally, he felt their attitude drove a wedge between them that hindered cooperation in matters of mutual interest. "It would be a triumph of Satan," according to McQuilkin, "if we should break fellowship with one another and fight one another."[2]

Although the division between McQuilkin and Dillard was something less than a victory for the devil, their dispute reflected a debate that raged within fundamentalist circles in the 1930s and 1940s. These debates were not only carried out in the North but also conducted among Southerners with equal fervor. Significantly, they were more than simple disagreements over the fine points of fundamentalist theology, but insofar as separatists acted on their interpretation of the relevant Biblical passages the resulting divisions reshaped alliances among Southern fundamentalists and the institutional structure of the movement in the South. Furthermore, these disputes represented the appearance of another Northern pattern of fundamentalist controversy in the South, one not concerning liberalism within the denominations but over the very definition of fundamentalism itself.

The separatist impulse was sourced in changing understanding of what the Bible taught concerning holiness. During the 1920s and 1930s fundamentalists expanded the interpretation of these teachings beyond the emphasis on personal piety and obedience to fundamentalist norms for individual behavior to include an application that justified

---

[2]RCM to E. A. Dillard, 9 October 1943, in ibid.

withdrawal from denominations controlled by liberals.[3] Quoting a verse from the Bible that referred to the Jews' separation from the pagan religious practices of their neighbors in biblical times, some fundamentalists roared, "Come out from their midst and be separate" from the theological sinners in the denominations. According to these militant separatists to remain in the denominations condoned the liberals' abandonment of orthodox Christianity and compromised the fundamentalist stand for truth. On the other hand, withdrawal was a means of exposing the liberals' theological errors and maintaining a faithful testimony to the doctrines that the modernists denied.[4] Anything less imperiled the fundamentalists' stand for a supernatural and biblical Christianity and one's credentials as a fundamentalist. Moreover, some separatists saw their departure as a means of influencing the orthodox left in the denomination to follow the separatist example. Many of the theologically conservative were unconvinced and denied that the circumstances in the denominations demanded such drastic steps. Disturbed by the critical and censorious rhetoric of the separatists and loyal to their denominational heritage, they believed that their duty was to reform their denominations from within. This debate in some ways represented a reexamination of an old question in American Protestantism, of the point at which the corruption of ecclesiological institutions required the creation of new

---

[3]See chapter 1, for a discussion of holiness as a central element in defining fundamentalism and chapter 3, 92-96, for how fundamentalist schools tried to inculcate these norms in their students.

[4]Written from the separatist perspective, George W. Dollar's *A History of Fundamentalism in America* 2nd ed. (Orlando Fl: Daniels Publishing Co., 1983) frequently evaluates the fundamentalist character of groups and individuals on their willingness to "expose" modernism; see in particular, 213–62. Those who do not adopt this tactic are denied membership in the fundamentalist camp. In "Toward an Honest Portrait of Fundamentalism, 1930–1980: An Historical Study of Progressive Development in the Working Definition of Fundamentalism" (Ph.D. diss., Bob Jones University, 1982) 283–91, Peter James Blakemore suggested that in the early 1930s the definition of who belong in the fundamentalist community changed from one which focused on the defense of particular doctrines to one which retained the doctrinal element but added the principle of ecclesiological separation.

ones.[5] The Pilgrims and the Disciples of Christ represent American Protestants who preceded the fundamentalists and applied the principle of separation to their situations.[6]

Eschatology also helped shape the perspective on conditions within the church and on the response to those conditions. Premillennialists believed that the Bible foretold a great apostasy, or massive abandonment by the Church of its teachings. Premillennial fundamentalists interpreted the growing acceptance and toleration of liberal interpretations of Protestant doctrine as a sign of the coming apostasy; indeed, for some these developments were proof of the apostate condition of some American denominations and vindication of their interpretations of prophecy. Furthermore, these fundamentalists believed that the Bible enjoined Christians to judge this apostasy and remove it from the church. If the effort to maintain the doctrinal purity of a denomination and its agencies failed, then the duty of fundamentalists was clear: separate themselves from those that endorsed, supported, or tolerated the false teaching and form institutions faithful to a supernatural Christianity. Here the question of evidence became paramount. At what point did the growth of apostasy justify schism? For some, any failure to rid all apostasy from a denomination necessitated withdrawal, and with their interpretation of prophecy telling them that such developments were an inescapable part of God's plans, they believed efforts to stop the trends were doomed. Thus the burden of proof that reform was possible fell on the orthodox that remained in the denominations. Moreover, the decision of when to obey the biblical teachings on separation was made for some fundamentalists because their efforts to eliminate

---

[5]Such is the suggestion of George Marsden in *Reforming Fundamentalism: Fuller Seminary and the New Evangelicalism* (Grand Rapids MI: Eerdmans Publishing Co., 1987) 6. Some fundamentalists looked further back in history to the Protestant Reformation for precedents justifying separation from liberal-controlled denominations. For example, see Carl McIntire, *Twentieth Century Reformation* (Collingswood NJ: Christian Beacon Press, 1945).

[6]For a brief review of this issue in American church history, see John D. Woodbridge, Mark A. Noll, and Nathan O. Hatch, *Gospel in America: Themes in the Story of America's Evangelicals* (Grand Rapids MI: Zondervan Publishing House, 1979) particularly the chapter entitled "The Division of the Church," 183–203.

apostasy resulted in their excommunication for disturbing the peace of the denomination. Separatists interpreted such actions as another piece of evidence confirming the apostate character of the church.

Whether they were driven out or left because they believed they were obeying scriptural injunctions, separatists often continued attacking what they believed to be continued development of liberalism in their former denominations to prove its apostasy. Though these assaults may have been nothing more than continued attempts at self-justification or born out of simple spite and bitterness, they hoped that their endeavors would convince others to forsake the apostasy with each such validating their position. And what of the relationship to those who did not read the evidence in quite so stark terms or who remained unconvinced by the separatists' interpretations? By the early 1940s some fundamentalists believed this doctrine required separation not only from liberals but also from fellow conservatives who remained in the denominations. Furthermore, they believed that only those who followed this interpretation were truly fundamentalist. Such a radical application effectively ended fundamentalist hopes for interdenominational cooperation among conservatives in projects of mutual concern and interest, and the consequence was further fragmentation of the movement.[7]

In the South, Baptist fundamentalists perhaps had the easiest path in following the injunctions of separatism. Their congregational polity emphasized the autonomy of the local church, hence loyalty to particular denominational institutions were not strong nor did the Convention have effective institutional means to control the separatist impulse. On the other hand, Presbyterian and Methodist fundamentalists left traditions where allegiance to a particular structure was an important part of their heritage thus becoming an independent Methodist or Presbyterian was something of a

---

[7]In "The Fundamentalist Leaven and the Rise of an Evangelical United Front," in *The Evangelical Tradition in America*, ed. Leonard I. Sweet (Macon GA: Mercer University Press, 1984) 274–87, Joel Carpenter shows how the issue of separation troubled evangelical efforts in the 1940s and 1950s to create a national organization to voice evangelicals' concerns and to cooperate in evangelistic campaigns.

contradiction in terms. To be sure, a few such congregations developed, but most chose either to join in creating a fundamentalist denomination or to align themselves with Northern separatist traditions. Caught in the middle of these controversies were the denominational and interdenominational fundamentalists. The former found themselves under fire from the separatists for remaining aligned with apostasy and discovered that their efforts at reform were tarred with accusations of trying to split the denominations in a separatist fashion. On the other hand, interdenominational fundamentalists faced a difficult choice: to continue to offer their schools as servants to all denominations, incurring the wrath of the separatists, or to commit to the separatist camp with whom they had much in common, alienating their denominational allies.

The exchange between McQuilkin and the piedmont pastors is worth closer inspection because it reveals both the theological parameters of the debate over separatism and its impact on fundamentalism among Southern Presbyterians. When McQuilkin moved to Columbia in the 1920s to assume the presidency of the Southern Bible Institute, he moved his membership to the Southern Presbyterian church and began to develop friendships with some of its ministers. Flournoy Shepperson was one. Born and raised in Arkansas, he earned his theological degree from Union Seminary in Virginia, graduating in 1908. After seventeen years in rural Arkansas and South Carolina churches, he became pastor of Second Presbyterian Church in Greenville.[8] With a membership in 1925 of just under five hundred, the church nearly doubled its membership over the next fourteen years under Shepperson's leadership.[9] During these years he became friends with McQuilkin and directed his congregation into supporting the college. Exactly when and under what circumstances the association began are not clear, but by the late 1920s and early 1930s young people from the church began enrolling

---

[8]PC-US, *Ministerial Directory of the Presbyterian Church in the United States, 1865–1941*, rev. and sup., 1942–1950, E. C. Scott, compiler, 613.

[9]Shepperson said the membership totaled 477 when he took over the pulpit and grew to 904 in 1939. "Answer to the Petition of January 19, 1940," no date, mimeographed copy in RCM Papers, Shepperson File.

in the college, and McQuilkin had spoken in Shepperson's pulpit.[10] Moreover, the relationship was close. At one point Shepperson characterized it as one between pupil and teacher, while McQuilkin confessed in 1943 that "my heart's love and loyalty has been with you from the beginning."[11]

Over the course of the 1930s Shepperson became increasingly critical from the pulpit of developments in the denomination, denouncing the liberal tendencies he saw in its seminaries, literature, and missions. Also beginning in the mid-1930s Shepperson's preaching on premillennial themes started attracting, in the words of the congregational faction who opposed him, "Baptists, Methodists, and various others who, while they have joined our church, may never become true Presbyterians."[12] These changes along with Shepperson's attacks on the denomination incited some members to petition the presbytery in January, 1940, to take over jurisdiction of the congregation. The presbytery refused but appointed a committee to investigate the charges. The petitioners sent the committee the same list of complaints and added a few new ones.[13] Equally troubling in their eyes was Shepperson's efforts to prevent the church's young people from attending Presbyterian summer camps, his substitution of Sunday school literature from an interdenominational press for Presbyterian-published lessons, and his encouragement of financial support for missionaries serving under interdenominational boards.[14] Columbia Bible College figured prominently in some of these

---

[10]Among the first students to enroll in Columbia Bible College's four-year program were two girls from Greenville's Second Presbyterian. Columbia Bible College Applications File, Library, Columbia Bible College, Columbia, South Carolina. Robert McQuilkin's Appointment Calendar indicate that he scheduled preaching engagements at the church in November 1931, and in May 1936.

[11]Flournoy Shepperson to RCM, 4 March 1943; and RCM to Flournoy Shepperson, 30 January 1943, in RCM Papers, Shepperson File.

[12]"Petitioners to the Presbytery's Committee," 19 January 1940, mimeographed copy, in ibid.

[13]Compare ibid., with "Petition from Members of Second Presbyterian Church, Greenville, to Enoree Presbytery," 8 January 1940, and F. McG. Kincaid to Second Presbyterian Church, 10 January 1940, mimeographed copies in RCM Papers, Shepperson File.

[14]"Petitioners to the Presbytery Committee."

complaints in that Shepperson sent the young people to Ben Lippen, the college's summer retreat, and that the college trained the interdenominational missionaries seeking support from the congregation.[15] Significantly, Shepperson did not deny these accusations but defended himself on several fronts. He pointed out that the missionaries were members of the church and that he was not alone in his concerns about the worldliness of the church youth camps and the liberalism of other Southern Presbyterian institutions. Moreover, according to Shepperson, the church's session approved the change in Sunday school literature, and in any case, the denomination did not require that churches use its material, only that they teach its catechisms, a practice Second Presbyterian continued to follow.[16] The committee recommended no presbyterial action but admonished Shepperson, the session, and the petitioners to work together for the peace of their church. Specifically, it told Shepperson to give his loyalty to Presbyterian rather than interdenominational institutions. "You will recognize at once," the committee chided in ministerial circumlocution, "that we have in mind a particular college."[17]

While responding "cheerfully and wholeheartedly" to the committee's suggestions and promising not to support nonpresbyterian institutions through the church's budget,[18] Shepperson escalated the conflict by having the congregation vote out of office church leaders opposed to him and replace them with people willing to follow their pastor's lead.[19] At this point, the presbytery intervened and ordered an

---

[15]Ibid.

[16]"Answer to the Petition."

[17]N.a., "Advice of the Committee," no date, mimeographed copy in RCM Papers, Shepperson File.

[18]N.a., "Pastor's Response to the Advice," 26 January 1940, mimeographed copy in RCM Papers, Shepperson File.

[19]This vote indicates some measure of Shepperson's support within the congregation: 225 members voted to oust the leaders while 96 opposed the move. RCM to J. H. Viser, 7 March 1940, in RCM Papers, Shepperson File. Exactly which group of leaders was involved is not clear. According to J. H. Viser, pastor of Greenville's McCarter Presbyterian Church, the vote concerned the removal of elders from the session. J. H. Viser to RCM, 7 March 1940, in RCM Papers, Viser File. In "Petitioners

investigation. After hearing testimony from both sides the Enoree
Presbytery voted to remove Shepperson from the pastorate of the
church "because the interests of religion imperatively demand it."[20]
The minutes of the meeting were not more specific because the
Presbytery conducted most of the debate in executive session, but a
majority of the Presbytery seems to have interpreted Shepperson's
action against dissident leaders as a sign of his unwillingness to abide
by his promise to work for the peace of the church.[21] But the
undercurrent involved Shepperson's criticisms of denominational
agencies and his disloyalty evidenced in his support of
nonpresbyterian institutions. Other Presbyterians feared that these
issues laid the foundation, and Shepperson's case set the precedent for
purging denominational fundamentalists who voiced complaints
similar to Shepperson. For example, J. H. Viser, pastor of Greenville's
McCarter Presbyterian Church confessed:

I am NOT using Presbyterian literature. I am NOT
supporting the Presbyterian Committee of Publications. I am
NOT giving to the Foreign Missions treasurer—but direct to
sound missionaries. I am not only PERMITTING my young
people to go to Columbia Bible College, but positively

---

to the Presbytery" and "Answer to the Petition," both sides indicate that Shepperson
was in the process of implementing a plan by which his supporters would gradually be
rotated onto the Board of Deacons. It may be that Shepperson sought to shore up his
support on the Session before trying to change the Board of Deacons.

[20]*Minutes of the Enoree Presbytery*, March 1940, 8. The division for and against
Shepperson was not recorded in the minutes.

[21]Ibid. Perhaps another factor working against Shepperson was a question
concerning his personal finances. The details are not clear, but apparently the
Presbytery loaned Shepperson some money, and he was slow in repaying it. Knowledge
of this situation led one minister, J. H. Viser, who in other circumstances would have
given Shepperson his unqualified support, to consider not attending the meeting.
Robert McQuilkin convinced Viser to attend and speak on Shepperson's behalf insofar
as the issue revolved around Shepperson's criticisms of the denomination. RCM to J.
H. Viser, 7 March 1940 in RCM Papers, Shepperson File; J. H. Viser to RCM, 7 March
1940; and J. H. Viser to RCM, 9 April 1941, in RCM Papers, Viser File. The *Minutes*,
8–9, record that Viser did voice support on this point and that the presbytery cleared
Shepperson of "any misconduct which would detract from his Christian character."

URGING them to go there.... I am NOT patronising the Clinton's young people's conferences but have gone "Ben Lippen" beyond all recall! In other words, I am FAR WORSE than Shepperson in these respects. And the Presbytery has the right to INITIATE proceedings against me even tho [sic] no one in my group would complain to the Presbytery about me.[22]

The presbytery took no action against Viser, though he felt that his activities cast suspicions on his loyalty to the denomination.[23] Shepperson, on the other hand, remained in Greenville and organized his followers into a new congregation associated with the Bible Presbyterian Church.

The choice of affiliation is not without significance because it reveals Shepperson's identification with the separatist wing of Northern Presbyterian fundamentalism. Organized by Carl McIntire, pastor of a Presbyterian church in Collingswood, New Jersey, the Bible Presbyterian Church contained the premillennialists that left the Northern Presbyterian denomination in 1936.[24] Adopting a rigid definition of ecclesiological separation, Bible Presbyterians required that its churches and ministers disassociate themselves not only from organizations that either endorsed or tolerated liberalism but also from orthodox individuals that remained affiliated with those

---

[22]J. H. Viser to RCM, 11 March 1940, in RCM Papers, Viser File.

[23]J. H. Viser to RCM, 26 March 1940; and J. H. Viser to RCM, 9 April 1941, in RCM Papers, Viser File.

[24]McIntire supported J. Gresham Machen in his battle the Northern Presbyterians over the organization of the Independent Board for Presbyterian Foreign Missions, a fundamentalist alternative to liberal-tainted denominational agency. Machen and his followers were excommunicated, and they formed what eventually became the Orthodox Presbyterian Church. Machen died in January 1937, and by June this church split over eschatology, with the amillennialists forming the Orthodox Presbyterian Church and the premillennialists following McIntire into the Bible Presbyterian Church. Louis Gasper, *The Fundamentalist Movement, 1930–1956* (The Hague: Netherlands: Mouton and Company, 1963; reprint, Grand Rapids MI: Baker Book House, 1981) 16.

institutions.[25] The Bible Presbyterians believed that the action of Northern Presbyterians in excommunicating orthodox leaders like J. Gresham Machen and McIntire while maintaining membership in the Federal Council of Churches and ordaining ministers that denied belief in cardinal Christian doctrines like the Virgin Birth and the inspiration of the Bible was a sign that this denomination was officially apostate.[26] Shepperson came to construe the action that the Presbytery took against him in much the same way, that his stand for traditional Southern Presbyterian doctrine was the cause of his persecution. And in at least one part of this analysis, Shepperson was encouraged by Robert McQuilkin. Writing before the Presbytery's vote, McQuilkin opined, "The irony of the situation, and the pathetic thing about it, is that a seminary or other institution may wholely [sic] deny some of the most vital 'Presbyterian' truths. Then when a true Presbyterian, who holds to the teachings of the Word as expressed in the Confession of Faith, voices any opposition to this denial of Presbyterianism, he is attacked on the grounds of being 'unpresbyterian.'"[27] But Shepperson went beyond McQuilkin's position by interpreting the presbytery's action as evidence of the denomination's apostasy. Furthermore, the dismissal from the denomination had the effect of opening Shepperson's eyes. Two years later he told McQuilkin, "I can see more clearly now that I am apart from these things" how deeply apostasy affected Southern Presbyterians.[28]

This analysis meant that the path of the denominational fundamentalists was not open to Shepperson. He believed conditions in the Southern Presbyterian church were such that he could no longer work from within to restore it to its theological heritage. To remain a minister in this denomination would compromise his stand for orthodox Christianity and call into question his own adherence to

---

[25]Though written in explanation of the American Council of Christian Churches' position on separation, McIntire's discussion reflects that of the Bible Presbyterians. See McIntire, *Twentieth Century Reformation*, 193–98.

[26]Ibid., 210–12.

[27]RCM to Flournoy Shepperson, 15 January 1940, in RCM Papers, Shepperson File.

[28]Flournoy Shepperson to RCM, 4 March 1943, RCM Papers, Shepperson File.

Presbyterian doctrine. He saw that his efforts to expose error and convince his fellow Southern Presbyterians to drive out liberals had fallen on deaf ears; indeed his campaign made him appear disloyal to the denomination and cast him as a disturber of its peace. In Shepperson's eyes, the presbytery in particular and the leadership of the Southern Presbyterian church in general were more interested in securing the denomination's peace than in maintaining its doctrinal purity. Because Shepperson criticized developments within the denomination, he became seen as an outsider even though by education and career he had the pedigree of loyal Southern Presbyterian. This perception of Shepperson was expressed best in the petition members of his congregation sent to the Presbytery. Its authors asserted that they were "Presbyterians of long standing, most of us reared in this church. We love the Presbyterian Church and respect the sacredness that should adorn its pulpit. We believe in its teachings and in its agencies and causes.... What we have done...is, we believe, our Christian duty, and is, in our opinion, necessary to preserve the peace and purity of our beloved Church and its institutions."[29] The action taken against Shepperson by the presbytery suggests that its members believed themselves acting out of similar perspective as the petitioners. Thus the fight within the congregation simply served as the pretext for the presbytery to intervene and remove a troublemaker. If Shepperson wished to carry on the fight against Southern Presbyterian liberalism, he would have to do so from the outside. Therefore his tactics became public attack, exposure of the errors, and negative criticism in order to convince others to leave the denomination in protest of its failure to discipline heterodoxy.

But such efforts could prove counterproductive. For example, J. H. Viser agreed with Shepperson that conditions in the denomination were troubling, and Viser even considered leaving but was very much influenced by the fact that McQuilkin kept his membership in the church. "So I like the fundamentalists INSIDE," he wrote McQuilkin, "better than the ones who have gone OUTSIDE.... And *if I am going to remain 'in,'* I certainly am not going to jeopardize my remaining

---

[29]"Petitioners to the Presbytery."

'standing' in the Presbyterian church by giving my hearty fellowship and support to an 'outlaw' denomination and its preacher."[30] Furthermore, Viser found that Shepperson's censorious broadsides on the Southern Presbyterian church had undermined denominational fundamentalists' efforts to secure reform. In Viser's eyes, Shepperson's activities reached beyond their impact on Viser's personal standing and denominational politics. "Personally," Viser commented, "I do not approve of this as it puts the whole cause of fundamental Christianity—especially prophecy and the Lord's return—in a bad light in this community.... This whole thing reflects on the honor of the Gospel."[31]

Shepperson was a not a voice crying alone in wilderness of Southern Presbyterian apostasy; already others had reached similar conclusions, had withdrawn from the denomination, and were involved in a campaign to convince other Southern Presbyterians to leave their denomination. One such minister was E. A. Dillard of Charlotte, North Carolina. Born in South Carolina in 1899, he attended college in his home state in addition to two years of study at Moody Bible Institute before going to Columbia Theological Seminary for three years.[32] After pastoring two rural South Carolina churches and serving as assistant pastor in Greenville's First Presbyterian, Dillard moved into the pulpit of Charlotte's Tenth Avenue Presbyterian in 1928, a church that had some association with itinerant fundamentalists that toured the South earlier in the decade.[33] Dillard continued this tradition when he had Robert

---

[30]J. H. Viser to RCM, 3 April 1940, in RCM Papers, Viser File.

[31]J. H. Viser to RCM, 9 April 1941, in RCM Papers, Viser File.

[32]*Ministerial Directory*, rev. and sup., 180. He spent a year at the Presbyterian College of South Carolina and two at the University of South Carolina. The *Directory* did not indicate if Dillard earned any degrees.

[33]Ibid. See chapter 2, p. 59, for an account of James Gray's 1921 Bible conference. The pastor at this time was Daniel Iverson who had attended Moody Bible Institute during the course of his ministerial training. Succeeding Iverson and preceding Dillard in the Tenth Avenue pulpit was J. Frank Ligon. Both Iverson and Ligon appeared as members of the *Southern Presbyterian Journal*'s advisory committee in 1945.

McQuilkin visit the church for a three-day Bible conference in 1933.[34] During the 1930s Dillard became disillusioned with the denomination over the same developments that troubled Shepperson: reunion, liberalism in denominational institutions and literature, and the failure to maintain the doctrinal standards of the church.[35] As he publicly voiced his criticisms in the late 1930s, Dillard found opposition growing in his congregation, particularly among the elders, to the point where a majority of the Session voted to restrict his use of church funds and to reject his suggestions for guest speakers.[36] In these circumstances Dillard decided to resign in 1939 and organize his faction into a Bible Presbyterian Church. He explained his reasons in "Facing the Issue." This pamphlet was more than simple self-justification with parting shots at the denomination. Dillard argued that the problems that led him to speak out were still present and sent a message to other Presbyterian ministers: by remaining members of the Southern Presbyterian church they were complicitous in the failure to redress them. In other words, he sought to convince those with similar concerns that they, too, should leave the denomination. For example, he reminded his readers that "the Presbyterian Church is *one*" and pointed out that Hay Watson Smith continued preaching his liberalism from the pulpit of Little Rock's Second Presbyterian Church. "So in *your* Church in Little Rock," Dillard concluded, "stands a man who has attacked the truth of God and has been whitewashed by the courts of *your* Church."[37]

---

[34]Appointments Calendar, RCM Papers.

[35]E. A. Dillard, "Facing the Issue; or Why I Resigned as Pastor of the 10th Avenue Presbyterian Church," pamphlet, no date, in RCM Papers, Presbyterian Church File. While the major issues remained the same, some of the specific details changed. For instance, as an example of worldliness in church literature, he noted that the Publication Board accepted advertisements for *Gone with the Wind*, a book Dillard denounced as reeking "with sexuality and profanity."

[36]In ibid., Dillard indicated that the Session objected to the fundamentalist connections of the speakers. He specifically mentioned that the Session refused to invite Charles Woodbridge, a Northern Presbyterian excommunicated with Machen in 1936.

[37]Ibid.

While in the long run hindering his efforts, Dillard's negative attacks, like those of Shepperson, were not simply vindictive assaults but had a positive purpose: to expose the liberalism in the denomination and convince the orthodox remaining within in the denomination that the Bible required them to leave. Such a mass withdrawal, in the thinking of separatists like Dillard and Shepperson, would serve as a powerful testimony against liberalism and for the Gospel. Moreover if acknowledged theologically conservative leaders withdrew their decision might influence others to follow their example. But such leaders had to be convinced on a case by case basis. Dillard and Shepperson, along with Robert Cox, the pastor of a Bible Presbyterian Church in Concord, North Carolina, and Carl McIntire, the leader of the Bible Presbyterian movement, joined forces in such an effort in 1942–1943.[38] The object of their campaign was Robert McQuilkin, and the exchange between these men reveals not only the issues and the shape of the debate that was joined among theologically conservative Southern Presbyterians but also the peculiar tensions interdenominational fundamentalists faced in offering their institutions as servants to both fundamentalist factions within Southern denominations and the emerging groups of independent and separatist fundamentalists.

They employed a variety of arguments to convince McQuilkin to resign from the Southern Presbyterian church. First and foremost, they rehearsed the evidence that led them to conclude that their denomination was apostate, a condition that required them to sever

---

[38]Born in New Jersey in 1911 and educated at Wheaton College (BA in 1936) and Union Theological Seminary in Virginia (M.Div. in 1939) Robert Cox began his ministerial career in 1939 at Bayless Memorial Presbyterian in Concord. Within two years he was pastoring a Bible Presbyterian congregation, presumably formed from a split in the Bayless church. Presbyterian Church in America, *Yearbook of the Presbyterian Church in America*, 1984–1984, 166. Cox probably became acquainted with McQuilkin through McQuilkin's preaching engagements at Wheaton College in 1933, 1935, and 1936. Appointments Calendar, RCM Papers. How McIntire became involved is not clear except that part of the debate centered on an article by Cox to be published in McIntire's *Christian Beacon* that explained Cox's analysis of relevant Biblical passages. Probably Cox and possibly Dillard sent copies of their exchange with McQuilkin to McIntire who then joined in the fray.

their ties with it.[39] For the most part McQuilkin did not dispute that some developments suggested apostate tendencies. In other correspondence he clearly indicated that he was troubled by the failure of the denomination to take action against Ernest Trice Thompson and the decision to rejoin the Federal Council of Churches.[40] In his eyes, the latter "certainly is a sign of apostasy. However it is not a sign that the men who voted for it are apostate. They are, many of them, just ignorant and nondiscerning and unspiritual."[41] McQuilkin doubted that the evidence warranted the drastic step of separation. "That the visible Church is heading to apostasy," he bluntly told Dillard, "I have no doubt; that apostasy is here in the Southern Presbyterian Church to such an extent that God's command is to come out...I do not believe."[42] Moreover, to McQuilkin, the growth of the denomination, especially in its overseas missions, the presence of large numbers of ministers faithful to the Confession of Faith concentrated in certain presbyteries, and the appearance of the *Southern Presbyterian Journal* showed that God's favor still rested on the denomination.[43]

Dillard and Cox dismissed such evidence, arguing that the toleration of any apostasy required the faithful to separate from it. According to Dillard the Bible taught that "if there is *one known*

---

[39]A detailed restatement of their evidence would be redundant, but it included the efforts at reunion, rejoining the Federal Council of Churches, and the failure to maintain the doctrinal purity of the church by not disciplining what they believed to be the heterodox teachings of some pastors, seminary professors, and some denominational literature. See E. A. Dillard to RCM, 21 January 1942, 20 August 1943; Robert H. Cox to RCM, 22 July 1943, in RCM Papers, Bible Presbyterian File; and Flournoy Shepperson to RCM, 4 March 1943, in RCM Papers, Shepperson File.

[40]See chapter 4, note 62, for a discussion of the controversy surrounding Ernest Trice Thompson, and chapter 4, 164-66, for the debate over the Federal Council of Churches.

[41]RCM to J. Oliver Buswell, 2 June 1941, in RCM Papers, Buswell File.

[42]RCM to E. A. Dillard, 27 August 1943; cf., RCM to Carl McIntire, 24 December 1943, in RCM Papers, Bible Presbyterian File.

[43]RCM to Robert H. Cox, 6 August 1943; and RCM to E. A. Dillard, 27 August 1943, in RCM Papers, Bible Presbyterian File. McQuilkin did not mention the *Journal* by name, but references in these letter imply that this newspaper was what he had in mind.

Modernist and the Church does not put him out the believer should withdraw from fellowship. How much money does one have to steal to become a thief?"[44] Furthermore, Dillard and Cox drew the conclusion that the failure to obey the Bible's teaching on this point meant that those who remained in the church were sinning.[45] McQuilkin agreed with them on the biblical teaching concerning the church's responsibility to discipline doctrinal deviance but denied that failure to do so required an absolute break. He explained to Cox, "But if and when any individual congregation or church in any city or any denomination did not obey God perfectly in those respects, the Bible does not command all Christians to forthwith leave that church. Putting out the sinner is one thing. Putting ourselves out because of the sinner who is not properly or immediately judged is another."[46]

Denominational fundamentalists may have lost a battle or two, but the war for the soul of the Southern Presbyterian church was not over. McQuilkin also pleaded for charity and tolerance from the separatists. He pointed out that Dillard remained in the church when unjudged modernism was present and then asked, "why may not the Lord be gracious with me and others and give us several years to work out these matters?" McQuilkin continued:

You see my point of view, Archie, is that you were not sinning during these years. You were loyal to Christ....Then you got new light on the situation and new guidance for yourself personally. You are seeking to turn that into a universal question of Biblical interpre-tation and applying it with the absolute rigidity of a

---

[44]E. A. Dillard to RCM, 20 August 1943; cf., Robert H. Cox to RCM, 22 July 1943, in RCM Papers, Bible Presbyterian File. In the latter Cox was unequivocal: "The Bible does not say how much modernism is necessary to make a church apostate because it says: tolerate *NONE!*...The Bible does not make it necessary to endure discussions of when to come out for it says: judge unbelief and if it cannot be judged, forsake it!!"

[45]Robert H. Cox to RCM, 20 May 1943; and E. A. Dillard to RCM, 29 September 1943, in RCM Papers, Bible Presbyterian File.

[46]RCM to Robert H. Cox, 27 August 1943, in RCM Papers, Bible Presbyterian File.

decision on right or wrong to every other minister in the church. In this I think you are dangerously wrong and unscriptural.[47]

Failing to persuade McQuilkin that based on the evidence the Bible required separation, Dillard, Cox, and Shepperson appealed to their friendship with him. All confessed that Mc Quilkin's teaching had influenced their beliefs with Shepperson confessing that what he learned from McQuilkin had "a major share" in helping him "discern the apostasy."[48] But McQuilkin's refusal to follow the logic of his teachings puzzled Shepperson. He wrote, "Now the pupil cannot understand why his teacher is not out here where his teacher's instructions led him to go!"[49] The crux of the problem was that as a representative of fundamentalist beliefs McQuilkin's decision to stay in the denomination hampered the separatists' efforts to convince others to leave. J. H. Viser admitted McQuilkin's presence influenced him to remain a Southern Presbyterian. Shepperson reported that McQuilkin's stand confused his young people, some of whom were considering attending his college.[50] Moreover, Carl McIntire suggested that the leadership of the denomination used McQuilkin's membership to counter the accusations of the separatists: "People everywhere are using you as an excuse to remain in fellowship with the Modernism of the Southern Presbyterian Church. The leaders of the Southern Presbyterian Church do not want you, and yet they are using you to keep people in the fold supporting their organization and propaganda. 'If the Southern Church is good enough for Bob McQuilkin, it is good enough for me,'...say many."[51]

---

[47]RCM to E. A. Dillard, 27 August 1943; cf., RCM to Robert H. Cox, 27 August 1943; RCM to Carl McIntire, 4 November 1944, in RCM Papers, Bible Presbyterian File; and RCM to Flournoy Shepperson, 13 September 1943, Shepperson File.

[48]Flournoy Shepperson to RCM, 4 March 1943, in RCM Papers, Shepperson File.

[49]Ibid. For the other's acknowledgement of McQuilkin's influence see Robert H. Cox to RCM, 22 July 1943; and E. A. Dillard to RCM, 20 August 1943, in RCM Papers, Bible Presbyterian File.

[50]Flournoy Shepperson to RCM, 10 September 1943, in RCM Papers, Shepperson File.

[51]Carl McIntire to RCM, 17 December 1943, in RCM Papers, Bible Presbyterian File.

In other correspondence, McQuilkin indicated that he was well aware of this point and hoped that his association with the Southern Presbyterian church had precisely the effect McIntire feared. Writing to J. P. McCallie, McQuilkin argued that "Southern Presbyterian leaders ought to recognize" that his position represented "a bulwark" against separatists like Dillard and Cox. "Instead," McQuilkin complained, the leaders "accuse us of the very thing that we helping to save them from, namely, a forthwith repudiation of the whole denomination as unspiritual and modernistic."[52] He believed that Columbia Bible College was a "great blessing" not only to Presbyterians but to other Southern Protestants by graduating students with a zeal for missions and evangelical interpretations of the Bible.[53] By accepting the college's graduates as candidates for missionaries and pastors, theological conservatives in Southern denominations would find their factions strengthened.

Thus, McQuilkin in some ways represented a mediator between denominational fundamentalists and the separatists, in essence pleading the case of the former to the latter. But it was a position increasingly difficult to maintain as separatists argued that the Bible required breaking off not only official ties to institutions tainted with liberalism but also fellowship with orthodox individuals who continued their affiliation with such organizations. For McQuilkin and leaders of other interdenominational fundamentalist schools and agencies, such a stand would mean a loss of financial support and possibly a decline student enrollment. Dillard, Cox, and Shepperson did not bluntly suggest that they would withhold their support if McQuilkin did not follow their advice. Rather they suggested that the Bible college would benefit in a variety of ways not the least of which would be freedom from the criticisms of denominational leaders as well as the ability to serve the needs of churches and organizations in

---

[52]RCM to J. P. McCallie, 6 January 1944, in RCM Papers, in Dispensationalism—Southern Church File. The occasion for this letter was McQuilkin's attempt to help McCallie convince a young woman to remain in the Southern Presbyterian church and serve as one of its missionaries.
[53]Ibid.

the separatist camp.[54] McQuilkin doubted the advantages would be worth the cost of alienating the college's supporters within Southern denominations. He pointed out that the logic of the separatists' position would mean that, if he left the Southern Presbyterian church on their terms, he eventually would have to demand that all of the college's faculty, trustees, employees, and students to withdraw their denominations, a requirement McQuilkin believed impractical.[55]

Nevertheless, the separatists perhaps had better insight into the changing shape of the broader fundamentalist movement, particularly that the mission of schools like Columbia Bible College was that of a servant not to fundamentalist factions within the denominations but to the growing independent and separatist wing of fundamentalism. Dillard quite correctly told McQuilkin that denominational criticism of him stemmed not from the college's opposition to liberalism but from "jealousy" that the college divided "the loyalty of the people" and received "money that the leaders think should be given to the Church and its agencies."[56] Moreover, the constituency of the school was changing. During the 1920s the college attracted many of its students from Presbyterian churches, but by the 1950s independent and Baptist churches sent more students that any other groups.[57] Though the

---

[54]Flournoy Shepperson to RCM, 21 January 1943, in RCM Papers, Shepperson File; and E. A. Dillard to RCM, 5 November 1943, in RCM Papers, Bible Presbyterian File.

[55]RCM to E. A. Dillard, 27 August 1943; and RCM to Carl McIntire, 24 December 1943, in RCM Papers, Bible Presbyterian File. RCM to Flournoy Shepperson, 13 September 1943, in RCM Papers, Shepperson File.

[56]E. A. Dillard to RCM, 5 November 1943, in RCM Papers, Bible Presbyterian File.

[57]This observation is based on lists in Columbia Bible College's *Catalogues* that recorded the breakdown of the students' denominational affiliation. These lists did not record exact numbers nor did they specify distinct denominations (i.e., Southern Presbyterian church or Southern Baptist Convention) but simply ranked denominational families (Presbyterian, Baptist, etc.) according to the number of students enrolled. From 1929–1934 the catalogs included no lists. In 1935–1942 Presbyterians topped the lists. From 1943–1954 the lists had Baptists as the largest group. What is interesting is that the early lists did not have a category for students from independent churches and just noted that some students came undenominational congregations. Beginning in 1941, though, the category "independent" appeared and by 1951 was consistently in second place on the lists.

correspondence ended with neither side convincing the other of its position, the break with the separatists was not final. For example, young people from Shepperson's church continued to choose McQuilkin's school for their college education. In fact, Shepperson's son attended for two years before transferring to and graduating from Furman University in his hometown.[58]

McQuilkin's consideration of the question of separation did not end with the conclusion of this correspondence, for by the early 1950s he had decided to resign from the Southern Presbyterian church. Significantly, he did not quit the denomination as the separatists would have him leave, in protest of membership in the FCC and of the alleged liberalism. Though these issues were part of the decision, he wished to remain on good terms with his supporters within the PC-US. In the letter to his presbytery requesting dismissal he explained that, though he "deplored" the denomination's membership in the FCC, "I have not considered that a minister should necessarily leave the Southern Presbyterian Church" for that reason.[59] Rather, he felt that since his work with the college denied him the time to participate fully in presbyterial affairs he could "render more service to the cause of Christ by affiliation with a group of men who are seeking to help and strengthen the various independent churches."[60] The presbytery granted his petition, and McQuilkin joined the Fellowship of Independent Evangelical Churches (FIEC).

In the early 1940s McQuilkin expressed a belief that "a crying need" existed "for a new denomination or at least a fellowship of churches," one that would unite missionary-minded independent and denominational churches.[61] Such an organization would be an

---

[58]Sam G. Shepperson received his theological training at Fuller Theological Seminary and was ordained a minister in the Bible Presbyterian Church in 1949. Presbyterian Church in America, *Yearbook of the Presbyterian Church in America,* 1984–1985, 272.

[59]RCM to Congaree Presbytery, 9 January 1951, in RCM Papers, Congaree Presbytery file.

[60]Ibid.

[61]RCM to [Harold John] Ockenga, 17 April 1943; cf., comments in RCM to Oswald J. Smith, 24 April 1943, in RCM Papers, Independent Church file.

association that pastors and churches uncomfortable with denominational affiliation could join without endorsing the negative stance of the separatists by emphasizing a positive program of "aggressive evangelism and soul winning at home and a Spirit-filled life of separation from the world."[62] McQuilkin took concrete steps toward this goal when he participated in a series of meetings in 1949 that led to the formation of the FIEC. Pastors of several independent churches in the piedmont participated as well as McQuilkin's assistant at the college, Donald Hoke, and the vice-president of its board of trustees, Vernon Patterson.[63] The doctrinal statement of the FIEC affirmed the Bible's inerrancy and premillennialism along with the doctrines of the Trinity, the deity of Christ, the fallen nature of mankind, and the importance of the Church's mission to proclaim the Gospel.[64] The FIEC's primary functions were to provide a forum for mutual encouragement, to promote evangelism, and to license and ordain ministers of independent churches and missionaries for interdenominational boards. The FIEC would not establish its own schools, missions, or publications but "shall endeavor to work through already existing agencies in these fields."[65]

Membership was small in its early years, but it did attract some interest from men like G. Allen Fleece, who left the Southern Presbyterian church in 1951 to teach at the college, and William Lautz, a Dallas Seminary graduate preparing to be a missionary to Japan for the Evangelical Alliance Mission.[66] McQuilkin's involvement was cut short by his untimely death in 1952. Nevertheless the

---

[62]Ibid.

[63]Pastors included the Dallas Theological Seminary graduates L. P. McClenny of Charlotte's Calvary Independent Presbyterian Church and William P. Jones who split Greensboro's Westminster Presbyterian Church. "Minutes of the FIEC", 21 October 1949, in RCM Papers, FIEC file.

[64]Constitution of the FIEC, Article III, in RCM Papers, FIEC file.

[65]Ibid., Article VII.

[66]Columbia Bible College, Catalog, 1953–1954, 8; William F. Lautz to RCM, 15 September 1951; RCM to William F. Lautz, 20 September 1951; and John G. Spurrier to RCM, 12 December 1951 in RCM Papers, FIEC file. "Minutes of the FIEC," 26 October 1951, in ibid., indicate both men were received into membership pending letters of dismissal from their presbyteries.

FIEC is important because it represents the efforts of some fundamentalists in the South to distinguish themselves from the negative image of separatist activities while not being identified through denominational affiliation with liberalism.

While Robert McQuilkin sought a middle way between the extreme separatists and denominational fundamentalists, J. Frank Norris followed his own trail. Though he was forced onto the separatist path when the local and state Baptist organizations refused to seat messengers from his church, once there, he found separatist doctrines and tactics useful tools to continue his campaign against the Southern Baptist Convention (SBC). In fact, Norris is perhaps the best representative of the strain among Southern fundamentalists that waged an ongoing crusade against their former denominations. At times, Norris seemed utterly lacking in the positive purpose separatists used to justify such endeavors: they were trying to convince those that remained in the denomination of the necessity of withdrawing. Often, his attacks seemed directed at only disrupting and destroying the SBC. To be sure, Norris was delighted when denominational fundamentalists like E. P. Alldredge added their voice to criticizing developments that Norris had already attacked. He made use of their material but only to validate and confirm his analysis not to acknowledge new allies nor to enlarge his coalition.[67]

One of Norris's favorite uses of separatist tactics was to try to discredit SBC leadership with the goal of convincing Southern Baptists to separate from the Convention. Perhaps his best opportunity to strike out at the Convention came after World War II when its president, Louie Newton, offered a few mild words of approbation concerning the religious situation in Russia. Norris hoped not only to score some points concerning Newton's worthiness as leader of the SBC and, by general association, cast suspicion upon the leadership of the SBC, but also to tie his crusade against the Convention to the

---

[67]See chapter 5, for discussion of the relationship between Norris and denominational fundamentalists. Detailed analysis of the final years of Norris's career can be found in Barry Hankins, *God's Rascal: J. Frank Norris and the Beginnings of Southern Fundamentalism* (Lexington: University Press of Kentucky, 1996) 118–60.

rising tide of anticommunism at the beginning of the Cold War. Furthermore, Norris's assault gained some extended regional notice over a libel suit concerning an Atlanta *Constitution's* editorial criticizing Norris's attacks on Newton. This incident not only shows how Norris shaped his tactics to capitalize on the changing political mood of the country but also how utterly impervious Southern Baptists were to being convinced to leave their denomination by his methods.[68]

Louie D. Newton had only been President of the Southern Baptist Convention for a few days when he learned he was invited to be its representative on a tour of Russia sponsored by the American Society for Russian Relief in the summer of 1946.[69] Born in 1892 and raised in rural Eastern Georgia, Newton took an unusual path to the pastorate. Earning his bachelor's degree at Mercer University and a Master's from Columbia University but having no training in a seminary, he worked for Georgia Baptists in a variety of ways in the 1910s and 1920s. He began by teaching history at Mercer from 1913–1917. Next he directed publicity for an effort to raise money from Georgians for the Convention, and then he edited for most of the 1920s the *Christian Index*, the newspaper of the Georgia Baptist Convention. Called and ordained in April 1929 to lead the Druid Hills Baptist Church in a wealthy Atlanta suburb, Newton enlarged the scope of his work by serving in several capacities in the Convention bureaucracy as well as a Secretary in the Baptist World Alliance. In May 1946 the messengers to the annual meeting of the SBC elected Newton their President, the youngest man to serve in that office.[70]

---

[68] For an analysis of how the emerging Cold War consensus helped shape this incident, see William R. Glass, "Southern Fundamentalism and Anticommunism at the Beginning of the Cold War: The Controversy Between J. Frank Norris and Louie D. Newton," *Studies in the Social Sciences*, 36 (May 1999): 81–97. Material reprinted with permission of the State University of West Georgia, Carrollton, GA 30118.

[69] Newton chaired the SBC committee that coordinated the collection of funds for the distribution of 175,000 kits of household items to Russian families in 1945. N.a., "Dr. L. D. Newton Will Tour Devastated Areas of Russia," *Christian Index* (Atlanta GA), 30 May 1946, 11.

[70] N.a., "President Louie DeVotie Newton," *Christian Index*, 30 May 1946, 4.

On his twenty-five-day tour of Russia, in addition to observing how Russians used American relief and conferring with Soviet officials on the people's needs, he met with Baptist pastors in nine different cities and preached in their churches, including those in Moscow, Leningrad, Stalingrad, Kiev, and Tbilisi.[71] The pastors in Moscow told him that "we are now enjoying a measure of freedom unknown by the Baptists in all the years of our witness in Russia" and that "we are free to preach what we believe."[72] He also met with Joseph Stalin, giving him a pocket New Testament in English. Upon his return to America Newton sent a Russian version with the inscription, "From one Georgian to another Georgian."[73] Based on these experiences Newton suggested, "Religiously we should regard Russia as our great ally. It is a virgin field for freedom...because Russia never knew freedom of religion until the present regime." Moreover, Newton found some similarities in principles between Baptists and Russians: "The Baptists stand for the same thing as the Russian Government—renouncement of resistance to coercion in matters of belief."[74] Additionally, he told a crowd of 3,500 Baptists gathered in Atlanta's Municipal Auditorium that "the Soviet Government has at last recognized that religion is a vital thing" and that it was "smart enough to grant what appears to be complete freedom of worship."[75] *Time* was reasonably generous in suggesting

---

[71]Newton gave an account of his tour in a series of articles published in Baptist newspapers. See Louie D. Newton, "What I Saw and Heard in the Union of Soviet Socialist Republics," *Christian Index*, 12 September 1946, 5–6; 19 September 1946, 5, 23–24; 26 September 1946, 5–6; and 3 October 1946, 5–6, 28.

[72]Ibid., 26 September 1946, 6.

[73]N.a., "Dr. Newton Welcomes Discussion of His Report on Russia," *Baptist and Reflector* (Nashville TN), 2 January 1947, 5.

[74]N.a., "Innocent Abroad," *Time*, 26 August 1946, 68.

[75]Louie D. Newton, "Baptist Leader Makes Official Report on His Russian Visit," *Constitution* (Atlanta GA), 26 August 1946, 9. Newton also affirmed that he return to America "more deeply committed to the doctrine of Democracy than ever before" and that he believed "Communism is not the answer to the world's greatest need." In "3,500 Hear Dr. Newton in Report on Russia," 26 August 1946, 1, 4, the *Constitution* reported that two white supremacists picketed the meeting with a banner charging Newton with "selling Communism to the USA."

that Newton's remarks resulted from his "holy innocence,"[76] while some mainstream Southern Baptists sought to dissociate the Convention from them. Frank Tripp of Montgomery, Alabama, told *Time* that Newton was "not authorized to speak as a representative of the Convention but...has a perfect right to express himself as an individual."[77]

Newton's words, though, were too easy of a mark for Norris to pass up, and perhaps sensing a division he could exploit, Norris first called for Newton to resign his office.[78] But he overplayed his hand by waiting to force the issue at the next annual convention held in St. Louis in May 1947. Renting an auditorium for the same days as the Southern Baptist meetings, Norris planned to hold rallies and preach in a counter-convention.[79] Moreover, he had a special surprise for Newton and alerted the press to attend a particular session of the Convention.[80] As a part of a pre-convention program at Second Baptist Church, Newton rose to report on his Russian trip and found that Norris had slipped in and began shouting out a list of questions designed to embarrass Newton and to challenge his loyalty to America.[81] He questioned Newton's description of religious freedom, pointing out that the state owned all church property, sent spies into

---

[76]Ibid. The Louisville *Courier-Journal* agreed and suggested that Newton had seen what the Russians had wanted him to see and therefore "innocently" wanted to believe "the best of another fellow," even if he was Stalin. Quoted in n.a., "Louie and the USSR," *Time*, 9 September 1946, 80.

[77]N.a., "Louie," 79.

[78]Ibid; n.a., "Baptist Pastor Urges Dr. Newton to Resign Post," Atlanta *Constitution*, 29 August 1946, 13.

[79]J. Frank Norris to Luther C. Peak, 19 March 1947 (J. Frank Norris Papers, Southern Baptist Historical Commission, Southern Baptist Historical Library and Archives, Nashville TN), box 34, file 1508 (hereinafter cited as JFN Papers).

[80]According to an anonymous letter sent to Ralph McGill, 23 May 1947, in JFN Papers, 28-1318.

[81]Norris gained access by having his church donated $50 to the Cooperative Program designated for foreign missions that entitled First Baptist to send two messengers to the convention. The church selected Norris and William Fraser, an evangelist who was a member of the church. E. P. Buxton to F. Mattison, 31 March 1947; and Jane Hartwell to the Southern Baptist Convention, 30 April 1947, in JFN Papers, 29-1356.

church services, and forbade criticism of the government. Under these circumstances, shouted Norris, "how then can there be religious freedom?"[82] Drowned out by congregational singing, Norris renewed his harassment at the end of the hymn. By this time police were on the scene, and Norris retreated claiming he had successfully revealed Newton and other Southern Baptist leaders as "appeasers of Moscow."[83]

Rallying to defend Newton was Ralph McGill, editor of the Atlanta *Constitution*.[84] In an editorial dated 8 May 1947, he called Norris "a Ku Klux yelper and a loud mouth shouter in many demagogic political and hate rallies" and denounced as ridiculous Norris's accusations that Newton was sympathetic to communism. Knowing Newton through his ministry at the Druid Hills church McGill suggested that Newton may have been duped by the Russians into making his "naive" comments but that Newton was no "appeaser." McGill reviewed Norris's career, incorrectly locating his church in Austin and suggesting that Norris's attacks were motivated by his desire to become president of the Convention. Calling him a "pistol-toting divine," McGill reminded his readers of Norris's murder trial. McGill concluded by noting his regret in not being able to attend the Convention and "to shout with the ministers."[85]

Disturbed and angered by McGill's characterizations, Norris turned on him, first writing to accuse him of including false statements then cryptically warning that "you will hear from me

---

[82]J. Frank Norris to Louie D. Newton, 7 May 1947, in JFN Papers, 29-1356. Norris sent the press a copy of the questions he tried to ask which were publish in various newspapers including the Dallas *News* and the Fort Worth *Star-Telegram*. J. Frank Norris to J. Wesley Edwards, 20 May 1947, in JFN Papers, 29-1355.

[83]N.a., "St. Louis Blues," *Time*, 19 May 1947, 70. See also C. Allyn Russell's account in "J. Frank Norris—Violent Fundamentalist," in *Voices of Fundamentalism: Seven Biographical Studies* (Philadelphia: Westminster Press, 1976) 42–43.

[84]The previous year, McGill came to Newton's side by affirming editorially that Newton was "right" in suggesting that Russia had more religious freedom under the Soviets than under the czars. Ralph McGill, "Religion Can Be a Club," Atlanta *Constitution*, 29 August 1946, 10.

[85]Ralph McGill, "J. Frank Norris Gets Shouted Down," Atlanta *Constitution*, 8 May 1947, clipping in JFN Papers, 28-1318. McGill also noted, "As a Ku Klux shouter, J. Frank Norris naturally exhibits the Ku Klux ideal."

again."[86] Within a week a Fort Worth District Attorney indicted McGill for criminal libel, but on the advice of his Atlanta lawyer, Samuel Hewlett, Norris did not pursue aggressively the charges but let Hewlett file a civil libel suit.[87] Nevertheless, Norris did not drop the criminal side because he believed it provided an extra measure of pressure on McGill. "As long as the indictment hangs over him," Norris explained, "he will be more willing" to publish a retraction.[88] By the end of the summer of 1947 Hewlett negotiated an agreement that McGill would publish an apology and retraction in return for Norris dropping the criminal complaint and any claims for monetary damages.[89] Norris did not indicate his approval until the following February, so the retraction appeared in the 20 March edition of the *Constitution*.[90] Apparently Norris was more upset with McGill's characterization of him as a gun-bearing minister than the comments linking him to the Klan. In addition to correcting the misinformation concerning Norris's career, the only retraction and apology in the column concerned the "pistol-toting divine" remark. "There is no evidence," McGill wrote, "that Dr. Norris carried or 'packed' a pistol.... The Constitution retracts that statement and regrets it."[91] Pleased with the fact that Newton's hometown newspaper published his accusations concerning Newton's procommunist leanings, Norris called his $500 lawyer fee "the best investment I ever made."[92]

---

[86]J. Frank Norris to Ralph McGill, 10 May 1947, in JFN Papers, 28-1318.

[87]Samuel D. Hewlett to J. Frank Norris, 22 May 1947, in JFN Papers, 2-60. Hewlett explained that Georgia law prevented criminal libel actions until a newspaper had the chance to correct misstatement of facts.

[88]J. Frank Norris to Samuel D. Hewlett, 24 May 1947, in JFN Papers, 2-60.

[89]Allen Post to Samuel D. Hewlett, 15 August 1947, typed copy in JFN Papers, 2-60.

[90]J. Frank Norris to Samuel D. Hewlett, 27 February 1948, in JFN Papers, 2-60; and J. Frank Norris to Samuel D. Hewlett, 4 March and 8 March 1948; and Samuel D. Hewlett to J. Frank Norris, 12 March 1948, in JFN Papers, 2-61. In the first letter Norris explained the delay resulted from his extended tour of Palestine.

[91]N.a., "Concerning a Previous Article," Atlanta *Constitution*, 20 March 1948, clipping in JFN Papers, 2-61.

[92]J. Frank Norris to Samuel D. Hewlett, 31 March 1941 [sic, 1948], in JFN Papers, 2-61.

Little evidence can be mustered to suggest that this incident had much effect on realigning factions among Baptists in the South or persuading Southern Baptists to leave the Convention. The results, nonetheless, are instructive for understanding Norris's tactics and ability to influence Convention affairs. Indicating his desire to take advantage of the disaffection with Newton he saw among Southern Baptists, Norris wrote in March 1947 that "there is a perfect storm on concerning Louie Newton. The laymen are up in arms and several Southern Baptist editors are demanding that he be fired."[93] The following month, in typical overstatement, Norris predicted, "We are winning a most glorious war among Southern Baptists. This fight at St. Louis will bring a thousand churches into our Fellowship."[94] Thus if Norris intended his performance at the convention to rouse opposition to Newton by embarrassing him and so deny him the customary second term as the Convention's president, he misread the mood of the Convention. His effort failed as Newton easily won reelection.[95] To Norris, the vote demonstrated the apathy of the rank and file Southern Baptist pastors to the issues before the Convention. Writing to E. P. Alldredge, he observed, "But the most serious thing of that 23,000 [orthodox Southern Baptist pastors] is their absolute indifference. Proof of their indifference is that when Louie Newton was out with his appeasement campaign for Russia, not a one opened their [sic] chops. They told me privately that they were with me and then turned around and voted to elect him."[96]

Perhaps the response was due not to indifference to the message as reaction to the messenger and his tactics of character assassination. Harold Frey, an observer at the 1947 convention for the Northern liberal newspaper *Christian Century*, believed that Norris's attacks

---

[93]J. Frank Norris to Luther C. Peak, 19 March 1947, in JFN Papers, 34-1508. Norris did not specify which editors. Three of the larger Baptist papers—*Baptist Standard* of Texas, *Baptist and Reflector* of Tennessee, and *Christian Index* of Georgia—did not comment editorially on Newton's remarks.

[94]J. Frank Norris to Luther C. Peak, 19 April 1947, in JFN Papers, 34-1508.

[95]Victor I. Masters to J. Frank Norris, 14 March 1948, in JFN Papers, 27-1229. N.a., "Convention Head Re-Elected," *Baptist Standard* (Dallas TX), 22 May 1947, 1.

[96]J. Frank Norris to E. P. Alldredge, 31 August 1948, in Alldredge Papers, 1-30.

"solidified" Newton's support so that he won by an "overwhelming vote."[97] In their coverage of the convention Southern Baptist newspapers did not describe the incident and carried Newton's report that his lasting "impression" of this meeting was that the SBC was "united in Conviction, Purpose, and Method."[98] Furthermore, Norris's dreams of mass defections from the Convention did not occur. Nor did Convention pastors seem much influenced by Norris's attempt to capitalize on McGill's retraction. Norris printed enough copies of the column to send to every Baptist pastor in the country, some 35,000–40,000, but the effort seemed to do little more than confirm the recipient's predisposition. Writing to ask Norris to send 500 extra copies, a Texas pastor proclaimed that "this retraction is the greatest blow Louie Newton and his followers could receive," while a Charlotte pastor asked for 1,000 copies, declaring, "Truly, this is V-C Day for Fundamental Baptist[s]."[99] Most Southern Baptists pastors probably threw Norris's mailing into the trash.

While this incident revealed his inability to convince Southern Baptists to separate from the Convention, Norris also faced a rebellion within his own empire during the same years. The issue centered on his control and dictatorial direction of the Fellowship, mission board, and seminary. This division is significant because it played a key role in reshaping the alignment of independent fundamentalist Baptists in the South and because it indicates the inherent fractiousness in the separatist ideology. Moreover, the irony of the situation should not be overlooked because one of the central issues around which Norris built his following and tried to convince Southern Baptists to leave the

---

[97]Harold E. Frey, "Why They Behave like Southern Baptists," *Christian Century* (21 May 1947): 649.

[98]Louie D. Newton, "The Convention," *Christian Index*, 15 May 1947, 1. This theme was conveyed in the various detailed reports of the meeting carried by Baptist papers. See for example, James W. Merritt, "Southern Baptists Gather in St. Louis of Ninetieth Convention Session," *Christian Index*, 15 May 1947, 5–6; R. E. Dudley, "St. Louis Convention Tops Attendance Record of 1920," *Baptist Standard*, 22 May 1947, 1, 5; and n.a., "The St. Louis Convention," *Baptist and Reflector*, 22 May 1947, 3–5.

[99]Roscoe Turner to J. Frank Norris, 15 April 1948; Maylon D. Watkins to J. Frank Norris, 9 April 1948, in JFN Papers, 2-61. Both men indicated they wanted to send the copies to each person on their mailing lists.

Convention was the concern over the centralization and growth of the denomination's agencies. He alleged this development reduced the freedom of local congregations because the test of a congregation's Baptist character ceased being adherence to Baptist principles and theology and became support of "machine-sponsored" programs like the Cooperative Program and use of "machine-published" literature from the Sunday School Board. The rebels shifted the focus to Norris, arguing that he made the test of an individual's fundamentalist credentials support of his policies in the institutions associated with First Baptist of Fort Worth.[100] In short, the rebels argued that what led them to separate from the Convention now justified their separation from Norris.

While the conflict concerned many aspects of his administration, it centered over the seminary Norris founded in his church.[101] Beginning as a Bible institute in 1939 with an enrollment of sixteen, the school became the Bible Baptist Seminary in 1944, but it remained an institute in spirit and curriculum.[102] Its 1948 catalog described its purpose as "first and fundamentally...to give a thorough knowledge of the entire Bible...to laymen and young women who want to give their lives to Christian service."[103] Offering no courses in biblical languages, the curriculum focused on a detailed study of the English Bible. Such emphasis was sufficient to train church workers because, according to

---

[100]In an interesting reversal of the Convention leaders' efforts to discredit denominational fundamentalists by linking them to Norris, I. W. Rogers accused his opponents of being like Norris in their authoritarian methods of running the denomination. Thus he saw in this split a lesson for Southern Baptists. Noting that the division arose over the "alleged dictatorial policies" of Norris, Rogers suggested that "if the same sort of high handed rule is continued for two or three more years, a major split in the Southern Baptist convention is almost certain." I. W. Rogers, "Baptist Groups Breaking Up," *The Faith* (Mayfield KY), July 1950, 3.

[101]For an extended discussion of the conflict written from the perspective of the dissidents, see Billy Vick Bartlett, *The Beginnings: A Pictorial History of the Baptist Bible Fellowship* (Springfield MO: Baptist Bible College, 1975) 39–57.

[102]Bible Baptist Seminary, *Catalog*, 1948–1949, 11–12, in JFN Papers, 15-703. The *Catalog*, 17, made clear the dependence of the school on the church for its facilities. The seminary had a 199-year lease on all the property of the church for which it paid no rent.

[103]Ibid., 16.

the catalog, "while we require a study of Theology, it is required in connection with the study of the Bible itself. The same is true of Biblical Introduction or Eschatology of the Study of the New Testament church. And the same is true of Missions."[104]

Like the interdenominational schools, the Seminary expected its students to be involved in Christian service; in fact, it required that all students spend at least two hours a week in "visiting and personal soul winning." So important was this part of the program that the catalog promised that "special consideration" would be given to students pastoring churches or conducting evangelistic meetings so they would avoid "being penalized for unavoidable conflict with class attendance."[105] Though it offered a Bachelor of Divinity degree along with a Masters and Doctorate of Theology, the seminary did not require a college degree for admission, thus it was a graduate school in name only.[106] By the late 1940s the school's enrollment grew to several hundred.[107]

Norris served as President until 1948 when at Norris's "request" the Trustees chose for his successor G. Beauchamp Vick, the Sunday school superintendent at Norris's Temple Baptist Church in Detroit.[108] The *Catalog* claimed that the change was necessary to allow Norris to

---

[104]Ibid., 37. The catalog practically apologized for requiring a textbook other than the Bible in its missions course.

[105]Ibid., 21. Students were required to sign a form indicating their agreement with the rules governing the Christian service requirements. This form warned that "no credit will be given to any student for any subject who fails to do his practical work." Undated form in JFN Papers, 15-706. So strict was the enforcement of this rule that Luther Peak had to have approval from Norris for a student who was a member of Peak's church to fulfill his obligation at his home church. Luther C. Peak to J. Frank Norris, 14 September 1949; and J. Frank Norris to Luther C. Peak, 15 September 1949, in JFN Papers, 34-1510.

[106]Two unusual degrees included a Bachelor of Sacred Music, presumably for those wanting to become choir directors in churches, and a Masters in Church Building for students planning on careers in establishing new churches. Ibid., 34–35. The catalog does not make clear if the Seminary awarded degrees who entered without an undergraduate education or awarded certificates upon completion of the program.

[107]In *History*, 133, Dollar recorded that by 1945 enrollment stood at 224 and peaked at 305, while Russell, in "J. Frank Norris," 30, put the figure at over 500.

[108]Bible Baptist Seminary, *Catalog*, 1948–1949, 7, in JFN Papers, 15-703.

devote more time and energy to his "world-wide ministry,"[109] but rather than simply relieving Norris of administrative duties Vick's main task was to solve the Seminary's serious financial problems. Within two years Vick had cut its $250,000 debt by half but found that Norris opposed further cost-saving measures like reducing the salaries of the faculty and staff.[110] Furthermore, in the spring of 1950 Norris unilaterally expelled students supporting Vick and then in May fired Vick, blaming him for the unrest among the students and charging him with disobedience and disloyalty. These actions precipitated a split at the annual meeting of the Fellowship with the dissidents leaving to form the Baptist Bible Fellowship (BBF).[111]

Norris's allies rallied to his defense. For example, R. D. Ingle of Jacksonville, Florida, sent a telegram for publication in *The Fundamentalist* asserting that Vick's actions were a part of a carefully planned conspiracy to take over the Fellowship and the Seminary. Moreover when Ingle tried to dissuade him, Vick replied that the dispute "had gone too far.... It is like trying to stop a Texas cyclone."[112] Norris's protégé at Central Baptist in Dallas, Luther Peak, remained loyal and sent Norris a notarized letter verifying that Norris did not try to "browbeat" the students into submission but "pleaded with them as a father would plead with his own son."[113] Additionally Peak wrote to other ministers in an effort to keep them on Norris's side. He explained to Dallas Billington, pastor of Akron's Baptist Temple that Vick had "a case of pure and undiluted jealousy" and "objected to Dr. Norris running everything." Peak suggested that Billington would exercise the same kind of concern and control if he had an institution like the Seminary associated with his church. Peak also accused Vick and his "conspirators and double-crossers" of making "disparaging remarks" about the success of Billington's ministry. Peak concluded by mentioning that only a few of the larger

---

[109]Ibid.
[110]Dollar, *History*, 217–18.
[111]Ibid.
[112]R. D. Ingle to *The Fundamentalist*, 8 June 1950, in JFN Papers, 15-707.
[113]Luther C. Peak to whom it may concern, 29 May 1950, in JFN Papers, 34-1511.

churches followed Vick and that most of the smaller churches would remain loyal.[114]

Peak did not convince Billington who eventually took his church into membership in the BBF. Furthermore, these two men roughly represent the regional lines along which the schism occurred with churches in the Midwest and upper South following Vick and Norris retaining the loyalty of those in the Southwest.[115] The splinter group also moved quickly to establish its own institutions. As early as June 1950 it announced plans to open a school in Springfield, Missouri, in the fall. Dropping the pretensions to graduate theological education, the Baptist Bible College assured prospective students that most of the faculty and administration of the Seminary joined the College's staff and that its three year program was approved for G. I. benefits.[116] From the original 119 churches, the BBF grew to over 1,200 and eclipsed the old organization with close to one million members by the early 1960s.[117] Perhaps one factor accounting for the vitality of the splinter group was the fact that Norris was not leading it. Those Southern Baptists worried about conditions in the Convention but also alienated from fundamentalism by Norris's reputation and tactics now had a group to join that allowed them to separate from the Convention without appearing to endorse Norris. Even some denominational fundamentalists approved the developments. E. P. Alldredge recommended the BBF's mission agency as an alternative to Cooperative Program for Southern Baptists' money, while I. W. Rogers told the readers of the *Faith and Southern Baptists* that the BBF was "a fundamentalist group that bids fair to make a deep impression

---

[114]Luther C. Peak to Dallas Billington, 3 June 1950, typed copy, in JFN Papers, 34-1511.

[115]Dollar, *History*, 217–18, 226.

[116]R. O. Woodworth to William M. Harris, 9 June 1950, in JFN Papers, 15-707. This letter notes that Vick was the school's president and Woodworth its Business Manager, a position he held at the Seminary.

[117]Dollar, *History*, 219. Dollar also reports on 226, that the World Baptist Fellowship, the successor to Norris's organization, had only 566 member churches by the early 1970s.

on the religious life of America."[118] In part, the inability of Norris to maintain control or to rebuild his Fellowship resulted from his failing health in the early 1950s and death in the summer of 1952, but a more significant factor may have been Norris himself and the tactics he used to build it in the first place.[119]

While separatism reshaped alliances among conservative Southern Presbyterians and divided fundamentalist Baptists in the South, it was also a significant factor in shaping the development of fundamentalism among Southern Methodists. As among Southern Presbyterians, reunion with the Northern denomination played a pivotal role in stimulating fundamentalist discontent among Southern Methodists, but Northern fundamentalists influenced that dissatisfaction into separatist response.

On 29 April 1938, following the lead of their bishops, the delegates to the General Conference of the Methodist Episcopal Church, South (MEC-S) voted to reunite with the Methodist Episcopal Church (North) and the Methodist Protestant Church, with the union to become official in one year at the first General Conference of the new denomination.[120] This decision transformed the debate among Southern Methodists about the propriety of reunion into a battle to stop it. Opponents voiced many of the same objections to reunion that appeared in Presbyterian circles in the 1940s.[121] But there were

---

[118]E. P. Alldredge, "Shall We Continue to Support the Co-operative Program?" *The Faith and Southern Baptists* (Mayfield KY), November 1950, 11; and I. W. Rogers, untitled article, *The Faith and Southern Baptists*, October 1950, 8.

[119]Russell, "J. Frank Norris," 229–30, note 93.

[120]The Annual Conferences of the MEC-S voted during the previous year to approve the merger by a combined total of 7,650 to 1,247. Only in the North Mississippi Annual Conference did a majority reject the plan. Walter McElreath, *Methodist Union in the Courts* (New York: Abingdon-Cokesbury Press, 1946) 24.

[121]Interestingly, one of the few connections between the Methodists and Presbyterians was B. W. Crouch, a layman from Saluda, South Carolina, who was a leader among Methodists opposing reunion in the late 1930s and early 1940s. Transferring his allegiance to the Southern Presbyterian church, he contributed two articles to the *Southern Presbyterian Journal* (*SPJ*), one suggesting that reunion would mean the loss of congregational control over its property and the other affirming the biblical basis of segregation. See B. W. Crouch, "The Proposed Plan of Union," *SPJ*, September 1944, 9 and "Dr. Palmer on Racial Barriers," *SPJ*, 2 December 1946, 5–6.

significant differences. First, organized opposition developed after the decision had been made to reunite; Methodist denominational fundamentalists waged a different battle, to reverse a decision already made rather than the Presbyterian effort to stop it from being made in the first place. Second, few clergy participated in the effort. In fact, the vote of the delegates at the 1938 conference, most of whom were ministers, was 434 to 26 in favor of union.[122] This movement was one of laypeople who resented their lack of influence in church affairs. Third, Methodist opponents appealed more directly to regional pride than Presbyterians. "Are you a Southern Methodist," asked one opponent, "or do you prefer to become a Yankefied [sic] Methodist?"[123] Fourth, leaders of the movement shamelessly exploited fears of racial integration resulting from reunion to win support for their cause. Another opponent suggested that the eventual result of reunion would be "racial amalgamation" and then asked, "ARE YOU SOUTHER-NERS READY FOR THIS?"[124] Fifth, failing in their effort to reverse the decision for reunion and in part influenced by Northern separatists, the opponents quickly moved to separate from the new denomination and form their own to preserve the traditions and doctrines of Southern Methodism. In other words, a prolonged controversy between denominational fundamentalists and liberals over control of the church did not occur. Ironically, the Northern separatist connection was one factor in limiting the acceptance of fundamentalism among Southern Methodists.

The opposition took institutional form as various groups of laypeople met across the South in 1938 in an effort to mobilize

---

Crouch did not appear as a member of the Board of Directors of the *SPJ* or as leader in the Presbyterian lay organizations that developed in the 1940s. In general, the editors and authors of the *SPJ* did not acknowledge any debt to the Methodists. For example, not one article used the Methodist situation as an warning to Southern Presbyterians as an example of what might happen to their church unless reunion was stopped.

[122]F. Mildred Huggins, "Early Southern Methodism," pamphlet (no publisher, no date, internal evidence suggests late 1940s) 1.

[123]N.a., Untitled article, *Southern Methodist Layman* (Atlanta GA), no date (c. June 1938) 2 (hereinafter cited as *SML*).

[124]N.a., "Prejudice against the Negro," *SML*, 25 November 1938, 10.

opposition to reunion.[125] Though antiunion sentiment found some
support in most parts of the South, it was the strongest in Georgia and
South Carolina. From this region eventually emerged The Layman's
Organization for the Preservation of the Methodist Episcopal Church,
South and a newspaper, *The Southern Methodist Layman*, edited by
John A. Manget of Atlanta.[126] While carrying a few articles on
Methodist piety, the *Layman* devoted most of its space to justifying
and describing the campaign to stop reunion.[127] Various articles
attacked the modernism of the Northern Methodist church and
suggested that reunion would encourage the liberal tendencies already
present in Southern Methodist seminaries and publications.[128] One
correspondent to the *Layman* believed the consequences of reunion
had significance beyond its impact on the MEC-S. This letter to the
editor apocalyptically warned that if reunion occurred "it will be a
hopeless surrender of the evangelical Christianity in the Southern
states to the counterfeit Christianity called modernism."[129] Not only
was the Northern church theologically suspect, but the politics of some
of its leaders cast doubt on the wisdom of reunion. One aspect of this

---

[125]John C. Smith, "Organizational History of the Southern Methodist Church,"
The Southern Methodist (Nashville TN), January 1971, 6.

[126]The hometowns of the Organization's first officers give some indication of the
regions where antiunion sentiment was the strongest. President J. W. Lipscomb came
from Columbus, Mississippi; vice president S. J. Summers from Cameron, South
Carolina; secretary G. G. Pike from Columbia, South Carolina; and treasurer Miller
R. Bell from Milledgeville, Georgia. McElreath, *Methodist Union*, 47.

[127]For general articles opposing reunion combining many of the objections, see
n.a., "Mississippi had Gone to Work," *SML*, 11 November 1938; and C. E.
Weddington, "Laymen Warned," *SML*, 17 February 1939, 9. See also the eleven points
from a declaration published by the Layman's Organization quoted in Smith,
"Organizational History," 6.

[128]On modernism in the Northern Methodist church, see n.a., "From a Brilliant
Mississippi Woman," *SML*, 2 September 1938, 6; and J. F. Yarborough, "Criticized
and Condemned," *SML*, 25 November 1938, 6–7. For complaints about liberal
theological trends among Southern Methodists, see L. M. Beacham, "Quo Vadis," *SML*,
5 August 1938, 5; Allen L. Rogers, "Why I Resigned as General Superintendent of the
Sunday School of the Bethel MEC-S," *SML*, 21 October 1938, 7–8; and n.a., "A
Revealing and Ominous Memorial," *SML*, 13 January 1939, 4–5.

[129]Anonymous letter, *SML*, 8 July 1938, 2; cf., n.a., "Excerpts from the Laymen,"
SML, 29 July 1938, 2.

issue was Northern Methodists' active support of the Federal Council of Churches (FCC). One article noted that while the MEC-S contributed to the FCC it was not as outspoken as the Northern church "in sponsoring the ideals of radical groups."[130] More troubling than the FCC, though, was the communist leanings contributors saw in some of the Northern Methodist leaders. Articles charged E. Stanley Jones, G. Bromley Oxam, and Ivan Lee Holt with endorsing communism.[131] Thus "the burning question" was will Southern Methodists "allow themselves to be dragooned in to supporting...[an] assault upon the constitution and free institutions of our republic in order that a collectivist, communistic social order may be set up on their ruins?"[132] Couched in these terms, the only answer was for Southern Methodist laypeople to awaken to the dangers and resist reunion.

But detailed criticism of theology and politics played only a minor role in the *Layman*'s propaganda campaign against reunion. As its name implied, the paper shaped its message to appeal to the laypeople in the MEC-S, and a central element was an effort to capitalize on lay resentment of the clergy's control of the denomination. This attitude emerged most clearly in the *Layman*'s efforts to explain why more clergy did not oppose reunion. Contributors alleged that the lopsided vote favoring reunion at the 1938 General Conference resulted from the power bishops had over the denomination's ministers. Bishops determined which church a pastor served, and all but one of the bishops supported reunion. According to opponents, the roll call vote on the proposition required each minister to declare his position on the plan whereas a secret ballot would have allowed the clergy to vote their consciences without fear of reprisal

---

[130]N.a., "The Federal Council of Churches," *SML*, 6 January 1939, 4.

[131]N.a., "More about Communism," *SML*, 2 September 1938, 2; Rembert Gilmore Smith, "Redism Rushes on in American Methodism," *Tomorrow*, no date, reprinted in *SML*, 14 October 1938, 5; n.a., "Communism," *SML*, 2 December 1938, 12; and James W. Lipscomb, "Is the 'New' Methodist Church to Help Pave the Way for a Communistic Government in Our Country," *SML*, 24 February 1939, 9.

[132]James W. Lipscomb, "Is the 'New' Methodist Church to Help Pave the Way for a Communistic Government in Our Country," *SML*, 3 March 1939, 7.

from the bishops. The latter method, opponents confidently claimed, would have resulted in the defeat of reunion.[133] Thus, according to one editorial, many ministers were nothing more than "political 'yesmen' of the bishops used by them in maintaining the machinery over which they rule with Czaristic power."[134] Articles also emphasized that the procedure for approving reunion denied Southern laypeople a voice in the decision, that the movement for union was a plot by the "czars" of the MEC-S, and that their leaders deliberately withheld information from the laity and misled them as to consequences of reunion.[135] One frequently cited result involved the fate of the denomination's property at both the local and regional level. Significantly, it yoked the sense of betrayal by their leaders among Methodist laypeople to regional pride and fears of Northern influence. Editorials and articles asserted that because Northerners would have numerical superiority in the new church Southern Methodists effectively lost control of their denomination's property to Yankees, even the buildings housing local congregations and constructed with funds raised by those congregations.[136] One contributor tied these objections together in a burst of frustration with the MEC-S's leadership:

> The attitude of the machine, composed of Bishops and other Czars, toward laymen...appears about like this: YOU pay the money IN, WE pay it OUT. YOU build churches and establish loan funds for the MEC, S, WE manipulate the machinery so that your property is placed under the absolute control of the

---

[133]N.a., "A Significant Omission," *SML*, 2 September 1938, 7

[134]N.a., Editorial, "Where Are We?" *SML*, 24 February 1939, 2; cf., a similar attitude expressed by one minister who confessed "We are doing little more than running a corrupt political institution in the interest of the 'plums.'" N.a., "Unification by a Methodist Preacher," *SML*, 4 November 1938, 4.

[135]N.a., "General Conference Observations," *SML*, 8 July 1938, 5; n.a., "Special Notice," *SML*, 22 July 1938, 2; G. G. Pike to J. Marvin Post, reprinted in *SML*, 22 July 1938, 3; n.a., "The Same Old Story," *SML*, 30 September 1938, 3; J. F. Yarborough, "Money vs. Christianity," *SML*, 21 October 1938, 2.

[136]N.a., "General Conference Observations," *SML*, 8 July 1938, 5; n.a., "Union Propaganda: Slandering the Nation's Courts," *SML*, 19 August 1938, 1; and n.a., "From a Florida 'Loyalist,'" *SML*, 11 November 1938, 8.

Church, North; in addition to that we will drive you like dumb animals into an organization under absolute control of said Northern Church, without permitting you to be informed much less express yourself.[137]

While capitalizing on the disaffection of the laity with their leaders, the *Layman* exploited as its most potent reason for stopping reunion the fear that these plans meant a racially integrated denomination. This exploitation in part resulted from the structure of the denomination. Unlike Presbyterian and Baptist congregations that chose their own ministers, Methodists had theirs assigned to them by bishops. Therefore the possibility existed that a black minister could be assigned to a white church and a black bishop have oversight of Southern white churches. One contributor bluntly pointed out that "white SOUTHERNERS do not wish Negro Bishops over them and will not stand for it."[138] Readers of the *Layman* heard many stories about activities among Northern Methodists that indicated support for "race mixing." For example, the *Layman* reported that Northern Conferences encouraged interracial youth group meetings, that a Northern white bishop took a minister into his home because no hotel would rent a room to an African-American, and that plans for a reunion celebration included seating black and white bishops at the same table.[139] Moreover, the *Layman* claimed that plans for restructuring the denomination included eliminating the Central Jurisdiction of the MEC-S for its black members. Finally, the *Layman* linked these actions and policies to the theologically-suspect character of the Northern church by pointing out that modernists among

---

[137]N.a., "'Benevolences' Again," *SML*, 14 October 1938, 4.

[138]N.a., "Correction for Memphis Papers Regarding Bishop's Estate," *SML*, 3 March 1939, 10. In "A Open Letter to Bishop Charles Edward Locke of the M. E. C., Santa Monica, Cal.," *SML*, 27 January 1939, 5–6, T. C. Keeling warned that schism would result when African-Americans began applying for membership Southern Methodist churches.

[139]N.a., Untitled article, *SML*, 16 September 1938, 7; n.a., Editorial, "Why Not Tell the Plain Truth, Bishops?" *SML*, 9 December 1938 2; and n.a., "Northern Bishops Practice Social Equality," *SML*, 24 February 1939, 10.

Northern Methodists promoted integration of the races.[140] The message to Southern Methodists was clear: reunion would be "a driving force toward the social equality" of the races and would undermine the Southern system of race relations.[141] *Layman* authors denied racial prejudice motivated their opposition to reunion and affirmed that they lived "in peace" and had "friendly relations" with their "colored brethren."[142] Nevertheless, the attitude that undergirded most of the *Layman*'s commentary linking reunion with Southern race relations was encapsulated in a remark by T. Hicks Fort at a meeting to establish a local committee of the Layman's Organization. He told his audience, "I love darkies in their place, but their place is not with a man or woman who wears white skin."[143]

While the *Southern Methodist Layman* waged a propaganda war, the Layman's Organization encouraged and coordinated resistance to reunion. In the summer and fall of 1938 it held mass rallies to explain to Methodist laypeople why the proposed union was wrong and how to fight it. According to reports in the *Layman* over 400 people attended a meeting in Dillon, South Carolina, to hear B. W. Crouch, a judge and Vice President of the Layman's Organization, while a similar number listened in Brownsville, Tennessee, to Collins Denny, Jr., the son of the Methodist Bishop from Virginia.[144] The message at the

---

[140]N.a., "More about the Race Question," *SML*, 23 September 1938, 6. One contributor blamed the increase of racially mixed marriages in the North on the presence of communist teachers in schools. N.a., "Northern White Woman and Southern Negro Marry in Staid, Aristocratic 'Hub,'" *SML*, 7 December 1938, 11.

[141]N.a., Editorial, "Race Discrimination," *SML*, 23 September 1938, 6. Another contributor suggested that Southern Methodist colleges would be controlled by a board dominated by Northerners who would force the colleges to integrate. N.a., "Methodist Leaders Form Single Board to Handle Schools," *SML*, 16 December 1938, 4.

[142]N.a., "Excerpts from the Laymen," *SML*, 29 July 1938, 2; n.a., untitled article, *SML*, 16 September 1938, 7; n.a., "Negroes and Crime," *SML*, 14 October 1938, 9; and n.a., Editorial, "Racial Problems," *SML*, 21 October 1938, 6.

[143]N.a., "Report of South Carolina Meeting," *SML*, 5 August 1938, 3.

[144]The *Layman* based its accounts on newspaper clippings describing these meetings. See the reprint of an article from the Columbia (South Carolina) *State*, 24 October 1938 in *SML*, 4 November 1938; and C. E. Weddington, "From Brownsville, Tenn.," *SML*, 11 November 1938, 2, 8. The 4 November issue carried accounts of three other South Carolina meetings on 2–3, 8.

meetings presented many of the themes evident in the pages of the *Layman*. For example, Denny opposed reunion because of the modernism of Northern Methodists, especially their "preaching sociology and economics" instead of fulfilling the "spiritual mission of the church." He noted that Northerners would dominate the new denomination and feared that superiority to force white churches to accept African-American members.[145] Speakers urged the creation of local and state branches of the Organization and recommended a variety of tactics, including the passage by congregations of resolutions expressing opposition to reunion and the withholding of money collected at the local church from the denomination.[146]

One interesting development in this campaign was the growing tie to Northern fundamentalists, especially the Presbyterian Carl McIntire. Beginning in late 1938 and based on information and analysis from McIntire's newspaper, *The Christian Beacon*, the *Layman* began portraying the Southern Methodist struggle as paralleling McIntire's fight with Northern Presbyterians.[147] For example, it told the stories of a layman, A. L. Lathem, who cited modernism among Northern Presbyterian leaders as his reason for withdrawing from the church, and it told of a minister, Clarence Lamen, who was excommunicated for contumacy in denouncing the apostasy of the Northern denomination. Then, employing separatist rhetoric, the *Layman* commented, "If Methodism North and South does not soon have some Lathems and Lamens 'to come out from among them,' it

---

[145]Weddington, "From Brownsville," 2, 8.

[146]N.a., Untitled article, *SML*, no date (c. June 1938) 7; n.a., "Report of South Carolina Meeting," 1–3; and n.a., Letter to the Editor, 25 November 1938, 8.

[147]In *SML*, 9 December 1938, 8, the *Layman* published a letter from Carl McIntire offering an exchange of newspaper subscriptions and support for efforts to establish a continuing MEC-S. In "Presbyterians Are Pulling Away from 'Union,'" *SML*, 24 February 1939, 6, and based on information gleaned from McIntire's *Christian Beacon*, the *Layman* described how some Cumberland Presbyterian congregations refused to follow their denomination's decision to unite with the Northern Presbyterian Church and suggested that reunion would drive hundreds of Southern Methodist churches to the same course of action.

will not be long until our youth will not know what to believe."[148] Some Methodists in the South had already made that decision. In one instance, ninety-five percent of the membership of a Methodist Protestant church in Charlotte, North Carolina, withdrew to form an independent community church.[149] In both Davis Station and Spartanburg, South Carolina, laypeople alarmed at the prospect of reunion left MEC-S churches to establish independent churches.[150] To demonstrate its fundamentalist ecumenicity, the Spartanburg group had a graduate of Eastern Baptist Seminary as its preacher and adopted for its motto, "to know him and to make him known," the phrase the Presbyterian Robert McQuilkin used to describe the educational mission of Columbia Bible College.[151]

Despite the efforts of the *Layman* and the Layman's Organization, reunion became a reality in 1939. More laypeople began leaving the churches of the new denomination, but not the thousands predicted. Moreover, during 1939 the Layman's Organization encouraged this development and shifted its activities toward creating a denomination that would "continue" the traditions and doctrines of the MEC-S. While it portrayed its efforts as one that had significance for Methodists in all parts of the South, the Organization apparently had little success in mobilizing support for its cause outside of South Carolina.[152] In January 1940 supporters of the Layman's Organization met in Columbia, South Carolina, to create the South Carolina Conference of the MEC-S. Not surprisingly under the provisional plan approved by the delegates, laypeople had full control

---

[148]N.a., "Lo, the Poor Presbyterians!" *SML*, 3 March 1939, 9; cf., n.a., "Dr. A. L. Lathem, Ph.D., DD, to Withdraw from Presbyterian Church in the USA," in ibid. Both articles cited the 23 February 1939 issue of the *Christian Beacon* as its source.

[149]According to G. H. Hendry, pastor of the church. Letter to the Editor, *SML*, 9 December 1938, 3.

[150]N.a., Letter to Editor, *SML*, 23 December 1938, 3; and n.a., "Methodist Forms 'Independent Non-Denominational Church at Spartanburg, SC," *SML*, 20 January 1939, 2.

[151]N.a., "Methodist Group," 2. This article notes that McQuilkin had preached recently to the congregation.

[152]Records of the Organization could not be found, so this observation is based reports of its activities in the *Layman*.

over the affairs of the conference. For example, three clergymen and four laypeople comprised the Ministerial Committee that determined assignments of preachers to local congregations, while ten laypeople and no clergy served on the Finance Committee.[153] In its early years it considered itself to be the true successor to the MEC-S and hence claimed the right to use the name of the old Southern denomination and, more significantly, the control of all its property, including schools, publishing facilities, campgrounds, denominational buildings, and, most important, the property of local churches. Court cases denied these claims forcing congregations out of buildings and the denomination to change its name to the Southern Methodist Church in 1945.[154]

In terms of organization, doctrine, and affiliation, it institutionalized many of the complaints raised in objection to reunion while indicating its growing fundamentalist character. It adopted the 1934 Discipline of the MEC-S and gradually revised it to conform to its practices by eliminating bishops and affirming the congregations'

---

[153]N.a., *Biennial Journal of the S. C. Conference of the M. E. Church, South*, 1940–1941, 6. Methodist clergy were not completely absent from the opposition to reunion, but the evidence from the *Layman* and the records of the Southern Methodist Church clearly indicate the leading role played by the laity. This provisional plan allowed for bishops to preside at Conference meetings. Only the elderly Collins Denny of Virginia opposed reunion and allowed his name to be listed as the bishop for this conference. His death in 1943 prevented him from taking an active role in these endeavors. The 1945 Discipline changed the representation slightly so that equal numbers of laity and clergy served on the various committees. The head officer of the denomination became a president elected from the clergy serving a one year term and unable to serve more than four terms in a row.

[154]Smith, "Organization History," 7. The lawsuits revolved around the efforts of fundamentalist factions in local churches to retain the use and control of the buildings in which they met. They argued that the property was held in trust for the exclusive use of the majority faction in local congregations and that they represented the continuation of the MEC-S. The courts ruled that the new denomination resulting from the merger was the lawful successor to the MEC-S and that therefore the property rights of the MEC-S were transferred to the new church. McElreath, *Methodist Union*, recounts at some length from his perspective as the legal counsel of the united church the legal arguments.

rights to their property.[155] Doctrinally, the Discipline took on a fundamentalist tone with sections affirming premillennialism, advocating separation, and denouncing apostasy.[156] Significantly, one section stated that Southern Methodists believed that "the holy writ teaches the separation of peoples" while warning that "God has set the boundaries, and woe be unto man if h∘ attempts to cross these boundaries."[157] The fundamentalist alignment of the denomination was developed in a variety of ways, most notably and directly in it membership in Carl McIntire's American Council of Christian Churches, a separatist organization to oppose the activities of the FCC.[158] Links to the broader fundamentalist movement also were made in a different fashion. Because Southern Methodists in the early 1940s lacked their own publication board, their leaders recommended the use of Sunday school literature from interdenominational publishers like David C. Cook.[159]

---

[155]See the Discipline changes adopted by the 1945 conference listed in Southern Methodist Church, *Journal of the General Conference*, 1945, 26–29.

[156]In general, the statement of faith of the Southern Methodist Church remained very close to the 1934 Discipline except that it eliminated that document's inclusion of the Federal Council's Social Creed of the Churches. Also omitted was the section affirming the biblical basis for the former denomination's episcopal structure. In its place was one describing a congregational polity. See *Journal*, 1945, 26; D. S. Moore, "Doctrine of the Southern Methodist Church," mimeographed pamphlet (no date); and n.a., *What, Why, How? History, Organization, and Doctrinal Belief of the Southern Methodist Church* (Greenville SC: Foundry Press, 1956).

[157]N.a., *What, Why, How?* 16. The references to "boundaries" was taken from Acts 17:26, a verse frequently cited to justify segregation.

[158]Beginning in the late 1940s the South Carolina Conference of the church sent representatives to the meetings of the ACCC with Mid-South Conference following suit in the early 1950s. See *Annual Journal of the South Carolina Conference of the Southern Methodist Church*, 1947, 7; 1950, 7; and *Annual Journal of the Mid-South Conference of the Southern Methodist Church*, 1952, 5–6. On the ACCC, see Gasper, *The Fundamentalist Movement*, 23–25.

[159]As early as 1939 B. W. Crouch told readers of the *Layman* to use Cook's Sunday school material because "it is free from many of the objectionable 'isms' that have crept into the literature of our church." N.a., Letter to the editor, *SML*, 13 January 1939, 2. The literature of the first General Conference made a similar recommendation. *Biennial Journal*, 1940–1941, 12.

After failing in their legal battles to retain control over MEC-S institutions, Southern Methodists focused on developing their own. Already in place was a newspaper, but it needed a new name. In the late 1940s the *Layman* became simply *The Southern Methodist*, the official newspaper of the church. Also, in 1946 the General Conference directed the Board of Christian Education to develop and distribute literature that reflected the distinctive Wesleyan tradition of its Discipline for use in the denomination's Sunday schools and youth groups.[160] Perhaps most important for development of leadership was the establishment of a college in which to train its ministers. As early as 1946 the Board of Education urged the General Conference to open a school in order to address the problem of recruiting and training clergy.[161] Part of the problem was that the interdenominational schools, while doctrinally acceptable in general fundamentalist terms, did not provide adequate instruction in Methodist theology and history.[162] The General Conference, though, needed ten years before it had the resources to open Southern Methodist College in a rented house in Greenville, South Carolina.[163] As the college grew, its debt to the Bible colleges became apparent in its curriculum and student life. While offering courses of study in the liberal arts and teacher education, the focus of the school's educational efforts resided in

---

[160]*Journal of the General Conference*, 1946, 10. The problem with some of the interdenominational material was reflected in comment from the Mid-South Conference's Board of Education that the literature of the May Press sponsored by the ACCC was "very sound and fine" but also "very Calvinistic in doctrine." *Journal of the Mid-South Annual Conference*, 1952, 15.

[161]*Journal of the General Conference*, 1946, 11.

[162]According to Dale Linder, "The History of Southern Methodist College" (research paper in Term Paper File at Southern Methodist College, December 1972) 1–2, candidates for ministry in Southern Methodist Churches attended during the 1940s the interdenominational Bob Jones University and Columbia Bible College. Linder based this observation on information from an interview with Lynn Corbett, a president of the denomination who attended Columbia Bible College for two years after World War II. The catalogs of both interdenominational schools indicate that courses on the history and beliefs of broad Protestant denominational families were not a part of their curriculum in the late 1940s.

[163]Southern Methodist College, *Bulletin*, 1960–1961, 6. The college eventually settled in Orangeburg in 1961. Linder, "History," 5–7.

Christian education, missions, and theology programs.[164] Daily chapel services, Bible and missionary conferences, prayer to begin each class, and Christian service assignments served to promote piety and build Christian character among the students.[165]

Membership of this denomination remained small and largely concentrated in South Carolina. In 1945 the Southern Methodist Church had 44 congregations and 3,811 members. By 1950, the figures stood at 53 and 4,634; for most of the 1950s they hovered around 50 and 4,500.[166] Administratively, the denomination had two conferences, the South Carolina Conference with approximately two-thirds of its members in small towns of rural Eastern South Carolina and the Mid-South Conference with small churches in urban areas like Nashville and Memphis, Tennessee, and Birmingham and Montgomery, Alabama.[167] These figures raise the question of why more Southern Methodists did not leave. If the threat was as serious as claimed, why did not more Southern Methodists join the church that claimed to be the true continuation of their heritage? Those who left suggested a variety of factors, but the most important was the denomination's control over the press preventing them from explaining their concerns to the Methodist laypeople.[168] Moreover, most well-respected leaders of Southern Methodism urged the laity to accept the decision for reunion. For example, the elderly Bishop Warren A. Candler

---

[164]Southern Methodist College, *Bulletin*, 1958–1959, 28–39.

[165]Ibid., 12–13.

[166]Figures taken from Joan Stanley, "A Brief History of Southern Methodist Missions" (research paper in Term Paper File, Southern Methodist College, Orangeburg SC, December 1972).

[167]See the statistical reports contained in *Annual Journal* of the South Carolina Conference of the Southern Methodist Church, 1947, 13; and *Minutes* of the Proceedings of the Mid-South Conference, 1945, 13.

[168]N.a., Untitled articles, *SML*, June 1938, 1–2; n.a., "General Conference Observations," *SML*, 8 July 1938, 5; n.a., Letter to Editor, *SML*, 22 July 1938, 4; n.a., "Important Notice," *SML*, 2 December 1938, 4; and n.a., "From a Southern Methodist Minister," *SML*, 2 December 1938, 8. Jesse Huggins, a lay leader, believed most Methodist laypeople were apathetic. Like frogs dying in slowly warming water, they did not sense the dangers of the growing acceptance of liberalism by their bishops and ministers. Jesse Huggins (taped interview, library, Southern Methodist College, Orangeburg SC, no date (c. early 1970s)).

issued a statement that the time for debate had passed. Appealing to both regional pride and Christian virtue, Candler upheld Robert E. Lee as one who knew "how to surrender" and counseled opponents that the time had come "to exercise that humility of spirit that knows how to cooperate, to play the game, and submit to authorized expression of the Church."[169] But the general lack of response is perhaps best interpreted as that most Southern Methodists did not agree with the analysis. Perhaps the shrill tone put off some, perhaps many saw opponents of reunion as divisive, perhaps the ties to Northern fundamentalists cast doubts on opponents' loyalty to Southern Methodist traditions. Some Methodists left the united church but did not join the separatists preferring membership in a larger Southern denomination. For example, B. W. Crouch, vice-president of the Layman's Organization in the late 1930s, led over fifty members of two Methodist churches in Saluda, South Carolina, into forming a congregation in the Southern Presbyterian church.[170] In short, the separatist ideology and practice did not appeal to most Methodists in the South.

By the early 1950s the separatist impulse recast Southern fundamentalism into the pattern that would characterize it for the next several decades. In essence, it was three movements, each with several branches. One part still remained within the denominations and sought to stall if not reverse the influence of liberalism within their traditions. Another part broke away to form separate denominations and fellowships along the lines of the theological traditions they left. Some of these joined already-established Northern fundamentalist groups while others created Southern versions. The third part was interdenominational in character, but divided on the issue of ecclesiological separation with one faction identifying with

---

[169]Warren A. Candler, "Agitation in Some Sections," *Nashville Christian Advocate*, reprinted in "Enthusiasm Shown for Re-United Methodism," *Wesleyan Christian Advocate* (Atlanta and Macon GA), 29 July 1938, 2.

[170]*Minutes* of the Congaree Presbytery, July 1941, 11–12. The various statistical reports in the *Minutes* of the South Carolina Conference do not record a Southern Methodist church in Saluda. In a taped interview Jesse Huggins believed Crouch dropped out because "he just got tired of the fighting."

separatist organizations and another trying to remain faithful to its principles of cooperation with all theologically conservative factions regardless of denominational affiliation.

7

CONCLUSION:

SOUTHERN FUNDAMENTALISTS

I have fought the good fight; I have finished the course; I have kept the faith.
—2 Timothy 4:7

In May 1952 Robert McQuilkin invited Lewis Chafer to give the baccalaureate sermon for the graduation ceremonies at Columbia Bible College despite misgivings about Chafer's dispensationalism. In an irenic spirit Chafer avoided the controversial eschatological scheme and focused his sermon on a topic dear to McQuilkin's heart, the cause of world missions.[1] Both men had busy summers planned, with Chafer touring the Pacific Northwest and McQuilkin supervising a full schedule of conferences at Ben Lippen in the mountains of North Carolina. Unfortunately neither lived to see the end of the summer. Chafer died after an illness of several weeks at age eighty-one, and

---

[1]Donald E. Hoke to LSC, 10 December 1951 (Lewis Sperry Chafer Papers, in Mosher Library, Dallas Theological Seminary, Dallas TX) (hereinafter cited as LSC Papers); and n.a., "Bible College Commencement Begins with Missionary Rally, "*The State* (Columbia SC), 24 May 1952, 8.

McQuilkin, age 66, from a heart attack.[2] Coincidentally, two days before Chafer's death, J. Frank Norris suffered and died from a heart attack while preaching at a youth rally in Florida.[3] In many ways their deaths mark the passing of the first generation of fundamentalists in the South.

In very different fashions, all three contributed significantly to the development of Northern patterns of fundamentalism in the South. Both Chafer and McQuilkin were a part of the group of Northern itinerants that toured the South in the first three decades of the twentieth century while Norris's pulpit became an occasional stop on other fundamentalists' itineraries. These travelling preachers were instrumental in introducing Southerners to the fundamentalist doctrinal formulations emerging in the North thus developing a Southern constituency for these teachings.

Moreover, the schools founded by Chafer and McQuilkin were important in several respects. McQuilkin's Columbia Bible College typified the development in the South of fundamentalist Bible institutes and colleges modeled after those in the North. Chafer's Dallas Theological Seminary expanded the scope of fundamentalist educational endeavors by creating a school for the graduate training of ministers. Both men believed their schools would contribute to the broader fundamentalist cause by graduating students to serve in churches and mission agencies cross the country and around the world. They hoped the alumni would contribute to the fundamentalist cause in the North by helping to restore the conservative theological character of Northern denominations. For Southern churches, they hoped their graduates would aid in preventing the penetration of liberalism. Some graduates did enter Southern churches as ministers, missionaries, and lay workers and helped to form and lead factions of fundamentalists within Southern denominations. But both men found that over the years their schools came to serve only occasionally

---

[2]N.a., "Dr. Lewis Chafer, 81, Dies in Seattle," *Morning-News* (Dallas TX), 23 August 1952, 4; and n.a., Editorial, "Dr. R. C. McQuilkin," *The State*, 18 July 1952, 4.

[3]C. Allyn Russell, "J. Frank Norris—Violent Fundamentalist," in *Voices of Fundamentalism: Seven Biographical Studies* (Philadelphia: Westminster Press, 1976) 25.

the conservative factions within the denominations while more frequently provided workers for a growing network of independent churches and mission agencies. Both schools prospered during the 1950s and 1960s so that Dallas Seminary by the early 1970s had a student body of over 700, while Columbia Bible College had over 8,600 alumni located in ninety different countries.[4]

Itinerant preachers, the interdenominational schools, and their graduates did not form isolated outposts of fundamentalism in the South, but they helped shape the controversy over theological liberalism within Southern denominations. Significantly, the parameters of this debate followed those of 1920s battles in the Northern denominations. For example, when Chafer and McQuilkin settled in the South during the 1920s they joined the Southern Presbyterian church. Though not leaders of the fundamentalist faction that formed in the 1940s, their sympathies clearly lay with its efforts to thwart liberal agenda of reuniting the church with the Northern denomination and of moving the Southern church to a less rigid theological position. Their work with interdenominational schools and identification with the wider fundamentalist coalition raised questions about their loyalty to the denomination. Moreover, in Chafer's case, his dispensationalism cast suspicion on his adherence to the church's beliefs, especially after it was condemned as inconsistent with Southern Presbyterians' Confession of Faith. Despite attack on his theology by Southern Presbyterians, Chafer remained a member of the Southern Presbyterian church, though he was not very comfortable in the association.

Denominational fundamentalists in the Southern Presbyterian denomination were much more successful than their Northern counterparts in thwarting liberal domination their church. They were particularly effective in frustrating achievement of the liberals' main

---

[4]John A. Witmer, "'What Hath God Wrought'—Fifty Years of Dallas Theological Seminary; Part II: Building Upon the Foundation," *Bibliotheca Sacra* 131 (January 1974): 4, 9. Robert Kallgren, *Alumview* '80 (Columbia SC: Columbia Bible College, 1980) 1; and J. Robertson McQuilkin, "Postscript," in R. Arthur Mathews, *Towers Pointing Upward*, classroom edition (Columbia SC: Columbia Bible College Press, 1972) 123.

goal of reuniting with the Northern denomination. The *Southern Presbyterian Journal* continued as the voice of this faction, but with the defeat of union in 1955 the anti-union organizations disbanded. Revived efforts at reunion and the continued growth of theological liberalism within the church sparked the creation of new organizations to combat these trends in the 1960s.[5] By the early 1970s some leaders of these groups essentially admitted defeat in denominational politics by concluding that the Southern Presbyterian church was beyond reform and that the only way of continuing its theological traditions was to create a new denomination. In 1973 the Presbyterian Church in America was organized and had 346 churches with over 55,000 members by the end of 1974, most of whom came from old denomination.[6]

J. Frank Norris is perhaps more well known if only because his flamboyant, confrontational style garnered so much attention. Also Norris embodied many of the characteristics so frequently associated with Southern fundamentalists: loud, intransigent, sanctimonious, and self-promoting with a touch of hypocrisy. Nevertheless, Norris played an important role in bringing Northern patterns of funda-

---

[5]Two of the more important were the Presbyterian Evangelistic Fellowship, for the purpose of promoting evangelism within the Southern Presbyterian church and of supporting conservative Southern Presbyterian missionaries and Concerned Presbyterians, Inc., for the purpose of organizing lay resistance to liberal clergy and reunion. For descriptions see Frank Joseph Smith, *The History of the Presbyterian Church in America: The Continuing Church Movement* (Manassas VA: Reformation Educational Foundation, 1985) 22–41. Morton H. Smith's *"How is the Gold Become Dim:" The Decline of the Presbyterian Church, US, as Reflected in Its Assembly Actions*, 2nd ed. (Jackson MS: The Steering Committee for the Continuing Presbyterian Church, 1973) is a fundamentalist interpretation of General Assembly actions concerning theology. According to Smith, *History*, 41, L. Nelson Bell, one of the leaders of the 1940s and 1950s campaign against reunion, refused to be identified with the new anti-union groups because they renounced secrecy. Moreover, Bell's election as moderator in 1972 was probably an effort to forestall schism by electing a noted conservative as leader of the denomination.

[6]See Smith, *History*, 62ff., for a description of the organization of the new denomination. Its leaders reject the label "fundamentalist." Nevertheless their concern for doctrine and their decision to separate certainly mark their activities as fundamentalistic. Church membership statistics come from Presbyterian Church in America, *Yearbook*, 1974, 154.

mentalism when he tried to bring Southern Protestants into the broader fundamentalist cause through his work with the World Christian Fundamentals Association and the Bible Baptist Union. In this endeavor he was instrumental in introducing Southerners to the issues dividing Northern denominations in the 1920s. He saw little success, in part because personal scandals and his critical, negative assaults often undermined any serious consideration of the issues on their merits alone. Similar factors also weakened his ability to lead an effective fundamentalist faction within the Southern Baptist Convention. The central question was usually Norris himself not those of unorthodox teachings in Baptist schools, the growth of the Convention's bureaucracy, or participation in cooperative Protestantism. George Dollar may be overestimating Norris's influence, as well as the degree of liberalism in the Convention, in suggesting his tirades "slowed down the Southern Baptist capitulation to out-and-out liberalism."[7] But even if his tactics alienated more than they won to his cause, Norris defined the issues and kept them before the Convention in such a way that few could ignore.

The considerable attention given to Norris, though, has obscured the fundamentalist discontent within the Convention outside of those in his orbit. While direct ties to Northern Baptist fundamentalists were weak, the denominational fundamentalists in the Southern Baptist Convention nonetheless introduced a pattern of controversy similar to the disputes that troubled Northern Baptists. Perhaps the most important development, but one not prominent in Northern Baptist circles, that sparked anxiety and suspicion among some pastors and laypeople was the growth of the Convention agencies and their intrusions into the life of local congregations. These initial concerns prompted a closer inspection of other conditions, with the resulting investigation broadening into a fundamentalist style critique of doctrinal deviation and cooperative Protestantism. But denominational fundamentalists among Southern Baptists had a difficult time making their voices heard and giving their movement

---

[7]George W. Dollar, *A History of Fundamentalism in America*, 2nd ed. (Orlando FL: Daniels Publishing Co., 1983) 129.

continuing institutional structure. In part, the problem of sounding like a follower of Norris drowned out their complaints. Furthermore, the traditional Baptist belief concerning the independence of local churches undermined efforts at mobilizing a coalition to attack these problems while the absence of a sharply defined confession of faith and of a system of church courts left fundamentalists without an avenue to prosecute those they accused of holding unorthodox views. Because many Southern Baptists dismissed fundamentalist complaints and viewed the critics as uncooperative and disloyal, some denominational fundamentalists in the Convention simply gave up the fight and followed the separatist trail to form independent congregations. These circumstances stand in marked contrast to the success that Southern Baptist fundamentalists had during the 1980s in developing and implementing a strategy that put them in a position to control the overall direction of the denomination. With the 1991 decision of the "moderate" faction to form a separate fellowship and mission board, Southern Baptists fundamentalists appear to have done what no other group of fundamentalists have done in denominational political battles: they won.[8]

The debates over separation that racked Northern fundamentalists and further fractured their movement also troubled Southerners and served to reshape alliances among conservative Southern Protestants. A good illustration of the difficult choices that the issue forced upon some fundamentalists in the South is Robert McQuilkin. He had a fairly good working relationship with denominational fundamentalists among Southern Presbyterians because of

---

[8]For analysis of the 1980s battles, see Joe Edward Barnhart, *The Southern Baptist Holy War* (Austin: Texas Monthly Press, 1986); Ellen M. Rosenberg, *The Southern Baptists: A Subculture in Transition* (Knoxville TN: University of Tennessee Press, 1989); and Nancy T. Ammerman, *Baptist Battles: Social Change and Religious Conflict in the Southern Baptist Convention* (New Brunswick NJ: Rutgers University Press, 1990). The best narrative of the strategy's development is David T. Morgan's *The New Crusades, the New Holy Land: Conflict in the Southern Baptist Convention, 1969–1991* (Tuscaloose: Unifersity of Alabama Press, 1996). All four are rather weak on the historical antecedents of the 1980s battles, and none consider what connections, if any, existed between the patterns described here and the fundamentalist tactics of the 1980s.

his careful cultivation of support for the college from conservative Presbyterian churches in the piedmont. At the same time the college catered to the needs of separatist churches and denominations too small to sustain their own institutions. But their support came with a price: adherence to what they believed was the biblical requirement to disassociate from apostate individuals and organizations and from the orthodox who remained so affiliated. For McQuilkin, such terms were unacceptable. He believed that such an interpretation misrepresented what the Bible taught and that, as a practical matter, compliance would mean identifying the college with a branch of fundamentalism too small to sustain his institution. Yet he clearly was troubled by developments in the denomination and the apparent inability of denominational fundamentalists to reverse the trends. McQuilkin left the Southern Presbyterian church but not on the separatists' terms in a negative protest. Rather he cast his decision as a positive effort to create a new association that would bring a measure of formal organization to the independent congregations in the South. In this endeavor McQuilkin reflected the transformation of some fundamentalists into evangelicals who hoped to shed the negative image of fundamentalism by moderating their militancy without compromising their stand for a supernatural Christianity and an inerrant Bible and by reclaiming the heritage and spirit of nineteenth century evangelicalism. The separatist impulse continued to divide fundamentalism's heirs so that only those who followed the most rigid interpretation of separation could claim to be fundamentalists. In fact these separatists at times appear to consider evangelicals Christianity's most dangerous enemy.[9]

The penetration of these Northern fundamentalist theological traditions into the Southern religious scene and the reflection of Northern patterns of fundamentalist controversy in Southern

---

[9]For discussion of the emergence of an evangelical coalition, see Joel A. Carpenter, *Revive Us Again: The Reawakening of American Fundamentalism*, (New York: Oxford University Press, 1997) 141–60. On the separatists' definition of evangelicalism as an enemy, see *History*, 203–262, where George Dollar uses adherence to separation as the test of an organization's or individual's fundamentalist credentials.

denominations are not the entire story of Southern fundamentalism, but they do represent significant and substantial chapters. More broadly, this account reveals the necessity of acknowledging the variety of fundamentalists, that what has developed is not a united fundamentalist coalition but a variety of movements divided along denominational, theological, and regional lines. This last factor points to the importance of recognizing that the Southern contribution to the fundamentalist cause was more than the participation of individuals but must include the development of institutions in the South that expanded fundamentalist educational endeavors and the stories of fundamentalist controversies within Southern denominations. Finally, the South provided fundamentalism with a region where cultural values generally sustained and nurtured conservative interpretations of Protestant doctrine. From here arose the next generation of fundamentalism's leaders, but their appearance built on the foundation built by this first generation of fundamentalists in the South.

Sources Consulted

Primary Sources

Manuscript Collections

Columbia Bible College Library. Columbia, South Carolina.
Robert C. McQuilkin Papers.
Mosher Library. Dallas Theological Seminary. Dallas, Texas.
Lewis Sperry Chafer Papers.
Rollin T. Chafer Papers.
Presbyterian Church (USA). Department of History. Library and Archives. Montreat, North Carolina.
Marion A. Boggs Papers.
James R. Bridges Papers.
Southern Baptist Historical Commission. Southern Baptist Historical Library and Archives. Nashville, Tennessee.
E. P. Alldredge Papers.
J. Frank Norris Papers.
Records of the Executive Committee of the Southern Baptist Convention.

School Publications, Records, and Miscellanea

Birmingham School of the Bible. Birmingham, Alabama.
"Announcement," 1934.
Bob Jones University. Greenville, South Carolina.
Announcements, 1927, 1938–1951.
Bulletins, 1951–1961.
Bryan College. Dayton, Tennessee.
"Bryan Memorial University." Pamphlet. No date.

Columbia Bible College. Columbia, South Carolina
Alumni Directory, 1956.
Applications File, 1929–1955.
Catalogues, 1931–1954.
Kallgren, Robert. *Alumnview '80*. Columbia SC: Columbia Bible
  College, 1980.
Dallas Theological Seminary. Dallas, Texas.
Alumni Records, 1935–1955.
Bulletins, 1936–1960.
Chafer, Lewis Sperry. "The Founding of Dallas Theological
  Seminary." Recording of Chapel message. No date.
Evangelical Theological College. Dallas, Texas.
Bulletins, 1924–1936.
"Doctrinal Statement," Pamphlet. 1924.
John Brown University. Siloam Springs, Arkansas.
Bulletins, 1925, 1939–1942, 1948–1949, 1953–1954.
Southeastern Bible School. Birmingham, Alabama.
Bulletins, 1942–1943, 1948–1949, 1952–1953.
Gateway (yearbook), 1949.
Southern Methodist College. Orangeburg, South Carolina.
Bulletins, 1958–1959, 1960–1961.
Jesse Huggins. Taped interview. No date.
Term Paper File.

Religious Periodicals

Baptist and Reflector. *Nashville, Tennessee.*
Baptist Standard. *Dallas, Texas.*
Bibliotheca Sacra. *Dallas, Texas.*
Bob Jones Magazine. *Panama City, Florida.*
Christian Fundamentals in Church and School. *Minneapolis,
  Minnesota.*
Christian Index. *Atlanta, Georgia.*
Christian Worker's Magazine. *Chicago, Illinois.*
The Faith. *Mayfield, Kentucky.*
The Faith and Southern Baptists. *Mayfield, Kentucky.*

Golden Age. *Atlanta, Georgia.*
Moody Bible Institute Monthly. *Chicago, Illinois.*
Northfield Echoes. *Northfield, Massachusetts.*
Our Hope. *New York, New York.*
Presbyterian Outlook. *Richmond, Virginia.*
Presbyterian Standard. *Charlotte, North Carolina.*
Record of Christian Work. *Northfield, Massachusetts.*
The Searchlight. *Ft. Worth, Texas.*
Southern Methodist. *Memphis, Tennessee.*
Southern Methodist Layman. *Atlanta, Georgia.*
Southern Presbyterian Journal. *Weaverville, North Carolina.*
Sunday School Times. *Philadelphia, Pennsylvania.*
Wesleyan Christian Advocate. *Atlanta and Macon, Georgia.*
Western Recorder. *Louisville, Kentucky.*

Denominational Records and Publications
Presbyterian Church in America
Yearbooks, *1973–1974, 1984–1985.*
Presbyterian Church in the United States
Ministerial Directory of the Presbyterian Church, US, 1861–1941. *E. C. Scott, complier.*
Ministerial Directory of the Presbyterian Church, US, 1861–1941. *Revised and supplemented, 1942–1950. E. C. Scott, compiler.*
Ministerial Directory of the Presbyterian Church, US, 1861–1967. *E. D. Witherspoon, compiler.*
Minutes of the Congaree Presbytery, *1941.*
Presbyterian Church in the United States General Assembly. Minutes of the General Assembly, *1934, 1940–1941, 1943–1944, 1948, 1955. Augusta GA: Constitutional Job Office.*
Minutes of the Enoree Presbytery, *1940.*
Minutes of the Nashville Presbytery, *1938.*
Minutes of the Orange Presbytery, *1936–1937, 1948.*
Presbyterian Church in the United States of America
Minutes of the General Assembly, *1910.*
Southern Methodist Church
Annual Journal of the Mid-South Conference, *1952.*

Annual Journal of the South Carolina Conference, *1947.*

Biennial Journal of the S. C. Conference of the M. E. Church, South, *1940–1941.*

Huggins, Mildred F. "Early Southern Methodism." Pamphlet. No date.

Journals of the General Conference, *1945–1946.*

Minutes of the Proceedings of the Mid-South Conference, *1945.*

Moore, D. S. "Doctrine of the Southern Methodist Church." Pamphlet. No date.

What, Why, How? History, Organization, and Doctrinal Belief of the Southern Methodist Church. *Greenville SC: Foundry Press, 1956.*

Wilmington (NC) Baptist Association.

Minutes of the Annual Meeting. *1914–1925.*

Newspapers

Atlanta, Georgia. Constitution.

Atlanta, Georgia. Journal.

Augusta, Georgia. Chronicle.

Birmingham, Alabama. News.

Charlotte, North Carolina. Observer.

Chattanooga, Tennessee. Daily Times.

Columbia, South Carolina. The State.

Dallas, Texas. News.

Ft. Worth, Texas. Star-Telegram.

Gainesville, Florida. Daily Sun.

Macon, Georgia. News.

Memphis, Tennessee. Commercial-Appeal.

Wilmington, North Carolina. Morning-Star.

Government Documents

US Department of Commerce. Bureau of the Census. Seventeenth Census: US Summary, Number of Inhabitants, *1950*

———. 1950 Census of the Population, *vol. 2: Characteristics of the Population.*

SECONDARY SOURCES

Books and Articles

Abell, Aaron. *The Urban Impact on American Protestantism, 1865–1900*. Cambridge MA: Harvard University Press, 1943. Reprint, Hamden CT: Archon Books, 1962.

Ahlstrom, Sidney E. *A Religious History of the American People*. 2 volumes. New Haven: Yale University Press, 1975; Image Books edition, Garden City NJ: Doubleday and Co., 1975.

Alldredge, E. P. *Unionizing Southern Baptists: A Survey of the Past and Present Efforts to Bring Southern Baptists into "Cooperative Christianity" and the "United Church of America."* Revised edition. Nashville TN: privately published, 1948.

————. *While Southern Baptists Sleep*. Nashville: privately published, 1949.

Allen, Frederick Lewis. *Only Yesterday: An Informal History of the 1920s*. New York: Harper and Row, 1931. Reprint, New York: Perennial Library, 1964.

Alvis, Joel L. *Religion and Race: Southern Presbyterians, 1946 to 1983*. Tuscaloosa: University of Alabama Press, 1994.

Ammerman, Nancy. *Baptist Battles: Social Change and Religious Conflict in the Southern Baptist Convention*. New Brunswick: Rutgers University Press, 1990.

"Announcements." *Alabama Christian Advocate*. 7 February 1907, 16.

Aspects of Pentecostal-Charismatic Origins. Edited by Vison Synan. Plainfield NJ: Logos International, 1975.

Baggott, James L. *Meet 1000 Atlanta Baptist Ministers, 1843–1973*. Atlanta: self published, 1973.

Bailey, Kenneth K. *Southern White Protestantism in the Twentieth Century*. New York: Harper and Row, 1964.

Baker, Robert. *The Southern Baptist Convention and Its People, 1607–1972*. Nashville: Broadman Press, 1974.

Barlett, Billy Vick. *The Beginnings: A Pictorial History of the Baptist Bible Fellowship*. Springfield MO: Baptist Bible College, 1975.

Barnhart, Joe Edward. *The Southern Baptist Holy War*. Austin: Texas Monthly Press, 1986.

Bear, James E. "Dispensationalism and the Covenant of Grace." *Union Seminary Review* 49 (July 1938): 285–307.

Bendroth, Margaret Lamberts. *Fundamentalism and Gender, 1875 to the Present*. New Haven: Yale University Press, 1996.

Brereton, Virginia Lieson. *Training God's Army: The American Bible School, 1880–1940*. Bloomington: Indiana University Press, 1990.

Boles, John B. *The Great Revival, 1787–1805: The Origins of the Southern Evangelical Mind*. Lexington: University Press of Kentucky, 1972.

Broughton, Leonard G. *Up from Sin: The Rise and Fall of a Prodigal*. Chicago: Fleming H. Revell, 1909.

Bruce, F. F. *The New Testament Documents: Are They Reliable?* Grand Rapids MI: Eerdmans, 1959.

Bradbury, John W. "Curtis Lee Laws and the Fundamentalist Movement." *Foundations* 5 (January 1962): 52–58.

Cable, John H. "Education." In *After Fifty Years: A Record of God's Working through the Christian and Missionary Alliance*. Edited by Robert B. Ekvoll, Harry M. Shuman, Alfred C. Snead, John H. Cable, Howard van Dyck, William Christie, David J. Fant. Harrisburg PA: Christian Publications, 1939.

Carpenter, Joel. "Fundamentalist Institutions and the Rise of Evangelical Protestantism, 1929–1942." *Church History* 49 (March 1980): 62–75.

———. "The Fundamentalist Leaven and the Rise of an Evangelical United Front." In *The Evangelical Tradition in America*. Edited by Leonard I. Sweet. Macon GA: Mercer University Press, 1984, 279–87.

———. *Revive Us Again: The Reawakening of American Fundamentalism*. New York: Oxford University Press, 1997.

Carter, Paul A. "The Fundamentalist Defense of the Faith." In *Change and Continuity in Twentieth Century America: The 1920s*. Edited by John Braeman, Robert H. Bremner, and David Brody, 179–213. Columbus: Ohio State University Press, 1968.

————. "The Negro and Methodist Union." *Church History* 21 (March 1952): 55–70.

Cartledge, Samuel A. *A Conservative Introduction to the New Testament.* Second edition. Athens: University of Georgia Press, 1944.

————. *A Conservative Introduction to the Old Testament.* Grand Rapids MI: Zondervan Publishing House, 1943.

Cauthen, Kenneth. *The Impact of American Religious Liberalism.* New York: Harper and Row, 1962.

Chafer, Lewis Sperry. *True Evangelism.* New York: Gospel Publishing House, 1911.

Cole, Stewart. *The History of Fundamentalism.* New York: Richard R. Smith, 1931.

Collins, Marjorie C. *To Know Him and to Make Him Known: The Leadership and Philosophy of Columbia Bible College.* Columbia SC: Columbia Bible College, 1978.

Cromwell, Patricia Daniels. *A Time for Remembering: The Story of Ruth Bell Graham.* New York: Harper and Row, 1983.

Dalhouse, Mark Taylor. *An Island in the Lake of Fire: Bob Jones University, Fundamentalism, and the Separatist Movement.* Athens: University of Georgia Press, 1996.

Damron, Troy. *A Tree God Planted.* Toccoa GA: Cross Reference Books, 1982.

D'Antonio, Michael. *Fall from Grace: The Failed Crusade of the Christian Right.* New Brunswick: Rutgers University Press, 1992.

Dayton, Donald. *Discovering an Evangelical Heritage.* New York: Harper and Row, 1976.

Dollar, George W. *A History of Fundamentalism in America.* Second edition. Orlando FL: Daniels Publishing Co., 1983.

Dornbusch, Sandford B., and Roger D. Irle. "The Failure of Presbyterian Union." *American Journal of Sociology* 64 (January 1959): 352–55

Ellis, William E. "Evolution, Fundamentalism, and the Historians: An Historiographical Review." *The Historian* 44 (November 1981): 16–23.

"Evangelical Schools and Colleges, 1950." *United Evangelical Action* (15 June 1950): 12–16.

"Fading Fundamentalism." *Christian Century* (16 June 1927): 742.

Fass, Paula S. *The Damned and the Beautiful: American Youth in the 1920s.* New York: Oxford University Press, 1977.

Faust, Drew Gilpin "Christian Soldiers: The Meaning of Revivalism in the Confederate Army," *Journal of Southern History* 53 (February 1987): 63–90.

Findlay, James. *Dwight L. Moody: American Evangelist, 1837–1899.* Chicago: University of Chicago Press, 1969.

―――. "Moody, 'Gapmen,' and the Gospel: The Early Days of Moody Bible Institute." *Church History* 31 (September 1962): 322–35.

Frey, Harold E. "Why They Behave like Southern Baptists." *Christian Century,* 21 May 1947:649.

Friedman, Jean. *The Enclosed Garden: Women and Community in Evangelical South,1830–1900.* Chapel Hill: University of North Carolina Press, 1990.

Fuller, Daniel P. *Give the Winds a Mighty Voice: The Story of Charles E. Fuller.* Waco TX: Word Books, 1972.

The Fundamentals. Volumes 1–12. Chicago: Testimony Publishing Co., 1910–1915.

Furniss, Norman F. *The Fundamentalist Controversy, 1918–1931.* New Haven CT: Yale University Press, 1954.

Gasper, Louis. *The Fundamentalist Movement, 1930–1956.* The Hague: Mouton and Company, 1963. Reprint, Grand Rapids MI: Baker Book House, 1981.

Getz, Gene A. *MBI: The Story of the Moody Bible Institute.* Chicago: Moody Press, 1969.

Ginger, Ray. *Six Days or Forever? Tennessee v. John Thomas Scopes.* Boston: Beacon Press, 1958.

Glass, William R. "Liberal Means to Conservative Ends: Bethany Presbyterian Church and the Institutional Church Movement." *American Presbyterians* 68 (Fall 1990): 181–92.

―――. "From Southern Baptist to Fundamentalist: The Case of I. W. Rogers and *The Faith,* 1945–57." *American Baptist Quarterly* 14 (September 1995): 241–59.

———. "The Ministry of Leonard G. Broughton at Tabernacle Baptist Church, 1898–1912: A Source of Southern Fundamentalism." *American Baptist Quarterly* 4 (March 1985): 35–60.

———. "Southern Fundamentalism and Anticommunism at the Beginning of the Cold War: The Controversy between J. Frank Norris Louie D. Newton." *Studies in the Social Sciences* 36 (May 1999): 81–97.

Goen, C. C. "Jonathan Edwards: A New Departure in Eschatology." *Church History* 27 (March 1959): 25–40.

Gordon, Ernest B. *Adoniram Judson Gordon: A Biography, with Letters and Illustrative Extracts Drawn from Unpublished or Uncollected Sermons and Addresses.* New York: Fleming H. Revell, 1896.

Graham, Ruth Bell. *It's My Turn.* Old Tappan NJ: Fleming H. Revell Co., 1982.

Handy, Robert T. "The American Religious Depression, 1926–1935." *Church History* 29 (March 1960): 3–16.

Hankins, Barry. *God's Rascal: J. Frank Norris and the Beginnings of Southern Fundamentalism.* Lexington: University Press of Kentucky, 1996.

Harrell, David Edwin, ed. *Varieties of Southern Evangelicalism.* Macon GA: Mercer University Press, 1981.

Harvey, Paul. *Redeeming the South: Religious Cultures and Racial Identities among Southern Baptists, 1865–1925.* Chapel Hill: University of North Carolina Press, 1997.

Headley, C. P. *George F. Pentecost: Life, Labors, and Bible Studies.* Boston: James H. Earle, 1880.

Hefley, James, and Marti Hefley. *Uncle Cam: The Story of William Cameron Townsend, Founder of Wycliffe Bible Translators and the Summer Institute of Linguistics.* Waco TX: Word Books, 1974.

Hehl, Alleene Spivey, with John Hehl. *This Is the Victory.* Columbia SC: privately published, 1973.

Heyrman, Christine Leigh. *Southern Cross: The Beginnings of the Bible Belt.* Chapel Hill: University of North Carolina Press, 1997.

Hill, Samuel S. *Southern Churches in Crisis.* New York: Holt, Rinehart, and Winston, 1967.

Hopkins, Charles Howard. *The Rise of the Social Gospel in American Protestantism.* New Haven: Yale University Press, 1940.

Howard, Philip E. *The Life Story of Henry Clay Trumball: Missionary, Army Chaplain, Editor, and Author.* Philadelphia: Sunday School Times Co., 1905.

Hudson, Winthrop S. *American Protestantism.* Chicago: University of Chicago Press, 1961.

————. *Religion in America: An Historical Account of the Development of American Religious Life.* Second edition. New York: Charles Scribner's Sons, 1973.

Hulsether, Mark. *Building a Protestant Left: Christianity and Crisis Magazine, 1941–1993.* Knoxville: University of Tennessee Press, 1999.

Hunter, James David. *American Evangelicalism: Conservative Religion and the Quandary of Modernity.* New Brunswick NJ: Rutgers University Press, 1983.

Hutchison, William R. *The Modernist Impulse in American Protestantism.* Cambridge MA: Harvard University Press, 1976.

Interpreting Southern History: Historiographical Essays in Honor of Sanford W. Higginbotham. Edited by John B. Boles and Evelyn Thomas Nolen. Baton Rouge: Louisiana State University Press, 1987.

"Innocent Abroad." *Time* (26 August 1946): 68.

Johnson, R. K. *Builder of Bridges: The Biography of Dr. Bob Jones, Sr.* Murfreesboro TN: Sword of the Lord, 1969.

Kennedy, Jr., Ralph C., and Thomas Rothrock. *John Brown of Arkansas.* Siloam Springs AR: John Brown University Press, 1966.

Ladd, George E. *The Blessed Hope.* Grand Rapids MI.: Eerdmans, 1956.

Laird, Landon. "Evangelist, Editor, and College President." *American Magazine* (February 1923) 63.

Larson, Edward J. *Summer for the Gods: The Scopes Trial and America's Continuing Debate over Science and Religion.* Cambridge: Harvard University Press, 1997.

"Leonard Gaston Broughton." *Baptist Biography*. Edited by B. J. W. Graham. Atlanta: Index Publishing Co., 1917, 45–49.

LeTourneau, R. G. *Mover of Men and Mountains: The Autobiography of R. G. LeTourneau*. Chicago: Moody Press, 1967.

Leonard, Bill J. *God's Last and Only Hope: The Fragmentation of the Southern Baptist Convention*. Grand Rapids: Eerdmans, 1990.

Lienesch, Michael. *Redeeming America: Piety and Politics in New Christian Right*. Chapel Hill: University of North Carolina Press, 1993.

Lindsey, Hal. *The Late Great Planet Earth*. Grand Rapids MI: Zondervan, 1970.

Lingle, Walter L. "What Does Presbyterianism Stand For?" *Christian Observer* (10 May 1939): 3, 7.

"Louie and the USSR." *Time* (9 September 1946): 80.

Loveland, Anne C. *Southern Evangelicals and the Social Order, 1800–1860*. Baton Rouge: Louisiana State University Press, 1980.

Magnuson, Norris. *Salvation in the Slums: Evangelical Social Work, 1865–1920*. Metuchen NJ: The Scarecrow Press, 1977.

Mariner, Kirk. "The Negro's Place: Virginia Methodists Debate Unification, 1924–1925." *Methodist History* 18 (April 1980): 155–70.

Marsden, George. "Defining Fundamentalism." *Christian Scholar's Review* 1 (1971): 141–51.

————. *Evangelicalism and Modern America*. Grand Rapids MI: Eerdmans, 1984.

————. *Fundamentalism and American Culture: The Shaping of Twentieth Century Evangelicalism, 1870–1925*. New York: Oxford University Press, 1980.

————. "Fundamentalism as an American Phenomenon: A Comparison with English Evangelicalism." *Church History* 46 (June 1977): 215–32.

————. *Reforming Fundamentalism: Fuller Seminary and the New Evangelicalism*. Grand Rapids MI: Eerdmans, 1987.

Marty, Martin A., and R. Scott Appleby, "Introduction: The Fundamentalism Project: A User's Guide." In *Fundamentalisms*

Observed, edited by Martin E. Marty and R. Scott Appleby. Chicago: University of Chicago Press, 1991.

Maser, Frederick E. "The Story of Unification, 1874–1939." *The History of American Methodism*. Edited by Emory Stevens Bucke. Volume 3. New York: Abingdon Press, 1964, 407–78.

Mathews, Donald G. *Religion in the Old South*. Chicago: University of Chicago Press, 1977.

Mathews, R. Arthur. *Towers Pointing Upward*. Classroom edition. Columbia SC: Columbia Bible College Press, 1972.

May, Henry F. *Protestant Churches and Industrial America*. New York: Harper and Brothers, 1949.

McIntire, Carl. *Twentieth Century Reformation*. Collinswood NJ: Christian Beacon Press, 1946.

McLoughlin, William G. *Modern Revivalism: Charles Grandison Finney to Billy Graham*. New York: Ronald Press Co., 1959.

McPheeters, W. M. *Facts Revealed by the Records in the So-Called Investigation of the Rumors Abroad Concerning the Soundness in the Faith of Rev. Dr. Hay Watson Smith*. Decatur GA: privately published, 1934.

McQuilkin, Marguerite. *Always in Triumph: the Life of Robert C. McQuilkin*. Columbia SC: Columbia Bible College, 1956.

Mead, Sidney E. *The Lively Experiment: The Shaping of Christianity in America*. New York: Harper and Row, 1963.

The Meaning of the Millennium: Four Views. Edited by Robert G. Clouse. Downers Grove IL: Inter-Varsity Press, 1977.

Meyer, F. B. *Steps into the Blessed Life*. Philadelphia: Henry T. Altemus, 1896.

Minnix, Kathleen. *Laughter in the Amen Corner: The Life of Evangelist Sam Jones*. Athens: University of Georgia Press, 1993.

Moberg, David. *The Great Reversal: Evangelism versus Social Concern*. Philadelphia: Lippincott, 1972.

Moody, William R. *D. L. Moody*. New York: Macmillan, 1930.

————. *The Life of Dwight L. Moody*. New York: Fleming H. Revell, 1900.

Moore, LeRoy. "Another Look at Fundamentalism: A Response to Ernest R. Sandeen," *Church History* 37 (June 1968): 195–202.

Morgan, David T. *The New Crusades, the New Holy Land: Conflict in the Southern Baptist Convention, 1969–1991.* Tuscaloosa: University of Alabama Press, 1996.

Murch, James DeForest. *Cooperation Without Compromise: A History of the National Association of Evangelicals.* Grand Rapids MI: Eerdmans, 1956.

Noll, Mark A., David W. Bebbington, and George A. Rawlyk. *Evangelicalism: Comparative Studies of Popular Protestantism in North America, the British Isles, and Beyond, 1700–1990.* New York: Oxford University Press, 1994.

Noll, Mark. A., ed. *The Princeton Defense of Plenary Verbal Inspiration.* New York: Garland Publishing, 1988.

Norris, J. Frank. "The Dilemma of the Southern Baptist Premillennial Fellowship." *The Fundamentalist* (1 April 1949). Reprinted, *Information Bulletin of the Conservative Baptist Fellowship* (March 1949) 6–7.

————. *Inside History of First Baptist Church, Fort Worth and Temple Baptist Church, Detroit: Life Story of Dr. J. Frank Norris.* Ft. Worth: privately published, 1938.

Nutt, Rick L. *Toward Peacemaking: Presbyterians in the South and National Security, 1945–1983.* Tuscaloosa: University of Alabama Press, 1994.

Ownby, Ted. *Subduing Satan: Recreation and Manhood in the Rural South.* Chapel Hill: University of North Carolina Press, 1990.

Ottman, Ford C. *J. Wilbur Chapman: A Biography.* Garden City NJ: Doubleday, Page, and Co., 1920.

Perkins, Vivian, and William F. Doverspike. "The Baptist Tabernacle." In *History of Atlanta Baptist Churches.* Edited by James L. Baggott. Atlanta: privately published, no date.

Pierson, Delavan Leonard. *Arthur T. Pierson: A Spiritual Warrior, Mighty in Scripture, a Leader in the Modern Missionary Crusade.* New York: Fleming H. Revell, 1920.

Pollock, John C. *A Foreign Devil in China: The Story of Dr. L. Nelson Bell, an American Surgeon in China.* Crusade edition. Minneapolis MN: World Wide Publications, 1971.

Rabinowitz, Howard N. "More than the Woodward Thesis: Assessing *The Strange Career of Jim Crow*," *Journal of American History* 75 (December 1988): 842–56.

Rausch, David A. "Arno C. Gaebelein (1861–1945): Fundamentalist Protestant Zionist." *American Jewish History* 68 (September 1978): 43–56.

———. *Arno C. Gaebelein, 1861–1954, Irenic Fundamentalist and Scholar*. Studies in American Religion. Volume 10. New York: Edwin Mellen Press, 1983.

———. *Zionism within Early American Fundamentalism, 1878–1918: A Convergence of Two Traditions*. New York: Edwin Mellen Press, 1979.

Reimers, David M. "The Race Problem and Presbyterian Union." *Church History* 31 (June 1962): 203–15.

Roberson, Lee. *Double-Breasted*. Murfreesboro TN: Sword of the Lord Publishers, 1977.

Rogers, Jack, and Donald K. McKim. *The Authority and Interpretation of the Bible: An Historical Approach*. San Francisco: Harper and Row, 1979.

Rosenberg, Ellen M. *The Southern Baptists: A Subculture in Transition*. Knoxville: University of Tennessee Press, 1989.

Rozell, Mark J., and Clyde Wilcox. *Second Coming: The New Christian Right in Virginia Politics*. Baltimore: Johns Hopkins University Press, 1996.

Rudnick, Milton L. *Fundamentalism and the Missouri Synod: A Historical Study of Their Interaction and Mutual Influence*. St. Louis MO: Concordia Publishing House, 1966.

Russell, C. Allyn. *Voices of Fundamentalism: Seven Biographical Studies*. Philadelphia: Westminster Press, 1976.

Ryrie, Charles C. *Dispensationalism Today*. Chicago: Moody Press, 1965.

Sandeen, Ernest R. *The Roots of Fundamentalism: British and American Millenarianism 1800–1930*. Chicago: University of Chicago Press, 1970. Reprint, Grand Rapids MI: Baker Book House, 1978.

————. "Toward a Historical Interpretation of the Origins of Fundamentalism." *Church History* 36 (March 1967): 66–83.

Sankey, Ira, James McGranahan, George T. Stebbins, and Philip P. Bliss. *Gospel Hymns, Nos. 1 to 6, Complete.* New York: Da Capo Press, 1972.

Schlesinger, Sr., Arthur M. "A Critical Period in American Religion, 1875–1900," *Massachusetts Historical Society Proceedings* 64 (October 1930–June 1932): 523–47.

Shelly, Bruce. "The Rise of Evangelical Youth Movements." *Fides et Historia* 18 (January 1986): 47–63.

————. "Sources of Pietistic Fundamentalism," *Fides et Historia* 5 (Fall 1972–Spring 1973): 68–78.

Signal, Daniel Joseph. *The War Within: From Victorian to Modernist Thought in the South, 1919–1945.* Chapel Hill: University of North Carolina Press, 1985.

Smith, Frank Joseph. *The History of the Presbyterian Church in America: The Continuing Church Movement.* Manassas VA: Reformation Educational Foundation, 1985.

Smith, Gary Scott. "The Cross and the Social Order: Calvinist Strategies for Social Improvement, 1870–1920." *Fides et Historia* 17 (Fall–Winter 1984): 39–55.

Smith, Hannah Whitall *The Christian's Secret to a Happy Life.* Westwood NJ: Revell, 1952.

Smith, Morton H. *"How is the Gold Become Dim:" The Decline of the Presbyterian Church, US, as Reflected in Its Assembly Actions.* Second edition. Jackson MS: The Steering Committee for the Continuing Presbyterian Church, 1973.

Smith, Timothy L. *Revivalism and Social Reform: American Protestantism on the Eve of the Civil War.* New York: Abingdon Press, 1957. Reprint, Gloucester MA: Peter Smith, 1976.

Snay, Mitchell. "American Thought and Southern Distinctiveness: The Southern Clergy and the Sanctification of Slavery." *Civil War History* 33 (December 1989): 311–28.

Sobel, Mechal. *Trabelin' On: The Slave Journey to an Afro-Baptist Faith.* New York; Greenwood Press, 1979. Reprint, Princeton: Princeton University Press, 1988.

Sosna, Morton. "More Important than the Civil War? The Impact of World War II on the South." In *Perspectives on the South: An Annual Review of Society, Politics, and Culture*. Volume 4. Edited by James C. Cobb and Charles R. Wilson. University: University of Mississippi Press, 1987, 145–58.

Sparks, Randy J. *On Jordan's Stormy Banks: Evangelicalism in Mississippi, 1773–1876*. Athens: University of Georgia Press, 1994.

Strong, Josiah. *Our Country: Its Possible Future and Its Present Crisis*. New York: Baker and Taylor, 1885.

Sweeny, Douglas A. "Fundamentalism and the Neo-Evangelicals." *Fides et Historia* 24 (Winter–Spring 1992): 81–96.

Synan, Vinson. *The Holiness Pentecostal Movement in the United States*. Grand Rapids MI: Eerdmans, 1971.

Szasz, Ferenc Morton. *The Divided Mind of Protestant America, 1880–1930*. University: University of Alabama Press, 1982.

Thompson, A. E. *The Life of A. B. Simpson*. New York: The Christian Alliance Publishing Co., 1920.

Thompson, Ernest Trice. *Presbyterians in the South*. 3 volumes. Richmond VA: John Knox Press, 1973.

———. *The Spirituality of Church: A Distinctive Doctrine of the Presbyterian Church in the United States*. Richmond VA: John Knox Press, 1961.

Torrey, R. A. *The Person and Work of the Holy Spirit as Revealed in Scripture and in Personal Experience*. Chicago: Fleming H. Revell, 1910. Reprint, Grand Rapids MI: Zondervan, 1968.

Trollinger, Jr., William Vance. *God's Empire: William Bell Riley and Midwestern Fundamentalism*. Madison: University of Wisconsin Press, 1990.

Waldrep, B. Dwain. "Fundamentalism, Interdenominationalism, and the Birmingham School of the Bible, 1927–1941." *The Alabama Review* 49 (January 1996): 29–54.

Walvoord, John F. *The Blessed Hope and the Tribulation*. Grand Rapids MI: Zondervan, 1976.

Weber, Timothy. *Living in the Shadow of the Second Coming: American Premillennialism, 1875–1982*. Revised edition. Grand Rapids MI: Zondervan, 1983.

Wells, David F. and John D. Woodbridge, eds. *The Evangelicals: What They Believe, Who They Are, Where They Are Changing*. Revised edition. Grand Rapids MI: Baker Book House, 1977.

Wilson, Charles Reagan. *Baptized in Blood: The Religion of the Lost Cause, 1865–1920*. Athens: University of Georgia Press, 1980.

Witmer, John A. "'What Hath God Wrought'—Fifty Years of Dallas Theological Seminary; Part I: God's Man and His Dream." *Bibliotheca Sacra* 130 (October 1973): [PAGE].

————. "'What Hath God Wrought'—Fifty Years of Dallas Theological Seminary; Part II: Building Upon the Foundation." *Bibliotheca Sacra* 131 (January 1974): 3–13.

Witmer, S. A. *The Bible College Story: Education with Dimension*. Nanhasset NY: Channel Press, 1962.

Wood, Nathan R. *A School of Christ*. Boston: Gordon School of Theology and Missions, 1953.

Woodbridge, John D. *Biblical Authority: A Critique of the Rogers/McKim Proposal*. Grand Rapids MI: Zondervan, 1982.

Woodbridge John D., Mark A. Noll, and Nathan O. Hatch. *The Gospel in America: Themes in the Story of America's Evangelicals*. Grand Rapids MI: Zondervan Publishing House, 1979.

Woodward, C. Vann. *The Strange Career of Jim Crow*. Third edition. New York: Oxford University Press, 1974.

World Conference on Christian Fundamentals. *God Hath Spoken*. Philadelphia: Bible Conference Committee, 1919.

Dissertations, Theses, and Unpublished Papers

Allem, Warren. "Background of the Scopes Trial at Dayton Tennessee." MA thesis, University of Tennessee, 1959.

Anderson, Richard James. "The Urban Revivalists, 1880–1910." Ph.D. dissertation, University of Chicago, 1974.

Boon, Harold W. "The Development of the Bible College or Institute in the United States and Canada since 1880 and Its Relationship to the Field of Theological Education." Ph.D. dissertation, New York University, 1950.

Carpenter, Joel A. "The Renewal of American Fundamentalism, 1930–1945." Ph.D. dissertation, Johns Hopkins University, 1984.

Ellis, Walter Edmund. "Social and Religious Factors in the Fundamentalist-Modernist Schisms among Baptists in North America, 1895–1934." Ph.D. dissertation, University of Pittsburgh, 1974.

Ellison, Roger Carroll "A Foundational Study of the Development of Tennessee Temple Schools." Ph.D. dissertation, Bob Jones University, 1973.

Glass, William R. "Religion in Southern Culture: Southern Methodists and Reunion, 1920–1940." Paper presented at the annual meeting of the Popular Culture Association, New Orleans LA, 22 April 2000.

Gurney, Gordon F. "A History of the Dallas Bible Institute." Th.M. thesis, Dallas Theological Seminary, 1964.

Hart, Nelson Hodges. "The True and the False: The Worlds of an Emerging Evangelical Protestantism in America, 1890–1920." Ph.D. dissertation, Michigan State University, 1976.

Hannah, John David. "The Social and Intellectual History of the Evangelical Theological College." Ph.D. dissertation, University of Texas at Dallas, 1988.

Herman, Douglas, Edward. "Flooding the Kingdom: The Intellectual Development of Fundamentalism, 1930–1941." Ph.D. dissertation, Ohio University, 1980.

Hubbard, Kenneth Cordell. "Anti-Conventionism in the Southern Baptist Convention, 1940–1962." Ph.D. dissertation, Southwestern Baptist Seminary, 1969.

Lasley, Jess Willard. "The History of Bryan College." Ph.D. dissertation, Baylor University, 1960.

McKinney, Larry James. "An Historical Analysis of the Bible College Movement during Its Formative Years." Ph.D. dissertation, Temple University, 1985.

Olansky, Marvin N. "When World Views Collide: Journalists and the Great Monkey Trial." Paper presented at the annual meeting of the Association for Education in Journalism and Mass Communication, Norman OK, 3–6 August 1986.

Renfer, Rudolf A. "A History of the Dallas Theological Seminary." Ph.D. dissertation, University of Texas, 1959.

Rensi, Raymond Charles. "Sam Jones: Southern Evangelist." Ph.D. dissertation, University of Georgia, 1972.

Scripture, Milton John. "A History of Toccoa Falls Institute Where 'Character Is Developed with Intellect.'" MA thesis, University of Georgia, 1955.

Showers, Renald E. "A History of Philadelphia College of Bible." Th.M. thesis, Dallas Theological Seminary, 1962.

Sledge, Robert Watson. "A History of the Methodist Episcopal Church, South, 1914–1939." Ph.D. dissertation, University of Texas at Austin, 1972.

Szasz, Ferenc Morton. "Three Fundamentalist Leaders: The Roles of William Bell Riley, John Roach Straton, and William Jennings Bryan in the Fundamentalist-Modernist Controversy," Ph.D. dissertation, University of Rochester, 1969.

Tinder, Donald George. "Fundamentalist Baptists in the Northern and Western States, 1920–1950." Ph.D. dissertation, Yale University, 1969.

Unger, Walter. "'Earnestly Contending for the Faith:' The Role of the Niagara Bible Conference in the Emergence of American Fundamentalism." Ph.D. dissertation, Simon Fraser University, 1982.

Wells, David Austin. "D. L. Moody and His Schools: An Historical Analysis of an Educational Ministry." Ph.D. dissertation, Boston University, 1972.

Wenger, Robert E. "Social Thought in American Fundamentalism, 1918–1933." Ph.D. dissertation, University of Nebraska, 1973.

Zopfi, David Noel. "Forward through Faith: The Founding of William Jennings Bryan Memorial University." Senior thesis, Bryan College, Spring 1979.

INDEX

Aiken, Warwick 142
Ainsworth, W. N. 71, 72
Alexander, Charles T. 78
Allan, D. Maurice 161-162, 173 n
   130, 174 n. 135
Alldredge, E. P. 187-190, 191, 204-
   205, 248, 254, 259
American Council of Christian
   Churches 27, 236 n. 25, 270, 271
   n. 160
Ammerman, Nancy x
Anderson, William 110, 141
anticommunism 249, 250 n. 75, 263
antievolution xvi-xv, 3, 31, 75-76, 87,
   122, 124
Appleby, R. Scott xii
Arkansas Presbytery 75, 76
Ashland Avenue Baptist Church
   (Lexington, KY) 212 n. 97, 214
Association for the Preservation and
   Continuation of the Southern
   Presbyterian Church 175-176,
   177, 178 n. 152
Athens Presbytery 125
Atlanta *Constitution* 249, 252-253
Baptist and Reflector 192, 209-212
Baptist Bible College 259
Baptist Bible Fellowship 213 n. 100,
   258, 259-260, 279
Baptist Bible Tribune 213 n. 98
Baptist Bible Union 63-64, 66-67, 79
The Baptist Challenge 186, 191
Baptist Standard 66, 67, 199
Baptist Tabernacle (Chattanooga, TN)
   53
Barnhart, Joe x
Barnhouse, Donald Gray 25

Bayless Memorial Presbyterian
   Church (Concord, NC) 240 n. 38
Baylor University 87 n. 22, 188
Bear, James 144-146, 147 n. 35, 151
Belhaven College 170 n. 121
Bell, Eugene 73
Bell, L. Nelson 146 n. 33, 156, 157-
   158, 174 n. 133, 176, 179-180, 278
   n. 5
Bellevue Baptist Church (Memphis,
   TN) 219 n. 121
Ben Lippen Conference Center 128,
   144 n. 23, 233, 235, 275
Bendroth, Margaret Lamberts viii
Bennett, William 125, 129 n. 194
Biblical authority and inspiration, 6-
   11, 46-47, 91-92, 247
Bible Baptist Seminary 198, 255-258
Bible conferences xvii-xviii, 20, 24,
   31, 34-36, 51-54, 79, 88, 97, 98,
   127-128, 133
Bible Institute of Los Angles 24, 25
Bible institutes and colleges xviii, 24,
   31, 84-84, 88-91, 107, 111, 145,
   192-193, 213-217, 271
Bible Presbyterian Church 27, 226,
   235-236, 239, 240
Bibliotheca Sacra 149
Billington, Dallas 258-259
Birmingham School of the Bible 96-97
Blanchard, Charles 53, 86, 109-110
Bob Jones College and University x,
   85, 91 n. 35, 92, 94, 95, 96, 100-
   101, 102, 106-107, 129 n. 193,
   193, 216, 271 n. 162
Boggs, Wade H. 180-181
Boone, W. C. 65-66

Boston Missionary Training School 89-90

Bridges, James R. 74, 75-76

Broughton, Leonard 11, 12 n. 33, 33-34, 37-39, 52, 79 leadership of Tabernacle Bible Conference, 40-51 passim

Brown, John 103, 104-105, 118-119, 126, 216 n. 113

Brown v. Board of Education 180

Browne, Fred Z. 75, 126, 143

Bryan College 85, 95 n. 53, 102 n. 80, 122-124, 129 n. 193

Bryan, William Jennings xiv-xv, 87-88, 122-123

Burgess, W. A. 181

Calvary Baptist Church (Roanoke, VA) 37

Calvary Baptist Church (Wilmington, NC) 59-60

Calvary Independent Presbyterian Church (Charlotte, NC) 247 n. 63

Candler, Warren A. 70, 71, 272-273

Carpenter, Joel viii, 107 n. 110, 230 n. 7

Carroll, W. Irving 110 n. 119, 126

Carter, Paul A. 3

Cartledge, Samuel 163-164

Central Baptist Church (Dallas, TX) 197,

Central Presbyterian Church (Little Rock, AR) 75

Chafer, Lewis Sperry 28, 52, 57, 78 n. 175, 95 n. 53, 97 n. 58, 120, 126, 134, 156 n. 69, 193, 275-276, leadership of Dallas Theological Seminary 108-117; role in dispensationalism controversy 140-142, 144, 149-153

Chafer, Rollin 52, 113, 149

Chapman, J. Wilbur 50, 108

China Inland Mission 28

Christian and Missionary Alliance 98-99, 102, 119, 121, 125, 127

Christian Century 1-2, 254-255

Christian Index 47, 66, 249

City Temple Presbyterian Church (Dallas, TX) 142

Clark, Robert 90

closed communion 202, 206

Coate, Lowell 85-86

Cobern, Camden 46

Coffin, Henry Sloan 168

Columbia Bible College 81-82, 85, 93, 94 n. 49, 97, 100, 101, 105-106, 127, 130-132, 145 n. 29, 231-234, 244-246, 268, 271 n. 162, 275-277

Columbia Theological Seminary 73, 163, 238

Committee on Cooperation and Reunion 154, 179, 180 n. 159

Conservative Baptist Association 27

Continuing Church Committee 178-180

Cooperative Program 187, 200, 207-208, 218, 219-220, 251 n. 81, 259

cooperative Protestantism 138, 154, 155, 185-186, 187, 190, 205-207, 209-210, 279

Cousar, R. Wilbur 169-170

Cox, Robert 240, 241-244

Crouch, B. W. 260 n. 121, 266, 270 n. 159, 273

Crowe, Robert McFerran 170 n. 121

Cumberland Presbyterian Church 172

Dalhouse, Mark Taylor x

Dallas Bible Institute 85, 97, 125, 127, 129 n. 194,

Dallas Theological Seminary 28, 78 n. 175, 85, 92, 97, 107-117, 124, 127, 128-130, 134, 139, 145 n 29, 146, 158 n. 76, 193, 247, 275-277

Darby, John Nelson 20

Dendy, Henry B. 157, 166, 179

Denny, Jr., Collins 266-267

Dick, Emily 99-100

Dillard, E. A. 226-227, 238-240, 241-245

dispensationalism xix, 19-21, 55, 117, 138, 194 n. 26, controversy in the

Presbyterian Church in the
United States 22 n. 58, 139-153,
156, 275, 277
Dixon, A. C. 30, 42, 46, 62
Dodds, Alfred 142
Dollar, George W. 223, 228 n. 4, 279,
281 n. 9
Dornbusch, Sanford 181
Druid Hills Baptist Church (Atlanta,
GA) 249
Dunn J. F. 98-99
Eggleston, J. D. 140-141
Enoree Presbytery 233-235
Evangelical Theological College 57
evangelism 11-16, 43-44, 93-96, 165,
215, 247, 257, 275
The Faith, 187 n. 7, 201-209, 212
The Faith and Southern Baptists 187
Federal Council of Churches 154, 155,
164-166, 173-174, 186, 189 n. 16,
206, 223, 226, 236, 241, 246, 263,
270
Fellowship of Independent Evangelical
Churches 246-248
First Baptist Church (Atlanta, GA) 48
First Baptist Church (Ft. Worth, TX)
77, 198-199
First Baptist Church (Winston-Salem,
NC) 219
First Presbyterian Church (Charlotte,
NC) 150
First Presbyterian Church (Dallas,
TX) 110, 141
First Presbyterian Church (Jackson,
MS) 175
First Presbyterian Church (Marshall,
TX) 110 n. 119, 126
First Presbyterian Church (Meridian,
MS) 58
First Presbyterian Church (Siloam
Springs, AR) 126
First Presbyterian Church
(Texarkana, TX) 75, 126
First Presbyterian Church (Toccoa,
GA) 125

Fitt, A. P. 46
Fleece, G. Allen 247
Flow, J. E. 172, 177
Floyd Street Presbyterian Church
(Lynchburg, VA) 58
Forrest, Robert A. 50 n. 65, 92, 94 n.
46, 98-99, 102, 119, 121, 125, 216
n. 113
Fort, T. Hicks 266
Fortna, Ray 142
Fosdick, Harry Emerson 211
Fuller, Charles 25-26
Fundamentalism Project xiii, xv
fundamentalism, definition x-xiii, 2-
23, 227, 230
fundamentalism, denominational
conflict xii-xiii, xviii, 1-2, 18, 23,
47-48, 68-79, 109, 133, 135-136,
140, 190, 199-200, 217, 220-223,
232-234, 237
fundamentalism, historiography viii-
x, 3 n. 7, 91 n. 35, 107 n. 110,
fundamentalism, institutional
networks 23-29, 79-80, 82-84,
118-119, 128, 132-133, 190-191,
201, 212, 218, 223, 224, 227, 248,
261
fundamentalism, southern xvii-xix,
30-32, 34, 191-192, 215, 216, 218,
224, 282
The Fundamentalist 77, 188 n. 13,
189 n. 15, 198, 258
The Fundamentals 7, 121
Gaebelein, A. C. 52, 54-56, 87, 90, 97,
113, 115
Gainesville Winter Bible Conference
51
Galilean Baptist Church (Dallas, TX)
125
Garret, Willis 129 n. 194, 130 n. 198
Gear, F. B. 146 n. 43, 150-151
General Association of Regular
Baptists 27

General Conference for Christian
Workers (Northfield, MA) 35-36,
38, 47, 52, 108
Gilmer, Graham 135, 149, 151
Glasgow, Tom 155 n63, 158 n. 76, 165
Gordon, A. J. 47, 89
Gordon, S. D. 44
graduate education 105-107
Gray, James 8 n. 20, 24, 42, 46, 53, 59,
61, 81, 97, 100
Green Street Presbyterian Church
(Augusta, GA) 56
Griffith-Thomas, W. H. 107 n. 109,
109
Groner, F. S. 67
Guille, George 56-58, 60, 61, 62, 95 n.
53, 97, 113, 124
Gulf Bible Conference (Galveston,
TX) 56
Gutzke, Manfred 141
Hamilton County Baptist Association
220-222
Hankins, Barry x
Harris, Elmore 46
Hawkins, W. E. 68
Herring, Ralph 219
Hewlet, Samuel 253
Highland Park Baptist Church
(Chattanooga, TN) 54, 213 n. 98,
215-216, 219, 220, 222
Hodge, A. A. 7 n. 19, 8 n. 23, 9 ns. 24,
25, 27, 10 n. 28
Hoke, Donald 247
holiness 16-18, 44-45, 92-93, 96-97,
227-229
Hough, R. E. 164
Hudson, Winthrop S. 6-7
immersion 202, 206, 223
Independent Board for Presbyterian
Foreign Missions 28
Independent Fundamental Churches
of America 27
Ingle, R. D. 258
institutional churches 12 n. 33
Inter-Varsity Christian Fellowship 28

Inwood, Charles 44
Irle, Roger 181
John Brown University 85, 92, 94 n.
49, 95, 96, 100-101, 104-105, 129
n. 193
Johnson, Albert Sidney 128, 150
Johnson, Wil R. 128
Jones, Jr., Bob 50 n. 65
Jones, Sr., Bob 94, 95 n. 51, 118, 128,
193
Jones, William P. 130 n. 198, 134-136,
152 n. 55, 225, 247 n. 63
Keswick (England) holiness
conferences 35, 44, 47, 107 n. 109
Keyes, Kenneth S. 170
Landrum, W. W. 48
Laws, Curtis Lee xii
Lawson, J. F. 75
Layman's Organization for the
Preservation of the Methodist
Episcopal Church South 262, 266-
267
Lee, R. G. 219 n. 121
Lee, Randolph E. 170, 171-172
Leonard, Bill J. x
LeTourneau, R. G. 102-104, 121
liberalism x, xii-xiii, xviii, 2, 4-7, 10-
11, 23, 26, 27, 30, 32, 34, 46-47,
62-63, 65, 66, 68-70, 73-76, 77,
83, 85-87, 108, 137, 138-139, 140,
147 n. 35, 148, 154-155, 162-164,
167-168, 187, 190, 206, 208, 209-
212, 221 n. 128, 226-227, 232,
236, 239, 246, 261, 262, 277
Lingle, Walter 145-146
Machen, J. Gresham 18 n. 49, 30, 86,
116-117, 124, 168, 235 n. 24, 236
Marsden, George M. x, xi n.9, xv, 13
n. 34, 18 n. 48, 29 n. 79, 31, 107 n.
110, 153, 229 n. 5
Marty, Martin E. xii
Massinger, Martin O. 129 n. 194
Masters, V. I. 191, 198
Mathes, F. A. 177

McCallie, J. P. 146 n33, 147-148, 150
n. 48, 156, 158 n. 76, 245
McCarter Presbyterian Church
(Greenville, SC) 233 n. 19, 234
McClenny, L. P. 247 n. 63
McGill, Ralph 252-253, 255
McIntire, Carl 211 n 93, 235-236,
240, 244, 245, 267, 270
McQuilkin, Robert C. 82, 94 n. 49,
119, 120-121, 125, 126, 128, 144
n. 23, 145 n. 29, 147-148, 226-
227, 231-232, 234 n. 21, 236, 237,
238-239, 240-248, 268, 275-276,
280-281
Meek, Robert 68-70, 73
Methodist Episcopal Church 70-71,
Methodist Episcopal Church, South
xviii-xix, 31, 68-73, 87 n. 22, 99,
230-231, 260-262, 263-264, 268,
269 n. 154
Meyer, F. B. 44-45
Miami Bible College 129 n. 194
Miller, R. V. 45
Miller, William 19
Missionary Training Institute 90
Moody Bible Institute 24, 25, 39, 42,
50, 81, 85, 88, 99, 100, 126-127,
158 n. 76, 238
Moody Bible Institute Extension
Department 57, 58-61, 79, 97, 124
Moody Bible Institute Monthly 24, 60,
85
Moody, Dwight L. 13-14, 35-36, 89,
108
Moody, William 42, 50
Mooney, James 119-120, 152
Morgan, David T. x
Morgan, G. Campbell 40
Nash, Charles A. 126
Nashville Presbytery 142
National Association of Evangelicals
27
Nelson, W. A. 47
New Orleans Presbytery 142

Newton, Louie 66, 219 n. 122, 248-
252, 254-255
Norris, J. Frank x, xix, 31 n.80, 63,
64, 67, 77-78, 87 n. 22, 94, 115,
185, 187, 188-189, 190, 191 n. 17,
195-196, 197-201 passim, 209,
212, 220 n. 124, 248-249, 251-
260, 276, 278-279
Orange Presbytery 135-136, 152 n. 55
Orthodox Presbyterian Church 27
Ostrom, Henry 58-59
Patterson, H. T. 100
Patterson, Vernon 247
Peacock, J. N. 71
Peak, Luther 197-201, 258-259
Phillips, J. B. 53-54, 60, 79, 216,
Piedmont Bible College 213 n. 101,
214-215, 217 n. 116
Plymouth Brethren 20, 102
Poe, Floyd 142
Pope, H. W. 43-44
postmillennialism 19, 46, 50, 218
premillennialism 18-23, 45-46, 47-48,
66-67, 78, 114, 139, 146-147, 149-
150, 153, 194-195, 215, 218-220,
223, 229-230, 232, 235, 247, 270
Presbyterian Church in America 278
Presbyterian Church in the United
States xviii-xix, 31-32, 73-76,
116-117, 226-227, 230-231, 240,
244, 245, 248, dispensationalism
controversy 22 n. 58, 139-153,
156; denominational
fundamentalists in 154-182, 224
Presbyterian Church in the United
States of America 116-117, 141,
149 n. 43, 167-168, 170, 180,
Presbyterian Outlook 159-160
Presbyterian Standard 73, 74
Putnam, C. E. 58-59
race relations xvi, xix, 40-41, 71-73,
127, 165, 172-177, 261, 265-266
Rankin, Brice 40
Reeves, E. C. 72, 73

Reinhardt Bible Church (Dallas, TX) 130 n. 198

reunion, Methodist 68-73, 260-268

reunion, Presbyterian 138, 154, 155, 166-182, 224, 239, 260, 277-278

Rice, John R. 68

Richardson, John R. 178

Riemers, David 181

Riley, William Bell 26, 27, 30, 58, 62, 63, 64, 68, 86-87, 114-115, 123

Rivermont Presbyterian Church (Lynchburg, VA) 135

Roberson, Lee 50 n. 65, 213 n. 98, 218, 220-223, 225

Robertson, A. T. 78

Robinson, J. S. 176

Robinson, William Childs 171,

Rogers, I. W. 187 n. 7, 201-209, 212-213, 219, 256 n. 100, 259-260

Routh, E. C. 66

Russell, Margaret 58-59

Salem Baptist Church (Winston-Salem, NC) 212 n. 98, 215

Sandeen, Ernest x n. 7, 3 n. 7, 9 n. 25, 18, 107 n. 110

Scarborough, L. R. 67

Schlesinger, Arthur M. 4, 5

Scofield, C. I. 20, 44, 45, 52, 55, 89, 108-109, 144

Scofield Memorial Church (Dallas, TX) 110, 125, 127

Scofield Reference Bible 20, 148, 153 n. 56, 195 n. 27

Second Presbyterian Church (Greenville, SC) 231, 233,

Second Presbyterian Church (Little Rock, AR) 74, 75

Second Presbyterian Church (Nashville, TN) 143-144

separation xix, 227-231, 235, 236, n. 25, 240-246, 247, 248, 249, 255-256, 260, 261, 267-268, 273-274, 280

Shepperson, Flournoy 231-238, 243, 244, 246

Shields, T. T. 63, 192-193,

Signal, Daniel Joseph xv-xvi

Simpson, A. B. 89, 90, 121

Slighter, Harold 222

Smith, Hay Watson 74-76, 239

Smith, Noel 188 n. 13, 189 n. 15

South Highland Presbyterian Church (Birmingham, AL) 177

Southeastern Bible School 85, 93, 125, 127, 129 n. 194,

Southern Baptist Convention ix-x, xviii-xix, 32, 47-48, 64, 66-67, 76-79, 138, 185-224 passim, 230, 248-249, 254-255, 279-280

Southern Baptist Fellowship 222-223

Southern Baptist Premillennial Fellowship 218-220

Southern Baptist Seminary 188, 201, 206 n. 74, 207

Southern Bible Institute 82, 98, 99-100, 119-120,

Southern Methodist 68, 72

Southern Methodist Church 268-273

Southern Methodist College 271-272

Southern Methodist Layman 262-265

Southern Presbyterian Journal 153, 155-159, 161-177 passim, 241, 260 n. 121, 278

Southern regional identity 70-1, 169-175, 261, 264, 272

Southern religion ix-x, xvi-xvii, 65-66, 137

Southfield Bible Conference (Crescent City, FL) 52-53, 109

Steel, S. A. 69

Stevens, Charles 212 n. 98, 215

Stone, Merwin A. 126

Strong, Josiah 12 n 32, 36 n 7

Stroud, Fred 142, 143-144

Strouse, Clarence 51

Sudan Interior Mission 28

Sunday School Times 24, 82, 86, 120, 147 n. 35, 213 n. 98

Sutcliffe, B. B. 109

Sutherland, James 58-59, 59-60

Szasz, Ferenc xiv, 4-5,

Tabernacle Baptist Church (Atlanta, GA) 33, 38, 40, 49, 63

Tabernacle Baptist Church (Greenville, SC) 222

Tabernacle Bible Conference 33, 38-51

Taylor, O. W. 192, 193-195, 199, 209-212, 219 n. 123

Temple Baptist Church (Detroit, MI) 196, 257

Tennessee Temple Schools 213 n. 101, 215-217, 220

Tenth Avenue Presbyterian Church (Charlotte, NC) 59, 238-239

Third Baptist Church (Atlanta, GA) 38

Thompson, Ernest Trice 31, 145 n. 29, 154 n. 63, 159, 181-182, 226, 241

Thompson, James J. 78

Tinder, Donald George 15-16, 18

Toccoa Falls Institute 85, 92, 98-99, 100, 102-103, 127, 128

Torrey, R. A. 14 n 38, 44, 53

Trollinger, Jr., William Vance viii

Trumball, Charles 86, 147 n. 35

Tuscaloosa Presbytery 177

union meetings 202, 205

unionism 205-207, 208, 215

Unionizing Southern Baptists 185-186, 204-205

Vance, James 50

Varley, Henry 46

Vick, G. Beauchamp 257-259

Vining, Robert 165

Viser, J. H. 233 n. 19, 234-235, 237-238, 244

vocational training 102-105

Wake Forest College and University 37, 221

Walker, Clarence 212 n. 97, 214, 215

Warfield, B. B. 7 n. 19, 8 n. 23, 9 ns. 24, 25, 27, 10 n. 28

Wells, John 73

Wesleyan Christian Advocate 41, 71

Western Recorder 66, 78, 191 n. 17, 198, 201

Westminster Presbyterian Church (Ft. Worth, TX) 125, 141

Westminster Presbyterian Church (Greensboro, NC) 135, 152 n. 55

Wheaton College 28, 86, 109-110, 116 n. 145, 240 n. 38

While Southern Baptists Sleep 186

White, W. P. 62

Williams, Virginia 58-59

Wilson, Robert Dick 46-47

Winchester, A. B. 109

World Christian Fundamentals Association 26-27, 61-63, 64, 79, 87 n 22, 88, 114-116, 123, 279

World Fundamental Missionary Baptist Fellowship 196, 198, 254, 255

Wycliffe Bible Translators 28

Young Life 28, 143

Youth for Christ 28